REGULATI

Some Recent Titles from the *Perspectives on Gender* Series

Series Editor: Myra Marx Ferree, University of Wisconsin, Madison

Black Feminist Thought: Knowledge, Consciousness, and the Politics of Empowerment
Patricia Hill Collins

Feminisms and the Women's Movement: Dynamics of Change in Social Movement Ideology and Activism
Barbara Ryan

Black Women and White Women in the Professions: Analysis of Job Segregation by Race and Gender, 1960-1980
Natalie J. Sokoloff

Gender Consciousness and Politics
Sue Tolleson Rinehart

Mothering: Ideology, Experience, and Agency
Evelyn Nakano Glenn, Grace Chang, and Linda Rennie Forcey, Editors

For Richer, For Poorer: Mothers Confront Divorce
Demie Kurz

Integrative Feminisms: Building Global Visions, 1960s-1990s
Angela Miles

Rock-a-by Baby: Feminism, Self-Help, and Postpartum Depression
Verta Taylor

School-Smart and Mother-Wise: Working-Class Women's Identity and Schooling
Wendy Luttrell

Community Activism and Feminist Politics: Organizing Across Race, Class, and Gender
Nancy A. Naples, Editor

Grassroots Warriors: Activist Mothering, Community Work, and the War on Poverty
Nancy A. Naples

Complex Inequality: Gender, Class, and Race in the New Economy
Leslie McCall

Maid in the U.S.A.: 10th Anniversary Edition
Mary Romero

Home-Grown Hate: Gender and Organized Racism
Abby L. Ferber, Editor

Stepping Out of Line: Becoming and Being Feminist
Cheryl Hercus

REGULATING SEX

The Politics of Intimacy and Identity

Edited by

Elizabeth Bernstein and Laurie Schaffner

ROUTLEDGE
NEW YORK AND LONDON

Published in 2005 by
Routledge
270 Madison Avenue
New York, NY 10016
www.routledge-ny.com

Published in Great Britain by
Routledge
2 Park Square
Milton Park, Abingdon
Oxon OX 14 4RN U.K.
www.routledge.co.uk

Library of Congress Cataloging-in-Publication Data

Regulating sex : the politics of intimacy and identity / Elizabeth Bernstein and
Laurie Schaffner, editors.
    p. cm. — (Perspectives on gender)
  Includes bibliographical references and index.
    ISBN 0-415-94868-1 (hardback) — ISBN 0-415-94869-X (pbk.)
1. Sex—Political aspects. 2. Sex and law. I. Bersnstein, Elizabeth, 1968–
II. Schaffner, Laurie. III. Series: Perspectives on gender (New York, N.Y.)
    HQ23.R43 2004
    306.7 — dc22
                                                        2004008237

To the PBs, and community at the margins

Table of Contents

Acknowledgments

This volume emerged out of the proceedings of a workshop supported by the International Institute for the Sociology of Law in Oñati, Spain in the summer of 2000. We are tremendously grateful to the numerous friends and colleagues who so powerfully contributed to the cultivation and shaping of this text during the intervening years. We would first like to offer our thanks to Malen Gordoa and Pierre Guibentif for graciously tending the workshop, and to Will Rountree for taking on special duties at the conference (including the overseeing of late-night impromptu hors d'oeuvres and assistance with the comings and goings of participants). Throughout the course of this project, Sea-Ling Cheng, Janet Jakobsen, Jason James, Mindie Lazarus-Black, Corinne Louw, Katalin Makkai, Greg Matoesian, Kelly Moore, Mark Padilla, Lucinda Ramberg, Gayatri Reddy, Beth Richie, Miryam Sas, Penelope Saunders, Steven Seidman, Robert Smith, Wendy Ward, and Paige West offered multiple forms of intellectual and emotional support, while Blaise Carter-Garber, Clare Corcoran, Lorena Diaz de Leon, Nirali Shah, Janna Thomure, Hsiu-Ann Tom, and Eddy U provided invaluable editing, research, and bibliographic assistance. We are especially thankful to Logan MacLeod, whose acuity and stamina helped to bring this book to completion, and at Routledge, to Myra Marx Feree, whose sponsorship and feedback were crucial in helping us to transform an unruly manuscript into a polished text. Elizabeth would like to offer special, heartfelt thanks to Kerwin Kaye, who contributed so much to this project at every stage—from intellectual input to pep talks to help with crude mechanics. Laurie appreciates the support from David Perry and the Great Cities Institute at the University of Illinois at Chicago. We are grateful to all of you for helping us to realize some of the forms of collaboration and community that were the inspiration for this book.

Elizabeth Bernstein and Laurie Schaffner
New York and Chicago,
December 2003

Regulating Sex: An Introduction

ELIZABETH BERNSTEIN AND LAURIE SCHAFFNER

Writing about sexuality is like writing about last evening's news. By the time one's thoughts are formulated, they may seem hopelessly out of date —vis-à-vis the world at large or vis-à-vis one's own political convictions. In recent years, a vast array of social transformations falling under the broad banner of globalization have served to radically recraft not only economic activities, but also kin networks and paradigms of intimacy. While the spread of global capitalism has exacerbated social inequalities, fragmented families, and severed individuals from traditional social ties, it has also given rise to transnational feminist activism, a burgeoning lesbian-gay-bisexual-transgender-queer (LGBTQ) movement, a renewed commitment to international human rights, and myriad new forms of eroticism and community. Within this context of cultural upheaval, the best means by which to advocate for sexual freedoms—while at the same time protecting vulnerable parties from violation—can be difficult to assess.[1]

Bold and rapid transformations force a continual reevaluation of social and political questions, including those that have plagued us as scholars and activists working in the field of sexuality studies. Is the flourishing of sexual commerce one domain among others in an expanding global service economy, or the manifestation of gross inequalities of gender, class, race, and nation? Should the pursuit of marriage and other forms of legal domestic partnerships for same-sex couples be seen as a vital stepping stone toward civil rights and state recognition, or as assimilation to heteronormative ideals? Are children more in need of protection from sexual exploiters than of direction and encouragement in their quest for erotic forms of intimacy? The purpose of this volume is to address questions such as these via a series of spirited dialogues among scholars from diverse disciplines, methodologies, and regions.

Sexuality as Social Politics

Over the last several decades, a large and important body of scholarship has developed within the growing interdisciplinary field of sexuality studies, a primary aim of which has been to problematize naturalistic understandings of sexuality and to highlight the influence of cultural diversity and historical change upon sexual identities and behaviors. Recent scholarly work has served as a corrective to the tendency in Western social thought to relegate questions of sexuality to the domain of the personal and the presocial —a trend that has prevailed over the last century. In contrast to the avowed moralism of Christian theological discourse, which situated questions of sexuality within the domain of ethics and the political, the fields of sexology and psychoanalysis emerged in the late nineteenth century to articulate the natural and instinctual underpinnings of sexual behavior.

It was not until the middle of the twentieth century that social scientists fully embraced sexuality as an object of analysis, systematically charting the ways that sexuality was "socially constructed" (i.e., labeled, molded, and experienced in accordance with social institutions and with history). Kinsey (1948), a pivotal figure in the transition from a biological "drive" model to a social constructionist one, conducted sweeping social surveys to reveal a tremendous amount of sexual diversity among the so-called "normal" heterosexual middle classes, thereby countering the perception that sexual identity was in any way innate. In the late 1960s and early 1970s, a new spate of sexuality studies were conducted under the purview of the sociology of deviance, pioneering the analysis of sexual roles and social identities, particularly in the newly visible, post-Stonewall homosexual community.[2] A decade later, Foucault would famously argue that not only modes of sexual expression were socially constructed (or rather, discursively produced), but also the very notion of "sexuality" itself as an "especially dense transfer point" for relations of power (1978, 103).

By the 1980s, sexuality had become not only a site of empirical investigation, but also of reinvigorated political contest, as feminists debated the ways that states facilitated the sexual and social control of women and children.[3] Lesbian and gay studies pursued a similar empirico-normative project—both by investigating the texture and meaning of same-sex intimacies in different cultural and historical milieu, and through documentation of the dearth of civil rights and liberties for gay, lesbian, and bisexual individuals.[4] Over the last two decades, the field of queer studies has emerged to critically interrogate not just socially marginalized sexual identities and practices, but also heterosexuality as a cultural institution and heteronormativity as a system of social control.[5] As with feminist theories and with gay and lesbian studies, queer theory is explicitly political in intent. Queer theorists aim to articulate ethical ideals of intimacy and sociality that do not confine individuals to the institution of the nuclear family. Yet they have often been leery of attempts to enlist the liberal state in this agenda, aspiring to radical social change rather than rights-oriented reform.

Recently, sociolegal scholars have joined this conversation in order to consider the impact of specific laws and social policies upon community forms and identities, as well as upon the subjective experiences of body, self, and desire.[6] From the decriminalization of sodomy to the legal recognition of same-sex unions, to laws that seek to curtail children's exposure to sexual experiences and images, the state serves to shape our erotic possibilities and to impart a particular normative vision. The state, in short, has a sexual agenda. Thanks to an accumulating lineage of scholarship and activism, this is an assertion that is much easier to make and to understand now than it would have been 30 years ago.

Debates around sexuality often serve as a barometer of more generalized social tensions—in times of economic and cultural flux, sex may become an easy and frequent target of campaigns for state regulation. As with the religious disputes of earlier centuries, contemporary conflicts around intimate relations "acquire immense symbolic weight" (Rubin 1999, 143).[7] Popular concerns about the legitimacy of gay marriage embody anxieties about changes in family structure, the coherence of national identity, and a social world in which erotic experience no longer derives its primary cultural and emotive meanings from procreation, but rather from intimacy and pleasure.[8] In similar fashion, contemporary debates over the problem of human trafficking fuse broad concerns about geographic and moral borders, the dividing line between childhood and adulthood, and the proper scope and reign of the market. In order to understand the regulation of sexuality, we must situate it within its broad political context, exploring the mutual constitution of public and private, family and nation, and sexual and social life.

Beyond Public and Private

Liberal theory locates questions of politics squarely within the realm of the state—they are negotiated, contested, and fundamentally social phenomena —while sexuality is secluded in the asocial and naturalized private sphere. Yet a growing body of literature regarding the concept of *sexual citizenship* has drawn attention to the ways in which the liberal state serves to guarantee the very privacy of the private.[9] The valorization of privacy by liberal states is itself premised upon a particular social configuration of sexual intimacy. This fact was made abundantly clear by the U.S. Supreme Court's 1986 ruling in *Bowers v. Hardwick*, in which consensual homosexual activity in the home was denied constitutional protection precisely because it did not support the norms of heterosexual marriage and family. More recently, in the celebrated decision *Lawrence v. Texas* (2003), the decriminalization of sodomy and the overturning of *Bowers v. Hardwick* hinged upon the fact that the particular activities taking place within the private realm were now deemed worthy of protection. Influenced, in part, by "values shared with a wider civilization" (specifically, the European Court of Human Rights), a majority of U.S. Supreme Court justices could determine that, in contrast to prostitution or sex with minors, homosexual intimacy constituted "a personal relationship . . . within the liberty of persons to choose without being punished as criminals" (*Lawrence v. Texas* 2003).

The public constitution of privacy often presents difficulties for those who seek to challenge the status quo merely through an invocation of liberal rights. As various contributors to this volume point out, the right to privacy has disparate effects for individuals who live their lives in apparent accordance with middle-class familial ideals, as opposed to those who violate conventions of gender and domesticity. The right to privacy does not imply a right to erotic expression outside the home, for example, or the rights of transgender individuals to even the most basic of civil freedoms. Nor does it enable children, the asexual apprentices within family life, to develop their own sexual practice.

Critical analyses of sexuality and the state are powerfully indebted to a long tradition of feminist engagement with related and overlapping themes, but they are not subsumable within it. Feminists have problematized the notion of the private as a realm where women and children have been subject to the rule of rights-endowed husbands and fathers, and they have pointed to the ways in which the liberal legal categories of contract and consent can be particularly troubling for women, who were regarded as property, not participants, within the original social contract (Pateman 1988). Because women remain in structurally subordinate positions to men, some feminist legal scholars have argued that the very notion of their consent to (hetero)sexual encounters is rendered all but meaningless (MacKinnon 1989; Pateman 1988).

While many of the pieces presented here build on this lineage of feminist scholarship, one crucial point of departure is the interrogation of aspects of sexual and social life that are deeply enmeshed with, yet irreducible to, the gendered power relations that have been the primary focus of feminist thinking. In this volume, we view sexuality and gender as separate—if at times interlocking— "vectors of oppression," to use Gayle Rubin's phrase (Rubin 1999). Inspired by the insights of recent work in queer theory, we foreground the institutions that undergird the cultural mandate of reproductive heterosexuality—in particular, the family, the couple, childhood, and ideals of eroticism premised upon romance and domesticity. One feature that unites the diverse contributions in this volume is a refusal to take for granted social norms and institutions such as these. In dialogue with both feminist scholarship and queer theory, we extend them in new empirical directions, bringing feminist and queer critiques of public and private, and the non-self-evidence of heteronormative configurations of intimate life to areas of inquiry such as age of consent laws (Schaffner, Chapter 11), lesbian parenting arrangements (Rountree, Chapter 2), and child sexual abuse (Kaye, Chapter 9), to name but a few examples from this text.

In this era of global flows of capital and culture, some have questioned the extent to which the geographic boundaries and legal regimes of the nation-state continue to shape the contours of sexual experience (Povinelli and Chauncey 1999; Altman 2001). Rather than reify the state as a disembodied conglomeration of laws and social policies, we situate it as an intricate web of discourses, social actors, and institutions. Policy makers, interpreters, and administrators who work in the various branches of government (legislative, executive, and judicial) and at a variety of levels (municipal, national, and transnational), as well as the police and other criminal justice officials, all form a part of the state apparatus, but these various actors do not form a seamless whole.[10] State regulatory strategies often contain gaps and contradictions. We regard state power as not simply censorial, but also as a productive force, noting the ways in which it is enmeshed with a vast array of cultural institutions and authorities that are "neither actually nor functionally part of 'the state'" (Rose 1989, xxi). Sexuality is regulated—governed, directed, and made more uniform—through the rule of law as well as through media, nongovernmental organizations (NGOs), educators, and others engaged in the "helping professions." Sexuality is also regulated by diffuse state policies seemingly unrelated to questions of gender and erotic intimacy. These policies range from decisions regarding municipal zoning and redevelopment (E. Bernstein, Chapter 7) to the laws and enforcement practices that surround questions of immigration (Chapkis, Chapter 4), to the international lending guidelines of the World Bank and IMF (O'Connell Davidson and Sánchez Taylor, Chapter 6).

Contributions to This Volume

The idea for this volume first emerged during a 2000 workshop entitled "Sexuality and the State" at the International Institute for the Sociology of Law in Oñati, Spain. We came together to raise probing questions about the regulation of intimate life, rather than to formulate concrete models of policy. Many of the essays we present here articulate perspectives that have often been relegated to the margins of gender studies and the sociology of law. We deliberately brought to the table scholars working at the cutting edge of diverse fields within the social sciences and the humanities, where parallel conversations had begun to take place around questions of sexuality and social justice. By juxtaposing arguments grounded in different methodological traditions (historical and cultural analysis, interviews and field observations, surveys of national legislation, and interpretations of case law), the chapters that we have assembled stand in provocative contrast to one another, balancing empiricist foundations with interpretive nuance.

As with any workshop, this one, too, was limited in scope. A comprehensive treatment of sexuality and the state in all of its diverse facets would require inclusion of a number of substantive topics and theoretical questions that we do not articulate in sufficient detail here. For example, both the politics of AIDS and questions of sexual violence (state-facilitated and interpersonally driven) are only fleetingly addressed.[11] The potential for disembodied forms of intimacy and community that have been brought about by new information technologies and the attendant legal and moral conundra that these new cultural formations have produced is, likewise, minimally explored.[12] New, postmodern identity formations (transgender and intersex identifications, queer youth mobilizations) and their regulatory configurations certainly merit a fuller discussion than the one we have provided.[13] Much remains to be considered about the sexual and gendered dimensions of the national security state, which have come into particularly sharp focus in the wake of September 11th (its fortifications and modes of surveillance, and the visions of sexuality implied by state-promulgated notions of terror and safety).[14] Perhaps the most significant limitation of the pieces assembled here is that the overwhelming majority focus upon the neoliberal nation-states that comprise the driving force behind cultural and economic globalization. As such, this volume stands in conversation with the expanding domain of new scholarship on sexuality, postcolonialism, and neo-imperialism.[15]

Underlying the diverse contributions to this volume are some common premises. Where official liberal doctrine holds that Western democracies serve to protect citizens' freedom, to afford them privacy, and to provide equal justice, the authors in this volume point to numerous ways in which these promises fall short. The state's lack of protections or recognition for those who defy conventional sex and gender norms, its ambivalent facilitation and curtailment of the global sexual marketplace in accordance with corporate-capitalist interests, and its disparately gendered policing of the sexual boundaries between childhood and adulthood are the themes around which the chapters in this book cluster. Although the majority of authors depart from certain shared assumptions regarding the potentials and limits of the liberal state, our aim has been less to persuade our readers to a particular point of view than to structure a number of energetic theoretical encounters. To this end, we have brought together scholars whose work encourages controversial dialogues. While we do not endorse all of the authors' interpretations or prescriptions, each chapter offers an innovative consideration of the subject matter at hand.

In Part I, "The Regulation of Queer Identities and Intimacies," M. Bernstein, Rountree, Currah, and Minter turn their attention to the first of three substantive topics—one in which the liberal state's continued presumption of heterosexual familial units and a binaristic, stable gender system is made most evident. As the pieces in this section suggest, states find same-sex intimacies and transgender rights particularly difficult to regulate precisely because they push up against some of the gendered status arrangements that lurk behind liberalism's core assumptions. In the United States, recent Supreme Court rulings have sparked heated controversy around the decriminalization of sodomy and the legal recognition of gay marriage, throwing the tension between liberal ideals of equality and a singular configuration of gender and sexuality into sharp relief. Within the context of this challenge, the authors assess the viability of particular legislative and litigative strategies for achieving sexual justice for lesbian, gay, bisexual, and transgender individuals.

Through a discussion of efforts to decriminalize sodomy in the United States, Mary Bernstein argues that social movements, such as the lesbian and gay rights movement, should be deemed successful not merely by dint of their ability to change particular laws and statutes, but also by the extent to which they are able to change dominant cultural values. In accordance with New Social Movement Theory, she argues that community formation and group empowerment are as important to the assessment of movement outcomes as are more overt measures of legal and political change. Although the 1986 ruling in *Bowers v. Hardwick* seemed to spell crushing defeat for gay and lesbian activists, in fact, the decision spurred a more organized and powerful social movement, which helped to change the cultural climate around same-sex intimacy and to usher in the 2003 *Lawrence* decision.

At a time when many heterosexuals are opting out of marriage, lesbian and gay activists have mobilized to gain access to the institution. Given that legal marriage is unavailable to the overwhelming majority of lesbian and gay couples,[16] in Chapter 2, Will Rountree offers a consideration of individually negotiated contracts as a means of providing legal and cultural mooring to relationships between persons of the same sex. Rountree argues that contract can serve as a tool for achieving the goal of state recognition, while allowing partners to flexibly tailor their individual agreements. He furthermore maintains that contract may in some ways actually be preferable to the institution of marriage, since fully contractual unions are forged in an expressly articulated way that heterosexual marriage, premised upon an unspoken gendered division of labor, cannot be.

In Chapter 3, Paisley Currah and Shannon Minter discuss both the failures of litigation and the legislative gains that transgender people in the United States have made in their efforts to secure basic civil protections. Although transgender discrimination might appear to fall squarely within the parameters of discrimination based on sex, sexual orientation, or disability, litigation has proven to be an unsuccessful political strategy for transgender individuals because courts typically dismiss their claims out of hand. Currah and Minter argue that transgender individuals have been denied their civil rights not because of doctrinal error or failures in legal reasoning, but because they have not even been deemed worthy of protection. As a result of the animosity transgender people have encountered in the courts, they have turned to the legislative branches of government—city councils, state legislatures, and Congress—to secure basic civil rights protections. Transgender people have begun to organize as a political constituency and, for the first time, to lobby for the passage of nondiscrimination laws. Currah and Minter conclude their chapter by surveying some of the political dilemmas entailed by the crafting of such legislation.

In Part II, "The Regulation of Sexual Commerce," Chapkis, Agustín, O'Connell Davidson, Sánchez Taylor, and E. Bernstein discuss the impact of market forces upon sexual migrations, modes of labor and exchange, and the meanings that accrue to commodified intimate relations. Rather than reengaging a well-worn controversy about the political significance of prostitution,[17] or debating whether prostitution should be decriminalized, legalized, or criminalized,[18] the authors analyze the burgeoning sexual marketplace in terms of its enabling social conditions. Specifically, they investigate the ways in which the social meaning of sexual commerce has been inflected by transnational travel and migration, and the growing disparities in material resources between the West and developing nations, as well as within Western cities. To this end, each of the four pieces assembled challenges axiomatic understandings of what is politically at stake in the commercial sexual encounter. Together, the contributions to this section reveal that the protection of national borders, nuclear families, and middle-class consumer spaces are as much at stake in the regulation of sexual commerce as is the control of sex per se.

In Chapter 4, Wendy Chapkis begins by exploring the U.S. Trafficking Victims Protection Act (2000), revealing a covert reinforcement of punitive immigration policies lurking behind the state's professed aim of protecting women and children. Drawing upon the statutory text, she challenges official statistics that claim 50,000 victims are sexually trafficked into the United States each year. Chapkis argues that numbers such as these are not only empirically groundless but serve as a smokescreen for a bipartisan anti-immigration agenda.

Laura Maria Agustín provides an equally potent challenge to standard academic and interventionist discourses on migrant sex-work in Chapter 5, focusing her analytic gaze not on sex workers, but rather on their self-appointed middle-class "helpers." She interrogates unspoken norms of familialism in the rhetoric and ideals of white European feminists, NGOs, and social workers who seek to save prostitutes from their fate. Agustín traces the ways in which nineteenth-century bourgeois women came into the helping professions—attempting not only to rectify the lives of underprivileged individuals, but to preserve the boundaries of heterosexual monogamy and the modern nuclear family. She argues that, while middle-class helpers strive to reinsert prostitutes back into nuclear families, it is the nuclear family itself that produces clients' desires for nonfamilial modes of sexual exchange.

In Chapter 6, Julia O'Connell Davidson and Jacqueline Sánchez Taylor address the ways in which international lending and debt policies facilitate the creation of sexual playgrounds for Western tourists in the Caribbean. They explore the phenomenology of tourists' demand for sexual exotica, while highlighting the substratum of material inequality that leads tourists from affluent nations to expect—and to naturalize—easy sexual access to locals from impoverished regions. O'Connell Davidson and Sánchez Taylor redirect our attention away from those that perform sexual labor to the European and North American men and women who choose to pursue commodified intimate relationships in island settings.

Finally, in Chapter 7, the last of the chapters in this section, Elizabeth Bernstein confronts the paradoxical emergence of state efforts to criminalize male sexual clients alongside the increasing normalization of commercial sexual consumption. She argues that recent state efforts to problematize the border zones of male desire—via programs such as "John School" and stricter laws on the possession of child pornography—have not served to eliminate, but rather to respatialize and domesticate the widening sphere of sexual commerce in U.S. and Western European cities. The intensified policing of the street-level sex trade has been accompanied by a proliferation of indoor sex businesses, such as gentleman's clubs and striptease venues. Both phenomena have served to expel class and racial Others from gentrifying inner cities, while creating safe and accessible spaces for white middle-class men to indulge in commodified sexual relations.

Next, in Part III, "The Regulation of Childhood and Gendered Innocence," we address what is undoubtedly one of the most politically complex arenas of contemporary state intervention. The mere mention of *childhood* and *sexuality* in the same breath sparks controversy in legal doctrine as well as in the broad and diffuse domain of cultural politics. Within academic scholarship, a lacuna is especially noteworthy, given that it occurs in the context of an expansion of work in the sociology and anthropology of childhood,[19] and a rise in institutional and community advocacy for the rights of the child, initiated by the 1979 United Nations declaration of "The Decade of the Child." Glaringly absent from the majority of these interventions are empirically driven, theoretically engaged discussions of children's rights or needs as sexual beings. Furthermore, in popular and political discourse, children's exposure to sexuality has predominantly been framed as a grave social danger, necessitating staunch preventative measures and clear legal protections. Rarely is childhood sexuality viewed as encompassing experiencec that are worthy of being nurtured or encouraged.[20]

The construction of children's sexual needs and rights has more to do with the opinions of those who are in positions of legal, economic, and cultural authority than with any real reckoning of the "best interests of the child" (Woodhead 1997). Here, a glimpse from the anthropological research is instructive: millions of parents and families in villages around the world view their chief task of parenting the young as facilitating and preparing children for adulthood both in terms of labor and in terms of reproduction, in contrast to the predominant western notion of shielding and protecting children from adulthood well into their thirties (Boyden 1997).

Yet many commentators continue to write as if the categories of childhood and sexuality were stable and uncontested. Contemporary discussions of childhood in law and psychology rest upon the notion that the innocence of childhood ends irrevocably with the acquisition of sexual knowledge (Levesque 2000; Hymowitz 2000; Levine 2002). By contrast, the four chapters in this section challenge some of the normative assumptions that are implied when sexual experience is taken as the *de facto* boundary line separating childhood from adulthood—such as the disparately gendered assessment of this acquisition as good for boys, yet dangerous for girls.

To this end, Kjersti Ericsson explores the contradictory sexual agendas that have informed child welfare policy in Norway. In Chapter 8, Ericsson calls attention to the ways in which girls' (but not boys') sexuality has historically been contained and pathologized by state rhetorics of juvenile delinquency, rhetorics that were literalized into official state practice by child welfare facilities. She further observes that, since the 1980s, incestuous adult men have replaced sexually wild and uninhibited girls as the main specter of danger in the discourse and literature of the Norwegian social welfare system.

In Chapter 9, Kerwin Kaye further deconstructs the state's role in the social construction of childhood sexuality and gender. He traces shifting accounts of childhood sexual abuse in feminist, psychological, and state discourses. Kaye notes the ways in which recent psychological and state discourses have served to naturalize both the moral worth of the male-dominated nuclear household and the sexual innocence of children. These interventions have diverted attention away from earlier feminist critiques of the family that emphasized gendered power differentials and structural inequalities, rather than the stigmatizing consequences of early sexual knowledge. In order to truly empower children, Kaye argues, change must occur at both discursive and material levels, so that children would have a means to sustain themselves outside the confines of the male-dominated nuclear family.

Penelope Saunders similarly calls into question notions of sexual innocence, as well as the normative constructions of gender that undergird contemporary NGO discourses around children's rights. In Chapter 10, she traces the recent transition from *child prostitution* to the more encompassing category of the *commercial sexual exploitation of children* (CSEC) among community-based workers at NGOs who advocate on behalf of children. Though broader in some respects than its predecessor term, Saunders argues that the notion of CSEC remains beholden to the same narrow visions of gender and sexual conformity.

Then, Laurie Schaffner discusses divergent trends in two key legal arenas that construct the boundary, and thus the social meaning, dividing childhood and adulthood: statutory rape prosecutions and juvenile waivers to adult court. Whereas in statutory rape cases, girls are typically constructed as juvenile victims who are incapable of granting consent, in cases of violent crime, boys are presumed to be calculating, clear-thinking individuals who are competent to stand trial as adults. Schaffner concludes with an appeal for the adoption of the international standard of adulthood set out in the *United Nations Convention on the Rights of the Child* (1989), so that all children below the age of 18 might be afforded the unique and special protections they require, while decriminalizing their sexual practices and preserving their sexual freedom.

We end our volume with a section entitled "Beyond Regulation: Towards Sexual Justice," in which we suggest some directions for future activism and theorizing. In this section, Hekma, Seidman, Jakobsen, and Kennedy provide diverse assessments of the current struggle for sexual justice in the United States and Western Europe. Despite their distinct vantage points and substantive foci, the chapters converge around a number of key questions: If a liberal rights model is not an adequate tool for late capitalist societies to fashion inclusive visions of equality and justice, what is? How might we articulate a political vision that is not beholden to liberalism's limited renditions of tolerance and privacy? Must we reject the liberal state entirely, or is there a way that we can use it towards better ends?

Gert Hekma begins this section by amending the common misperception of the Netherlands as the libertarian seat of sexual justice, highlighting the gaps that exist between official state policy, attitudinal tolerance, and embodied sexual practice. Although the Netherlands appears progressive at the levels of attitudes and policy, Hekma draws on an analysis of social survey data to argue that the actual range of pleasure-seeking activities available to most Dutch citizens is quite narrow. Hekma concludes his chapter by highlighting the need for alternative forms of sexual infrastructure that might challenge restrictive norms of sexual behavior, such as the provision of public spaces for erotic activity, and more ample versions of state-sponsored sex education.

In Chapter 13, Steven Seidman seeks to provide resolution to the tension between assimilationist and liberationist approaches to sexual justice among lesbian and gay activists. Whereas assimilationists have tried to impel liberalism to fulfill its promise of equality and rights by advocating for legal reforms, liberationists have espoused a radical sexual agenda that challenges the very terms of liberal freedom (including norms of gender, the public-private divide, and marriage as the legitimating paradigm of sexual intimacy). Since the 1960s, gay rights have received greater endorsements by cultural elites as well as by the state.[21] Yet the pursuit of liberal equality has also run up against some important limits, most notably vis-à-vis the institutions of marriage and the military—the twin emblems of full American citizenship. Seidman suggests that the standstill in attaining full citizenship for gays and lesbians might be resolved by blending elements from both the assimilationist and the liberationist activist agendas. Though the pursuit of a liberal rights agenda remains crucial, Seidman argues that, by itself, it is insufficient. Like other authors in this volume (especially M. Bernstein, Chapter 1 and Kaye, Chapter 9), Seidman argues that the simultaneous pursuits of legal, cultural, and institutional change must go hand in hand.

Jakobsen and Kennedy conclude the volume by pointing toward the contradictions that contemporary social justice activists face in demanding state protections from various forms of sex and gender domination on the one hand, while opposing the state's overzealous interventions into matters of sexual freedom on the other. In a neoliberal economy such as ours, this dilemma is further complicated by the fact that the very notion of freedom can feel tainted by its associations with the market, the military, and U.S. neo-imperialism. Yet Jakobsen and Kennedy remind us that the struggle for freedom formerly served as a rallying point for diverse progressive movements, such as the women's liberation, lesbian and gay rights, and civil rights movements. Through genealogies of African-American movements for social justice and of early twentieth-century lesbian life, they aim to recover a vision of freedom that stands in contrast to individualistic, privacy-based conceptions of the term, one that is premised upon the ideal of struggle rather than choice, and embedded in community relations. As Jakobsen and Kennedy argue, the liberal state should not be mistaken for the site of freedom, but neither should it be simply eschewed. A radical and reinvigorated understanding of freedom could serve as a means of both negotiating with and resisting the limitations of liberalism.

Many of the chapters in this edition point to additional axes of inquiry that are vital to a full understanding of sexual regulation. These include considerations of reproductive rights, intersections between state processes of sexualization and racialization, and the salience of international human rights law to the pursuit of sexual justice. Each one of these arenas could be the subject of another volume of essays. We offer this text as an invitation to further dialogue among the expanding field of scholars and activists who are concerned with engaging the dilemmas, questions, and challenges that we have outlined. It is our hope as the editors of this volume that these essays will incite vigorous debate and broaden our political visions.

Notes

1. On the consequences of new economic and cultural formations for intimate life, see, for example, Giddens (1992), Stacey (1996), Altman (2001), Ehrenreich and Hochschild (2002), Jakobsen (2002), and Hochschild (2003).
2. See, for example, Douglas (1970), Henslin (1971), Winick and Kinsie (1971), and Bell and Gordon (1972).
3. The literature is voluminous, but see generally Luker (1975, 1984, 1996), Smart and Smart (1978), MacKinnon (1979, 1987), Davis (1983), Joffe (1986), Pateman (1988), and Gordon (1989, 1990). On the intertwining of sexuality and power more generally, see Snitow, Stansell, and Thompson (1983); Lorde (1984); and Vance (1984).
4. Overviews can be found in D'Emilio (1983a), Duberman, Vicinus, and Chauncey (1989), Abelove, Barale, and Halperin (1993), Katz (1995), Duberman (1997), and Seidman (2002).
5. See, for example, Butler (1990), Epstein (1993), Stein (1993), Warner (1993, 2000), and Seidman (2002).
6. See, for example, Duggan and Hunter (1995), Eskridge (1999), and Brown and Halley (2002).
7. Social historians have similarly documented the ways in which cultural upheavals associated with modernization and urbanization were manifest in early modern moral reform movements. See, for example, Walkowitz (1980), Rosen (1982), Beisel (1997), and Luker (1998).
8. See Chapters 2 and 13 in this volume, as well as Knight (1999).
9. On sexual citizenship, see Evans (1993), Weeks (1995a), and Bell and Binnie (2000).
10. For a useful typology of varieties of masculinist state power, see Brown (1995), Chapter 7.
11. Socio-political perspectives on AIDS include Farmer (1993, 2001), Schneider and Stoller (1995), Epstein (1998), Cohen (1999), and Patton (2002). For theoretical and empirical treatments of sexual violence, see MacKinnon (1989), Chancer (1992), Olujic (1995), Richie (1996), Heise (1997), and O'Toole and Schiffman (1997).
12. For treatments of these issues, see Lane (2000) and Jenkins (2001).
13. The literature on transgender and interesex individuals and the state is unfortunately quite sparse. On queer youth, see Herdt (1989, 1997), Plummer (1989), Owens (1998), and Warner (1993). On the relationship of transgender individuals to the state, see Chapter 3, this volume, and accompanying citations.
14. See, for example, Enloe (2000), Lutz (2001), Eisenstein (2002), Puar and Rai (2002), Hawthorne and Winter (2003), and Orr (2004).
15. See Manderson and Jolly (1997), Sychin and Herman (2001), Cruz-Malavé and Manalansan (2002), and Sunder Rajan (2003).
16. Following the Netherlands, Belgium became the second nation in the world to recognize gay marriages on January 30, 2003. Unlike the Netherlands, however, Belgium did not go so far as to allow such couples to adopt children. Several Scandinavian nations, such as Denmark, Finland, Iceland, Norway, and Sweden have laws recognizing same-sex "unions" and granting substantial legal, tax, and property rights to these couples (Wintemute 2001; "Gays to Marry in Belgium" 2003). On July 19, 2003, following approval by Ontario's highest court, Canadian Justice Minister Martin Cauchon authorized Canadian provinces to begin blessing same-sex marriages while the Supreme Court completed a review of new federal legislation defining marriage as the "lawful union of two persons to the exclusion of all others" (Thibodeau 2003; Tibbetts 2003). On November 19, 2003, Massachusetts became the first U.S. state to rule that gay couples have the right to marry under the state's Constitution (*Goodridge v. Department of Public Health,* 2003). The states of Hawaii, Vermont, and California do not currently allow gay marriage, but allow some form of civil union (see Human Rights Campaign 2003).
17. For a sampling of perspectives and overviews, see Delacoste and Alexander (1988), Barry (1995), Chapkis (1997), Jeffreys (1997), Nagle (1997), and O'Connell Davidson (1998).
18. Chapkis (1997) and Alexander (1998) provide cogent summaries of different state regulatory strategies around prostitution.

19. Significant recent works include West and Petrik (1992), Stephens (1995), James and Prout (1997), Jenkins (1998), Scheper-Hughes and Sargent (1998), Fass and Mason (2000), Weis and Fine (2000), and Brown, Larson, and Saraswathi (2002).
20. For notable exceptions, see Nathanson (1991), Tolman (1994), Thompson (1995), Lamb (2000), and Levine (2002).
21. Although two landmark decisions for lesbian and gay activists, *Lawrence v. Texas* (2003) and *Goodrich v. Department of Public Health* (2003), occurred after the writing of this chapter, they aptly illustrate its claims.

1
The Regulation of Queer Identities and Intimacies

CHAPTER 1

Liberalism and Social Movement Success:
The Case of United States Sodomy Statutes

MARY BERNSTEIN[1]

In 1960, every state in the United States had a sodomy law that banned certain consensual sex acts between adults in private. In addition to statutes regarding anal sex, the sodomy statutes, either by express statutory language or judicial interpretation, prohibited any oral-genital contact. In some states, these laws applied to opposite-sex as well as same-sex couples, and to married as well as single people (Apasu-Gbotsu et al. 1986). During the last half-century, however, these laws have primarily been used to control lesbians and gay men, despite the fact that they were originally enacted to prohibit any nonprocreative sex (Halley 1994; Greenberg 1988; M. Bernstein 2004). Lesbians and gay men have been arrested in undercover sting operations in gay bars, cruising places, and hotel rooms, as well as in their own bedrooms as recently as the 1980s and 1990s (Robson 1992). Sodomy laws have also signified support for a heteronormative order that posits distinct gender and sexual roles for men and women (M. Bernstein 2001).

How should social movement theorists assess the success of movements that seek to profoundly alter dominant cultural values as well as achieve concrete legal change? Political opportunity theory along with much of the social movement literature tells us that changing laws or policies, in this case the sodomy statutes, constitutes movement success. But should we count these legal victories as successes when, rather than challenging the symbolic dimensions of these laws that discursively mark lesbian and gay sexuality and identity as inferior to heterosexuality, activists appeal to a right to privacy that leaves the symbolic meaning of these laws intact? Or do we need an alternative way to understand movement success?

Elsewhere (M. Bernstein 2003), I argue for a multidimensional approach to understanding movement outcomes (see also Staggenborg 1995), which identifies three categories of movement impact: political and policy outcomes, which include changes in laws and policies, as well as new benefits for a constituency; mobilization outcomes that correspond to organizational successes that result in the ongoing ability of movement organizations to engage in collective action; and cultural outcomes that, among other things, include discursive impact. In this chapter, I argue that liberal notions of success underlie political opportunity and political process theory and inhibit an understanding of movement impact. I examine the relationship between lesbian and gay movement strategies and outcomes along with a particular discursive frame: the right to privacy. I show both the strength of hegemonic discourse on privacy and illustrate the potential to challenge this discourse. The impact of social movements is varied, and liberal notions of success only partially capture their impact.

Political Opportunity, Liberalism, and Social Movement Success

Political opportunity theory focuses on the external political environment in order to explain the emergence of social movements, their strategies, and their outcomes. As political access opens, influential allies seek new constituents, and divisions among elites magnify, activists have better opportunities for mobilization and success.[2]

Implicit in political opportunity theory is a notion of success derived from liberal political theory. Movement success is generally defined as new benefits for a constituency and/or recognition by elites (Gamson 1990). Thus, an alliance with elites' lobbying strategies may result in policy change. In this view, legal or policy change should be considered the end of collective action and the mark of a successful movement. But a liberal conceptualization of success does not take into account a movement's cultural and mobilization goals. Divisions among which types of goals to seek are apparent in many social movements, including civil rights and Black Power movements, liberal and radical feminism movements, and gay liberation and gay rights movements. Although alliances with elites may lead to legal change, they may also demobilize a movement and promulgate a conservative discourse. Therefore, the effects of "opportunity" are contradictory, so that political change, mobilization, and other movement goals may be inversely related, suggesting the importance of a multidimensional approach to movement success that does not assume that political, cultural, and mobilization goals line up in a one-to-one fashion (M. Bernstein 2003).

Sociolegal scholars ask to what extent the courts can serve as a vehicle for meaningful social reform by examining the discursive and ideological effects of the law. According to McCann (1998), studies of the impact of legal reform begin with legal norms or actions and examine their impact on target populations. With few exceptions, such studies are critical of the promise of legal justice (76). For example, critical legal theorists argue that formulating claims in terms of rights is problematic because such claims can, in turn, generate competing rights claims (for example, the rights of the woman versus the rights of the fetus; see Hunt 1990). Queer legal theory stresses that the legal categories dictated by the law inadequately describe lesbian, gay, bisexual, transgendered (LGBT) or queer people, and contribute to the suppression of differences within queer communities (Bower 1997). Put simply, legal change generally fails to alter existing power relations.

Skepticism by sociolegal theorists about the benefits of legal change is matched by social movement scholars who question the passage of legislation as an adequate gauge of success. If we assume policy or legal change is an instrumental good, we also assume that these policies are materially meaningful. But Paul Burstein (1985) argues that the implementation of equal employment opportunity legislation was as important as its passage. Entman and Rojecki (1993) find that nuclear-freeze legislation was passed to quell protest, but due to lack of enforcement was ultimately an impotent measure. Often policy reform is symbolic in nature, having little impact in the real world. In fact, most recent studies of movement outcomes focus strictly on explaining why policy changes occur (e.g., Amenta, Dunleavy, and M. Bernstein 1994; Gamson 1990). While this remains a critical question, the achievement of new policies should be considered one aspect of success—a starting point, not an endpoint. Thus, even within a liberal political framework, a multidimensional approach to movement success is justified.

New Social Movement (NSM) theory, like critical legal studies, conceptualizes the goals of collective action in a fundamentally different way from resource mobilization and political opportunity theories, thus offering an alternative way to understand movement success. NSM theory views the generation of social movements that emerged in the 1960s and 1970s as challenges to dominant cultural patterns. Recent work argues that the ontological role of NSMs is to challenge the way markets and regulations "threaten, destroy, or manipulate self-identity" (Touraine 1997, 765). In this view, the challenges presented by collective action to dominant beliefs and the new identities created by political action are more significant than instrumental political change. Despite the many problems with the distinction between "new" and "old" social movements (e.g., Calhoun 1993; M. Bernstein 1997; Pichardo 1997), it makes sense for social movement actors to challenge both the fact of, as well as the stigma embodied by, the sodomy statutes.

The extent to which the courts can produce meaningful social change depends on whether movement outcomes are conceptualized as narrowly defined legal change and policy reform or by their impact on culture, including the development or deployment of identities, discourse, and community-building. Although NSM theory has not underscored the importance of law to social movements, it shows a concern with the impact of NSMs on transforming broad cultural patterns and norms.

Therefore, I argue that theorists must understand not only a movement's political impact, but its mobilization and cultural effects, including the creation of alternative discourse, community-building, and empowerment as well. Political campaigns are often as important for their effect on communities, organizations, and identities as for the laws they change. For example, despite the fact that abortion is still legal in the United States, the antichoice movement has made safe abortions unattainable for many American women. The antichoice movement has also had a tremendous discursive impact. For example, the terms "unborn children" and "partial birth abortion" are now routinely used by the media and the culture more broadly. I am not arguing that changing laws and policies is unimportant, but rather that certain goals are often privileged at the expense of others. Because shifts in the political environment privilege some forms of collective action over others, the state and the law influence which types of goals movements seek.

Political opportunity theorists argue that access to the structure of political bargaining leads activists to constrain or limit their claims, but the underlying assumption is that such censoring is the price to be paid for policy change. In contrast, I argue that when legal and political elites share movement goals, rather than being an unequivocal good for social movements, such openings may sometimes limit mobilization efforts, that is, dampen the development of a more progressive discourse and slow community-building. Similarly, the price of admission to the courts can be framing arguments in ways that often prevent the cultural challenge of social movements. "Opportunities" may privilege a liberal political agenda, but activists often have other goals, leading them to act in ways not envisioned by political opportunity theory. By understanding movement agendas, we can better understand movement responses to their environment and how the environment shapes those agendas.

Following both NSM and critical legal theory, I advocate caution when viewing legal or political change as the end of collective action. A movement may not achieve legal change, but it may build lasting organizations that can influence dominant cultural values or produce a new generation of activists. Alternatively, legal change may be a catalyst for increased movement and opposing movement activism. In this chapter, I adopt a multidimensional approach to movement success and de-center the focus on legal and policy change as the primary marker of movement impact. This does not mean that I dismiss the importance of legal change. Instead, I suggest that legal decisions and policy outcomes must be analyzed according to their impact on movement and opposing movement mobilization, as well as on dominant cultural values.

In the following section, I draw on two examples from a larger research project that examines the lesbian and gay movement and the decriminalization of sodomy.[3] I explore the impact of activists' strategic choices on agenda-setting, the production of discourse, movement- and community-building, and legal and legislative change. I then consider the *Lawrence v. Texas* (2003) decision (which occurred after my period of data collection), its cultural meaning, and its possible impact on mobilization and on future legal and policy decisions.

The Alliance of Elites and Social Movements

> In return for removing the formal threat of severe criminal sanctions for *hidden and discreet* acts (which society had rarely enforced in any case), dominant heterosexual society has sought the quiescence of sexual nonconformists—their tacit agreement to hide themselves from view and spare the beneficent dominant culture the disgust of any type of public presence. (Backer 1993, 759)

From 1961 to 1977, elite and movement interests in sodomy law reform coincided. In 1955, the American Law Institute (ALI) set out to rationalize this country's laws, publishing a Model Penal Code (MPC) as a blueprint for states to follow when revising their laws. Although maintaining penalties for the solicitation of sexual acts, the MPC removed sodomy from its list of crimes and misdemeanors.

The ALI's rationale for decriminalization (*American Law Institute* 1980; *American Law Institute* 1955) rested on the divided opinions of medical elites and contemporary debates over whether or not crimes without victims should be considered crimes. Medical elites were uncertain about whether homosexuality was genetic or psychological, and even less sure about the prospects for a cure. As a medical condition, homosexuality was better treated by medical authorities than by the criminal justice system. Alternatively, if homosexuality were genetic, then punishment would be pointless. The ALI also wanted to eliminate victimless crimes, that is, crimes that lacked a complainant and from which no quantifiable harm resulted. Because of the mostly private nature of the offense, the ALI reasoned that sodomy laws were unenforceable.

The fledgling National Gay Task Force (NGTF), later the National Lesbian and Gay Task Force (NGLTF), ceded initiatives to state legislators. The reigning wisdom was to avoid drawing public attention to the reform. For example, Jean O'Leary, then co-executive director of the NGTF, recommended that the best strategy for success was to work quietly, behind the scenes, and to assist states in recodifying their penal codes (O'Leary 1978). If the code had already been revised, then a more "frontal" strategy could be necessary. During this time period, the NGTF newsletter rarely mentioned sodomy law reform.

The ALI's commentary provided a number of scripts that lesbian and gay activists could adopt to advocate for change, most notably, the right to privacy. Each script played on dominant political and cultural themes that simultaneously allowed for the moral condemnation of homosexuality and sodomy, but argued that the state need not be a moral arbiter. The normative status of homosexuality could remain intact and, above all, homosexuality would remain in the "private sphere." By the 1970s, the feminist claim that "the personal is political" directly conflicted with privacy arguments, which did little to challenge dominant cultural norms about homosexuality.

Today, the negative ramifications of privacy arguments are apparent in the military's "don't ask, don't tell" policy, where one is allowed to *be* gay as long as that "fact" is not made public. Similar reasoning about organizational rights to privacy allowed the Supreme Court to rule that the Ancient Order of Hibernians as well as the Boy Scouts of America had the right to keep identified lesbians and gay men out of their parades and organizations (Currah 1997), despite the apparent "public" nature of these groups.

What effects did leaving the decision making to elites have on discourse, organizing, and legal change? A survey of legislative reference librarians (Apasu-Gbotsu et al. 1986) shows that when legislators first considered decriminalizing private, consensual, sexual conduct between adults in the early 1970s, they either felt law and morality should be separated or they chose to equate legal sanctions with moral disapproval. Even when states voted to decriminalize, their arguments rested on an absence of harm, and the fact that the behavior in question took place behind closed doors.

Penal review committees and state legislatures adopted one of two views about the relationship between law and morality. Those who saw law as a symbolic tool equated decriminalization with condoning sexual conduct they found morally offensive. By 1977, one legislator equated decriminalization with a "gay rights bill." Others cited reasons to separate the spheres of law and morality. Testimony in favor of decriminalization claimed that issues of morality should be left to spiritual or other authorities, that the law did not signify moral countenance or approval of sexual conduct, that immorality was not the same as criminality, and that the law should not be used to enforce purely religious or moral standards, or, finally, that these laws had no relationship to "family values." Thus, although the moral status of homosexual behavior was left unchallenged, an albeit more tolerant, but nonetheless heteronormative, order was maintained.

Passive strategies did little to foster organizational development and even less to challenge negative stereotypes of homosexuality or dominant cultural beliefs. Because the agenda was set by law review committees, often little controversy surrounded repeal (Cohn and Gallagher 1984). When elite agendas incorporate movement concerns, activists will often ignore those issues and leave the framing to elites. Thus, political opportunities often *do* lead to policy success, but they may also demobilize a movement and leave hegemonic discourse unchallenged.

Did these passive strategies lead to legal reform? Ceding the issues of penal code reform to elites resulted in the repeal of 18 sodomy statutes by the end of 1977.[4] Seven states decriminalized consensual sodomy between opposite sex partners while specifying homosexual acts for punishment,[5] and the rest retained their pre-Model Penal Code statutes or reduced penalties associated with the "crime" (Hunter 1992). Although repealing sodomy statutes removes an important legal weapon from the state that has been used to harass lesbians and gay men, it is not at all clear that the reformed states were more hospitable to lesbians and gay men. Statistical research finds that the repeal of sodomy statutes does not significantly predict the passage of hate crime legislation (Jenness and Grattet 1996) or lesbian and gay rights ordinances (Button, Rienzo, and Wald 1996; Haider-Markel and Meier 1996), nor do such laws reduce economic disparity between same-sex and opposite-sex couples (Klawitter and Flatt 1998). Although the sodomy statutes may have provided a convenient excuse to limit the rights of lesbians and gay men, it is likely that without altering the cultural climate, legal change was an important but limited benefit. Where the solicitation of sexual acts still remained a crime, because of its allegedly public nature, the state could continue to arrest gay men for cruising in parks, restrooms, and bookstores (Gallo et al. 1966; D'Emilio 1983b).

In sum, elite support for decriminalization led 18 of the 50 states to repeal their sodomy laws between 1961 and 1977 with a minimum expenditure of activist energy and resources. But while elite support sometimes led to legal change, it failed in more cases than it succeeded. Additionally, elite support came at the price of failing to combat the stigma associated with homosexuality. By adopting the dominant script and deferring activism to elites, lesbian and gay activists ceded control of the discursive terrain to the state. Antigay opponents routinely employ privacy arguments in order to limit lesbian and gay rights. Conceptualizing elite support for decriminalization as a "political opportunity" ignores the multiple implications of this political shift on activism and social change. Although elite support led to legal change (which may have eventually created a more gay-positive environment), such support also defused protest and dulled the edge of challenges to dominant cultural patterns.

The Absence of Elite Support

> To hold that the act of homosexual sodomy is somehow protected as a
> fundamental right would be to cast aside millennia of moral teaching.
> (*Bowers v. Hardwick*, opinion of Justice Burger 1986, 186)

In 1982, Michael Hardwick was arrested in the privacy of his bedroom for committing sodomy with a consenting adult male partner. Recognizing this as an ideal case, activist lawyers used the case to challenge existing sodomy statutes. Four years later, the lesbian and gay movement suffered its most visible and humiliating legal defeat, when the U.S. Supreme Court ruled in *Bowers v. Hardwick* (1986) that there was no constitutional right to privacy that included consensual sodomy by adults in private to be found in the Constitution. This much-criticized decision sent a clear message to the public that elites were not sympathetic to the cause of lesbian and gay rights. The lesbian and gay movement responded to *Bowers* by making sodomy law repeal a central focus of its political agenda and by engaging in a wide variety of strategies. In this section, I argue that the strategies and tactics employed by the NGLTF after *Bowers* never fully abandoned the discourse on privacy. Instead, the NGLTF modified the dominant discourse by linking private acts with public stigma and employing a more open approach to sexuality as it sought to organize in the unreformed states. This discussion is based on a thorough examination of the Privacy Project files.[6]

Furious over *Bowers*, the NGLTF embarked on a campaign to organize activists in unreformed states to challenge the sodomy laws. National lesbian and gay organizations called for a march on Washington, which took place the following year in 1987, bringing several hundred thousand people to the Capitol. The NGLTF issued a call to arms, appointing Sue Hyde director of its newly formed Privacy Project. The Privacy Project had three main goals: First, the Project was devoted to research, preparing materials, and working with existing groups around sodomy-law repeal. Second, the Project had an organizing mission: to create new organizations in the unreformed states, "the *raison d'etre* of the project itself" (Hyde 1987c). The third focus of the Project was "to promote and encourage discussion of sexuality among and between lesbians and gay men" (Hyde 1990). The link between cultural and legal change was clear. Hyde claimed:

> It was a consensus opinion of the [Ad Hoc Task Force to Decriminalize
> Sodomy] that the gay and lesbian community must now take a more
> proactive role in decriminalization of sexual behavior. The lesson of
> Hardwick may well be that decriminalization, because it is so inextricably connected to antihomophobia work, is unlikely to occur in a political vacuum. (1987a)

In contrast to previous strategies (and to the failure of privacy arguments in the Supreme Court), the NGLTF began to address the issue of sexuality directly. The NGLTF amassed statements supporting sodomy law repeal by professional and civic organizations, including psychiatric associations, civil rights groups, law enforcement officials, and churches. Substantial time was devoted to delinking sodomy law repeal from the spread of AIDS and arguing that continued criminalization would deter people from seeking HIV tests and treatment. Hyde attended many LGBT conferences to educate activists about sodomy laws and to give advice on repeal strategies. Even in their written materials, the lesbian and gay movement tried to find a way to talk about sex (Hyde 1987b). In its flyer "Eight Good Reasons to Decriminalize Sodomy," the NGLTF claimed, "Antisodomy laws define love and sexual intimacy as criminal, unnatural, perverse, and repulsive. That's the real crime" (n.d.).

In addition to actually overturning laws, the Privacy Project's philosophy was to build organizations and coalitions and to bring LGBT communities together. Hyde was sent to the "sodomy states" to help organize repeal efforts. The Project launched a series of annual events ranging from lobbying to rallies and protests to commemorate a "National Day of Mourning for the Right to Privacy" (Hyde 1989a, 1989b). These events often marked the first public emergence of LGBT people into politics. Strategies varied substantially according to locale, but in most places, post-*Bowers* sodomy law reform efforts showed a markedly more open approach to discussing and defending same-sex sexuality. Largely due to the Privacy Project's efforts, new lesbian and gay organizations developed in more than a half dozen states. Not all of these new organizations chose to underscore sodomy law repeal. Instead, many organized around AIDS-related policies and antidiscrimination legislation (Hyde 1987c; 1990), but their entry into the political realm was an important victory for the lesbian and gay movement.

Hyde convened several town meetings on "Sex and Politics" for LGBT people to discuss how to address sexuality in the political arena. The Project recognized problems with the right to privacy:

> Privacy-based arguments fail to support repeal of laws used to stigmatize and criminalize people who have no recognized right to privacy. Only when we change public consciousness so that gay and lesbian people are not vulnerable to attack-by-innuendo, and gay and lesbian sexuality is not untouchable and indefensible will we make lasting change in the social status of homosexuality. (Hyde n.d.)

Discursively, the NGLTF validated lesbian and gay intimacy while also demanding respect for the privacy rights of lesbians and gay men. At the 1987 March on Washington, the NGLTF sold T-shirts that read "So-Do-My Friends,

So-Do-My Neighbors" to raise pubic awareness that the acts prohibited by the sodomy statutes were engaged in by most people, gay or straight, married or single.

The Privacy Project, which lasted from 1986 until 1991, helped mobilize and empower people at the grassroots level to build lasting organizations and create a discourse around sexuality that defended lesbian and gay intimacy. During this time period, activists often refused to sacrifice movement-building or challenging dominant cultural norms for the sake of legal change. Yet when the NGLTF disbanded the Privacy Project in 1991, it had repealed no sodomy statutes. Because (or in spite) of a hostile organized opposition, activists challenged the symbolic dimensions of the sodomy laws. The Privacy Project's failure to change any laws led to its disbandment. Nonetheless, new organizations formed and activists created a language with which to discuss sexuality and politics that acknowledged the relationship of sodomy laws to sexual orientation, while pointing out that most people, regardless of sexual orientation, engage in such acts.[7] Activists continued to gain the support of other institutions, expanding the campaign's reach and its potential cultural impact. Activists adopted, modified, and challenged the discourse on privacy, responding discursively in a way that confronted public phobias about sexuality, even at times when that risked achieving concrete policy change.

Postscript: Private Acts, Public Consequences, and the *Lawrence v. Texas* Decision

> To say that the issue in Bowers was simply the right to engage in certain sexual conduct demeans the claim the individual put forward, just as it would demean a married couple were it to be said marriage is simply about the right to have sexual intercourse . . . When sexuality finds overt expression in intimate conduct with another person, the conduct can be but one element in a personal bond that is more enduring. The liberty protected by the Constitution allows homosexual persons the right to make this choice. (*Lawrence v. Texas* 2003, 17–18)

In a case eerily similar to *Bowers v. Hardwick*, John Geddes Lawrence and Tyron Garner were arrested while committing an act of consensual sodomy in the privacy of Lawrence's apartment, violating Texas's sodomy statute. In 2003, the U.S. Supreme Court, in *Lawrence v. Texas* invalidated not only the Texas statute, but the remaining sodomy statutes and overturned *Bowers v. Hardwick* as well. The Court ruled on privacy grounds, with privacy understood as a liberty interest arising under the due process clause of the Fourteenth Amendment. In contrast to the legislative repeal of sodomy statutes in the 1960s and 1970s, I would argue that *Lawrence* is the product of contradictions within the dominant discourse of privacy, which (falsely) relies on the separation of the private and public spheres. _Lawrence is also the result of a partial shift in the cultural climate regarding sexual orientation_. Like the NGLTF approach to sodomy law repeal after _Bowers_, the _Lawrence_ decision itself both validates same-sex sexual relations and demands respect for the privacy rights of those engaging in such acts. This decision has increased the mobilization of lesbian and gay rights proponents and opponents alike, as _Lawrence_ appears to pave the legal road to same-sex marriage.[8]

Elsewhere I have argued (M. Bernstein 2001) that the right to privacy allows activists to circumvent the challenge to dominant gender and sexual norms that underlie the opprobrium associated with homosexuality because the rubric of privacy allows the state to avoid sanctioning gender and sexual behavior that is nonnormative. However, _Lawrence_ manages to avoid making a moral judgment while simultaneously claiming that the values condemning homosexuality have changed. For example, the Court acknowledges long-standing opposition to homosexual conduct, but suggests that the majority cannot impose its own moral code (25). Yet rather than stop there, the Court goes on to suggest that the moral condemnation of homosexual conduct is abating. To substantiate this claim, the Court cites the Model Penal Code; recent state court and legislative decisions that overturned sodomy statutes; Britain's Wolfenden Report (1963), which recommended decriminalizing sodomy committed between consenting adults in private; and a recent decision by the European Court of Human Rights, which invalidated any remaining sodomy laws in the now 45-nation Council of Europe. Thus, _Lawrence_ casts doubt on _Bowers_' claim that decriminalization is at odds with Judeo-Christian moral and ethical standards.

Lawrence also corrects the historical errors of _Bowers_ in order to claim that the condemnation of homosexuality per se is relatively recent. The Court argues that sodomy statutes were originally intended to prohibit any nonprocreative sexual activity, not to target "homosexual conduct" as such. _Laws that single out homosexual sodomy, the Court points out, are very recent inventions._ So while the Court claims not to be making a moral judgment, _Lawrence_ goes a long way toward showing that _moral condemnation of homosexuality is abating_. Nonetheless, the majority opinion dodges the issue of same-sex marriage by claiming that this decision does not involve granting legal formal recognition to same-sex relationships.

Although _Lawrence_ rests on an understanding of privacy, the decision, as is evident in the quote at the beginning of this section, transforms the discursive field by suggesting that _private_ acts carry _public_ stigma, which the Court declares, is unacceptable. Therefore, the Court openly acknowledges the existence of same-sex sexuality and finds and interprets a privacy right within the liberty clause of the due process clause of the Fourteenth Amendment to include autonomy in choosing one's intimate relationships. In this way, the *Lawrence* decision directly challenges heteronormativity, in contrast to previous rulings (see M. Bernstein 2001).

In a strange twist on the right to privacy, the Court acknowledges the public stigma and attendant discrimination that attaches when private conduct is made criminal. The Court explains that this is why the decision was based on privacy and due process rather than on equal protection grounds (since the Texas statute only criminalized sodomy between same-sex partners).[9] The Court states:

> Were we to hold the statute invalid under the Equal Protection Clause, some might question whether a prohibition would be valid if drawn differently, say, to prohibit the conduct both between same-sex and different-sex participants . . . When homosexual conduct is made criminal by the law of the State, that declaration in and of itself is an invitation to subject homosexual persons to discrimination both in the public and in the private spheres. The central holding of *Bowers* has been brought in question by this case, and it should be addressed. Its continuance as precedent demeans the lives of homosexual persons. (30–31)

Thus, the Court echoes the claims of the NGLTF's Privacy Project and of other lesbian and gay rights activists in decrying the opprobrium signified by the sodomy laws by linking public stigma and discrimination to private acts. Since 1983, the national legal networks of Lambda Legal Defense and Education Fund's cooperating attorneys,[10] ACLU affiliates, nonaffiliated activist lawyers, and some statewide lesbian and gay organizations have mounted judicial challenges to the sodomy statutes, often innovating novel arguments. In *State v. Morales* (1994), the Texas Human Rights Foundation argued that the stigma that accrued to lesbians and gay men as a result of the mere existence of the sodomy statutes as well as the real danger of loss of housing or employment entitled them to standing. Although the case was successful in the lower courts, the Texas Supreme Court ultimately reversed the Court of Appeals decision (*State v. Morales* [1994]; see also *City of Dallas v. England* [1993]). Similarly, in a series of cases brought by activist attorney John Rawls in Louisiana, Rawls argued in *State v. Baxley I & II* (1994, 1995) that the stigma of the mere existence of the law should give the plaintiff standing, but this was rebuffed by the Louisiana Supreme Court (Wolfson and Mower 1994). Rawls made a similar argument on behalf of named plaintiffs in *Louisiana Electorate of Gays and Lesbians Inc. v. State of Louisiana* (2002) but did not succeed in having the Louisiana law invalidated. By adopting lesbian and gay arguments regarding the public consequences of private acts, the Court was able to exploit the contradictions within the right to privacy that assumed the separation of the private and public spheres. Although the dominant discourse of privacy continues to frame what can and cannot be said in certain arenas, the boundaries of what is contained in that discourse have expanded.

By reversing *Bowers* and claiming that the cultural and legal consensus that condemns homosexuality has changed, *Lawrence* has generated alarm in conservative circles and excitement among lesbian and gay activists and their allies. Greenhouse (2003), for example, reports that "By the time [Justice Kennedy] referred to the dignity and respect to which he said gays were entitled, several [gay and lesbian lawyers] were weeping, silently, but openly." Since the decision, numerous commentators have predicted that this decision will open the door to same-sex marriage.

Responding to the same news, gay and lesbian opponents have introduced the "Marriage Protection Amendment" into Congress. This proposed amendment to the U.S. Constitution defines marriage as strictly between one man and one woman to stave off the specter of same-sex marriage. If passed, this amendment would also invalidate any existing civil union and domestic partner legislation (ACLU 2003). In addition, President Bush instituted a "Marriage Protection Week" to galvanize opposition to same-sex marriage. As conservative activist Phyllis Schlafly put it, "President Bush has proclaimed October 12 through 18 [2003] as Marriage Protection Week because it is becoming clearer all the time that the institution of marriage needs protection from the courts. Gay lobbyists have made it clear that their aim is to litigate to get activist judges to accord the status of marriage to same-sex relationships" (Schlafly 2003).

Just as the moral shock of *Bowers* sparked renewed activism on the part of lesbian and gay activists, *Lawrence* has regalvanized their opponents and illustrates that while views on same-sex relations may be shifting, opposition remains strong. Yet *Lawrence* has also directly confronted heteronormativity and acknowledged the legitimacy of multiple expressions of sexual intimacy. This shift in discourse is already apparent in the newspaper coverage of the *Lawrence* decision and in subsequent agitation for same-sex marriage (e.g., Greenhouse 2003; Gibbs 2003).

Conclusion

This chapter has employed a multidimensional approach to understanding social movement success that, in contrast to liberal notions of success embodied in political opportunity theory, considers legal change to be only one element of movement impact. I first compared lesbian and gay political strategies around sodomy law repeal when political opportunities were auspicious and when they were lacking. Then I outlined the implications of *Lawrence v. Texas* for mobilization, culture, and future legal and policy decisions.

Within the context of relatively weak lesbian and gay political organizations during the 1960s and early 1970s, deferring the issue of sodomy repeal to elites appears to have been a wise decision. Using conventional understandings of movement success, the repeal of sodomy laws in 21 states (18 with little activist effort) was a considerable victory. However, the repeal of those laws did not necessarily signify a weakening of the moral consensus against homosexuality, as is evidenced by the lack of correlation between sodomy law repeal and other legal lesbian and gay rights victories. Nonetheless, the repeal of those laws meant that when lesbians and gay men did organize to pass antidiscrimination legislation, they could avoid the charge that they were advocating rights for people who, by definition, violated the law. The state avoided some cultural and discursive battles around sexuality by removing legal penalties on its own accord, although such cultural battles inevitably arose around other lesbian and gay legal issues such as lesbian and gay rights ordinances.

By contrast, the *Bowers* defeat ushered in a period of activism around sodomy-law repeal, which, by conventional standards, was an abject failure, because no laws were repealed. Yet lasting organizations were built, new activists joined the political process, and discourse was altered as activists directly confronted the symbolic meanings of the sodomy statutes. Many new organizations formed as a result of the Privacy Project's organizing efforts and of the 1987 March on Washington. The impetus for the lesbian and gay workers right's movement can be traced to the 1987 march, and *Bowers* provided the motivation to propel AIDS activists to engage in new and more daring strategies that ultimately changed policies surrounding HIV/AIDS (Raeburn 2000; Gould 2001).

In *Lawrence*, lawyers from lesbian and gay public interest organizations were able to persuade the U.S. Supreme Court to adopt a vision of privacy that acknowledged the public stigma and discrimination that inhered from the continued criminalization of sodomy. This decision echoed activist claims that the sodomy statutes disparage lesbian and gay sexuality and lead directly to discrimination in the public sphere. In addition to acknowledging that sodomy laws demean the lives of homosexuals, the Court reaffirmed the hegemonic discourse on privacy, but defined that privacy to include the choice of intimate relationships and intimate sexual conduct. This discursive shift has created more space for the discussion of same-sex marriage but has also contributed to substantial backlash, such as the introduction of the Federal Marriage Amendment and the declaration of "Marriage Protection Week."

These examples suggest that we must revise our understandings of political opportunity and of the impact of the state on movement activism. While political opportunities provided by state penal code revisions privileged a liberal political agenda during the 1960s and 1970s that stressed the achievement of new laws, the closing of opportunity in the 1980s followed by the *Bowers* decision in 1986 (see M. Bernstein 2003) sparked a political agenda that facilitated the movement's growth and challenge to dominant cultural norms. The decriminalization of the remaining sodomy statutes in 2003 has resulted in increased activism among both proponents and opponents of lesbian and gay rights. It also marks the end of a very long battle by lesbian and gay activists to challenge their status as criminals, and closes one important chapter on lesbian and gay politics. Studies of movement outcomes must take all these effects into account.

Notes

1. This research was supported by a National Science Foundation grant (9623937). Thanks to Elizabeth Bernstein, Nancy Naples, and Yvonne Zylan for comments and clarifications.
2. See, for example, Kitschelt (1986); Tarrow (1988, 1996, 1998); McAdam (1982); and Meyer and Staggenborg (1996).
3. This research is based on published accounts of the lesbian and gay movement, the newsletters of the national lesbian and gay organizations Lambda and the NGLTF, the *Sexual Law Reporter* and *Lesbian and Gay Law Notes* (two lesbian and gay legal periodicals), court decisions regarding sodomy, the NGLTF's Privacy Project files held by the Cornell University Human Sexuality Collection, and the Web sites of Lambda, the NGLTF, and the ACLU, which include press releases and discussion of strategy. Interviews with selected informants were also conducted.
4. The states included Illinois (1961), Connecticut (1969), Oregon (1971), Colorado (1971), Hawaii (1972), Ohio (1972), Delaware (1973), New Hampshire (1973), Maine (1975), Washington (1975), West Virginia (1976), South Dakota (1976), Indiana (1976), Iowa (1976), Nebraska (1977), North Dakota (1977), Vermont (1977), and Wyoming (1977); (Hunter 1992; Nice 1988). The dates in parentheses next to the states indicate the years the laws were changed, not the years they took effect. California and New Mexico also repealed their sodomy laws during this time. California's repeal was the result of the organized lobbying efforts of lesbian and gay activists (National Gay Task Force 1976). New Mexico repealed its sodomy law as part of a general package of reform regarding rape laws and was supported by feminists and gay activists (*The Gay Blade* 1975).
5. The states were Kansas (1970), Montana (1973), Texas (1973), Kentucky (1974), Arkansas (1977), Missouri (1977), and Nevada (1977) (Hunter 1992).
6. The Privacy Project files include newspaper articles, correspondence, minutes, action alerts and memos from local LGBT organizations, monthly reports by the Project's director, Sue Hyde, and NGLTF newsletters that discuss sodomy law reform.
7. Most public health authorities agree that engaging in such acts is "common" among married and unmarried heterosexuals as well as homosexuals (e.g., *American Psychological Association* 1986:2) This was a claim that was frequently echoed by activists (e.g., Nevins 1987).
8. Both Justice O'Connor in her concurring opinion and Justice Scalia in his dissent to *Lawrence* suggest that the majority's opinion provides legal justification for same-sex marriage.
9. The equal protection clause of the Fourteenth Amendment reads, "No State shall . . . deny to any person within its jurisdiction the equal protection of the laws." Had the Court ruled on equal protection grounds, then existing laws that prohibited consensual sodomy between same-sex and different-sex partners would have remained constitutional and only those sodomy statutes that prohibited such conduct between same-sex partners would have been overturned. Justice O'Connor's concurring opinion is based on equal protection grounds, but since it was not the majority opinion, it holds no precedential value.
10. Lambda is a public interest lesbian and gay law firm.

CHAPTER 2

Contract and the Legal Mooring
of Same-Sex Intimacy

WILLIAM ROUNTREE

Recent changes in laws pertaining to intimate relationships in North America and Western Europe have produced contradictory trends. On one hand, states have increasingly revealed an interest in providing binding legal structures for intimate relationships. The political battles over same-sex marriage in Hawaii, Vermont, and Massachusetts and the creation of a "covenant marriage" in Louisiana (which marked the return of fault-based divorce) reflect the widespread desire for states to provide structure to intimate relationships.[1] Though covenant marriage legislation reflects more traditional family values than the politics behind the same-sex marriage movement, these examples are similar in that each reflects a desire for structural constraints for intimate arrangements.

Although a desire exists for the constraints that legal structures provide, there also appears to be a countertrend—a desire for more flexibility in intimate relationships than the legal structure of marriage can provide. For example, in the United States, people are marrying much later in life. In 1970, the median age of first marriage was 22.2 years for men, and 20.8 years for women. By 2000, this rose to a historic high: 26.8 years and 25.1 years for men and women, respectively. Cohabitation appears as both a precursor and alternative to marriage. In 1960, 1.1 percent of all households were comprised of unmarried cohabitants. By 2000, this rose to 3.7 percent of all households (U.S. Bureau of the Census 2000).

19

French law also provides an interesting example. France's "*Pacte civil de solidarité*," or PACS, extends many of the rights and benefits included in marriage without the difficulties of gaining a divorce. Although PACS was created in order to extend legal recognition to same-sex couples, the more flexible arrangements that PACS offers are proving wildly popular with French heterosexual couples as well. Of the 14,000 PACS reported throughout France, 40 percent are heterosexuals who choose PACS instead of, or as a stepping stone to, marriage (Daley 2000). These developments reveal contradictory trends in laws that provide mooring to intimate relationships—a desire for structural constraints when seeking state recognition of intimate relationships, with a simultaneous desire to be free from the constraints that legal structures provide.

Lacking access to the traditional legal structures of marriage, same-sex couples in the United States have instead used a patchwork of contracts: written accords covering co-ownership of property, wills and trusts, donor insemination agreements, and coparenting pacts to govern child-bearing and child-rearing arrangements. The contracts that same-sex couples create most often attempt to achieve the legal terms that are a part of state-defined marital arrangements.

In this chapter, I present an in-depth case study from the United States of the uses of contracts in same-sex parenting arrangements. These contracts attempt to mimic the legal arrangements contained within state-defined marriage laws. For example, marriage laws create a paternity presumption for husbands of all married women who bear a child. The assumption that the spouse of a woman who bears a child is a legal parent to the child is not available to same-sex couples. This is true for several reasons. First and most obviously, same-sex couples cannot marry in the United States, and thus legal presumptions within marriage are not available to them. Second, the reproductive arrangements of same-sex couples do not mirror those of heterosexual couples because the partners are of the same sex. As a result, the material it takes to make a child (sperm and egg) is not present within the relationship. Since the legal framework of marriage that creates the presumptions that individuals in an intimate bond are the legal parents to children born within that union, same-sex couples must rely in part on contracts to gain legal recognition of their parenting relationships. Further, since same-sex couples use a patchwork of contracts to achieve what is available in the single, encapsulated structure of marriage, they must engage in lengthy discussions about the ways they want to structure their parenting relationships. These discussions are not necessary in marital relationships because the legal framework of marriage structures these relationships for them.

Thus, contracts serve as a tool for achieving the contradictory goals of providing state recognition of same-sex intimacy while also providing the opportunity for couples to define the legal content of the promises they create. At a cultural moment when there is both a desire for a structural recognition of different intimate forms, as well as a desire for more flexible intimate arrangements, contract emerges as a way of achieving both of these seemingly contradictory goals.

Critics of the contractual model suggest that the presence of contracts between intimates is evidence of the infiltration of market principles into the familial sphere. Scholars such as Margaret Radin (1996), Milton Regan (1993), Robert Bellah et al. (1985), and Barbara Katz-Rothman (1989) argue that contracts in familial contexts are part of two interrelated trends: (1) an increasing incursion of a market logic into more and varied domains of society, and (2) the tendency toward individuated understandings of social life that weaken conventional structures of family. These critiques are based in the heterocentric assumption that the state provides access to a single and unified structure to organize legal aspects of parenting. Because of this assumption, contracts that appear in familial relations are automatically associated with market principles and deemed incompatible with intimate life.

In this exploration of the use of contracts in same-sex relationships, I am not suggesting that contracts are preferable to state-defined legal arrangements, such as civil unions or marriage. Indeed, access to *pro-forma*, encapsulated legal structures like marriage serves important political, economic, and cultural ends for the lesbian and gay rights movement. My intent here is to illustrate ways in which contract offers the opportunity for couples to define the legal content of the promises that intimates create, while also providing couples with access to the state in order to enforce intimate promises between them.

The Role of Contracts in Gaining Legal Recognition for Both Partners in Same-Sex Relationships

In this section, I discuss the role of contract in lesbian and gay parenting arrangements. I draw from an interview with Naomi and Ruth, one of 12 lesbian couples I spoke with in which one or both of the partners were planning to have a child. This couple was chosen because they most comprehensively illustrate both the deeply embedded presumptions of traditional family structure within the law, and the way that contract can create a legal recognition of parenting arrangements outside of more traditional legal structures.

This research is part of a larger project exploring the role of contracts in both heterosexual and same-sex relationships (Rountree 2000). My research included interviews with 20 heterosexual and 30 same-sex couples, as well as an in-depth historical legal analysis of case law in California from 1850–1999. For heterosexual couples, I found that contract was overwhelmingly seen as a source of contention. Many who were asked to sign these contracts felt it was evidence of selfishness, or planning for the demise of the relationship before marriage. However for same-sex couples, the contracts were uniformly viewed in a positive light because the contracts were the only way the couples could gain legal recognition of their relationships. The planning and conversations that occurred in contractual negotiations were viewed as bringing individuals in these relationships closer together.

Yet the legal structures outside of marriage offer little opportunity for two persons of the same sex to be legal parents to a child. As of this writing, most states do not permit persons of the same sex to be legally recognized as parents. Only four states—New Jersey, Vermont, Massachusetts, and California—provide the legal possibility to have two parents of the same sex as legal parents. Massachusetts and California enacted state laws that permit two persons of the same sex to adopt a child in the 1990s, and many other states will likely follow. Although these states have allowed for two persons of the same sex to be named as legal parents to a child, the fact that there is not a presumption of parenthood makes coparent adoption much less secure than the rights available in marriage.

Laws that govern parenting are constructed around the presumption that a child has one male and one female parent. The parenting contracts that same-sex couples draft attempt to alter this deeply embedded legal assumption by creating legal rights for the non-biologically related parent, while extinguishing some of the legal rights of the biological parent. In the case of lesbian couples, contracts are often drafted to extinguish the legal rights of the sperm donor, while creating legal rights for the parent who is not biologically related to the child.

In what follows, I elaborate on the social, cultural, and legal attributes of same-sex reproductive arrangements, drawing connections between the cultural assumptions that are embedded in law and the ways same-sex reproduction violates these assumptions. Many of the "taken-for-granted" arrangements of marriage are exposed when looking at same-sex couples' use of contracts. With heterosexuals, the materials of reproduction are assumed to be present. The cultural organization of parenting arrangements where women are mothers and thus "primary" parents and men (if present) are fathers and secondary parents serves as a template that organizes heterosexual parenting. When we move to a consideration of same-sex parenting arrangements, adherence to a cultural script of primary parenting is no longer possible.

To provide an example of the role of contract in lesbian reproductive arrangements, I turn now to the story of Ruth and Naomi Cohen-Burns. Their account reveals how each step of the reproductive process is fraught with difficult legal decisions that need not occur in heterosexual reproductive situations.

Ruth and Naomi's Relationship

Ruth and Naomi had been together for seven years when I interviewed them in their San Francisco, California, home during the spring of 2000. Both appeared casual and unpretentious, each in a different way. Ruth had short hair and wore Levi's with a short-sleeved, button-down shirt when I spoke with her in her office. Naomi's hair was long and fell casually over one eye. Naomi had a frenetic air about her, while Ruth seemed calm, deliberate, and less eager to please. Ruth made me work during our interview, asking me questions about my questions, and sometimes answering either "yes" or "no" or "somewhat" or "Why that?" Naomi, on the other hand, would take the questions and run with them. Perhaps this was because Naomi, as a lawyer, was willing to see connections between the questions I was asking and the legal structures in which their relationship exists. Naomi had just gained a very prestigious clerkship, where she had been working for about a month. She was concerned about interviewing for this job while she was seven months pregnant and was surprised when she got it. She talked about how much she enjoyed being pregnant. Their phone rang every half-hour, and Naomi would answer it, have a brief conversation—sometimes in Hebrew, sometimes in English, sometimes both—and would seamlessly return to our discussion.

Ruth and Naomi were the only lesbian couple I spoke with who, by appearances alone, adhered to "butch/femme" gendered personae. Ruth's short hair and muscular build contrasted with Naomi's long hair, slight build, and chipper, stereotypically feminine personality. Nevertheless, the butch/femme role that was present in their appearances did not play itself out either in their professions or in their domestic division of labor.

Like all 12 lesbian couples I interviewed, the decision to have a child was the beginning of a long deliberative process much different than that entered into by most heterosexuals. For example, the first task of many lesbian mothers-to-be is to choose who is going to carry the child.

Who Goes First?

The decision to have children was something that occurred early in Ruth and Naomi's relationship. Naomi recalled their initial conversation as follows.

> I said to her, "I just want you to know that I'm first." And she said, "What are you talking about?" And I said, "I'm getting pregnant first." And she was like, "You are insane!" Then I said, "You know, you are going back to the States and I am going to be here, but we're going to be together and we're going to have kids, and I just want you to know that I want to get pregnant first."

In spite of the fact that Naomi made the claim to go first, circumstances were such that it made sense for Ruth to be the one to initially get pregnant. There were several aspects to this decision. First, Ruth was more ambivalent about having children than Naomi was. For Ruth, the decision to have children seemed to be connected more with her relationship with Naomi and less with her desire to be a parent.

> Four days after we get together, Naomi says, "I'm first." But I was pregnant with our first child, so obviously that didn't happen. But we knew from the beginning, we always knew that we wanted kids. Did I always want kids? No, but I won't even go into that; that's a whole other thing. We decided to have children [she paused contemplatively], but it was just a question of when.

Second, Ruth decided to go to graduate school, which was much more flexible than Naomi's law school program. Although the concerns of school and work presented important reasons for Ruth to go first, what proved to be the most important reason was their concern that the butch/femme roles might be played out in parenting arrangements. Since Ruth was, at least by appearances, the "butch" in the relationship, she noted that this would become exaggerated if Naomi were to go first. Since Naomi was outwardly more feminine than Ruth, and much more excited about carrying a child, Ruth feared that she would be cast into a secondary father role. Thus, the decision for Ruth to go first was partially motivated by an attempt to minimize what she referred to as the "butch/femme" polarity:

> I felt it would really polarize our relationship and accentuate and exaggerate the butch/femme qualities that are already in it. Naomi really wanted to be pregnant; she was really into being pregnant and nursing a baby and being a mom. If Naomi were pregnant first, I was afraid that would shut me out. Me, on the other hand, I was less into it. I felt that if I were the one pregnant first, I would be emotionally able to make room for her to participate in it. There were some difficulties in terms of jealousy and such while I was pregnant, but in hindsight I think it was a really good idea. It has changed the dynamic. [The fact that I went first] has not allowed butch/femme polarity to occur in our relationship. [This] has given us a model for the next child we are having.

Naomi also acknowledged how the decision that Ruth go first was a good one, in spite of the fact that it was she who really wanted to be pregnant and to be a mother. Naomi mused,

> Now, in retrospect, I think that there are good things about it in terms of the balance of our relationship. I am just sort of more maternal by nature. And being pregnant and giving birth and nursing and all that stuff forced Ruth to be maternal. It balanced our relationship with

Joshua in a way that I don't think it would have been balanced had I been the one who got pregnant first. I don't think I would have given her as much of a central role in the child's life as she gave me. She was so *not* possessive about being "the mother" at all. In fact, she didn't want to be the mother. And I don't think I would have been that generous with that role. I think I would have been like, "I'm the mother. You know, I mean, you are the mother too, but I'm *really* the mother." I would have had more issues about that than she did.

Naomi talked about being jealous while Ruth was pregnant, but the decision for Ruth to go first was something she saw as providing balance to the relationship. In fact, it turned out that Naomi's maternal feelings helped ease the transition to parenthood for both of them. Ruth's pregnancy had been a difficult one, and she described being less than enthusiastic about her maternal responsibilities. Though she clearly loved Joshua and was delighted to have him, she did not take to parenting immediately. Naomi talked about this period in more detail than Ruth did:

So, I just fell in love with him the minute they took him out. I just thought, "He's so beautiful! He's so beautiful!" And Ruth was like, "Leave me alone, I have to sleep." She always says that it took her four months to fall in love with Joshua, but I was in love with him right away. [Ruth] was having a really hard time because she was temporarily physically disabled by the birth and by the whole thing. So I was taking care of him. I mean, she was nursing, trying to nurse at least as much as she could, and I was taking care of him, you know, everything else other than nursing. She didn't have a good time nursing. It didn't feel good for her, and so a lot of times he would suckle on my breast just to be calmed. Seventy-five percent of nursing is more just like sucking and not eating. I felt just so bonded with him so fast. There was never any feeling of not being close to him.

Lesbian parents have decisions to make about pregnancy that are different from those of heterosexuals; the need to choose which partner is going to bear the child is foremost among these differences. Workplace and school concerns featured prominently in Ruth and Naomi's decision, but what proved even more important were concerns pertaining to the "butch/femme" roles in their relationship. That a decision about who should carry the first child had to be articulated gave their child-bearing decision more of a contractual character.

The contractual features of their relationship become even more apparent when we begin to look at another concern many lesbian couples who want to have children face: whether to have a known or an unknown donor.

How to Get Pregnant, and By Whom

Once they decided it was time to get pregnant, and who would be impregnated, Ruth and Naomi began the difficult process of deciding whether they wanted a known or an unknown sperm donor. Like other lesbian couples I interviewed, Ruth and Naomi provided a detailed discussion of the plusses and minuses of known versus unknown donors. The most frequently mentioned benefit of known donors is that they are more likely to be accessible to the children. All of the couples I spoke with planned for the day when their child would grow up and want to know who their donors were. With known donors, this is more easily arranged.

Though known donors are more likely to agree to be available to children, they are also more likely to be in a position to assert paternity rights, thus thwarting the desires of lesbian couples to have both women become legal parents to the child. In spite of this risk, four of the 12 lesbian couples I interviewed decided to choose a known donor. Two of the 12 couples opted for what is called a "yes" donor. These are donors the couple does not know, but who, through the sperm bank, have agreed to have their name released after the child reaches 18. Though six of the couples chose unknown donors, all of the couples were concerned about how children would react to not being able to find out who their donors were. "Yes" donors provide a balance between protecting the legal rights of the couple, and the anonymity of the donor, while also giving the child the opportunity to discover their donor's identity.

Ruth and Naomi began looking for a donor by having informal conversations with friends. Deciding to donate sperm can be an emotionally intricate decision, particularly when the context of the donation is not anonymous. It is a decision that potentially involves not just the couple and the donor, but also the donor's spouse or partner, as well as his family of origin. For example, many donors have told me that their parents found it difficult knowing they had a biological grandchild, yet did not have any connection to this child. Ruth and Naomi had numerous informal conversations with friends in which they talked about these difficulties. It was through these informal conversations with friends that Ruth and Naomi first met Stanley.

Stanley was dating a friend of Ruth and Naomi's. After he expressed a willingness to consider becoming a donor, they decided to invite him and his girlfriend over for dinner. Their discussion went well, so they decided to invite him over again, this time without his girlfriend, to talk about specifics. During this conversation, he expressed concern that they would change their minds and want him to economically contribute to rearing the child. However, Ruth and Naomi's main concern was that he would change his mind after the child was born and want to participate in the rearing of the child. Since they were all interested in maintaining an arms-length relationship, their interests were compatible and they easily arrived at an agreement.

The contract they drafted achieved three goals. First, it provided protections between the couple and the sperm donor who, in the case of known donors, may be able to offer a court a convincing argument that allows him to obtain legal rights because of his biological connection to the child. Second, the contract set the foundation for custodial arrangements in the event that their relationship should end either through the death of the biological mother or in a custody battle over the child. Third, the contract articulated the contours of "family," creating familial insiders and outsiders. The contract made the non-biological parent, Naomi, a familial insider, while extinguishing any legal rights that the donor, Stanley, might have, thus placing him in the category of familial outsider. Contracts such as the one between Ruth, Naomi, and Stanley are drafted in order to carve out legal recognition for what would otherwise, from the state's perspective, be considered a collection of legal strangers.

Like many of the lesbian couples in which both women planned to bear children, Ruth and Naomi wanted to have the same donor for both of the children they planned to have. Initially, Stanley agreed to this arrangement.

Once the sperm donor had been decided, the parties involved had a choice between a sperm bank, intercourse (never a consideration for Ruth and Naomi, or for any of the couples I interviewed), or doing what has come to be known as a "turkey-baster" insemination (where the sperm is inserted at home without a doctor present). Of these three possibilities, sperm banks offered legal protections that were appealing to Ruth, Naomi, and Stanley. In the state where Joshua was conceived, going through a sperm bank and having a doctor act as intermediary extinguished the parental rights of the donor. Ruth explained these protections, as well as additional protections they decided to take to ensure Stanley would not retain legal rights.

> The law here is that if you go through a licensed physician, meaning that if the sperm is handed to the doctor, then the donor's rights are extinguished and he is a donor and not a father.[2] However, we also learned that that's not necessarily the case because we did go through a doctor and, in spite of that, when we did our adoption for Joshua, the social worker had to meet with the donor and get his signed consent to have him give up his right.

Unlike many couples where it took as many as 12 attempts before pregnancy occurred, Ruth became pregnant on the second try. Joshua was born nine months later.

Two years later, as Naomi came to the end of law school, she and Ruth began to think about having another child. During this period, Stanley had ended his relationship with Ruth and Naomi's friend, married another woman, and fathered a child in a more traditional family setting. Ruth and Naomi had not had much contact with Stanley since he married, so they were a bit cautious about approaching him. Because of the changed circumstances in Stanley's intimate life, they decided a visit or a phone call would be inappropriate. They instead decided to send a letter to his office. In the lengthy letter written in both Ruth and Naomi's script, they thanked him for the gift he gave them. They talked about how much they loved Joshua, how beautiful he was, and how much joy he brought to their lives. After giving their thanks to Stanley, they then asked if he would be willing, as previously agreed, to make a donation for another child that Naomi would carry.

In less than a week, Ruth and Naomi received the letter they wrote to Stanley. It had not been opened. On the outside of the unopened envelope, Stanley had written, "Don't ever contact me again." Through a common friend, Ruth and Naomi found out that Stanley's new wife did not like that he had a child with a lesbian couple and requested that he not have any further contact with them.

Second Parent Adoption

In addition to terminating any parental rights that Stanley might have retained, Ruth and Naomi were concerned about creating legal rights for Naomi as the nonbiological mother. To do this, they had to go through what is referred to as a second-parent adoption. Second-parent adoption is different from typical adoptions because the parental rights of the initial parent are not extinguished. Second-parent adoptions frequently occur in heterosexual relationships when a parent remarries and the new spouse adopts the child from the previous union. Ruth and Naomi's second-parent adoption was different, however, because Stanley had relinquished parental rights prior to Joshua's birth.

The contracts that Ruth, Naomi, and Stanley negotiated were intended to ensure that Stanley could not successfully assert parental rights. However, these contracts were only an intermediate step until Naomi could formally adopt Joshua. When it came time for Naomi to become a legal parent through a second-parent adoption, Ruth and Naomi were presented with additional difficulties. A social worker came to their home on three different occasions to make sure that theirs was a good home for Joshua. Further, Stanley was again asked to sign away his paternal rights, even though he did not have parental rights to begin with. Naomi expressed her frustration as follows:

> I felt just so bonded with [Joshua] so fast—[so] I just got mad at the adoption. I got mad that we had to have a social worker come to our house and tell me that I could be his mother when I was already his mother. I felt totally pissed off at her and resentful. And she was condescending. I was relieved when the adoption went through . . . The very act of [Stanley] signing the relinquishment was sort of an acknowl-

edgement that he had rights that I didn't think he had. But on the other hand, the benefit of it is that he is doubly acknowledging that he doesn't have rights if he does sign it. So I was relieved after he signed it. And after the adoption I was relieved. I felt like, okay, we're equal. No matter what happens. If something happens to Ruth or if something happens between us, no one will be able to take [Joshua] away from me. But it didn't change my relationship with him. It just sort of changed my own sense that there wouldn't be a fight. But mostly, it just made me . . . mad that we had to go through it and pay so much money to do it.

The second-parent adoption gave Ruth and Naomi the security of a legal status that contract could not provide. Because contract is a disfavored tool in governing parental relationships, the contracts that Ruth and Naomi created with Stanley always rested on tenuous legal grounds. The contract between them was not enforceable in court, and until the second-parent adoption was finalized, Stanley would have been able to challenge the termination of parental rights articulated in the contract. In many jurisdictions, his challenge would have been successful. Ruth and Naomi are privileged to live in a jurisdiction where individuals of the same sex can be parents to a child. In most other jurisdictions, the only way to articulate legal intent for coparenting arrangements between people of the same sex is through contract.[3]

The "Darn Good Agreement"

Ruth and Naomi were devastated by Stanley's refusal to donate again, not just because it meant they would have to find another donor, or that their next child would not be biologically related to Joshua. Most of their sadness was for Joshua who would not be able to see Stanley who was instrumental in giving Joshua life.

Still wanting to have another child, Ruth and Naomi briefly thought about going to a sperm bank to find a "yes" donor. But this time Ruth and Naomi ultimately decided that having a man who would agree to be involved with their family was the preferred alternative. After a few weeks of thinking it over, they decided to approach a friend Naomi had met the previous year. Naomi initially had reservations because, as she put it, "he just seemed so far from our world." But the distance that she initially considered a minus turned out to be a plus because it allowed them to define the nature of the relationship without preconceived notions about what their relationship would be like. This initial distance eventually led them to agree to something a bit deeper than a mere donor.

We never approached him before even though he had offered, because he just seemed so far from our world. I mean, he's not queer, you know. But then we thought more and more that that was a good thing that he

is really far from our world. He could have that distance and we would-
n't be enmeshed. So we started meeting with him and talking about it,
and it has been really sweet. I mean, he actually wants more contact. He
wants to have contact with our family. He wants to be sort of part of our
family, in a way. And now that we have Joshua, we'd love that, if some
man wanted to be part of our family. We'd love it if [he] came and
played with our kids once a month or once every two weeks.

As for many of the lesbian couples I interviewed, the ideal situation would
have been to have the same donor for all of the children they planned to have.
But such relationships do not always work out as initially planned. Because
these contracts are dense with emotion and personal meanings, their terms
cannot always be realized.

When forming the contract with their second donor, Ruth and Naomi had
new concerns that did not exist with the first donor. They needed to specify
what relationship they and their son Joshua would have with the second donor.
Specifically, they wanted to avoid a scenario in which one child had a relationship with his or her donor while the other did not. Ruth explained this concern
as follows:

> We didn't want it to be where each child has a separate relationship with
> his or her separate donor. What if one person has a really bad relation-
> ship, and the other kid has a really good relationship? It's just really un-
> equal and potentially damaging. We wanted to make sure that if you
> can't have a consistent relationship with both children, then we prefer
> no relationship at all. We don't want you to start developing with the
> children, developing expectations and then not to show up. So if you
> want to be involved, you have to be involved consistently. If you want to
> send birthday gifts, then you have to send birthday gifts to both of
> them. If you want to take one to the zoo, then you have to take both to
> the zoo. It's a package deal. You have a relationship with the entire fam-
> ily. And he agreed to this.

Ruth acknowledged that while this was their desired arrangement, and that
one could agree or disagree on paper, there were nevertheless circumstances
that could not be completely accounted for within the contract. While a contract provides a model for articulating future intent, interpersonal relationships are, by nature, so fluid and emotionally laden that it is impossible for a
contract to actually lock a donor into a specific emotional arrangement.

Now, what that will all mean emotionally in the future, who knows. We
can't. We have no say, no control, you know; it's anyone's guess as to

what is going to happen. So the contract [with our second donor] was different [than] our agreement with our first donor. [With our first donor] when he first gave us the sperm, we would see him every once in a while because he was going out with a friend of ours. Since then, they have broken up; he is seeing someone else who is not in our lives. So our agreement was that we will see him if we see him in the course of our lives, but we will not make special arrangements because he gave us sperm. Our agreement was that we would contact him if and when the child would request to see him. And that hasn't happened so far. It isn't even close to happening at this point. With our second donor, who wants to be involved, we see him every once in a while, we talk to him, he calls and asks how Naomi is doing; it's definitely much more. He wants to be a part of our lives.

The nature of their contract with Stanley, their first donor, was a _transactional contract_ in that it did not govern an ongoing relationship. It was merely an exchange of semen for the relinquishment of paternal rights. Further, the contract was transactional because it lacked any significant emotional content and expectation. Ruth and Naomi had worked hard to maintain a transactional exchange with Stanley because they feared if they acknowledged the existence of a relationship with Stanley, they might be opening themselves up to paternity claims. Since they obtained a second-parent adoption with Joshua and were both named as his legal parents, Ruth and Naomi were less concerned about this issue the second time around. Thus, the agreement with their second donor was more of a _relational contract_ because it attempted to outline an ongoing familial relationship.[4] Because the contract attempted to make their second donor more of a member of their family than the first, the contract contained emotional weight. This was evident in the humor behind naming their contract, "A Darn Good Agreement."

> Well, it was funny because he wanted to call it "The Agreement for Life," but I was like, "Arrgh!" that has too many pro-life associations. We were laughing that if we called it the darn good agreement that, if there was ever any litigation over this, in the [court] opinion, it would say, "the 'Darn Good Agreement' between . . . " It was funny! We just decided that it would be funny. So I thought that was sweet. He's a very funny person in that way. There are a lot of jokes throughout the agreement, 'cause that's just the way he is.

Though Naomi resented what she felt as the state's intrusion on her parental relation with Joshua, many would not see this as the most problematic part of this arrangement. I reviewed with them the way that contract outlines the arrangements between donors and intended parents. The contract carefully articulates how the donor will not take on the responsibilities of being a "father" to the child, but also provides for the possibility that the donor will have a relationship with the child. The cultural connotations that come with being a "father" to the child operate in the background, making it necessary for Ruth and Naomi to outline the role the donor will play in their family's life. Though contracts potentially create arm's-length relationships, arms have elbows that bend to allow for both closeness and distancing. These contracts allow same-sex parents to articulate the nature of the relationship that they intend to have with their donors.

The nature of the agreement with their first donor was akin to the arm's-length model of contract. This first contract was an exchange of sperm for the termination of parental rights. This contract terminated legal rights that would have otherwise been present while creating legal rights that would have otherwise been absent. The agreement with their second donor was more complex. This contract included the exchange of sperm for the termination of parental rights, and also attempted to outline an ongoing relationship between the second donor and their family.

Conclusion

Critics of contract in familial contexts assert that contracts are a manifestation of rampant individualism and that market principles are infiltrating the sphere of familial relations. As a result, they assert that contract is inherently antithetical to familial principles. These critics assume that an alternative to contract, specifically the legal status of marriage, is available to all couples.

An empirical look into the use of contracts in same-sex relationships reveals a different picture. The contracts that same-sex couples draft often attempt to mimic some of the rights and privileges contained within marriage. For example, marriage laws contain a "paternity presumption" that any child born to a married couple is the legal child of the husband. This occurs without regard to whether the husband is the biological father or not. On the other hand, same-sex couples have a difficult time establishing parental rights for the nonbiological parent. Contract then becomes a way of severing the parental rights of the donor, and creating parental rights for the nonbiological partner in the relationship. In states where coparent adoption is available to persons of the same sex, these contracts serve as an intermediate step toward the more secure status of the legal parent. In states where coparent adoption is not available, these contracts serve as the only way of outlining parental intent.

A contract permits flexibility in defining relationships with donors. The contract with Ruth and Naomi's first donor was a transactional contract in that it did not attempt to articulate an ongoing relationship. Instead, the contract stipulated only that he would provide seminal fluid and would agree to terminate any parental rights he might have had upon the child's birth. This contract was akin to traditional models of contract in that it was conducted at arm's length and did not overtly contain emotional expectations.

Ruth and Naomi's contract with their second donor was a relational contract in that it attempted to outline an ongoing relationship between the donor and their family. Ruth, Naomi, and their second donor realized that the contract could not lock all of them into specific emotional states—that is, the contract was not going to make the second donor love Ruth and Naomi's first child, Joshua, whom they had with another donor. However, the contract outlined the expectation that the second donor would not treat Joshua any differently than he would treat his biological offspring. As such, the contract outlines ideals rather than attempting to dictate future emotional states. In same-sex contexts such as this, contract is a useful tool for providing legal mooring to intimate relations and for conveying family principles.

Ruth and Naomi voiced considerable ambivalence toward the institution of marriage. Like other same-sex couples I interviewed, they felt that drafting and negotiating the contracts brought them closer together, even as they lamented the fact that marriage was not available to them. Yet when asked if they would get married if it were available to them, they hesitated—mostly because marriage was not seen as flexible enough to meet their unique circumstances. Contract offered an effective compromise. The conversational ethos of contract provided them with clarity in defining the contours of their commitment to each other, as well as their relationship to each donor. It allowed them to gain legal recognition of their relationship while conveying their long-term commitment to each other.

Current debates surrounding same-sex marriage concern whether the privileges of marriage should be extended to gay and lesbian couples. These political debates have a tendency to obscure the legal content and cultural meanings of marriage. The legal content of marriage is revealed through the patchwork of contracts that lesbian and gay couples draft in order to mimic some of the legal rights of marriage. While contracts may perform much of the legal work of marriage, the cultural work—the public conveyance of long-term commitment—is not entirely achieved through the use of these contracts. Although contracts in and of themselves do not articulate the institutional significance of intimate commitment signaled by marriage, marriage may have a lot to learn from the specific articulation of unspoken assumptions that contracts do provide.

Notes

1. Louisiana Covenant Marriage Act (1999); For summaries of legal decisions pertaining to same-sex marriage, see Human Rights Campaign 2003.
2. The couples I spoke with were understandably concerned about referring to the donor as a "father" of their child. The term father is associated with a set of legal rights and responsibilities that are recognized by the state. These couples were clearly attempting to avoid these associations. The contracts they drafted were, in most instances, an attempt to alter the legal arrangements of fathering and transform it into the more articulated and arm's-length relationship of a donor.
3. For a state-by-state summary of adoption laws that pertain to same-sex couples, see Human Rights Campaign 2003.
4. Relational contracts are those contracts that are drafted to outline relationships that are ongoing and not discrete transactions. For a discussion and definition of "relational contracts" in commercial contexts, see Macaulay 1985 and McNeil 1985.

CHAPTER **3**

Unprincipled Exclusions:
The Struggle to Achieve Judicial and Legislative Equality for Transgender People

PAISLEY CURRAH AND SHANNON MINTER[1]

The Short, Unhappy Life of Transgender Jurisprudence

Transgender people face severe discrimination in virtually every aspect of social life—in employment, housing, public accommodations, credit, marriage, parenting, and law enforcement, among others (Currah and Minter 2000).[2] This discrimination is rooted in the same stereotypes that have fueled unequal treatment of women, lesbian, gay, and bisexual people, and individuals with disabilities—that is, stereotypes about how men and women are "supposed" to behave, and about how male and female bodies are "supposed" to appear (Currah and Minter 2000; Benjamin 1996). For the most part, in other words, antitransgender discrimination is not a new or unique form of bias, but rather falls squarely within the parameters of discrimination based on sex, sexual orientation, and disability (Holt 1997; Cain 1998; Greenberg 1999). From a strictly philosophical or doctrinal perspective, therefore, it might well seem that the most logical course for social activists would be to seek protection for transgender people through litigation under statutes that already prohibit discrimination on those bases, rather than attempting, legislatively, to create a whole new set of statutory protections (Franke 1999).

In practice, however, litigation alone has proved to be a singularly unsuccessful route to winning basic civil rights for transgender people. With few

35

exceptions, courts presented with sex or other discrimination claims on behalf of transgender people have simply dismissed those claims out of hand, with very little in the way of rational analysis or application of the law (Greenberg 1999; Storrow 1997). As a result, to the extent that there is now what Judge Richard Posner has called a "nascent jurisprudence of transsexualism" (*Farmer v. Haas* 1993, 320), it consists largely of decisions in which courts, including Posner's own, have summarily excluded transgender people from civil protections that are readily available to nontransgender persons.[3]

Legal scholars have put forward a variety of theoretical explanations for why courts have failed to deal with transgender people in a coherent or principled way (Valdes 1995; Case 1995; Franke 1995). Ultimately, however, it is probably not possible to identify any single doctrinal error or logical mistake that will fully account for—and thus provide a simple means of remedying—the historical exclusion of transgender people from equal protection in the courts. For the most part, transgender people have not been excluded from civil rights protections because of conceptual or philosophical failures in legal reasoning, but rather because they have not been viewed as worthy of protection or, in some cases, even as human.[4]

In the employment arena, that differential treatment has operated to exclude transsexual plaintiffs from any ability even to state a viable discrimination claim. As Richard Storrow has rightly pointed out,

> Employment discrimination jurisprudence at both the federal and state levels . . . captures transsexuals in a discourse of exclusion from social participation. This wide net, using a remarkably refined system of semantic manipulations, snags all claims launched by transsexuals and reveals that no matter how a transsexual frames her discrimination claim, it will fail. (Storrow 1997, 310)

The impact of these judicial exclusions has been particularly stark in sex discrimination cases. Thus, although it is difficult to see how an employer's decision to terminate an employee for changing her sex is not based on sex, courts have adopted the Orwellian notion that there is a meaningful legal distinction between discrimination because of sex and discrimination because of a *change of sex*. In *Holloway v. Arthur Anderson & Co.* (1977), for example, Ramona Holloway was fired for transitioning from male to female on the job. The Ninth Circuit held that Holloway was not discriminated against "because she is male or female, but rather because she is a transsexual who chose to change her sex. This type of claim is not actionable under Title VII." Similarly, in *Underwood v. Archer Management Services, Inc.* (1994), the plaintiff alleged that she had been terminated from her job because, as a transsexual woman, she retained some masculine traits. The court held that insofar as "she merely indicates that she was discriminated against because . . . she transformed herself into a woman" rather than for "being a woman," she had failed to state a viable sex discrimination claim.

The incoherence of that purported distinction is apparent the moment one imagines a court applying a similar distinction in a case involving discrimination on any other ground. It is unlikely, for example, that an employer who terminated an employee for changing her religious affiliation or nationality would be absolved of liability on the grounds that the employer did not object to the employee's new religion or national origin, but only to the *change of religion or national origin* (Holt 1997). The only difference between these situations and that of a transsexual person is that while changing one's religion or nationality is generally considered to be a legitimate personal choice, "the very idea that one sex can change into another" is likely to engender "ridicule and horror" (Storrow 1997; Garet 1991).

Perhaps because of the extreme discomfort that transgender people often evoke, courts have also relied on the dehumanizing argument that transsexual people cannot be classified as either male or female and therefore do not fall into a protected category under sex discrimination laws. In *Ulane v. Eastern Airlines Inc.* (742 F. 1984), for example, the Seventh Circuit held that Karen Ulane, a transsexual woman who was fired from her job as an airline pilot because she changed her sex, had failed to state a viable claim of sex discrimination under Title VII. In dismissing Ulane's claim, the court was openly derisive of her identification as a woman, which the court characterized as "pathetic" and "delusional":

> Ulane is entitled to any personal belief about her sexual identity she desires. After the surgery, hormones, appearance changes, and a new Illinois birth certificate and FAA pilot's certificate, it may be that society . . . considers Ulane to be female. But even if one believes that a woman can be so easily created from what remains of a man, that does not decide this case . . . [I]f Eastern did discriminate against Ulane, it was not because she is female, but because Ulane is a transsexual . . . a biological male who takes female hormones, cross-dresses, and has surgically altered parts of her body to make it appear to be female.[5]

As Professor Susan Keller has noted, the court's description of Karen Ulane not only excludes her from any definitive identification as either female or male, but in so doing, it effectively excludes her from the category of human as well.

> [The] court suggests that it may not be so easy to create a woman "from what remains of man," it also suggests that the transsexual litigant is

something less than either a man or a woman, and—since it has previously offered those as the only choices—something less than human. (Keller 1999, 373)

Transgender people who have sought protection under the rubric of gay rights statutes have been placed in a similar double bind. In jurisdictions that do not prohibit discrimination on the basis of sexual orientation, courts have cited decisions holding that lesbians and gay men are not protected under Title VII and comparable state laws as a rationale for excluding transsexual people as well.[6] Yet in jurisdictions that protect lesbians and gay men, courts have concluded that transsexualism is distinct from sexual orientation and have dismissed sexual orientation claims by transsexual plaintiffs on that basis.[7] The result, as Richard Storrow has pointed out, is that "no matter the wording of the statutory regime, transsexuals generally are not protected from employment discrimination on either the basis of their transsexualism or of their sexual orientation" (1999, 314; see also Valdes 1995).

Transsexual employees have also been largely unsuccessful in achieving protection under state disability rights statutes.[8] In *Doe v. Boeing Co.* (1993), for example, the plaintiff (a male-to-female transsexual) was discharged after she wore a string of pearls to work, in violation of Boeing's unwritten dress policy, which allowed Doe (and all other "male" employees) to wear male or unisex clothing but prohibited her from wearing female clothing until she had undergone sex reassignment surgery. The Washington Supreme Court acknowledged that gender dysphoria "is a medically cognizable condition with a prescribed course of treatment," including living as a member of the other gender before obtaining sex reassignment surgery. Nonetheless, the court concluded that "Boeing discharged Doe because she violated Boeing's directives on acceptable attire, not because she was gender dysphoric" (536), despite having recognized that Doe's "violation" was a direct result of the medically prescribed course of treatment for her gender dysphoria. Following the decision in *Doe*, other state courts have also interpreted their state disability laws to exclude transgender plaintiffs.[9]

In short, one does not have to look past the case law to find at least one powerful reason why transgender people have been motivated to lobby for civil rights protections. Because courts routinely have created a "transgender exception" to existing nondiscrimination laws, transgender advocates have concluded that one obvious solution is to create legislation designed to remedy these exclusions by explicitly designating transgender people as a protected group. Thus, it is at least in part because of the animosity transgender people have encountered in the courts that they have turned to the legislative branches of government—to city councils, state legislatures, and Congress—to secure basic civil rights protections.[10]

Legislative Struggles and Successes

In the past 10 years, transgender people have made unprecedented efforts to mobilize politically and to lobby for civil rights laws.[11] To date, those efforts have been most successful at the local level. In 1975, Minneapolis, MN, passed the first local ordinance prohibiting discrimination against transgender people (Minneapolis, Minn. 1975). Fifteen years later, only five additional cities had followed suit—Champaign and Urbana, IL; Harrisburg, PA; Seattle, WA; and St. Paul, MN. By the end of 2000, however, the number of localities protecting transgender people had multiplied exponentially. As of this writing, 60 such local laws have been enacted (Transgender Law and Policy Institute 2003).

Encouragingly for transgender advocates, progress in this arena has not been limited to large metropolitan centers, college towns, or any single geographic area. Jurisdictions that have passed local antidiscrimination laws include cities as culturally diverse as Ann Arbor, MI; Louisville, KY; and Tucson, AZ. They also include a healthy mix of small and midsized cities, such as York, PA, and Toledo, OH (with populations of approximately 19,000 and 333,000, respectively), alongside larger cities such as San Francisco, Pittsburgh, Atlanta, and New York City.

In 1993, Minnesota became the first jurisdiction to enact a statewide antidiscrimination law that includes express protections for transgender people in education, employment, housing, and public accommodations. Since then, Rhode Island, New Mexico, and California have followed suit.[12]

In 1998, California became the second state, following Minnesota in 1996, to include transgender people in its state hate crimes statute (Cal. Penal Code 2000; Minn. Stat. 2000). In 1999, the California Legislature incorporated the same language into the California Student Safety and Violence Prevention Act, thereby prohibiting discrimination against transgender students, teachers, and administrators (Cal. Ed. Code 2000). Also in 1999, Missouri and Vermont included transgender people in their state hate crimes statutes, and the governor of Iowa, Tom Vilsack, became the first governor to issue an executive order prohibiting discrimination against state employees on the basis of gender identity (Mo. Rev. Stat. 2000; 13 Vt. Stat. Ann. 2000). Unfortunately, a district court judge subsequently held that Vilsack lacked authority to issue the order, in a lawsuit filed by Republican state legislators (Chew 2000). In 2000, California became the first state to pass legislation removing "transsexualism" and "gender identity disorders" from the list of excluded impairments under state disability laws (Cal. Assembly Bill 2000). In 2003, California also enacted the country's first statute to prohibit discrimination against lesbian, gay, bisexual, and transgender youth in foster care (Cal. Assembly Bill 2003).

All told, almost 25 percent of the U.S. population now lives in a jurisdiction that prohibits discrimination against transgender people. As modest as these initial legislative gains may seem, their true significance lies in what they portend for the future. In the words of a recent news story, "the transgender community . . . appears to be gaining acceptance as a bona fide minority group" (Johnson 1998). For the first time, transgender people are forging a shared political identity and coalescing into a visible and increasingly significant political movement.

Four Key Issues in Drafting Transgender-Protective Legislation

After decades of losing in the courts, as described previously, transgender people have begun to organize as a political constituency and, for the first time, to lobby for the passage of nondiscrimination laws. One of the greatest challenges in that effort has been drafting statutory language for which there is little or no precedent, given the virtual absence of prior transgender-specific legislation anywhere in the world. Although now a number of such laws are on the books in the U.S., courts have not yet had time to provide much guidance as to problems or limitations that may be associated with particular kinds of statutory language.[13] In the meantime, this section examines some of the specific questions advocates and legislators have faced in drafting this type of legislation.

1. *Whether to add "gender identity" as a new category or, as the alternative, to include transgender people in the definition of sexual orientation or sex.* The first issue is whether to secure protection for transgender people by adding "gender identity" (or a comparable term) as a new protected category or, alternatively, by amending the statutory definition of sexual orientation or sex to clarify that transgender people should be included in one of those existing categories.[14] In San Francisco, for example, local legislators opted to recognize transgender people as a new group (San Francisco, Cal. 1994). The local ordinance, which already prohibited discrimination on the basis of sex, sexual orientation, race, religion, and various other attributes, was amended to add the category of gender identity. This approach has been adopted in many local nondiscrimination laws, as well as in the statewide hate crime statute in Vermont and the local hate crime statute in Ithaca, NY.

In contrast, the Minnesota statute includes transgender people in the definition of sexual orientation, which is defined, in relevant part, as "having or being perceived as having a self-image or identity not traditionally associated with one's biological maleness or femaleness" (Minn. Stat. Ann. 2000). Transgender people are also included in the definition of sexual orientation in the Missouri hate crimes statute (Mo. Ann. Stat. § 557.035) and in a number of local ordinances, including those in Evanston, IL; Minneapolis, MN; St. Paul, MN; Toledo, OH; York, PA; and Ypsilanti, MI.

In California, the legislature included transgender people in the California hate crimes statute (and subsequently, in the Fair Employment and Housing

Act) by clarifying that the term "sex" includes a person's "identity, appearance or behavior, whether or not . . . different from that traditionally associated with the [person's] sex at birth" (Cal. Penal Code 2000). The strategy of including transgender people in the definition of sex has also been used in Cambridge, MA; Champaign, IL; the city and county of Santa Cruz, CA; DeKalb, IL; Harrisburg, PA; New York City; Pittsburgh, PA; and Urbana, IL, among others. In sum, legislative protection for transgender people has been secured in one of three ways: (1) by adding gender identity and expression (or a comparable term) as a new protected status; (2) by including transgender people in the statutory definition of sex; or (3) by including transgender people in the statutory definition of sexual orientation.

The considerations that go into choosing one of these strategies over another may vary from place to place, and different concerns may come into play at the statewide as opposed to the local level. In general, however, the considerations militating in favor of adding gender identity as a separate category center on the benefits of increased visibility and the symbolic value of having gender identity given equal billing, so to speak, with other protected classifications. Designating gender identity as a freestanding classification sends a powerful message that transgender people are entitled to full equality and legitimacy.[15]

There are also potential downsides to establishing gender identity as a new category. Pragmatically, it may be easier to persuade legislators to amend the definition of an existing protection than to add a new category of protected persons to the law, which is likely to be seen as a more radical step (*It's Time*, 1999). In addition, identifying gender identity as a new category may reinforce the misperception, which is already so pervasive in the case law, that transgender people are somehow fundamentally distinct from—and by implication inferior to—nontransgender people (i.e., that transgender people are not men or women, but something other or in between).

A related concern is that creating gender identity as a new legislative category may be misinterpreted to mean that transgender people should not be protected under sex discrimination laws (Franke 1995). To avoid this possibility, some advocates and legislators have opted to amend the statutory definition of "sex" in existing statutes to clarify that transgender people should already be included in those laws. In New York City, for example, transgender activists introduced a bill amending the New York City Human Rights Law to add a transgender-inclusive definition of the term "gender," which is already included (without definition) as a protected category in the local law. The bill's legislative findings section states that this amendment is designed to clarify existing law.[16]

2. *How narrowly or broadly to define transgender people.* A second strategic issue concerns how broadly or narrowly to define the protected status or group. Regardless of whether transgender people are included in a new category or

under the rubric of sexual orientation or sex, advocates and legislators have faced the challenge of finding language that is specific enough to remove any doubt that transgender people are protected, and yet broad enough to encompass the full range of those who need protection. In Olympia, WA, for example, the statute defines the protected category very specifically, as "the status of being transsexual, transvestite, or transgender" (Olympia, Wa. 1997). On the one hand, naming specific groups is useful insofar as it leaves less room for ambiguity about the purpose of the law and may work to eliminate or at least restrain the kind of semantic manipulations that have led courts to exclude transgender people from Title VII and state sex discrimination laws. On the other hand, however, the enumeration of specific groups makes it more difficult to ensure that the law will be construed to include gender-variant people who may not identify or even necessarily be perceived as a specific "type" of transgender person. In Minnesota, the legislature sought to avoid this problem by defining the scope of protection in broad terms, as extending to all persons "having or being perceived as having an identity or self-image that is not traditionally associated with one's biological maleness or femaleness" (Minn. Stat. Ann. 2003).

Thus far, most localities have incorporated some variation of the broad language used in Minnesota and have avoided relying exclusively on a list of specifically protected groups.[17] In Tucson, AZ, for example, the ordinance combines the general and specific approaches by defining gender identity to mean "an individual's various attributes as they are understood to be masculine and/or feminine and shall be broadly interpreted to include pre- and postoperative transsexuals, as well as other persons who are, or are perceived to be, transgender" (Tucson, Ariz. 1999). This hybrid approach has the merit of ensuring protection for specific groups (such as transsexuals) while simultaneously avoiding any suggestion that other nonenumerated groups or individuals should not be protected as well.

Similar considerations were behind Seattle's decision to revise its ordinance in 1999. The original ordinance, which was first passed in 1986, limited protection to discrimination on the basis of "transsexuality, or transvestism" (Seattle, Wash. 1986). After extensive review, the City of Seattle Commission on Sexual Minorities concluded that "the terminology used by the City of Seattle on this matter could be changed to be made more accurate, inclusive, and more easily administered in its attempt to protect gender nonconforming persons" (Seattle Commission on Sexual Minorities 1999). Noting that "the words transsexuality [and] tranvestism, but not the word transgender appear [in the 1986 statute]," the Commission found that simply expanding the list to include new terms was not an adequate solution, because "doing so could allow the term "transgender" to be read in its narrowest definition and thus leave unprotected some other members of the gender-identity community." Instead, the

Commission recommended revising the law to include general language similar to that used in Minnesota, as well as a nonexhaustive listing of covered groups.[18] Commission member Marsha Botzer explained the reasoning behind the recommendation: "Every few years, there's a new word. When we did the law the first time in the 1980s, 'transgender' wasn't something anyone used. With all these words of the week, the real object is to find the most inclusive set of words" (Botzer 1999).

Some advocates and legislators have also been concerned that using clinical terms such as "transsexual" or "transvestite" may lead to an overly narrow interpretation of who is covered by the law (Green 2000). In particular, because transsexual people must usually receive a diagnosis of gender identity disorder to obtain medical treatment, using only the term transsexual may arbitrarily exclude transgender persons who are unable or choose not to obtain medical care.[19] In 1999, the city council in Boulder, CO, considered limiting the class of persons protected in a proposed nondiscrimination law to those who were undergoing or had completed sex reassignment, as certified by a licensed physician (Shilling 1999). Christa Kriesel, the coordinator for a Boulder County Health Department program for gay, lesbian, bisexual, and transgender youth, argued that the licensed physician requirement would be "tragic because . . . everyone does not have equal access to medical care" (Mills 1999). Boulder Human Relations Commissioner Liz Padilla agreed, stating: "I don't want to be responsible for somebody's pain just because they don't have the money for a doctor or they just haven't gone that route" (Dizon 1999). Transgender activist Kathy Wilson also argued against this limitation: "The idea of singling out people and making them carry a bit of documentation to have access to the most basic human rights—that is most offensive to me" (Shilling 1999). After a robust public debate on this issue, the Boulder City Council decided to omit this restriction (Boulder, Co. Ordinance 2000).

Limitations of the kind considered and ultimately rejected in Boulder have also been rejected in most other jurisdictions. Thus, despite the fears of some, the emergence of a transgender rights movement has not resulted in laws that protect only a narrowly defined class, such as transsexuals or even self-identified transgender people. Instead, advocates and legislators have developed statutory language that is broad, principled, and applicable to as wide an array of transgender people as possible. They recognize, for example, that female-to-male transsexuals often have different routes to transition than male-to-female transsexuals; that many female-to-male transsexuals may never have genital ("bottom") surgery; that many transsexuals are nonoperative, either because they cannot afford or choose not to undergo sexual reassignment or are prohibited from doing so for health reasons; that some transsexual people may transition with hormone therapy only; that some transgender people may choose to take hormones but not to transition from their birth sex, or may choose to take low doses of hormones to bring about some physical changes; that some transsexual people who are transitioning or have transitioned may not be under a doctor's care; that many transsexual people are not readily identifiable as such and do not challenge prevailing gender norms in any visible way; that other transsexual people are more visible, either because they cannot or do not wish to conceal their transsexual status; and that some transgender people do not fit easily into one of two gender categories. Moreover, the broader definitions also include people who may not identify as transgender, but whose gender identity or expression contravenes social norms in some way, such as feminine men and masculine women. In short, advocates and legislators have generally been sensitive to the dangers of misusing legislation to reinforce arbitrary social identities and divisions and have sought to respect both the diversity among transgender people and the commonality between transgender people and others, instead.

3. *How to avoid the status versus conduct trap.* A related issue concerns the tension between language that appears to define transgender identity solely as a status (such as "gender identity") and language that also includes appearances, conduct, and behavior (such as "gender expression"). Transgender activists generally agree that some status-based language is necessary to make the point that gender identity is a fundamental aspect of personhood and that transgender people are indeed a real and legitimate minority group, deserving of civil rights protections. At the same time, relying exclusively on status-based language runs the risk that some courts may misinterpret the language to exclude conduct such as undergoing sex reassignment or changing one's gender presentation, from protection (Currah and Minter 2000).[20] To alleviate that risk, the majority of ordinances that have been passed in the United States combine elements of both status and conduct. This has been accomplished either by using the term "gender identity and expression," or by otherwise defining the prohibited basis of discrimination to include discrimination on the basis of external as well as internal manifestations of identity.

4. *How to avoid cross-dressing exclusions.* A final strategic issue concerns so-called cross-dressing exclusions, which permit employers to impose gender-specific dress codes. These exclusions serve no purpose other than to pacify some legislators' fears about extending legal protection to the proverbial "man in a dress." Moreover, by capitulating to irrational animosity toward men who are deemed too "feminine," they harm women by reinforcing the devaluation of qualities and characteristics associated with femaleness.[21] These exclusions are also increasingly at odds with the growing body of cases holding that discrimination against masculine-appearing women and feminine-appearing men violates Title VII and similar state laws (see *Price Waterhouse v. Hopkins* 1989).

Unfortunately, activists in a few jurisdictions have been unable to fend off this type of restriction. In New Orleans, some local legislators were so concerned that the local law might protect a "man in a dress" that they insisted on adding broad exclusionary language stating: "nothing in this chapter shall prohibit an employer from prohibiting cross-dressing in the work place or while an employee is acting in the course and scope of his or her employment." The only exception is an additional provision requiring employers to accommodate transsexual employees who are undergoing sex reassignment:

> "Cross-dressing" shall not be deemed to include the regular wearing of clothing, cosmetics, footwear and or other accouterments which is appropriate to the gender other than his or her biological or legal gender at birth with which an employee or applicant identifies if the employee or applicant provides the employer with the written statement of a licensed doctor or other health care professional certifying that the employee or applicant presents the characteristics of gender identification disorder or another similar status or condition and that the employee or applicant intends prospectively to attire and conduct himself or herself for the foreseeable future in the employee's employment and workplace or workplaces in the manner appropriate for persons of the gender with which he or she identifies.

This provision effectively limits employment protection to those under a doctor's care, because it requires the employee to provide a written statement certifying that he or she "presents the characteristics of gender identification disorder" (New Orleans, La. 1998; see also Shilling 1999).

In Kentucky, local transgender advocates spoke out strongly against the unfairness of limiting protection to transsexual persons. F.M. Chester, a transgender lesbian, testified about the impact of gender-based dress codes on nontranssexual people at a city council hearing in Lexington:

> Many of the people in this room probably thought I was male when they first saw me. I am not. I am biologically female. However, my gender presentation is very masculine. I am a "mannish" woman. I also wear men's clothes. I cannot wear women's clothes comfortably. They feel wrong. When I wear women's clothes I feel anguish. I feel like I am in "drag" and that I am "passing" as a woman. I have always been like this . . . . I am not transexual [sic]. At this point in my life, I do not want to become a man. I have considered changing my sex and have rejected it for me right now. (Chester 1999)

Despite opposition from Chester and others, Louisville and Lexington both enacted ordinances that contain cross-dressing exclusions.[22] Shortly thereafter, Jefferson County, which encompasses the city of Louisville, passed a law defining gender identity as "manifesting an identity not traditionally associated with one's biological maleness or biological femaleness" (Jefferson County, Ky. 1999), which would at least ostensibly include dress. Although this ordinance explicitly allows employers to enforce a written employee dress policy, it does not require transgender people to prove their gender identity by providing documentation from a medical professional.[23] This wording clearly extends employment and other protections to gender-variant people who are not transsexual.

Ultimately, of course, no statute will be perfect and no amount of foresight or careful drafting will eliminate the reality that statutes are enforced by human beings and will ultimately be interpreted by the same judges whose hostility and resistance to accepting transgender people as fully human contributed to the need for transgender-specific laws in the first place. That being said, being aware of the pitfalls in drafting transgender-protective legislation can go a long way toward maximizing the chances of passage, minimizing the chances of causing harm to transgender people in other areas of the law, and ensuring the broadest and most comprehensive protections it is possible to achieve.

Conclusion

Although this chapter has focused on the historical failure of litigation as a ve-hicle for securing basic rights for transgender people and on the resultant need for political advocacy, there is of course no inherent or inevitable tension be-tween the two. To the contrary, as transgender people have begun to achieve some visibility and success in the legislative arena, the judicial climate has begun to shift as well. In the past five years, courts and human rights commis-sions in at least seven states have ruled in favor of transgender plaintiffs under state laws prohibiting discrimination on the basis of sex or disability.[24] In 2000, the Ninth Circuit awarded asylum to a transgender person from Mexico, con-cluding that gender identity and expression are fundamental to a person's iden-tity (*Hernandez-Montiel v. INS* 1999), and the Second Circuit held that a transgender person had stated a viable sex discrimination claim under the Equal Credit Opportunity Act (*Rosa v. Park West Bank & Trust Co.* 2000). In 2002, the Eighth Circuit rejected a Title VII claim by a female employee who ar-gued that being required to share a restroom with a transsexual woman amounted to sexual harassment (*Cruzan v. Special Sch. Dist. #1* 2002). Perhaps most dramatically, in 2001, a Massachusetts court held that a public middle school was required to permit a transgender youth to attend school dressed as a girl, despite her male anatomy (*Doe v. Yunits* 2001). The empathy displayed toward transgender litigants in these decisions is unprecedented; almost cer-tainly, it owes less to any developments in the law than to the emergence of an organized transgender movement.

Notes

1. Reprinted with permission from the *College of William and Mary Journal of Women and the Law*. We thank Jennifer L. Levi and Liz Seaton for help with the work upon which this chapter was based, and Monica Barrett, Robin Gilbrecht, and Courtney Joslin for their comments on earlier drafts. Paisley Currah's work researching and writing this chapter was supported by a fellowship from the Wolfe Institute for the Humanities at Brooklyn College and a grant from the PSC-CUNY Research Foundation.
2. This chapter uses the term transgender in its most inclusive sense, as an umbrella term encompassing: pre-operative, postoperative, and nonoperative transsexual people; cross-dressers; feminine men and masculine women; intersexed persons; and more generally, anyone whose gender identity or expression differs from conventional expectations of masculinity or femininity. In contrast, some legal scholars have used the term more narrowly, as a synonym for transsexual (Feldblum 1996; Green 2000).
3. *Ulane v. Eastern Airlines, Inc.* (742 F. 1984). See also Holt 1997, Greenberg 1999, and Storrow 1997.
4. In one case, for example, a court compared a male-to-female transsexual to a donkey (*Ashlie v. Chester-Upland School District* 1979). See also Keller (1999) and Storrow (1997).
5. In contrast, the trial court in *Ulane* had concluded that "sex is not a cut-and-dried matter of chromosomes, and that the term 'sex', as used in any scientific sense and as used in the statute can be and should be reasonably interpreted to include among its denotations the question of sexual identity and that, therefore, transsexuals are protected by Title VII" (*Ulane v. Eastern Airlines 581 F. 1984).*
6. See, for example, *Holloway v. Arthur Anderson & Co.* (1977) and *Ulane v. Eastern Airlines* (742 F. 1984).
7. See, for example, *Underwood v. Archer Management Servs.* (1994). The one exception is Minnesota, where the legislature has expressly defined sexual orientation to include transgender people (Minn. Stat. Ann. 2000).
8. Transgender persons are expressly excluded from protection under federal laws prohibiting discrimination on the basis of disability. See the *Americans with Disabilities Act* (1990) and the *Rehabilitation Act* (1973). As of this writing, some state disability statutes (IN, IA, LA, NE, OH, OK, TX, and VA) explicitly exclude transgender people as well.
9. See, for example, *Holt v. Northwest Pennsylvania Training Partnership Consortium, Inc.* (1997) and *Dobre v. National R.R. Passenger Corp.* (1983).
10. Although most legislative advocacy on behalf of transgender people is focused at the local and state level, some transgender advocates have lobbied for the inclusion of transgender people in the Employment Non-Discrimination Act (ENDA), and proposed federal legislation that would prohibit employment discrimination on the basis of sexual orientation (Holt 1997). In addition, transgender advocates and allies have also lobbied to include transgender people in the proposed federal Hate Crimes Prevention Act (see, for example, Suffredini 2000).
11. Although this chapter focuses on the United States, others have documented a similar surge in transgender activism internationally (see Whittle 2000).
12. These protections were passed as part of a bill that prohibits discrimination on the basis of sexual orientation, which was expressly defined to include transgender people. See Currah and Minter (2000) for a description of the history behind Minnesota's passage of the first statewide law protecting transgender people. See also R.I. Gen. Laws 11-24-2 (2001); N.M. Stat. Ann. 28-1-2 (1990); Cal. Assembly Bill 196 (2003).
13. To date, the only decision construing a transgender-specific statute is *Goins v. West Group* (2000).
14. According to Kessler and McKenna (1978), gender identity "refers to an individual's own feeling of whether she or he is a woman or a man, or a girl or a boy. In essence, gender identity is self-attribution of gender." The legislation in Boulder, Colorado, passed by City Council on January 20, 2000, uses the term "gender variance" rather than gender identity (Boulder, Co. 2000).

15. In Iowa City, for example, one transgender activist argued for the importance of including gender identity as a freestanding category by noting "most people in this community will never read the complete ordinance . . . What they will see . . . is the list that you give . . . If gender identity is subsumed under sexual orientation most of them will never know that" (Iowa City Public Hearing 1995).

16. New York City Bill 2000. The section reads, in part: "Included in the City's Human Rights Law is a prohibition of discrimination against individuals based on gender. The scope of this gender-based protection, however, requires clarification. This local law is intended to make clear that all gender-based discrimination—including but not limited to, discrimination based on an individual's actual or perceived sex, and discrimination based on an individual's gender identity, self-image, appearance, behavior, or expression—constitutes a violation of the City's Human Rights Law."

17. See for example, Toledo, Ohio, 1998.

18. The new law defines gender identity to mean "having an identity, expression, or physical characteristics not traditionally associated with one's biological sex or one's sex at birth, including transsexual, transvestite and transgender, and including a person's attitudes, preferences, beliefs and practices pertaining thereto" (Seattle, Wash. 1999).

19. For a definition of gender identity disorder, see American Psychiatric Association (1994).

20. See also *Kirkpatrick v. Seligman* (1981), which found that an employer who fired a transsexual woman for transitioning on the job did not discriminate against the plaintiff for being a transsexual, but rather for dressing as a female, and *Grossman v. Bernards Township Board of Education* (1975), which upheld the dismissal of a transsexual woman who "was discharged by the defendant school board not because of her status as a female, but rather because of her change in sex from the male to female gender."

21. Case (1995) explains that discrimination against women cannot be fully eradicated without also addressing discrimination against feminine men.

22. These ordinances define gender identity, in part, as "manifesting, *for reasons other than dress*, an identity not traditionally associated with one's biological maleness or femaleness." They also contain an express dress code provision which provides, "Nothing [herein] shall be construed to prevent an employer from . . . enforcing an employee dress policy which policy may include restricting employees from dress associated with *the other gender*" (emphasis added; Louisville, Ky. 1999; see also Lexington, Ky. 1999).

23. See R.I. Gen. Laws (2001); N.M. Stat. Ann. 1990; Cal. Assembly Bill 196 (2003).

24. For a complete list of these cases, see Minter (2003).

2
The Regulation of Sexual Commerce

CHAPTER 4

Soft Glove, Punishing Fist:
The Trafficking Victims Protection Act of 2000

WENDY CHAPKIS[1]

During the final months of the Clinton administration, the U.S. House, Senate, and Executive Branch joined together to pass legislation providing legal residency and welfare benefits to undocumented workers and foreign prostitutes. Only those who were defined as victims of "severe forms of trafficking" qualified, however. Nevertheless, the Victims of Trafficking and Violence Protection Act of 2000 (HR 3244) at first glance appears to be an inexplicable if welcome break from a continuing series of anti-immigration, antipoor, and antiprostitution policies in the United States. But a closer study of the law reveals that rather than being a significant departure from past practice on migration, poverty, and commercial sex, the new law actually serves as a soft glove covering a still punishing fist.

Historically, poor women, especially those suspected of participation in prostitution, have been the object of state scrutiny and disciplinary control. The first federal immigration law in the United States, the Page Law of 1875, specifically closed the border to those entering the country for "lewd and immoral purposes" from Asia. A few years later, additional legislation denied entry to "those likely to become public charges" (Luibheid 2002, 2). Such hostility to poor women—especially those not white, not native born, and not sexually restrained by marriage—has been a recurring theme in the United States. In 1996, the federal government approved a new round of sweeping welfare and immigration "reforms" (the Personal Responsibility and Work

51

Opportunity Reconciliation Act and the Illegal Immigration and Immigrant Responsibility Act), which further undermined the already precarious position of these groups.

Yet, almost simultaneously, the Trafficking Victims Protection Act of 2000 (TVPA) (HR 3244) was being drafted to specifically exempt a small class of abused and exploited migrants from those punitive measures. The most publicized objective of the Act was to combat "sexual slavery." But the legislation promised to offer protections to a broader class of victims. As the law observes, trafficking "is not limited to the sex industry—[it] also includes forced labor and involves significant violations of labor, public health, and human rights standards worldwide," (TVPA Section 102 [6] 2–3). The law was designed to not only increase penalties against traffickers but also to provide assistance to abused workers, including temporary residency and work permits, welfare support, and even the possibility of permanent residency for qualified victims and their families. These benefits are to be provided "without regard to the immigration status of such victims" (TVPA Section 107 [6] 1).

The question, then, is what motivated the near unanimous support for abused migrants and prostitutes under the TVPA by legislators characteristically hostile to immigrants and poor women, especially those engaged in commercial sex? As I will argue in this chapter, the answer lies, in part, in the usefulness of the law in creating a politically strategic exception to an otherwise punitive rule. A close reading of the debates surrounding the revisions and eventual passage of HR 3244 (expressed in legislative hearings and media reports) reveals how the law mobilized anxieties surrounding sexuality and gender in the service of immigration control. As Eithne Luibheid observes, feminist scholars must "examine how public discourses on sexuality legitimate the exclusion, condemnation, or acceptance of particular migrants . . . [and] how discourses about dangerous migrant sexualities legitimize the subordination of minoritized U.S. communities" (Luibheid 2002, 144).

In the case of the Trafficking Victims Protection Act, language within and surrounding the legislation neatly divides "violated innocents" from "illegal immigrants" along the lines of sex and gender. Trafficking victims, described as vulnerable women and children forced from the safety of their home or homelands into gross sexual exploitation, are distinguished from economic migrants who are understood to be men who have willfully violated national borders for individual gain.[2] The law justifies offering protection to the former and punishment to the latter through the use of three sleights of hand. First, it relies on a repressive moral panic about "sexual slavery" created through slippery statistics and sliding definitions.[3] Second, despite offering symbolic support to the notion that all prostitution is "sexual slavery," the law carefully differentiates between "innocent" and "guilty" prostitutes and provides support only to the innocent. And third, by making assistance to even "deserving" victims contingent on their willingness to assist authorities in the prosecution of traffickers, the legislation further seals U.S. borders against penetration by "undeserving" economic migrants. Protections offered to the innocent help to reinforce the suggestion that the punishments meted out to the "guilty" are justified. I argue, then, that although proponents have presented the bill as important for the people it rescues, it may be that its more important hidden effect involves the people that it excludes.

Moral Panic, Slippery Statistics, and Sliding Definitions

HR 3244 was presented both to legislators and to the American public as a necessary response to a massive violation of innocent women and children by depraved sex traffickers. The key sponsor of the bill, a conservative Republican, Christopher Smith of New Jersey, had previously distinguished himself in Congress primarily as a supporter of the rights of religious minorities and of the "unborn." Smith had exhibited relatively little concern for the plight of the poor, of migrants, or of women. As cochair of the House's "Pro-Life Caucus," Smith repeatedly authored legislation prohibiting U.S. financial support for family planning clinics in third-world countries that provide abortion services. In the U.S. as well, poor women attempting to support large families on inadequate incomes did not seem to be of much concern to Representative Smith; he strongly supported both the immigration and welfare reform acts of 1996. The phenomena of forced migration and sexual slavery, however, struck a deep chord with Christopher Smith. Like an endangered fetus, women and children trafficked into the United States, especially for purposes of sexual exploitation, were innocent victims in need of protection. The problem, according to Smith, was a moral outrage of enormous proportions:

> Each year, 50,000 innocent women and young children are forced, coerced, or fraudulently thrust into the international sex trade industry with no way out. This brutal, demeaning, and disgusting abuse of women and children is predicated on their involuntary participation in sexual acts . . . The image of a young, innocent child being forcibly sold into the sex trade for the fiscal gain of one sick individual and the physical gain of another is tragic. The idea that we would allow it to go unpunished is even more so. (Smith 2000)

Smith was not alone in calling attention to this problem or positioning it as uniquely abusive. He was joined in the call for action by the National Organization for Women, the country's largest feminist organization, which noted that "sex trafficking, referred to by many of us as *the* modern form of slavery, is thought to victimize 50,000 women and girls every year in the U.S. alone" (NOW 2000).

The figure of 50,000 victims of sex slavery is inaccurately based on data from a 1999 CIA briefing on "global trafficking" in which it was estimated that between 45,000 and 50,000 women and children are trafficked into the United States for sweatshop labor, domestic servitude, agricultural work, and prostitution each year (O'Neill Richards 1999, 3). The misleading claim that all these exploited undocumented workers were "sex slaves"—and that "global trafficking" was all about women and children—was useful in rallying public support for victims of migrant abuse in a climate generally hostile to undocumented workers in America's factories and fields.

HR 3244's conflation of migrant abuse, trafficking, and sex slavery is a common rhetorical device in antitrafficking discourse.[4] Definitions of "trafficking" are as unstable as the numbers of victims. This point is unintentionally made by the U.S. State Department in its discussion of "model antitrafficking legislation" (on which HR 3244 was based). The State Department argues that "trafficking in persons, predominantly women and children, is an insidious and growing global and translational [sic] crime and human rights problem" (U.S. State Department 2000).

Certainly little consensus exists on the meaning of "trafficking," and "translational" difficulties do abound. In some accounts, all undocumented migrants assisted in their transit across national borders are counted as having been trafficked.[5] In others, trafficking refers exclusively to victims of "sexual slavery." In some instances, all migrant sex workers are defined as trafficking victims regardless of consent and conditions of labor;[6] and in still others, abusive conditions of employment or deceptive recruitment practices in the sex trade are emphasized.[7]

One recent example of this problem of slippery statistics and sliding definitions can be found in a statement by Pino Arlacchi, director of the United Nations Office for Drug Control and Crime Prevention, who argues that globally "200 million people may now be, in some way, under the sway or in the hands of traffickers" (Crossette 2000, A-15). Here Arlacchi is making use of the most expansive definition of trafficking in order to strengthen the case for the enormity of the problem:

> We don't just have economic slavery, which includes two things: forced labor and debt enslavement. We also have a lot of exploitation of migrants. And we have classic slavery. *If you put all this together under the same concept,* you get the biggest violation of human rights in the world. (Crossette 2000, A-15; emphasis added)

This potentially useful linking of the problems and interests of all exploited migrants is, however, primarily used by Arlacchi to argue for more effective policing of immigration to stop what he considers a "slave trade." Arlacchi emphasizes the comparison with slavery by insisting that the modern manifestation of trafficking is an even more serious problem than the African slave trade: "Four centuries of slavery moved about 11.5 million people out of Africa, [while] in the last decade more than 30 million women and children may have been trafficked within and from Southeast Asia for sexual purposes and sweatshop labor" (Crossette 2000, A-15). By eliminating any distinctions between intentional (if exploitative) migration for work and forced enslavement of millions of Africans, Arlacchi creates a moral imperative to stop the flow of undocumented workers regardless of their desire to immigrate.

From this perspective, the abuse of migrants becomes fully the fault of "traffickers" who must be stopped, not the by-product of exploitive employment practices, restrictive immigration policies, and vast economic disparities between rich and poor nations. In the aftermath of Britain's worst smuggling disaster in June of 2000, when 58 Chinese migrants were found dead in an airtight freight compartment, Arlacchi condemned the practice of "trafficking" but not the immigration policies and poverty that led to such desperate attempts (Crossette 2000, A-15). British refugee advocates, on the other hand, noted that "tighter restrictions are forcing immigrants to take more dangerous routes into the country" (Miller 2000, 1-A). Prime Minister Tony Blair condemned only the smugglers and vowed to combat the "evil trade" in human beings (Miller 2000, 1-A). Subsequent attempts to restrict immigration can then be packaged as antislavery measures; would-be migrants are would-be victims whose safety and well-being are ostensibly served by more rigorously policing the borders.

This reasoning resonates especially strongly when "sex trafficking" is the focus. Antiprostitution legislation, which criminalizes all parties to the commercial sexual transaction, is most often presented as a strategy to stop the exploitation of vulnerable women—even when it entails their incarceration or deportation. Dutch antitrafficking activist Marjan Wijers argues, however, that this strategy actually intensifies the exploitation and abuse:

> Since there are practically no possibilities for poor, unskilled women to travel independently and to work legally in these countries, they are almost totally dependent on recruiting agencies and brokers, and are thus in imminent danger of falling victim to criminal networks. In receiving countries, the increasingly restrictive immigration laws . . . have clearly negative effects for women who attempt to migrate. The laws appear to benefit traffickers, who will always find ways to circumvent laws, while simultaneously working to the disadvantage of migrant women, increasing their dependence on third parties. (1998, 72)

The Trafficking Victims Protection Act of 2000, which strengthens law enforcement and increases penalties against those defined as traffickers, will likely increase the risk and cost of doing business for smugglers. This is a cost that undoubtedly will be passed on to the victims the law is designed to protect.

Fortunately, HR 3244 doesn't simply intensify the prosecution of traffickers; it also promises assistance to victims. It is this element of the law that helped to mobilize feminist and other progressive support for the legislation—and led conservatives to demand that the law be carefully drafted to restrict the numbers of qualified victims. In the writing and rewriting of the legislation, eligible "victims of trafficking" became increasingly narrowly defined. In the final version of the law, two distinct categories of victim are defined: "victims of trafficking" and "victims of a severe form of trafficking." Victims of trafficking are all those whose presence in the United States is due to sex trafficking—which is defined without reference to force, coercion, or deception. A victim of trafficking includes anyone who has received assistance with migration for the purposes of prostitution (TVPA—Section 103 [9]).

Significantly, however, although this category appears in the legislation, it is also made otherwise irrelevant to it. The law, in fact, only covers violations of a different sort: those involving a "severe form of trafficking." Severe forms are defined as either "sex trafficking in which a commercial sex act is induced by force, fraud, or coercion," or in which the person performing the act is under 18, or "the recruitment, harboring, transportation, provision, or obtaining of a person for labor or services through the use of force, fraud, or coercion for the purpose of subjection to involuntary servitude, peonage, debt-bondage, or slavery" (TVPA—Section 103 [8]).

In other words, severe trafficking deals with the conditions of labor coupled with abusive or deceptive forms of recruitment, whereas sex trafficking simply refers to the *kind of labor* to be performed (i.e., prostitution). All assistance under the new law is restricted to victims of so-called severe forms of trafficking. Despite the fact that sex trafficking itself is not covered by HR 3244, it is used to set a tone within the legislation. The repeated mention of sex trafficking reinforces the notion that migrant abuse is largely a problem of the sexual violation of innocent women and children.

In addition, the inclusion of voluntary migration for purposes of prostitution helps to swell the numbers of victims (though not those eligible for assistance) and thereby contributes to the claim of a massive moral and legal crisis. This focus on sex adds both urgency and drama to the demand that something be done. It also offers a symbolic nod to the concerns of antiprostitution feminists who were instrumental in getting the proposed legislation before lawmakers.

For antiprostitution feminists, anyone involved in performing prostitution is by definition a "victim" regardless of consent or conditions of labor. The National Organization for Women, for example, demanded that HR 3244 cover "all traffickers who lure or force women into prostitution regardless of whether or not their victims 'consent'" (NOW 2000). Victims are defined here not by abusive conditions, but by the form of labor they may have been lured into performing. As the quotation marks around the term "consent" suggest, in the context of commercial sex, consent is understood to be meaningless or impossible.[8]

Dividing the Innocent from the Guilty

The issue of consent has been a central problem in discussions of prostitution. Are all sex workers "victims," including those who consciously enter the trade? Are those who are forced into prostitution considered "innocent" when faced with abuse? Certainly, few workers in any trade fully consent to their labor, if by consent we mean "freely choosing" it from among an expansive range of occupational (or even survival) options. However, as sex workers' rights advocates have noted, making consent irrelevant in prostitution can further undermine the well-being of those in the sex trade by, for example, making the rape of a prostitute no more than redundant. Furthermore, by defining prostitution itself as violence, its prohibition and criminalization can be justified "for the workers' own good" (much as anti-immigration policies are presented as measures taken in the migrants' best interests). Sex workers thereby become both victims and criminals, suffering additional abuse at the hands of the state. For these reasons, since the 1970s, sex workers' rights activists have objected to the notion that all sex workers are victims and have challenged the idea that those who pay for their services or who assist them in securing work or arranging for migration should indiscriminately be defined as perpetrators, pimps, and traffickers.[9] They have insisted that antiprostitution legislation be focused on forced prostitution, not commercial sex per se.

However, in recent years, sex workers' rights activists have become as concerned as antiprostitution feminists with the dangers of the "forced" and "free" distinction, especially when it is used to determine which prostitutes deserve protection from abuse (Doezema 1998, 34–50). As prostitution researcher Jo Doezema points out, laws focusing only on victims of forced prostitution leave most sex workers outside of their protective umbrella: "It is one thing to save innocent victims of forced prostitution, quite another to argue that prostitutes deserve rights" (Doezema 1998, 45).

Thus, despite passionate ideological differences among feminists on the question of decriminalization of commercial sex, both antiprostitution activists (who see all sex workers as victims) and sex workers' rights activists (who demand rights for all those engaged in prostitution) have come to agree that the forced/free distinction should never be a factor in determining which victims of abuse deserve assistance. Sadly, this unusual consensus among feminists failed to find expression in the Trafficking Victims Protection Act of 2000.

As passed, the law relies heavily on the distinction between "innocent victims" of forced prostitution and "guilty sex workers" who had foreknowledge of the fact that they would be performing sexual labor. As such, the law neither empowers most migrant prostitutes by protecting their rights as workers, nor offers assistance to the majority of abused sex workers who may be interested in leaving the trade. As Dorchen Leidholt, director of the antiprostitution organization called the Coalition Against Trafficking in Women, notes, "The bill reinforces a distinction feminists have fought for decades: The good victims deserve assistance and protection versus the bad girls who have chosen their fate and are on their own" (Leidholt 2000).

Feminists failed to secure a law fully responding to their concerns in part because of a strategic decision to join forces with powerful conservative religious and political groups. The alliance behind HR 3244 was always, in the words of Michael Horowitz of the Hudson Institute, "an amazing, somewhat vulnerable, but remarkably cohesive coalition of feminists and church groups" (Carnes 2000). When the interests of the two partners conflicted, antiprostitution and anti-immigration conservatives seemed to have won out.

The problematic distinction written into the final version of the law separating the innocent from guilty reflects concerns of conservatives who feared that, unamended, the legislation would redefine abuse "until it is a catch-all phrase for expanding immigration" (Carnes 2000). Mark Krikorian, the executive director for the Center for Immigration Studies, an anti-immigration think tank, warned that the law could become part of "an ongoing trend to expand the grounds for asylum, especially for women. . . . The feminists as well as the homosexual rights organizations have begun to use asylum as another vehicle for promoting their interests" (Carnes 2000, online). Amendments restricting eligibility of victims to only the most severely abused and the most purely innocent were put forward by anti-immigrant representatives like Lamar Smith from Texas. Smith justified the restrictions on the grounds that they would "prevent hundreds of thousands of people claiming to be trafficking victims . . . [leading] to a massive amnesty for illegal aliens" ("Congressional debate over immigration" 2000).

Given these concerns, depictions of the model victim relied heavily on very graphic accounts of extreme sexual violation. In debates over the legislation, even progressive Democrats described victims not as "ordinary" abused migrants but rather as those who

> . . . are found behind dark, padlocked doors and hidden corridors. The deprivations of food, the beating with electrical wires, metal rods, and leather straps, the cigarette burns, and the brutal rapes are conducted in the hidden rooms and upper floors where, if you can get to them, you can find women and children locked in literal cages. (Minority Views 1999)

Such extreme portrayals of the problem allowed action to be taken against the abuses of [sexual] slavery while leaving in place policies that continue to punish the majority of "ordinary" prostitutes and abused and exploited migrants. In fact, HR 3244 serves to further cement the division between victims deemed deserving of sympathy and support and those eligible only for detention and deportation. The limited exception for victims of a severe form of trafficking helps to prove the rule that good women and men do not intentionally violate national borders and certainly not to deliberately engage in prostitution. In this way, the Trafficking Victims Protection Act helps to define "compassionate conservatism:" a willingness to provide assistance and protection for a few while reinforcing barriers to help for the many. The law insists that victims deserve support because they differ from economic migrants who have unfairly benefited from facilitated migration.

But, in fact, making such distinctions is difficult at best. Amy O'Neill Richards, a State Department analyst with the Bureau of Intelligence and Research, notes that over a million people are arrested each year by the U.S. Immigration and Naturalization Service (INS). She argues that, among this group, "it is tough to determine who has been severely victimized and trafficked" (O'Neill Richards 1999, 36). Indeed, according to O'Neill Richards, the INS "finds it is hard to 'play favorites' because there are countless other illegal aliens who are exploited by unscrupulous employers, and it is not easy to know where you draw the line in terms of who is being exploited" (O'Neill Richards 1999, 36). The need to "draw the line" at all is justified by the belief that, within a "continuum" of abuse, not all can be deserving victims:

> On one end of the continuum are trafficking cases, characterized by slavery or slaverylike treatment of the trafficking victims. On the other end is the criminal exploitation of smuggled economic migrants including fair labor and safety violations. The government seeks to address all types of exploitation, though the types of protection and assistance afforded the victims differ, depending upon where the victims fall within the spectrum. (O'Neill Richards 1999, 25)

Innocence becomes a key element in separating the violated from violators, but convincing the INS that any migrant is "innocent" may be an uphill battle:

> Distinctions regarding trafficking in women, alien smuggling, and irregular migration are sometimes blurred with INS predisposed to jump to the conclusion that most cases involving illegal workers are alien smuggling cases instead of trafficking cases. One INS agent recently stated that there are no innocent victims, they are all willing participants. Consequently, their focus is on deporting the women once they are discovered. (O'Neill Richards 1999, 31)

HR 3244, then, attempts to counter the expectation that all migrants are "guilty" by creating an utterly passive, entirely pure, and extremely vulnerable victim who is above reproach. Victims are portrayed as no more than unwilling goods exchanged between unscrupulous men. In the words of one anti-trafficking activist, they are just "commodities, they are nothing more than commodities . . . bodies exchanged on a market" (Barry 1992). Another anti-trafficking activist echoes this description, arguing that trafficked women are "goods and services in an industry without borders" (Raymond 1998, 5). "Innocent victims," in other words, are much more likely to be depicted as objects of exchange than as exploited workers. As such, they are not even guilty of ambition.

The innocence of trafficking victims is further established by the constant linkage of women and children, a phrase suggesting a special shared vulnerability (see also Schaffner, this volume). Women and children outside their home or homeland are separated from individuals and institutions described as necessary to their safety. HR 3244 explicitly warns that "traffickers often transport victims from their home communities to unfamiliar destinations, including foreign countries, away from family and friends, religious institutionc, and other sources of protection and support, leaving the victims defenseless and vulnerable" (TVPA—Section 102(b) 5). No acknowledgment is made that the protections offered by family and religious institutions might be oppressive or abusive in their own right. Another unfortunate effect of such rhetoric is, as sociologist Kamala Kempadoo points out, that third-world prostitutes become positioned "as incapable of making decisions about their own lives, forced by overwhelming external powers completely beyond their control into submission and slavery" (Kempadoo 1998, 12).

That victims should be seen as defenseless is, in any case, striking, given that the United States, like most nations, has many laws prohibiting kidnapping, rape, forced servitude, and debt-bondage that could be used to prosecute those who abuse migrants, including those engaged in prostitution. Yet language within the bill suggests that such laws are impotent in the face of sex trafficking. HR 3244 asserts, "even the most brutal instances of trafficking in the sex industry are often punished under laws that also apply to lesser offenses, so that traffickers typically escape deserved punishment" (TVPA—Section 102(b) 14). One explanation for why this might be true is that offenses against prostitutes and "illegal aliens" are routinely considered less serious than comparable crimes against more "innocent" victims. In HR 3244 it is specifically noted that, because "victims are often illegal immigrants in the destination country, they are repeatedly punished more harshly than the traffickers themselves" (TVPA—Section 102(b) 17). This acknowledgment of the extreme hostility and discrimination faced by most undocumented workers, let alone prostitutes, is left unaddressed in the legislation. As Jo Doezema observes, this is commonplace in laws and conventions on prostitution; tying punishment for abuse to the "innocence" of the victim "bears a frightening resemblance to rape trials in which victims' chastity status will determine the severity of the crime. . . . Human rights organizations and bodies in the United Nations seem content to let governments trample on the rights of sex workers as long as the morals of 'innocent' women are protected" (Doezema 1998, 46).

The line drawn between the innocent victim and the willful illegal immigrant used to determine punishment and protection is not only a dangerous one, it is also a distinction that does not hold. Most trafficking victims are also economic migrants. Their victimization most often involves high debts and abusive working conditions, not outright kidnapping and imprisonment. Amy O'Neill Richards notes that many victims, even of serious abuse, actually resist assistance, distrusting law enforcement and fearing deportation even more than continued exploitation (O'Neill Richards 1999, 32). Similarly, Licia Brussa, director of the migrant prostitute project TAMPEP in Amsterdam, observes that victims of sex trafficking often tell project staff, "I want to stop, I want to go back to my normal life—but with some money. Then I'll be able to start something else." The money is crucial; it is the reason they migrated in the first place. These are women with both serious economic problems and lots of ambition . . . .The thing is, the women in general are absolutely not interested in being defined as victims, including those like Eastern European women who certainly qualify. Even when we can guarantee that if they submit a complaint against a trafficker or a pimp they'll be given a shelter address, a temporary residency permit, and a welfare check, that doesn't address their real need. Their real need is to make money in any way they can (Interview, March 3, 1994).

Payback: Protecting the Borders

Not only does antitrafficking legislation like HR 3244 fail to benefit the majority of exploited undocumented (sex) workers, it also extracts a particular price from those it does assist: demanding their help in closing down smuggling networks used by other migrants. Participants in the program must assist in identifying, locating, apprehending, and prosecuting traffickers (TVPA—Section 107(2) C 3 and Section 107(E) I–iii).[10] Those seeking a T-visa must prove themselves "willing to assist in every reasonable way" in the investigation and prosecution of traffickers (TVPA—Section 107[E]). But even those victims most willing to assist cannot assume they will be awarded permanent residency. For that, victims must also demonstrate that they would "suffer *extreme* hardship involving *unusual* and *severe* harm upon removal from the United States" (TVPA—Section 107 (F) ii; emphasis added). The T-visa, then, is designed not so much as a means to assist the victim in securing legal residency as it is a device to assist prosecutors in closing down trafficking networks.

The names of those identified during the investigation as traffickers or suspected traffickers, or those believed to have aided, abetted, assisted, or colluded with a trafficker, are to be passed on to immigration officials who are authorized to deny them, their families, and their associates entry into the United States (TVPA—Section 111[d]). Because much illegal migration is "chain migration," this may work to pit friends and family members against one another as the state pressures illegal immigrants to reveal who trafficked them into the country in exchange for the (temporary) right to remain. In short, HR 3244 has many features of a protective law masquerading as a good cop to anti-immigration-policies' bad cop. As antitrafficking activist Marjan Wijers warns,

> We can distinguish between two types of strategies to combat trafficking in women. On one hand, there are repressive strategies, including more restrictive immigration policies, more penalization, and stronger and more effective prosecution. Repressive strategies have a strong tendency to end up working against women instead of in their favor. . . . At the same time, these repressive strategies are the most attractive for governments. . . . On the other hand, there are strategies that aim to strengthen the rights of the women involved, as women, as female migrants, as female migrant workers, and as female migrant sex workers. (1998, 77)

Some elements of the Trafficking Victims Protection Act do attempt to strengthen the position of women by addressing the reality that trafficking is not primarily a problem of forced migration of unwilling women but rather of economic desperation. One section of the law specifically considers the need for economic alternatives to prevent and deter trafficking by enhancing opportunities in labor exporter nations (TVPA—Section 106). The proposed initiatives include microcredit lending programs, training in business development and job counseling, programs to promote women's participation in economic decision making, programs to keep children—especially girls—in school, and grants to nongovernmental organizations to advance the political, economic, and educational roles of women (TVPA—Section 106(a) 1-5). Unfortunately, however, HR 3244 only authorizes appropriations of $15 million over two years to fund all of these initiatives (TVPA—Section 106(a) 1-5). In contrast, the federal government spends nearly 1 billion dollars annually to patrol the U.S./Mexican border (Smith 2000, 68).

Grossly underfunded programs, however innovative and important, are highly unlikely to stem the flow of migrants. As Carolyn Sleightholme and Indrani Sinha note about economic alternatives to prostitution programs in India, "income-generating projects with sex workers reflect one of the prejudices that pushes women into sex work in the first place: the myth that women only require 'pin money,' a small income . . ." (Sleightholme and Sinha 1996, xii).

The second component of the "prevention" effort built into HR 3244, "antitrafficking educational campaigns," is also flawed. The bill encourages domestic and international initiatives "to increase public awareness, particularly among potential victims of trafficking, of the dangers of trafficking and the protections that are available for victims," (TVPA—Section 106[b]). This presupposes that potential victims do not recognize the dangers and need only be educated about the risks in order to decide to abandon plans to migrate. Victims are understood, then, to be not only passive, but also deeply naive. The law thus proposes to warn them of the dangers of leaving home.

A comparable antitrafficking education campaign was developed in the Netherlands in the early 1990s to discourage sex workers from the Dominican Republic from migrating to Holland. Licia Brussa reports that the campaign was a failure on several fronts:

> The film they produced is a version of the "innocent from the third-world victimized in prostitution" story. . . . She decides to come to the Netherlands after hearing there's a lot more money to be made here. But once she arrives, it's one horrible experience after the other. In the course of a few months, every evil you can imagine happens: rape, racism, police brutality, you name it. . . . The film was made to be shown widely in the Dominican Republic as a kind of warning to just stay at home. You can imagine how worried the Dominican women who work here are about the impact the film could have on their lives. They are terrified that it will blow their cover back home, exposing them as prostitutes. But even in its own terms, I think the film won't work. It's meant to frighten off women, but anybody watching it would think, "I'm much smarter than that idiot; those things would never happen to me." Besides, for women who don't have many choices, survival mechanisms take over. And a warning film exposing migrant women workers as prostitutes won't really help with that problem. (1994)[11]

A more effective response to trafficking than sensationalized "education" campaigns and underfunded job training programs in labor-exporting countries would involve reducing barriers to legal immigration in destination countries. However, in contemporary "Fortress Europe" and anti-immigrant America, such a strategy seems remote at best. Indeed, the challenges facing immigrants and would-be immigrants are only intensifying. The *San Francisco Chronicle* reports that "As many as 20,000 refugees from across the world, cleared to come to the United States to escape persecution in their homelands, have had their arrival here delayed indefinitely in the aftermath of the September 11 terror attacks . . . in effect, a temporary moratorium on refugee admissions [is in place]" (Chronicle News Services 2001, A5). This closed door will only serve to increase the problem of trafficking according to some activists. Widney Brown of Human Rights Watch argues that, post-September 11, "as borders get tight in receiving countries, traffickers will tell desperate women they have ways to cross, and they (the women) will find themselves as trafficking victims" (Casert and Shepard 2001, A2).

Conclusion

The Trafficking Victims Protection Act does too little to strengthen the rights of most migrant workers, whether in the sex industry or outside of it. Insofar as HR 3244 attempts to address the very real problem of migrant and sex worker abuse, it is an honorable if inadequate effort. But any truly effective response demands more than symbolic action against the gross economic disparities between the world's rich and poor,[12] as well as a recognition that the criminalization of migration and the labor associated with it seriously endangers the well-being of vulnerable workers. HR 3244 may lead to increased convictions of traffickers, but it is unlikely to challenge deeply held and hostile attitudes toward poor women, undocumented workers, and prostitutes.

In the first two years after passage of the law, 36 convictions against traffickers resulted, a doubling of the number successfully prosecuted in 2001 (Marquis 2003). On the other hand, it may also be significant that the first recipient of a T-visa was neither a prostitute nor an exploited undocumented worker. Rather it was a 4-year-old boy from Thailand named Got. At age 2, Got was used as a decoy to help create the illusion of a proper nuclear family by a smuggler attempting to bring a Thai prostitute into the United States on tourist visas; the boy apparently had been rented for the occasion from his mother (described in the media as an HIV-positive prostitute and heroin addict) for $250 ("Boy used in smuggling scheme can stay in U.S." 2001, online). He was taken into custody by the INS when they ascertained that the couple was not married, the child was not theirs, and the boy was HIV positive. The woman was deported and the INS then spent the next two years attempting to deport the child as well, against appeals by the Thai American community in Los Angeles and antitrafficking activists. As one *Washington Post* reporter observed, the "Thai Elian Gonzales" became a cause celebre:

> For opponents of sex trafficking, Got was their spotted owl, their Polly Klaas . . . with trafficked women, there is always the question of their complicity. With a boy who cannot speak his own name yet, no one can say he agreed. (Rosin 2000)

After a federal judge blocked his deportation, Attorney General John Ashcroft declared that the boy would become the first recipient of a T-visa. Ashcroft described the child as the archetypal victim of trafficking: "Human trafficking victims are too often people like Got. Too young, too frightened, and too trapped in their circumstances to speak for themselves. This is a 4-year-old child" ("Boy used in smuggling scheme can stay in U.S." 2001).

Despite Ashcroft's assertion, most victims of migrant and sex worker abuse can speak for themselves when allowed to do so. However, their accounts do not always reduce to simple morality tales featuring evil traffickers, naive victims, and protective border guards. Instead, their stories are ones of enormous complexity that challenge easy distinctions between innocent and knowing, between mere exploitation and severe abuse. Feminists should look critically at legislation like the Trafficking Victims Protection Act, which relies heavily on narratives of female powerlessness and childlike sexual vulnerability. Certainly, no one should be forced to trade sex or safety to survive. The relevant social response, however, demands more open borders, not bigger fences, and more expansive state support for the poor, not its reduction or elimination. Addressing the abuses of women working in and outside of the sex industry requires an acknowledgment that women can consent to both economically motivated migration and to sex. The possibility of that consent, however, must never be used to excuse violation: There are no guilty victims. By institutionalizing such distinctions, the Trafficking Victims Protection Act of 2000 runs the risk of reinforcing barriers to help rather than removing them.

Notes

1. A condensed version of this article first appeared in *Gender and Society,* December 2003. I would like to express my gratitude to a number of people who commented on drafts of this paper: Erica Rand, Gabriel Demaine, Laurie Schaffner, Elizabeth Bernstein, and the members of the Sexuality and the State workshop held in Oñati, Spain. Special thanks, too, to Jill Hanson for research assistance and to Ann Jordan for her vision.
2. According to the most recent ILO figures, more than 50 percent of all labor migrants around the world are, in fact, women (Wijers 1998).
3. For a more general discussion of the question of "moral panics," see Wagner (1997).
4. See, for example, Barry (1979) and Raymond (1998).
5. Representative Lamar Smith—responsible for most of the restrictive amendments to HR 3244—was one of the two key sponsors for the 1996 Illegal Immigrant Reform Act, which, among other things, made "trafficking in humans" a felony punishable by up to 15 years imprisonment. Smith argued in favor of the new law by pointing out, "When we cracked down on drugs with harsher sentences, we inadvertently created an imbalance in the penal code that made immigrant smuggling more appealing. This law redresses that" (Gordy 2000, 5). Note that for Smith, "trafficking" is the definitional equivalent of "immigrant smuggling."
6. See, for example, materials by the Coalition Against Trafficking in Women (CATW 2003).
7. See, for example, materials by the Global Alliance Against Trafficking in Women (GATW 2003).
8. Antiprostitution activists Cecilie Høigard and Liv Finstad make this point in their study of Norwegian street prostitution when they argue against the relevance of the notion of consent in prostitution by asserting, "It is not mere rhetoric to counter the absurdity of the demand for legalization of prostitution with 'Legalize rape and incest. Recognize these as normal activities'" (Høigard and Finstad 1986, 183). The most important abolitionist legislation relating to trafficking in women is the "Convention for the Suppression of the Traffic in Persons and the Exploitation of the Prostitution of Others" adopted by the U.N. General Assembly in 1949. That document specifically prohibits and punishes anyone who "procures, entices or leads away, for purposes of prostitution, another person, even with the consent of that person; [or] who exploits the prostitution of another person, *even with the consent of that person*" (see United Nations 1949, Article 1 of the Convention; emphasis added).

     Recent international campaigns by American antiprostitution activists are similarly focused on defining prostitution as abusive regardless of consent; see demands for a new U.N. Convention "Against All Forms of Sexual Exploitation" regardless of "age, *consent*, race, or geography" (Raymond 1998, 5; emphasis added).
9. See, for example, Chapkis (1997); Delacoste and Alexander (1998); Nagle (1997); Pheterson (1989); Shrage (1994); and Weitzer (2000c).
10. In a number of ways, the "T-visa" provided to victims of trafficking resembles another program directed at undocumented immigrants: the so-called snitch visa that has gained prominence in post-September 11 America. In November of 2001, Attorney General John Ashcroft announced that visas would be available under the "Responsible Cooperators Program" to those who provide useful information on possible terrorists or terrorist activity (Lewis 2001). The program met with significant hostility in immigrant communities. Renee Saucedo, director of the Day Labor Program in San Francisco, for example, notes, "The same government that supports rewarding people for reporting other people . . . is the same government that makes it virtually impossible for illegal immigrants to legalize. This encourages scapegoating fellow immigrants . . ." (Ness and Kim 2001, A8).
11. For a discussion of the ways in which similar "disaster narratives" are evoked around questions of prostitution more generally, see the chapters by Agustín and Saunders in this volume.
12. For example, erasing the $100 billion in debt owed by the world's poorest nations to the world's richest through loans made by the World Bank, the International Monetary Fund, and Western nations. Now many destitute countries are spending more than half of their tax revenue on debt repayments (Pocina 2001, 2C).

CHAPTER 5

At Home in the Street:
Questioning the Desire to Help and Save

LAURA Mª AGUSTÍN

Western discourses of "prostitution" have changed little since the late eighteenth century, when populations outside nuclear-family units began to be feared by "society." Medical, sociological, criminological, and psychological discourses have been fixated on those selling sex rather than on those buying it, on women rather than men, on individuals rather than families or communities, and on particular body parts rather than whole persons. A wide variety of commercial-sexual relations are essentialized as "prostitution"—an isolated, two-party, sex-for-money transaction, which "deviate" from a supposed norm: sex with a loved partner or between spouses in a nuclear family. Yet vast numbers of people every day, all over the world, want to spend time, sometimes having sex, outside the family, and away from spouses. Not only state agencies of social control but nongovernmental organizations (NGOs), feminists, and others interested in bettering society continue to ignore the limitations of "home" and "family."

My own work during a number of years has concerned migrants (men, women, transgender people) who work in the West's domestic, "caring," and sex industries. I have interviewed migrants (potential, current, and returned) in Latin America, the Caribbean, Europe, Australia, and Thailand, and I have studied social agents (governmental, NGO, religious, academic, and other workers) proposing to support and "help" them (Agustín 2001a, 2002a, 2003).[1] I began studying the relationship between European supporters and non-Europeans looking for work in Europe when I noticed the disturbing difference between their accounts of these migrations; later, I discovered that this difference goes back a long time. In this chapter, I trace the development of this disparity in European ideologies of family and gender.

The Construction of "Victims"

For many migrants, Europeans appear to be confused about sex. At tourism sites away from home, they act sophisticated and tolerant about sex and affection, and later many invite new friends and facilitate their trips to Europe to visit or work. European embassies in third-world countries grant hundreds of visas every day for "artists" and "dancers," knowing the work will be sexual. Yet once in Europe, migrants find that, despite abundant opportunities to work—meaning their services are desired—they themselves are despised, pitied, and harassed, often even more than they would be at home. Around them have grown up a number of volunteer and NGO "helping" projects, particularly in cities. The most powerful are health programs aiming to contain epidemics of sexually transmitted disease by focusing on "high-risk groups;" others are feminist projects to save women from "traffickers." It is common for all projects to offer other kinds of information, such as legal references, along with condoms and sympathy.

But migrants have their questions: Why do Europeans facilitate people's trips only to demonize, chase, and deport them once they arrive? Why do police harry those selling sex and not those buying? Why do so *many* people give out condoms, and why do they talk about the possibilities of being "reinserted" into society through activities such as sewing and recycling, which are not interesting and pay little? Anyway, how can one be "reinserted" into a society that one was never part of in the first place? Why doesn't anyone help with what's really important—becoming legal to live and work? Why do feminists talk about traffickers when often it was people's own family and friends who helped them migrate? Why do they call many lovers and partners "pimps" instead of wondering why their own husbands leave home for sex? These questions reveal the contradictions between discourses of social control and the exclusion of "illegals" from Europe and discourses of pity and helping, in which migrants become objects to be discussed and moved about. Yet clients for sexual services abound, businesspeople continue to facilitate jobs, and helping projects proliferate.

Western feminist commentators sometimes talk as though migrants were naive women who only yesterday were carrying water on their heads in some remote countryside; the fact that many come from large postmodern cities and have planned their migrations to the best of their ability disappears.[2] As with many treatments of non-Western women in general, an evolutionary discourse is employed in which some countries are advanced and enlightened, while others are backward and ignorant (Amos and Pratibha 1984). Women selling sex become casualties of imperialism, development, and cruel men; all ambiguities of roles, the fact that many are transgender or men, and that clients and traffickers are also women are erased. This is an agency-free view of the poorer women of the world.

Migrants selling sex do not, however, tend to think of themselves as passive victims *until they learn to* from outsiders (Agustín 2002b). Many feel their current life is difficult, and they are trying to improve it—but not necessarily by getting out of the sex industry. They may be trying to find a better situation inside it, one where they are less vulnerable and controlled by others. Feminists who tell them they are suffering life's worst experience are assumed to be unfamiliar with other jobs available to poor women, such as live-in domestic service, cleaning public toilets, and caring for other people's babies and sick or elderly relatives. Sietske Altink shows how the word "victim" may be used in a technical way (when you are robbed you are legally a victim), but it is also a word that transmits shades of meaning that demand that *these* victims be chaste and ignorant. This concept

> ignores the sense of responsibility that leads women to migrate in search of work . . . "It hurts, but don't call me a poor thing," one woman . . . said. Victims can also be very tough, doing anything to avenge the damage done to them and make a better life for themselves. Some victims don't go to the police but start trafficking for themselves, or side with the traffickers to avoid reprisals. (Altink 1995, 2)

Meanwhile, other feminists focus on issues of identity, constructing sex workers as individuals who should be empowered with rights (Alexander 1995). This feminist strategy also involves much talking, writing, and attempting to influence governmental policies, but migrants tend to be uninterested in or excluded from these debates. This is so, I believe, because the continuing essentializing of "prostitution," whether as a sex act or a sex job, overlooks other aspects (such as flexible schedules and instant cash), which make possible supporting one's own relatives and enjoying such advantages as travel, meeting new people, and being admired and desired.

My questions, then, examine Western behavior, specifically that of middle-class women who concern themselves with helping.[3] Why do many feminists who want a different, better world propose solutions based on policing and punishment? Why do they appear to make no (personal) connection between a guilty class of men ("clients") and their own male friends and relations (Agustín 2001b)? Why do middle-class women assume they need to save working-class ones? Why are the diverse impulses that have led people to sell sex not taken into account? What would happen if we questioned the centricity of families and why many people wish to leave them? To understand better, I have studied the development of women's movements to help and save others.[4]

The Rise of the Social

My subject is Europe for two reasons: It is the physical site of a sophisticated sex industry employing hundreds of thousands of migrants, and it is the source of a technology called "research" that is driven by the will to know (and ultimately do something) about "prostitution." There were probably always differences of perception, description, and morality about selling sexual services—people who saw it as a problem and people who did not. Before the Enlightenment, however, it appears that the main discourse about the subject was primarily juridical, seeing it as a kind of unavoidable delinquency of not very great social consequence. But in the late-eighteenth and early nineteenth century, when concepts of absolute monarchy were being swept away or discredited in northern Europe, there was a change. Self-appointed observers and commentators conscientiously pronounced on the effects of the Industrial Revolution and the rise of the cities. Philosophers and new experts felt called upon to decide what should be the *right* way to live in civilized societies. In this period, the family, in its bourgeois definition, came to be defined as society's central unit and women as the figures responsible for holding families together (Donzelot 1979). For the nobility, lineage (and therefore pride) had been secured through the connection son-property. For the bourgeoisie, "family" had more emotional meanings—a way of life, domesticity, the *home* (Barber 1955).

With this identification of families as the good and the normal, large numbers of people were discursively converted into social misfits—people without proper places in a domestic structure. They were also seen as threats to normal society. As Friedrich Engels pointed out in his 1845 study of Manchester, the capitalist system made the ideal of family life impossible for workers to attain:

> The various members of the family only see each other in the mornings and evenings, because the husband is away at his work all day long. Perhaps his wife and the older children also go out to work and they may be in different factories. In these circumstances how can family life exist? (1958, 145)

In France, Jules Simon published popular works (*L'Ouvrière* 1861 and *La Famille* 1869) berating women who worked as "impious" and "sordid"—no longer women. They represented disorder, when order was defined as family and maternity (Scott 1987). Women selling sex, once viewed as conventional miscreants to be guarded against (capable of mugging men in the street), were now seen as pathological subjects capable of contaminating good citizens.

In the history of regulation and control, whether those helping are feminists, bureaucrats, doctors, legislators, police, nuns, or social theorists, an overwhelming majority of efforts have aimed to get "excess" people—those in streets or taverns, those who live in furnished rooms, those who eat out instead of cooking their own food—into family units. Such people and their desires were until recently labeled "deviant," a word that assumes the existence of a correct way that can be strayed from. Getting people into families means *placing* them in the proper locations of families—houses or homes. Social reformers who began regularly visiting the poor in the nineteenth century found dwellings that did not conform to middle-class standards. What followed involved the gradual evolution of a bourgeois ideology celebrating private life and the individual that went hand in hand with a morality in which the bourgeoisie sought to regulate the working class, teaching values of domesticity (Weeks 1981). Social thinkers debated such problems as the poor's lack of interest in marriage or sleeping arrangements that allowed children to see their parents in bed. If reform efforts didn't work inside the home, quasi-homes were to be provided: The institutionalization of prisons, hospitals, workhouses, children's homes, boarding schools, and asylums dates from this period, including those meant for "prostitutes."

Jacques Donzelot shows how this ideology was far from being utopian:

> Men placed at the head of business and government know how urgent it is to diminish and restrict not only the costs of policing and judicial action occasioned by the excesses that the depraved classes indulge in, but also all the expenses for the almshouses and hospitals that result from the mutual abandonment of fathers, wives, and children who should have helped one another as members of the same family, but who, not being united by any social tie, become strangers to one another. The task at hand is not only a social necessity and a highly moral endeavor; it is also an excellent piece of business, an obvious and immense saving for the state . . . When the man and woman of the people live in disorder, they often have neither hearth nor home . . . on the contrary, once a man and a woman . . . are married, they desert the filthy rooms . . . and set up their home. (Donzelot 1979, 32)

Mother was to be the axis of this family: She would always be at home, saving men from "dissolution" and holding the family together.[5] But untold numbers of women did not live this way.

Excess Women

We know more, obviously, about upper-class women, many of whom left written testaments to their way of life: producers of fine arts, holders of salons, writers of letters. These women managed to live independently and wield power in privileged social and political circles, without relying on a family identity. Women of any kind of financial means have always had a better chance of escaping forms of social control, but women at the bottom of the economic heap have not been doomed to passive immobility.

With the assumption by the bourgeoisie that the only "good" woman was a domestic(ated) one, the "bad" woman began to be defined (or attempts were made to define her). Yet plenty of women had long been outside the home, *working*. Natalie Zemon Davis writes of women's jobs in sixteenth-century France, apart from domestic service: ferrying people across rivers, attendance in bath-houses, digging ditches, and carrying loads at construction sites (1975). Joan Landes shows that such women as fishwives had a definite voice during the French Revolution, and she also points to the widespread female desire to go on the stage, this career being "one of the few professions in which a woman could hope to earn a living, practice a craft, and achieve some measure of social acclaim" (1988, 75). There were dressmakers, needlewomen, milliners, washerwomen, charwomen, milkmaids, circus women, shop assistants, chambermaids, and governesses. Women worked in the jute industry as machinists, in the textile and other mills, and as hawkers, flower sellers, message girls, and match girls. They brewed and sold beer. Outside the cities there were fieldworkers, flither girls who gathered birds' eggs and limpets, and women who hauled coal in the mines. When we get the chance to read the words of working women, any notion of their passivity is annihilated:

> I was a servant gal away down in Birmingham. I got tired of workin' and slavin' to make a living, and getting a _____ bad one at that; what o' five pun' a year and yer grub, I'd sooner starve, I would. After a bit I went to Coventry, cut brummagem, as we calls it in those parts, and took up with soldiers as was quartered there. I soon got tired of them. Soldiers is good—soldiers is—to walk with and that, but they don't pay' cos why they ain't got no money; so I says to myself, I'll go to Lunnon and I did. I soon found my level there. ("Swindling Sal," quoted in Bracebridge Hemyng, "Prostitution in London," In *London Labour and the London Poor*, ed. Henry Mayhew IV 1968, 23 [1851])

Later in the nineteenth century, more women were schoolteachers, office workers, waitresses, and attendants in toilets for the middle classes. Many working-class women left home; they migrated, looking for their "level." And they were not all *forced* to remain single; Michèle Perrot cites an 1880 study of female postal workers in France, which showed a majority choosing financial and professional independence rather than marriage. She comments: "Nineteenth-century women who wished to improve their position in society through work were obliged to sacrifice their private lives" (1990, 255). Such women may be viewed as more exploited and downtrodden or less powerful than other people of their day, but they remain human beings with will and desire who made decisions to move and change. And while some of them un-doubtedly exchanged some kind of sex for some kind of benefit, certainly not all did, and if they did, it may have been occasional and without anyone's iden-tifying them as a "prostitute."

The literary and historical writings of many middle-class men, of course, scarcely mention working women *unless* they were prostitutes. For F.F-A. Béraud, in an 1839 book on "public women" in Paris, "it does not take much acuteness to recognize that a girl who at eight o'clock may be seen sumptuously dressed in an elegant costume is the same who appears as a shop girl at nine o'-clock and as a peasant girl at ten" (51). Siegfried Kracauer's nineteenth-century Paris seems to be a great open-air theater for men, in whose backdrop carefree women romp, referred to affectionately as *vedettes, lorettes, cocottes,* and *grisettes* (1937). Looking past these male prejudices, however, we can see a di-versity of women sharing the same spaces as their patrons, friends, harassers, potential targets, and boyfriends: parks, taverns, theaters, and streets. Women also liked to dance, drink, take walks, make money, and have sex. As Elizabeth Wilson says,

> . . . although the male ruling class did all it could to restrict the move-ment of women in cities, it proved impossible to banish them from public spaces. Women continued to crowd into the city centres and the factory districts. (1995, 61)

Mannerisms such as loud voices, "garish" dress, drinking, and cursing were associated by the bourgeoisie with sexual promiscuity, but this was certainly often a cultural misunderstanding. Bourgeois women may not have been "per-mitted" to spend time in public until the arcades were built and "shopping" became an accepted activity, but working-class women were already there.[6]

Women as Helpers and Savers

Chaste virgins, virtuous mothers, and wives (including many early feminists), feeling sorrow, pity, disapproval, disgust, horror, and anger about the situation of poorer women (called wayward, common, unruly, disorderly), desired to "protect" them. While they may have had good intentions, various matters were not usually questioned: in the first place, the decision of these women that something had to be done, especially about women and children. Women who might once have made a charitable contribution to a workhouse designed to keep offenders out of the way, now found inspiration in *participating* in the raising up of "unfortunates."

Middle-class women's certainty of their ability to help may be understood as part of a discourse of social evolutionism, as discussed by Johannes Fabian, in which "all living societies were irrevocably placed on . . . a stream of Time—

some upstream, others downstream. Civilization, evolution, development, ac-
culturation, modernization . . . are all terms whose conceptual content derives
. . . from evolutionary Time" (1983, 18).

Mary Poovey discusses Adam Smith's belief that poor men were prevented
from developing self-government in the modern liberal state's division of
labor, a regime in which they were conceptualized as an aggregate and thus had
to be treated differently from those individuals capable of specular morality,
the ability to reflect on one's own moral character (1995, 34). In these schemes,
the bourgeois way of life was "advanced" and the poor's, like that of primitive
tribes, was "backward." Women were considered inherently inferior to men,
but within all possible classifications, bourgeois women, as members of the
most advanced class in the most advanced society, were placed ahead of poor
women. Some tried to prove through anthropometry that "prostitutes" were
biologically degenerate, born with a constitution and disposition to this particular evil (Lombroso and Ferrero 1895).

During the rise of the social, a theory of self-government also began to develop, but it was thought that it could only be carried out by those with sufficient capacity for rational thinking. Where this was lacking, other people were
called upon to help, and middle-class women were considered to have a "natural" duty to care for the poor, a "civilizing mission," which derived from the redefinition of the concept of virtue. Whereas eighteenth-century salon hostesses
had moral authority because of their "disinterestedness and generosity, an elo-
quent concern for the public welfare," it was now respectability that made
virtue, and only married women were seen as respectable (Marguerite Glotz
1945, 14–15, cited in Barber). As Martha Vicinus notes, these qualities

> . . . when appropriately applied, not only would give the family a hap-
> pier and better life, but also would help to eliminate the most grievous
> wrongs of society. Philanthropy had traditionally been women's partic-
> ular concern, and its definition during the . . . century . . . was broad-
> ened to include virtually every major social problem. It is from the
> narrow base of woman's special duties and obligations that women in
> the nineteenth century came to expand their fields of action and their
> personal horizons. (Vicinus 1977, x)

A discourse developed in which the virtuous domestic woman was (at least
superficially) accepted as knowing what was best for everyone; at the same
time, anxiety grew about women working outside the home. In France, the
term *femmes isolées* was used for both women wage earners living alone in furnished rooms and for women selling sex but not officially registered at one of
the known houses. *Femmes isolées* were considered potential prostitutes, their
economic "misery" contributing to their desires—to glitter and to have sex. To

the social sector, "there was only one cure for sexual license and that was control" (Scott 1987, 123).

But the new dedication of middle-class women was not altruistic. For a complex of reasons, there were now more educated women, with time to spare and/or the desire or need to work: widows, unmarried daughters, wives without access to their own property, and leisured women.[7] Female respectability was found in few occupations; the two most acceptable, lady's companion and governess, were isolating, boring, and poorly paid. The invention of "social work" provided dignified careers that in no way compromised notions of femininity. As Anthony Platt has argued, "philanthropic labour filled a vacuum in their lives" (1969, 98).

Middle-class women, finding the poor's family life deficient, undertook to inculcate in them an ideology of thrift, individual responsibility, and domesticity. Nancy Armstrong comments that "one can see [how] the notion of charity was inexorably linked to the female role of household overseer" (1987, 133).[8] The bourgeoisie advocated independence for themselves but not for the working class. And as Jeffrey Weeks points out, middle-class anxiety concerned work conditions less than "the moral and spiritual degradation said to accompany female employment. It was largely because of these alleged conditions that the working class was the recipient of sustained evangelism throughout the nineteenth century" (1981, 58).

The archetype of women outside the home and domestic role was, of course, the "prostitute," who began to receive large amounts of attention from bourgeois women. Linda Mahood describes the treatment of inmates in Glasgow's penitentiaries for women as "organized around the premise that inmates could only be reformed if order was put into their lives and a strict regime of mild, wholesome, paternal, and Christian discipline was enforced" (1990, 78). Inmates' own family ties were disapproved of and disrupted, and a secular education was provided in which

> what is striking . . . is the overall "gentility" and similarity to the manner in which middle-class women might spend their evenings. The emphasis on gentility reflects how closely penitentiaries associated middle-class manners with reform. It was not intended that inmates become learned, or "ladies," but rather they should appreciate the values associated with being a lady, in order to make them better servants . . . Inmates could act out their femininity by becoming servants, which conveniently enabled bourgeois women to protect their own femininity. (Mahood 1990, 84)

"Social" work became not only a suitable job for a woman, but the vehicle for creating a whole sphere of functions positioned as belonging "naturally" to women in society. These were paid occupations with prestige, something that had not existed before this period. There was now employment for women in charitable, educational, and correctional institutions, including as social investigators, district visitors, rent collectors, sanitary inspectors, poor-law guardians, fundraisers, public speakers, settlement house workers, superintendents, matrons, managers, probation officers, and adult-education teachers. F.K. Prochaska, historian of women's philanthropic work in the nineteenth century, has documented the significant numerical rise in numbers of women on charity subscription lists, in women's financial contributions to charities, in women's "district visiting" to the poor, in women's participation on management committees, and as managers and as volunteer helpers in a variety of sites from lying-in hospitals to village bazaars (1980).

Many women began as volunteers, defying ideas that their only place was the home, because charity work was a way to get a foot in the door of the "public" world. Later, there would be a move to professionalize, train, and struggle for recognition, but at the beginning, amateurs were essential. In London alone, 279 charities were founded before 1850, and 144 more during the following *decade* (Humphreys 1997). In the city of Aberdeen, with a population of less than 70,000 in the 1840s, rescue organizations included local branches of the Association for the Promotion of Social Sciences, the British Ladies' Society for Promoting the Reformation of Female Prisoners, and the Association for the Promotion of Social Purity, as well as the Aberdeen Association for Reclaiming Fallen Females and the Aberdeenshire Association of Ladies for the Rescue of Fallen Women (Mahood 1990, 116). In France, similar groups proliferated from the 1870s, and by the turn of the century, there were at least 1,300 associations devoted to the protection and "raising up" of girls (Corbin 1990, 280). It was an immense movement to succor poor women, but, as Anne Summers notes,

> In asserting a particular feminine point of view, women philanthropists made an indirect contribution towards the emancipation of women of their own class. However, their philanthropic initiatives were often diametrically opposed to the emancipation of women in the social classes beneath them. (1979, 33)

Indeed, the only approved job for a regenerated woman was domestic service.

Present-Day Helpers

Although movements to help women selling sex have always aimed at liberation (from exploitation), *how* they should be liberated has never been agreed upon. The conflict concerns whether to demand nothing less than the "abolition of prostitution" and the moral restoration of men, or to accept the existence of commercial sex as part of patriarchy and work to improve the lives of those doing the selling. This is the polemic that continues today.

Though everyone agrees that ubiquitous laws holding women selling sex responsible for "prostitution" constitute oppression of women in general, the battle on the subject is waged among feminists themselves. A veritable industry exists in writing articles and books, generally theorizing commercial sex as a problem of patriarchy and "violence against women." In conference after conference and in settings such the United Nations Commission on Crime Prevention and Penal Justice, lengthy, repetitive arguments and lobbying focus on which defining word will become part of legal instruments related to the sale of sex.

Linda Mahood describes "the social" as "the site where rival interpretations and discourses about people's needs are produced and played out" (1995, 63). In the debate over "what to do about prostitution," both sides employ discourses of laws and rights in the effort to know and express the truth about "prostitutes." It is the middle-class, self-nominated "supporters" (activists, lobbyists, NGO workers) who have become protagonists, not those selling sex, and the role that feminists play in this exercise of social control needs to be recognized. Some of this derives from the victimizing discourse that prevails, in which women selling sex are constructed as lacking agency and choices, but some of it comes about because the social sector is now an enormous area of government (whether public or private) that exists to service people with problems, among them "victims." Programs that were invented two hundred years ago have not left their roots behind, what Michel Foucault called "biopolitics," in which society is figured as a population that must be managed and regulated for its own health and welfare (1978, 139–43). Those who set out to administer the lives of others do so according to what they believe to be good, healthy, normal, and so on, so that *knowledge* is central:

> [G]overnment is intrinsically linked to the activities of expertise, whose role is not one of weaving an all-pervasive web of "social control," but of enacting assorted attempts at the calculated administration of diverse aspects of conduct through countless, often competing, local tactics of education, persuasion, inducement, management, incitement, motivation, and encouragement. (Rose and Miller 1992, 175)

Amidst the institutionalization of this social sector, helping careers have proliferated and are now completely conventional among middle-class women.

These careers continue to serve the interests of the people employed in them, just as they did when the social was first carved out as a sphere of legitimate work. Careers in the social sector are not only considered dignified but confer an implication of virtue, if not selflessness, on the people in them. In the institutionalizing of assistance, the professional tends to occupy at least as important a place as those she sets out to help, whose needs are defined by "programs." The voice of the object of help is rarely heard and, in victim debates, may even be disqualified, a consequence of false consciousness. "We don't have to talk to prostitutes to know what prostitution is" was the angry reply at one public forum I attended when a member of the audience asked to hear from them in Madrid. This is clearly taking "helping" a very long way.

The recognition of one's own interests does not have to mean abandoning all projects of helping others; one might seek instead an approach that attempts to understand the subjects of one's interests through listening to them, learning about their social and cultural contexts, and resisting the desire to project onto them one's own feelings. Theories of how to help, based more soundly on what subjects say, would be stronger theories. When Tobias Hecht studied homeless children in one Brazilian city, some children said that they could return to a house, or that they did return sometimes, but that they preferred to live in the streets.[9] The information that children say these things, however, is unacceptable to many people who want to save them. Hecht says:

> If one's goal in writing about street children is to offer ideas on how to *eradicate a problem* one can hardly view those people seen to *embody* the problem as autonomous beings in a social world. Reduced to something to be cured, *street children become objects in a distant debate* among adults. (1998, 188, emphasis added)

By the end of his project, Hecht had counted more people trying to help street children than street children themselves. And as he suggests, *studying* "victims" needs to be understood as part of the "helping" field.

Social Science: Social Justice?

Nancy Scheper-Hughes analyzed her own development as a feminist anthropologist interested in maternity and child mortality in a poor Brazilian town. Beginning from a premise that mothers were uncaring, she "wanted to know just what was necessary to propose and introduce 'appropriate' kinds of intervention" (1992, 269). Later, she learned to hear other values in the discourses of this community:

> My analysis and findings challenge the psychological infant attachment and maternal "bonding" theorists and those cultural feminists who argue for a singular conception of women's goals, interests, and moral visions . . . an essentially "womanly" ethic and ethos of maternal

responsiveness, attentiveness, and caring labor . . . Attempting to recover the muted and marginalized voices of women *can paradoxically
do violence to the different experiences and sensibilities* of poor and third-
world women whose moral visions may not conform to the feminist
paradigm. (341, emphasis added)

Both Hecht and Scheper-Hughes are Western academics who learned to
step out of the supposedly neutral tradition of social research and a familiar
feminist discourse of goodness and helping. Their insights offer an alternative
to the persistent academic colonization of non-Western, non-middle-class
subjects that Valerie Walkerdine calls voyeurism.[10] "Researchers" need to recognize our full participation in an apparatus of surveillance: the desire to know
and explain social phenomena. In fact, we research what is interesting or beneficial to ourselves.

Is there a way out of the bind of benefiting from one's desire to help? Gayatri
Spivak suggests we not be afraid of a "crisis" in which

your presuppositions of an enterprise are disproved by the enterprise
itself . . . *these are not* necessarily moments of weakness. It seems to me
that this is the only serious way in which crisis can become productive,
when one feels, for example, that the women's movement challenges the
project of feminism. On the other hand, one is not about to give up on
feminism, but the relevant outcome, either from the women's movement point of view, or from the feminism point of view, is a . . . moment when you must think about negotiating. (1990, 139)

Spivak goes on to propose that feminists examine their own privilege not in
order to feel guilty or to retire from working for a better world, but rather in
order to de-center their own importance in their work. Among the largely middle-class people who study commercial sex, this means examining assumptions
that a bourgeois family life is superior, assumptions that lead to feelings of pity,
disgust, disapproval, anger, or other emotions projected onto those involved in
the sex industry.

Leaving Home

Traditionally, the family home was assumed to be the site of love and commitment, and sex to be properly located only there, but nowadays more kinds of
relationships are accepted as meaningful, or, indeed, as "familial" (Davidoff
and Hall 1987; Sorrentino 1990; Weston 1997). Though these changes are not
universal and vary by generation, class, and ethnicity, it is fair to say that many
concepts of family now extend beyond the walls of houses (living together not

ending

being a requirement) and increasingly include non-blood or non-formal marriage relationships. For many people, "communities" acting through social movements have more symbolic meaning than families (Weeks 1995b, 44).

Although the dominant assumption continues to be that "home" is best, vast numbers of people of all ages do everything they can to *limit* time spent there, actively escaping a place where they feel—at least sometimes—alien, uncomfortable, unfree, unhappy, or unable to express some aspect of themselves. When the family is meant to both shelter and discipline its members, spaces for "self-realization" and risk-taking must be somewhere else than the home. For individuals with money and time to learn, exotic sports such as hang-gliding and scaling rock faces may fulfill this need; others will seek out more classic pastimes in more accessible spaces. People with less money, time, and perhaps hope may go to spaces that are labeled "marginal," such as "drug addiction," "drug-dealing," "addiction to gambling," "alcoholism," "anorexia," "juvenile delinquency," "gangs," "street children," "extramarital sex," and "prostitution." What happens outside the nucleus of "family life" demonstrates that the family is not sufficient to take care of all human desire. Is the nuclear family the best model for today's world, given its tendency to suppress rather than encourage the enormous diversity of human desires? If "family life" were considered only one possible normalized option, fewer people would be discursively constructed as "deviants" and "social problems." Might this lead to less social conflict and more individual satisfaction and peace?

In terms of the struggle to "help" people selling sex, we would do well to stop obsessing about *them* and about the "commercial moment"—the exchange of money for sex—and instead divert our gaze to a multitude of other questions: the market for their services, what happens besides sex at sex industry sites, concepts of sexuality that condemn those assumed to find "love" irrelevant, the presupposition that the client has all the power, the assumption that money contaminates sex, the surmise that vendors of sex cannot enjoy the sex they provide, the growing demand among women to purchase sexual services and the presumption—this above all, by Western feminists—that sex *matters* so much that its imperfection can damage a person's essence. With these kinds of questions, we also problematize the bourgeois vision of a family-centered state that prevailed in the West after the Enlightenment. We further open sexuality debates aimed at "equal opportunity" for homosexual love and sex that often claim the right to bourgeois family life. Those debates continue to exclude people not necessarily seeking that kind of home, among these—it is possible—both sex workers and their clients.

At the end of *Centuries of Childhood*, Philippe Ariès concludes that as society's pressures become unbearable, people isolate themselves at home and the house becomes a private space where before it was public. "Professional life and family life have stifled that other activity which once invaded the whole of life: the activity of social relations" (1962, 407).

Notes

1. I belong to several networks of researchers and outreach projects composed of both sex workers and supporters in Spain (Red Estatal de Organizaciones y Proyectos sobre Prostitución), the U.K. (U.K. Network of Sex Work Projects), and at the transnational level (Europap, Tampep, and the International Network of Sex Work Projects). I also created and moderate a transatlantic e-mail forum, Industria del Sexo, which for more than two years has brought together individuals selling sex in Latin America and Europe, and members of national Latin American sex worker networks and their researchers and supporters, including migrant associations in Europe. These fora provide continuous and continually renewed information on what people say about their lives.

2. For example: "Trafficking in women prevails especially in pre-industrial and feudal societies that are primarily agricultural, where women are excluded from the public sphere. Women's reduction to sex is a fact of their status as the property of their husbands" (Barry 1995, 51).

3. This is not to say that these contradictions and supervaluations of "family" are limited to Europe; on the contrary, they are ubiquitous. Nici Nelson, for example, writes of women who sell sex to migrant men in Mathare, Kenya: "It would be entirely understandable if many [married women], especially those left alone in the rural areas by migrant husbands, were resentful and morally indignant. After all, it is their husbands who are spending their money on such women in towns, money which would otherwise be expected to come to their family. This would explain the commonly expressed image of such women as rapacious bloodsuckers who squeeze men dry of all they have before they cast them aside. Men, in this stereotype, are seen as helpless victims of these women's charms who are almost bewitched into forgetting their homes and families . . . Certainly the [poorer] married women in Mathare whom I knew expressed great sympathy for women who sold sex . . . Perhaps it is a function of shared poverty . . . middle-class and elite urban women were more likely to moralize and be judgmental . . . than those living in squatter settlements" (1987, 217–239).

4. Another richer, more powerful group concerned with commercial sex is doctors. I do not address here the medicalization of women selling sexual services and their essentialization as disease-carriers; suffice it to say that doctors, too, have used a discourse of "helping" and "curing disease" in order to consolidate the social and economic status of their profession.

5. This vision masked her *vigilante* role. An entire tradition of women as suspicious monitors of family behavior begins here, where they are fused with "the home:" "Where were you last night?" "Why did you get home so late?" "Who were you with?"

6. Since the word "whore" has perhaps always been used to brand *any* woman who steps out of the bourgeoisie's respectable box, it may be that many texts about prostitutes were simply referring to women outside the home. In novels, the literary form most emblematic of late-eighteenth- and nineteenth-century mores in England and France, the assumptions about women are extremely clear. The classic *bildungsroman* depicted a young man from the country arriving in Paris or London to make his fortune, learning, loving, and in some way triumphing at the end. The equivalent theme for a young woman was nearly always disaster, failure, and death. Not safely ensconced in a home, she encountered enemies everywhere, some of the fiercest being those members of polite society who preferred to see women dead rather than unmarried and pregnant, or married and attempting to realize desires of their own outside the home. Archetypal examples include *Tess of the D'Urbervilles* and *Madame Bovary.*

7. Poovey cites the British census of 1851 with 42 percent of women between the ages of 20 and 40 unmarried and two million of a total six million British women self-supporting (1988, 4).

8. Armstrong goes on to point out how "the same logic that allowed women to carry the skills they possessed as women into the new world of work would eventually provide the liberal rationale for extending the doctrine of self-regulation and with it, the subtle techniques of domestic surveillance beyond the middle-class home and into the lives of those much lower down on the economic ladder. It was not uncommon for nineteenth-century conduct books to put forth a rather explicit theory of social control" (1987, 133).

9. See also Saunders in this volume.
10. "Observation . . . has been understood as, at worst, minimally intrusive on the dynamics and interaction unfolding before the eyes of the observer, who is herself outside the dynamic. My argument is that such observation, like all scientific activity, constitutes a voyeurism in its will to truth, which invests the observer with 'the knowledge,' indeed the logos. The observer then should be seen as the third term, the law that claims to impose a reading on the interaction. This is offered as an explanation to which the observed have no access and yet which is crucial in the very apparatuses that form the basis of their regulation" (Walkerdine 1986, 167).

CHAPTER **6**

Travel and Taboo:
Heterosexual Sex Tourism to the Caribbean

JULIA O'CONNELL DAVIDSON AND JACQUELINE SÁNCHEZ TAYLOR[1]

In this chapter we are concerned with "sex tourism" as a phenomenon involving sexual relations between tourists and local or migrant persons who are unequal in terms of economic, social, and political power. While these relations are sometimes organized as straightforward cash-for-sex transactions, sex tourism can involve a wider range of sexual-economic exchanges than those conventionally implied by the term "prostitution." We therefore consider the phenomenon by which local and migrant women, men, and children enter into fairly open-ended relationships with tourists in the hope of securing some material benefit (including gifts, meals, clothing, cash, and opportunities to migbate to affluent countries) to be as much a part of sex tourism as the phenomenon of brothel or street prostitution in tourist areas. This chapter draws on ethnographic research in Jamaica and the Dominican Republic to explore the phenomenon of heterosexual sex tourism as an outcome of both national and international laws and social and economic policies.[2]

Constructing Sexual Disneylands: Part 1

There is a strong association between travel and sex in affluent as well as economically underdeveloped countries (Oppermann 1998; Clift and Carter 2000). Some European holiday destinations, such as Ibiza, are renowned for the high level of tourist-tourist sexual interaction; tourists and foreign businesspersons provide a significant segment of demand for prostitution in most major cities of the world; and some European and American cities have sex sectors, which are tourist attractions in and of themselves, such as Amsterdam, Copenhagen, and Las Vegas. Sites of sex tourism in poor countries, however, are distinguished not only or even necessarily by the existence of a formally organized sex industry serving demand from tourist clients, but also by the existence of an informal sex sector, in which local and migrant people enter into a wide range of sexual-economic exchanges with tourists.

Sex tourist destinations in poor countries thus offer the tourist both extensive opportunities for sexual experience and opportunities for types of sexual experience that would not be readily available either back home or in tourist destinations in more affluent countries. For example, the American, Dutch, or British male tourist to sex tourist areas in Thailand, the Philippines, Brazil, or the Dominican Republic, will find it possible to secure powers of sexual command over the person of a prostitute for 24 hours for a sum that would not even purchase him five minutes of oral sex back home; he will find it relatively simple to secure sexual access to girls or boys of 13 and 14 years old; or to find an attractive young and racially Other woman who is willing to act as his girlfriend-cum-domestic servant for the duration of his holiday in exchange for a small amount of money and/or gifts and meals. Likewise, the European, North American, or Australian woman visiting sex tourist destinations in India, Indonesia, Latin America, or the Caribbean will be faced by opportunities either to enter into explicit cash-for-sex exchanges, one-night stands or quasi-romantic sexual relationships with local or migrant men and boys. This wealth of sexual opportunity leads both male and female sex tourists to describe such places as "sexual paradise," "Fantasy Island," and "Disneyland." Sexual Disneylands do not exist in nature, however. They have to be created.

In the Caribbean, a set of linkages between international debt, price fluctuations in global commodity markets, economic development policy, and prostitution, as well as particular laws and social policies adopted by individual countries, have been important to the construction of a sexual Disneyland for heterosexual tourists. Since the 1970s, world financial institutions have encouraged indebted nations, including Jamaica and the Dominican Republic, to respond to economic crises by developing tourism. One side effect of this is the creation of highly concentrated, effective demand for prostitution in the form of affluent tourists seeking "entertainment" (Kempadoo 1999; Bishop and Robinson 1998; Chant and McIlwaine 1995). At the same time, the International Monetary Fund agreements and World Bank structural adjustment loans, sector adjustment loans, and programs loans that the Jamaican and Dominican governments entered into have served to swell the prostitution labor market, for the policy packages tied to these loans have had a devastating impact on the poor. They have undermined traditional forms of subsistence economies and redirected subsidies away from social spending and basic commodities towards debt servicing. Furthermore, adjustment processes have also involved massive currency depreciation and a concomitant drop in the price of labor (Anderson and Witter 1994; Safa 1997; Kempadoo 1999).

Wages in both countries are among the lowest in the Caribbean region, and many Dominicans and Jamaicans now need alternative sources of income to supplement or substitute for extremely low-waged employment. Structural adjustment has created a surplus laboring population, as well as driving down wages of those in work, and has thus been associated with the growth of the informal economic sector in both countries (Le Franc 1994; Safa 1997; see also Black 1995). Though sex tourism represents only one segment of the tourism market in Jamaica and the Dominican Republic, and involves only a minority of local or migrant persons, expatriates, and tourists (Forsythe et al. 1998), it is nonetheless the case that in both countries, prostitution and other forms of tourist-local, sexual-economic exchange are among the wide range of activities that take place in the informal tourism economy. It is also the case that in both countries, workers employed in the formal tourism sector sometimes supplement low wages by entering into sexual-economic exchanges with tourists.

North American and European tourists' very presence in the Caribbean is predicated upon a particular, and vastly unequal, world political and economic order, and the individual tourist necessarily enters into relationships with poor and working-class locals or migrants as the politically and economically privileged party. Even the working-class, budget tourist from Europe, Canada, or the U.S. is in a position to spend about as much on a package vacation in the Caribbean as many locals or migrants will earn in a year. This not only makes commercial sex more affordable for the tourist, it also means that tourists are in a position to freely dispense gifts and sums of money that, though negligible to them, represent significant benefits to the average local person. Even the half-empty shampoo bottles, unused medicines, and uneaten foodstuffs that the tourist would throw away at the end of a vacation can make an important contribution to a household that is struggling to subsist. Small wonder then, that many local and migrant persons seek to befriend tourists and/or to enter into sexual relationships with them.

As citizens of affluent and politically powerful nations, tourists also enjoy rights and freedoms that are denied to most of the locals and migrants they meet. Their passports allow them to cross national borders virtually at whim, as obtaining a tourist visa is a mere formality for European, Canadian, or U.S. nationals visiting Caribbean countries. Indeed, U.S. citizens can even enter Jamaica for vacations simply by showing a driver's license. The holder of a Jamaican or Dominican passport attempting to enter Fortress First World will have a rather different experience, even when she or he merely seeks to attend the wedding or funeral of an immediate family member living in Europe or

North America. Given that European and North American countries endorse heterosexual relationships by extending citizenship rights (albeit often only partially and reluctantly) to the spouses of their nationals, it is unsurprising to find that marriage represents one of a dwindling number of migration strategies for poor and working-class Jamaicans and Dominicans.

Moreover, while tourists do not acquire formal citizenship by entering Jamaica or the Dominican Republic (and so do not have an automatic entitlement to vote, to work, to hold a passport, etc.), they nonetheless enjoy a range of social, economic, and cultural benefits that effectively amount to a degree of substantive citizenship far greater than that enjoyed by ordinary working-class citizens of either country. A tourist can, for example, expect to be housed in accommodations connected to a water supply, as well as to find a range of leisure facilities geared toward his or her interests, shopping facilities to meet his or her desires as a consumer, and so on. This is more than can be said of the average working-class Dominican or Jamaican, and tourists' privileges are not merely a reflection of their greater individual spending power. It results in large part from *government* spending on infrastructural development to support tourism (airports, roads, water supply, sewage systems, electricity, and telephones), something that actually diverts money from projects that might help ordinary Jamaicans and Dominicans to enjoy basic social, economic, and cultural rights of citizenship (Patullo 1996; Ferguson 1992; Howard 1999). Again, sexual relationships with tourists represent one of the few ways in which ordinary Jamaicans and Dominicans can tap into privileges reserved for tourists and elite locals.

The asymmetry of power between European and North American sex tourists and their local or migrant sexual partners is also racialized. Though discourses about race are very different in the two countries, one of the legacies of colonialism in both Jamaica and the Dominican Republic is a "pigmentocracy" (James 1993; Fennema and Lowenthal 1987). Although class position cannot be directly determined by a racialized identity, nonetheless a strong relationship exists between whiteness and economic and social privilege. The life chances of those who possess phenotypic characteristics associated with white European heritage (lighter skin tone, straighter hair, blue or green eyes, and so on) are generally greater than the life chances of those who possess phenotypic characteristics associated with black African heritage. There is certainly some upward mobility among persons of African descent, but there is little downward mobility among white people, and social hierarchies in both countries remain highly racialized. This means, for example, that white Jamaicans and Dominicans are involved in the tourism industry as owners and managers of businesses, not as low-paid manual employees, informal sector workers, prostitutes, or beach hustlers. Tourism thus provides many working-class Dominicans and Jamaicans of African descent with their first and only social or sexual contact with white people, something that, in the context of post-colonial racism, is often believed to promise a chance of upward social mobility for oneself or one's children.

In short, the tourist and the local or migrant are simultaneously brought together and separated by global inequality. Were it not for the huge disparity in terms of political and economic power between Europe/North America and Caribbean nations, the average North American or European tourist would never even get to Jamaica or the Dominican Republic, and those who did venture to the Caribbean would not find themselves automatically positioned as the local's superior in terms of social, political, and economic rights and freedoms. In a different and more equal world, North American and European tourists to the Caribbean would find it no harder and no easier to make contact (sexual or otherwise) with local people than they find it to strike up such acquaintances with locals when they visit New York, Nice, Seville, or Amalfi. As visitors to these latter vacation destinations, the individual tourist's ability to make friends, find romance or a one-night stand, and so on, is constrained by his or her personal qualities and physical appearance, as well as social markings and status.

Of course, it would be quite wrong to claim that Europeans' and North Americans' relation to each other is, in Marx's terms, a human one within which "you can exchange love only for love, trust for trust, etc." (Marx 1959, 124). Fellow Americans and Europeans are also divided by gender, race, class, and age. However, the average vacationer in an affluent country is not in a position to command any more or any less sexual access to local persons than he or she is able to command back home. The person who is considered too fat, too old, or too ugly to pull young, fit sexual partners in Chicago or Paris is also considered to be too fat, too old, or too ugly to pull young, fit sexual partners in Vancouver or Barcelona. Travel between and within affluent countries does not reposition the citizen of an affluent country on economic, gendered, or racial hierarchies of power. But travel to Jamaica or the Dominican Republic or other poor and indebted nations does. In the third world, even the "third-rate" American or European tourist is king or queen. The magic this repositioning works explains why sex tourists refer to such destinations as Sexual Disneylands (see Brace and O'Connell Davidson 1996).

Constructing Sexual Disneylands: Part 2

Jacqueline Alexander has explored the relationship between tourism, gender, heterosexuality, and the state in the Bahamas and describes a "process of heterosexualization," which has occurred as part of the construction of a "neo-colonial state" (1997, 83). Nationalism may have involved rejecting colonial rule but has not involved a rejection of European discourses on "nature" and "civilization," and as ever, nationalist politics are heterosexist politics.

Prostitutes, homosexuals, and HIV carriers are legally constructed as Other in the Bahamas, since they commit "unnatural crimes" against God and man:

> the neocolonial state continues [the] policing of sexualized bodies, drawing out the colonial fiction of locating subjectivity in the body (as a way of denying it), as if the colonial master were still looking on, as if to convey legitimate claims to being civilized. (1997, 83)

In socially and politically excluding and criminalizing those deemed to be sexual Others, the Bahamian state continues "to premise citizenship in physiognomy, the basis of colonial refusal to admit agency and self-determination" (1997, 88). At the same time, however, the state has used sex to sell the island as a vacation destination ("white imperial tourism would not be complete without eroticized blackness" [1997, 96]). Alexander argues that tourism is significant for the project of creating the neocolonial nation-state because it "draws together powerful processes of (sexual) commodification and (sexual) citizenship" in order to create a population of heterosexual "natives" that is servile both to the tourist industry and to the neocolonial state that depends on that industry (1997, 67).

Since the state is patriarchal and heterosexist, its response to the natives who service tourists is highly gendered. Female prostitutes are stigmatized and criminalized, but males who enter into sexual-economic exchanges with tourist women are not legally or socially constructed as "prostitutes." This is also true in Jamaica and the Dominican Republic, where the legal regulation of prostitution constructs local and migrant females, but not males, who enter into sexual-economic exchanges with tourists as "prostitutes." It also heightens female prostitutes' vulnerability to abuse, violence, and financial exploitation by clients and third parties. While the Dominican Republic attracts far larger numbers of male sex tourists than does Jamaica, and while Dominican law formally tolerates female prostitution to a much greater degree than Jamaican law, law enforcement practice is remarkably similar in each country. It is heavily focused upon female prostitutes who solicit in the streets and other public spaces, rather than on the abuse and exploitation of female prostitutes by third parties (Cabezas 1999; Campbell et al. 1999). In both countries, law enforcement practice frequently involves violations of local and migrant females' civil and human rights—women and girls are rounded up and taken to holding cells where they are often detained without charge for several hours or even days. Many report being subject to physical and sexual violence from police officers, who also often extort money from them.

The state's more general regulation of informal economic activity is also significant for the phenomenon of heterosexual sex tourism. Both Jamaica and the Dominican Republic have recently enacted legislation against "tourist hustling," introduced licensing systems for ambulant vendors and tourist guides, and set up special tourist police units to patrol resorts and enforce antihustling laws. Such measures are designed to protect tourists and the tourism industry rather than local and migrant people's interests, and they serve to further heighten the distance between tourists and locals in terms of civil rights and freedoms. The tourist's rights to security, free movement, and leisure are protected at the expense of the local and migrant people's economic rights and rights of access to public spaces. However, these forms of regulation do not have a uniform impact on local and migrant people. As well as increasing migrants' vulnerability to harassment and deportation, these measures have buttressed gender divisions in the informal economy. In particular, they reinforce the beach—a prime location for informal tourist-related economic activity— as a largely male terrain.

Only those who have a vendor's license or whose presence there is linked to their formal employment have "legitimate" access to the beach, and these trades and jobs are male dominated (e.g., lifeguard, watersports promoter, boat hand). Access to the beach means access to tourists, and so to opportunities to hustle, which may include procuring prostitutes for male tourists or entering into sexual relationships with female tourists in pursuit of cash, gifts, meals, drinks, or other benefits. The fact that male hustlers or "beach boys" are not usually wholly dependent upon these sexual-economic relationships for their subsistence but engage in a combination of income-generating activities (formal employment, ambulant vending, drug dealing, pimping, provision of tour guide services, etc.) is hugely significant for the social organization of such relationships and the meanings that are attached to them.

The sexual exchange between beach hustlers and tourist women is not normally constructed as a narrowly instrumental exchange of cash for commodified sex, and very few beach hustlers self-identify as prostitutes or sex workers. The material benefits that accrue from entering into sexual relationships with tourist women usually supplement income from other sources, and for many beach hustlers, this is an activity that more closely resembles playing the lottery than going to work. Indeed, beach hustlers in English-speaking Caribbean countries often refer to themselves as "players." Because measures to control informal economic activity restrict women's and girls' access to the beach, they make it difficult for a local or migrant female to take on the role of hustler or player. Local or migrant females' sexual encounters with tourist men are much more likely to be constructed as prostitution contracts (albeit often more diffuse and open-ended contracts than those traditionally associated with prostitution).

The state's regulation of prostitution and of the informal economy thus constructs sexual-economic relationships between locals or migrants and tourists in highly gender-stereotypical ways: The local or migrant female becomes a prostitute through her sexual contact with tourists, and the local or migrant male becomes a player (stereotypes that are all the more significant when viewed through the lens of European and North American racism, which reads the black body as hypersexual). The state's gendered regulation of the informal tourism economy thus contributes to the sex tourist's view of Jamaica and the Dominican Republic as Sexual Disneylands. The male tourist, constructed as King, gets to rule over a fairytale world of "dusky maidens," constructed as naturally sexual and sexually available prostitutes; the female tourist, constructed as Queen, gets to command a fairytale world of "hypermasculine" black men and boys, constructed as naturally sexually voracious and indiscriminate players.

Heterosexuality, Homophobia, and the Demand for Disneyland

The global processes and the national social and economic policies that bring tourists and locals face to face as profoundly unequal parties are clearly not enough, on their own, to create the phenomenon of sex tourism. Back home, the same North Americans and Europeans often find themselves, or could find themselves, face to face with individuals who are structurally positioned and socially constructed as their unequals, and yet do not necessarily feel the urge to pursue sexual contact with them. In London or San Francisco, for example, we do not see ordinary, middle-aged women flirting with homeless young men who sit on the pavement begging for spare change, or taking them to dinner and nightclubs and then back home to bed.

The European or North American sex tourist's wish to sexually experience local or migrant people in the Caribbean is clearly partly a function of the way Western discourses on race construct the Other as an object of sexual desire and Other cultures as closer to "the state of nature" regarding sexual practices and mores (Said 1978; Dollimore 1991; Mercer 1995; Bishop and Robinson 1998). It also reflects the way tourist destinations are discursively constructed as liminal spaces in which it is both possible and desirable to suspend normal routines and transgress the rules that govern daily life. Here, however, we want to focus on questions about the relationship between institutionalized heterosexuality in the tourist's home country and the desire to engage in sex tourism in the Caribbean.

Radical feminism, which views "prevailing definitions of eroticism . . . [as] the product of gendered patterns of domination and submission intrinsic to patriarchal societies and written into their cultural representations" (Jackson 1996, 23), could provide one perspective on such questions. However, because radical feminists are primarily concerned about revealing the patriarchal structures that underpin heterosexual expression and experience, they typically pay very little attention to the subjective meanings individuals attach to them. The latter is particularly problematic in Andrea Dworkin's (1987) and Kathleen

Barry's (1995) work, wherein the rapist, the prostitute's client, the incestuous father, and the husband sometimes appear to be all but indistinguishable (as do prostitutes, rape victims and the more general category of women).

Radical feminist theory also discourages an interrogation of diversity within heterosexual experience, and so pays little attention to the legal and social construction of "good" and "bad" heterosexuals. Any practice that can be read as involving an eroticization of gender power (whether it be penetrative sex between husband and wife, cross-dressing, vanilla sex with a prostitute, or sadomasochism [S/M] with a noncommercial partner) gets subsumed within the normative category of heterosexual desire, regardless of whether or not the practice transgresses the laws and social conventions that regulate sexuality (see for example, Jeffreys 1996). Such an approach obscures the specificity of heterosexual sex tourism as a sexual practice, and so cannot help us to understand its appeal for those who engage in it. It also makes it extremely difficult to explain the fact that women, as well as men, practice sex tourism.

A very different approach to questions about sexuality and the state, and one that is centrally concerned with the construction and control of "good" and "bad" sexualities, is provided by sex-radical theory (for instance, Vance 1984; Rubin 1999). Sex radicals locate oppression in the way that "society assigns privilege based on adherence to its moral codes" (Califia 1993, 11), rather than in patriarchal structures that subordinate women in general. Along with Foucaultian- or Lacanian-inspired theorists such as Judith Butler (1990), these writers have provided powerful deconstructions of the legal and social binaries of normal/abnormal, healthy/unhealthy, and pleasurable/dangerous sex, as well as of gender itself. This often leads to a positive view of sexual practices, which can be read as subverting such binaries. For sex radicals, prostitutes and clients and, boys and "boy-lovers," as much as drag kings, transsexuals, and S/M enthusiasts are understood as challenging oppressive norms through their transgressive sexual acts (Rubin 1999; Califia 1993; Leigh 1997).

Heterosexual sex tourists do not deviate from hegemonic gendered and heterosexist norms regarding the specific form of sexual relations they engage in, but they do generally transgress social conventions pertaining to the race, age and/or class identity of sexual partners; they often break codes against promiscuous or anonymous sex; and many also transgress hegemonic norms by entering into explicitly commercial sexual transactions with local or migrant persons. Some further break national and international laws against child sexual exploitation. Heterosexual sex tourism is simultaneously normative and transgressive, and for this reason, it is not easily accommodated within either radical feminist or sex radical frameworks. However, heterosexual sex tourists are not a homogenous group. Some of them (to whom we will refer as "hardcore sex tourists") attach a great deal more sexual value to the transgressive elements of their sex tourism than do others (to whom we will refer as "vanilla sex tourists").[3] It is therefore worth considering whether hard-core sex tourists (who would be deemed by their respectable fellow country-persons as "bad boys and girls," and who often fondly see themselves as such) could be accommodated within sex radicalism's realm of "benign sexual variation."

The worldview and sexual ambitions of hardcore male heterosexual sex tourists is well captured in the following passage from a posting on an Internet Web site run by and for male sex tourists. It describes Boca Chica, a resort town in the Dominican Republic:

> Boca is a place of [Western] men's dreams and [Western] women's nightmares. It finds the heart of desire within all of us. Boca . . . is a place where sexual fantasies become commonplace. A place where you can go into your room with a pack of multicolored girls and no one will blink twice. A place where an older man can convince himself that the young girl rotating on his lap cares for him and understands his needs more than the women from his homeland. It's a place where men come for lust and sometimes end up confusing it for love. It's where a man can be a star in his own adult videos. It's a place where a young pretty girl once offered me sex for a [plate of] lasagna. It's a place where every woman you see whether whore or maid or waitress, young or old, can be bought for a few hundred pesos. It's a place where you can have a girl, her sisters, and her cousins. (Travel & the Single Male message board, 3/19/98)

Perhaps sex radicals would find themselves in sympathy with such men's desire for anonymous sex, commercial sex, group sex, intergenerational sex, or sex with videos. It is doubtful that they would be so comfortable with the fact that such men describe their local sexual partners as "stupid" and "ignorant" and as "Little Brown Fucking Machines;" that they frequently try to cheat prostitute women and children of payment or take pleasure in trying to beat their prices down to the most paltry sum possible; that they openly explain their sex tourism as a response to what they see as the excessive powers now supposedly exercised by both prostitute and nonprostitute women in their home countries ("if you beat your wife—leave just one little bruise—she calls the police;" "if you don't pay a prostitute in Canada, you know what? They call it rape"); that they value countries like Cuba and the Dominican Republic because here, they say, "you can call a nigger a nigger and no one cares;" and that they frequently heap racist abuse upon their local female sexual partners (see O'Connell Davidson and Sánchez Taylor 1996, 1999).

Those who hold that the desire to purchase commercial sex should be accepted as just as much a legitimate feature of "erotic diversity" as sadomasochism or homosexuality do often acknowledge that clients can be abusive or disrespectful. But this is not an essential feature of clienting, they argue, and rather than trying to solve the problem by denying individuals the right to purchase sex if they so choose, we should try to educate clients to treat sex workers with respect and to appreciate the value of the emotional labor involved in sex work.

However, to imagine that it would be possible to "reeducate" the hardcore male heterosexual sex tourists in such a way as to encourage them to respect sex workers would be to entirely misunderstand their motivations, desires, and practices. The phenomenon of hardcore male heterosexual sex tourism does not simply involve men individually and privately pursuing particular kinds of sexual gratification. It is also a subcultural, and so a social and public, practice. Hardcore male sex tourists group together in the resorts they visit, and back home they form clubs, produce publications for each other, and chat with each other via the Internet. Their desire to bond with other men like themselves is a highly visible and significant feature of their sex tourism. They espouse and promote a worldview that is profoundly and explicitly racist, misogynist, and homophobic, for they believe in biologically essentialist models of difference that naturalize social and political inequalities based on gender, sexual orientation, and race (see O'Connell Davidson 2001b).

For these men, the ultimate and most significant taboo is the taboo against the sameness of men and women, since they accept dominant, traditional understandings of gender within which women's difference is vital to community formation (Chow 1999; Rubin 1975; Levi-Strauss 1971; Freud 1985). Shifts in the legal and political construction of hierarchies of gender, race, and sexuality in their own countries (such as affirmative action programs and equal opportunities legislation) are perceived as undermining the natural privilege of the straight white male. These men's sexual transgressions are better understood as an attempt to reinscribe the binaries of man/woman, Madonna/whore, white/black, heterosexual/homosexual than as an attempt to subvert them. They transgress only in order to reinstate taboos. They travel precisely to escape social and legal pressures to treat women, black people, gay people, and prostitutes with respect. If it were possible to enforce a system that imposed restraints upon them as prostitutes' clients and forced them to pay European/North American rates for the sexual services they consume, then travel to the Caribbean would quickly lose its appeal for these men. (Indeed, we have even interviewed men who say that they have stopped going to Thailand because sex workers there are becoming too powerful and imposing too many limits on the prostitution contract.)

Much the same can be said of the women who experience Jamaica and the Dominican Republic as Sexual Disneylands, because in these countries they can transgress laws and social conventions regarding promiscuous and/or commercial sex and/or the age and racialized identity of their sexual partners (Sánchez Taylor 2000, 2001). Hard-core female sex tourists we have interviewed want to transgress both the racialized and gendered codes that normally govern their sexual behavior, and yet maintain their honor and reputation back home. As one 45-year-old white woman from Chicago said of Jamaican men,

> (They) are all liars and cheats. . . . American women come to Negril because they get what they don't get at home. A girl who no one looks at twice at back home, she gets hit on all the time here, all these guys are paying her attention, telling her she's really beautiful, and they really want her . . . They're obsessed with their dicks. That's all they think of, just pussy and money and nothing else . . . In Chicago this could never happen. It's like a secret, like a fantasy and then you go home.

She explicitly stated that she would not take a black boyfriend home to meet her friends or parents, and it is hard to see how secretly transgressing white racist strictures against interracial sex can be read as an act of political resistance against those strictures. The previous quote also draws attention to another problem with sex-radical theory. Gayle Rubin has observed that

> in Western culture, sex is taken all too seriously. A person is not considered immoral, is not sent to prison, and is not expelled from her or his family for enjoying spicy cuisine. But an individual may go through all this and more for enjoying shoe leather. Ultimately, of what possible social significance is it if a person likes to masturbate over a shoe? (Rubin 1999)

In picking the example of a shoe fetishist, Rubin evades the more difficult issues that confront any theory of sexual ethics. What if, like the Chicago woman quoted previously, an individual likes to live out racist-sexual fantasies about black men as walking phalluses, or black women as pure, animalistic sexual beings? Does this not have social significance in a world where political, economic, and social inequalities are structured along lines of race, as well as of class and gender?

Not all sex tourists are inspired by such overtly hostile racist fantasies. Indeed, many sex tourists—both male and female—are not particularly sexually hostile. Vanilla sex tourists need instead to imagine their sexual encounters with local or migrant people as mutual and noncommercial in order to obtain sexual and emotional gratification from them. The sex tourist resorts they visit are Disneylands because here they experience themselves as desirable, and thus successful, heterosexuals. In the mirror of the Other, they find themselves reflected back at half their age or weight, or twice as beautiful. This feat is achieved by either ignoring the massive imbalance of economic, social, and political power between themselves and their local or migrant sexual partners, or by interpreting it in ways that do not suggest that their partner is acting on a purely instrumental basis. The vanilla sex tourist buys into exoticizing rather than denigrating racisms, and the binaries of self/Other help to explain why someone half their age or weight and twice as fit is attracted to them. In this culture, they will tell you, white bodies are valued over black, age doesn't matter, obesity is a sign of wealth, sex is natural, "they" are naturally eager heterosexuals, and so on.

Vanilla sex tourists may not be hostile, but they do not always treat their local or migrant sexual partners in the way that they wish to be treated. They sometimes refuse requests for financial help (i.e., payment), for example, or make paltry gifts of cheap clothing or cosmetics, which the local person views as incommensurate with the amount of time and emotional and sexual labor they have invested in the relationship. The men sometimes impregnate their local or migrant "girlfriends" but refuse to pay for an abortion or to provide child support payments. And vanilla sex tourists, perhaps more so than hardcore sex tourists, do not always observe safe sex precautions, despite coming from countries where resources have been invested in sexual health education. Again it is worth noting that campaigns to educate clients in such a way as to make them into good (responsible and respectful) consumers of commercial sex would not represent an answer to these problems. If it were possible to make the vanilla sex tourist comprehend the fact that sexual encounters with local persons have an economic basis, these sexual encounters would lose their appeal. The vanilla sex tourist does not want to enter into an explicit prostitution contract wherein he or she is constructed as a prostitute's client. As a male vanilla sex tourist once remarked to one of the authors,

> I wouldn't have gone off with just an out-and-out girl that was going to be with me just for money . . . Why? Because it wouldn't be a turn on. There would be no point to it, as attractive as they are . . . If I ended up in bed with someone, I'd have to feel there was more to it than [money]. (O'Connell Davidson 1998, 177)

Vanilla sex tourists often want to be "good" in many senses of the word. We have interviewed scores of male and female sex tourists who want to feel beloved, valued, or cared for; to feel beautiful and desired; or to feel kind and generous, because they do not feel any of these things back home.[4] These sentiments, of course, highlight much that is very wrong with North American/European societies—the way in which bodies are constructed as beautiful/ugly, the refusal to recognize people with physical disabilities as sexual beings, the sexual value that is attached to youth, the class inequalities that deny people the opportunity to be generous, and so on.

However, interview work with both hardcore and vanilla sex tourists has above all left us with a sense that dominant Euro-American discourses on gender and sexuality, founded as they are upon the taboo against the sameness of men and women, are bizarre, contradictory, and dysfunctional. They teach that to be male is to be less than fully human, for the male is expected to deny both his need for care and his capacity to give care. They encourage us to imagine that men's and women's biological sexual difference separates them completely, that there is and always has been a "war of the sexes"—that men are from Mars and women are from Venus. And yet we are also told that our highest destiny and overriding ambition should be to forge a lifelong relationship with one of our "enemies," with someone (or something) from another planet.

The heterosexual sex tourists we have interviewed, whether hardcore or vanilla, take these discourses at face value and interpret and give meaning to their experience through reference to them. The men talk about how terrible women are, how they humiliate men, manipulate men, exploit men's weaknesses, hurt and reject men. The women talk about what "bastards" all men are; how they use, abuse, and cheat on women; how they are only interested in one thing; and how they hurt and reject women. And yet at the same time they want, above all else, to be successful heterosexual men or women, a wish that is evidenced not just by their pursuit of sexual/romantic relationships with "opposite-sex" partners who will affirm them as such, but also in their attitudes towards homosexuality.

Both hardcore and vanilla male sex tourists often express overtly homophobic attitudes in interviews, but their homophobia is also expressed in their fear of failing to be, and be seen as, real (heterosexual) men. These fears and aspirations are also informed by ideas about race. Our research suggests that different patterns of demand for sexual-economic exchanges in Jamaica and the Dominican Republic are shaped by popular North American and European ideas about racial and cultural differences between the Hispanic and English-speaking Caribbean. White racist European and North American discourse constructs the black Jamaican in particular as violent, aggressive, and sexually potent. Jamaican men are popularly imagined as hypermasculine beings, and Jamaican women as lacking feminine attributes. The same discourses construct Dominicans as a "hybrid" rather than a black population and attribute feminine characteristics to both males and females (men are thought to be bisexual and effeminate, women to be passive and sexually receptive). One of the reasons that male sex tourists favor the Dominican Republic over Jamaica is because these discourses construct the Dominican male as less truly masculine than the European or North American man, while the Jamaican man represents a threat to the European and North American man's masculinity. It is easier for the European or North American man to imagine himself as a successful heterosexual man in the Dominican Republic than in Jamaica.

Meanwhile, one of the things we found striking about female sex tourists in Jamaica in particular was their tolerance not just of the intensely homophobic remarks that pepper the "sweet talk" of beach hustlers and other local men they meet, but also of extreme violence against homosexuals. Several American and European women who are frequent visitors to Negril reported to us, without horror or even disapprobation, an incident in the mid-1990s in which a Jamaican man was stoned to death by a crowd of local people because they believed him to be gay. Our female interviewees were also, without exception, quite happy to be in sexual relationships with men who advocate or instigate violence against gay men and lesbians. The more homophobic their sexual partner, the more he demonstrates himself to be a "real man," and through her capacity to attract or command the sexual attentions of a real man, the tourist woman demonstrates herself to be a successful heterosexual woman.

Although vanilla and hardcore sex tourists differ in terms of the sexual practices that interest them and the way in which they subjectively interpret their relationships with local people, the joy of sex tourism for both groups ultimately lies in the same thing—the fact that it affords them control over self and Others as sexual, racialized, and engendered beings. This control allows them to conform to highly gendered ideals of heterosexuality. They travel to reinscribe and realize the taboo against the sameness of men and women. The urgency of their desire to do so perhaps reflects an uneasy recognition of the perversity of their own sexual interest in the "opposite sex"—a group of people they imagine as essentially untrustworthy, hostile, and emotionally dangerous.

Conclusion

Sex radicalism claims to provide a critique of systems of sexual judgment that insist on "the need to draw and maintain an imaginary line between "good" and "bad" sex" (Rubin 1999, 152). Not everyone who refuses to adhere to society's moral codes is welcome at the sex-radical party, however. Rapists, as much as prostitutes or sadomasochists, stand outside society's charmed circle of good, normal, natural, blessed sexuality, for example, but Rubin does not consider them to be a legally persecuted sexual minority. She states that her discussion of sex law "does not apply to laws against sexual coercion, sexual assault, or rape," only to the "myriad prohibitions on consensual sex and the 'status' offenses such as statutory rape" (1999, 157). Despite an emphasis on diverse and morally commensurate sexualities, then, sex radicalism still ultimately draws a line between "good" and "bad" sex: "People who are sex-positive . . . don't denigrate, medicalize, or demonize any form of sexual expression *except that which is not consensual*" (Leigh 1997, 127, emphasis added).

An adage along the lines of "consensual foursomes good, nonconsensual twosomes bad" might be all very well were it not for the fact that concepts of coercion and consent are notoriously problematic. The nature and degree of coercion that can be said to nullify consent are always open to debate.

Individuals do not give consent (whether to a system of political governance, a wage-labor contract, or to sexual interaction) in a social, political, and economic vacuum, and consent cannot be meaningfully abstracted from the power relations that surround it. As soon as this is acknowledged, the boundary between the consensual and the nonconsensual begins to lose definition; a gray and ambiguous space opens up. Much of what happens in sex tourist destinations occurs within this space. Given the massive social, political, and economic inequalities that exist between local or migrant people and tourists from affluent countries, it is hard to see how the local or migrant person's sexual consent can be anything other than ambiguous.

If the sex-radical analysis of commercial sex is accepted, the logical response to sex tourism would be to defend the tourist's right to buy sex, but to exhort tourists to be "good," responsible, and respectful consumers. This seems a singularly inadequate political response to the phenomenon described in this chapter and highlights the far from radical implications of sex-radical theory. Critiquing Rubin and others who focus on sexual diversity per se, Stevi Jackson observes, "we each live our sexualities from different locations within social structures." Lack of attention to the structural bases of power, she continues, leaves us with "no way of establishing regularities underpinning diverse 'sexualities', of relating them to dominant modes of heterosexual practice or of locating them within power hierarchies" (1996, 25). Similar points are made by Diane Richardson, who reminds us that

> There are . . . other considerations that go beyond the currently fashionable concern with subversive performance as political strategy and social method. Whilst this may indeed be valuable in highlighting some of the contradictory meanings embedded in discourses of gender and sexuality, and the socially constructed and potentially unstable nature of identities and practices . . . we also need to ground this in the context of the material conditions of people's lives at local, national, and global levels. (1996, 9)

This injunctive is particularly apposite in relation to both the phenomenon of sex tourism in particular, and of commercial sex in general.

Notes

1. The support of the Economic and Social Research Council, which funded the research upon which this chapter is based (award no: R000237625), is gratefully acknowledged. We are also thankful to Elizabeth Bernstein and Laurie Schaffner for their encouragement and comments on the chapter.

2. We have been involved in research on sex tourism since 1994. As well as interviewing local and migrant women, men and children who are involved in tourist-related prostitution and other forms of sexual-economic exchange, we have conducted extensive interview work with male heterosexual sex tourists and expatriates in Latin America, South Africa, Thailand, India, and the Caribbean. Most recently we have undertaken Economic and Social Research Council-funded research on sex tourism in Jamaica and the Dominican Republic, which involves a survey on the sexual behavior of female sex tourists, as well as ethnographic research on both male and female heterosexual sex tourism.

3. We are dividing sex tourists into these categories purely on the basis of the different ways in which they eroticize their sexual encounters. It is not intended to imply any value judgment about the particular sexual acts that are generally classed as "vanilla" or "hardcore" (for instance, within the S/M subculture); indeed, this chapter is informed by the assumption that the moral evaluation of sexual behavior should focus on questions about the context in which sexual acts take place and the power relations that surround them, rather than upon the nature of the sexual acts themselves.

4. Two interviews in particular stand out. One was with a New York police officer who very genuinely seemed to want both to "do good" in the world and to be loved. But he was not wealthy, and he was also overweight, short, and, in terms of Euro-American ideals of physical beauty, not an attractive man. He liked visiting the Dominican Republic not simply because here he found it easy to find "girlfriends," but also because he could make a difference to local people's lives by bringing gifts or giving them money. The other was with a woman who suffered from a congenital muscle-wasting disease and had been wheelchair bound since the age of 10. She was on her third vacation in Jamaica where, she said, she found the care extended to her by a beach hustler who had befriended her infinitely preferable to that provided by professional caretakers back in the States.

CHAPTER **7**

Desire, Demand, and the Commerce of Sex

ELIZABETH BERNSTEIN[1]

Suddenly, the car takes off. We're moving again, but I'm not quite sure whom we're following. Apparently, a woman has gotten into the car ahead of us with a date. We proceed at full speed about a block or two, over train tracks, to a deserted stretch of territory with few cars or people. Indeed, the area is completely barren save for a few abandoned warehouses. Despite the gleaming California sunshine, the atmosphere is tense.

Everything happens in a flash. In mere minutes, it's all over; we slam the brakes on, and two of the officers hop out. They motion for me to join them.

The other members of the Street Crimes Unit are already on the scene. They stopped a blue Chevrolet truck and handcuffed the driver, a large but trembling man who is trying to be obsequious in spite of being terrified. Two of the officers have their guns pointed toward him. In addition to the arresting officer, the sergeant and another policeman also surround the suspect. Meanwhile, the female officers beckon the passenger, Carla, from her seat and begin to talk to her.[2] They are trying to get her side of the story so that they can use it as evidence. Carla is high on drugs and rather weary, but still lucid. She is apparently one of the numerous street prostitutes whom the officers know by name, because she has been arrested repeatedly during the 10 or so years that she has been working. But today she is not the main focus of their attention.

I hover in the background, absorbing the drama of the surrounded man, the drawn guns, the momentary displays of power and fear. My heart pounding, I try to listen, feeling vaguely guilty about being a part of this. The arresting officer delivers a rapid-clip, tough-guy, made-for-TV monologue:

> *I want you to tell me what happened . . . Remember, we've spoken to her so we know . . . What were you thinking? . . . Did you use a condom? . . . No? So you came in her mouth? . . . Did you even look at her? Did you see that disgusting shit she has on her hands? Now it's all over your wee-wee . . . Do you have a wife or girlfriend? Now you're going to go home and give whatever you just got to her. Every man's thought of it, but you don't need to take chances. Next time you're feeling horny, why don't you just buy some porn and jack off?*

Before releasing their detainee, the officers issue him a written citation and a court date.

Much later that same evening, I arrive at a famed "erotic theater" with a friend, tired but intrigued. The theater has a reputation for being one of the most upscale of the 14 legal sex clubs in the area, where striptease, lapdances, and, in recent years, hand jobs and blow jobs are widely, if unofficially, available for purchase. We wade through the small crowd of Asian businessmen standing outside and make our way to the entrance. A middle-aged man with glasses politely takes our money ($45 each) with no perceptible surprise that we should choose to come here —even though we are obviously the evening's only female customers. A basket of condoms sits prominently by the door.

Again in straightforward fashion, an employee proceeds to give us a tour and to describe the various shows. The rooms have names like the "VIP Club" and the "Luxury Lounge." The premises are dimly lit but clean, orderly, and rather spare. The floors are bare yet spotless. We head over to the main stage in the back room, where a young, tanned, and toned woman in a sparkly thong bikini is doing a dance to the accompaniment of strobe lights and disco. She twists and turns, gyrates and thrusts, opens and closes her legs. Her featured partner is a long, silver pole that protrudes upright from the floor. As the male customers watch the show, I watch them. They crane their necks to get a better view of the dancer. All of the seats are filled and it's standing room only. "Imagine coming home to that," gushes a 40-something white man in a dark business suit and red tie to one of his colleagues. The performance concludes with the dancer making her way into the audience and sidling up to individual customers who caress the surface of her body and push $20 bills under her garter.

Many of the customers are extremely young: under 25, perhaps under 20, white, baseball-capped, and sporting casual attire. These contingents have clearly come in groups. The 30- and 40-something, suited, white businessmen seem to comprise another category, and also cluster together in groups of three or four.

Then there are the loners—again, typically under 50 years of age, predominantly white, with a sprinkling of Blacks and Latinos. All are able-bodied, of average looks and builds. By mere appearances, they certainly belie the stereotype that the sex industry is geared toward older men who can't find partners.

In a room called "Amsterdam Live," a central stage is encircled by a sunken ring of little cubicles, each partitioned off from the performance area by fine, black mesh curtains. This design allows the heads and bodies of the customers to protrude through to the stage, and for the women to protrude back through to the booths in the other direction. A surrounding wall of mirrors above the cubicles means that each customer can see every other customer, as well as the performers. Two young, beautiful women come out, both with gleaming, waist-length hair and very high heels, naked but for black and white midriff corsets that leave their breasts and genitals exposed. They perform a highly choreographed and stylized sex act together, kissing and licking. Then, despite an earlier staff person's admonishment that body parts must remain within the booths, the women come over to each booth to ask if anyone would like a "show." Both of them soon descend into the dark cubicles where they are grasped by eager hands, momentarily disappearing from our line of vision.

[Fieldnotes, San Francisco Bay Area, May 1999]

Feminists and other scholars have debated theoretically what is "really" purchased in the prostitution transaction: Is it a relationship of domination? Is it love, an addiction, pleasure? Can sex be a service like any other? But they have scarcely tackled this question empirically. This chapter draws upon field observations of and interviews with male clients of sex-workers and state agents entrusted with regulating them in order to probe the meanings ascribed by different types of consumers to commercial sexual exchange and to situate such exchanges within the broader context of postindustrial transformations of culture and sexuality.[3]

I begin with the two paradoxical ethnographic images above. The first describes the new and growing phenomenon of the arrest of heterosexual clients of female street prostitutes, an unprecedented strategy of direct state intervention in the expression of male sexual desire. In the late 1990s, for the first time ever, U.S. cities such as San Francisco and New York began to boast arrest rates of male customers that approached those of female prostitutes, reversing a historical pattern that feminists have long criticized (Pheterson 1993; Lefler 1999).[4] The second takes us to a local sex club where sex acts are—legally, and to some extent, culturally—consumed as relatively unproblematic instances of sexual entitlement and male bonding.

In Western Europe and the U.S., recent state efforts to problematize heterosexual male desire—rising client arrests and re-education via diversion programs such as "John School," vehicle impoundment, stricter domestic and international laws on the patronage of underage prostitutes and the possession of child pornography–have occurred in the face of an increasingly unbridled ethic of sexual consumption. During the last 30 years, demand for commercially available sexual services has not only soared, but become ever more specialized, diversifying along technological, spatial, and social lines. As seen in Figure 7-1, the scope of sexual commerce has thus grown to encompass live sex shows; all variety of pornographic texts, videos, and images, both in print and online; fetish clubs; sexual emporiums featuring lap-dancing and wall-dancing; escort agencies; telephone and cyber-sex contacts; drive-through striptease venues; and organized sex tours of developing countries (Kempadoo and Doezema 1998; Weitzer 2000a; Lopez 2000). Sexual commerce has become a multifaceted, multi-billion-dollar industry, produced by and itself driving developments in other sectors of the global economy, such as hotel chains, long-distance telephone carriers, cable companies, and information technology.[5] Just as the availability of hardcore pornographic films on videocassettes led directly to the introduction of the home VCR, pornography on CD-ROM and over the Internet has been responsible for the acceptance and popularization of these new technologies (Schlosser 1997; Lane 2000). According to Internet research firms, a full one-third of the people who surf the Internet visit a pornography site (typically during workday hours) and, as late as 1997, almost all paid content sites on the Web were pornographic (Learmonth 1999; Prial 1999; "Sex, News, and Statistics" 2000).

These contradictory social developments reveal a tension between sex-as-recreation and the normative push for a return to sex as romance, a cultural counterpart of which can be found in the simultaneous emergence of Viagra and 12-step languages of masculine sexual addiction. "Sex" as cultural imperative and technical quest, now freed from the bounds of emotionality and romance, and the casting of nonrelationally bound erotic behavior as a pathological "addiction" are products of the same place and time. My goal in this chapter is to unravel this paradox.

Some have attributed recent attempts to reform male sexuality to the gains of second-wave feminism, and even described a shift in social stigma from the seller to the buyer of sexual services (Kaye 1999). Yet the influence of larger, structural factors has been neglected in most discussions. In fact, state interventions in (a typically lower-class tier of) male heterosexual practices, and the regendering of sexual stigma in certain middle class factions can both be linked to some of the broader transformations that produced the burgeoning demand for sexual services in the first place. In the industrializing nineteenth and early twentieth centuries, the "wrong" in prostitution was seen to reside in the female prostitute herself,[6] and in the classical writings of social science, prostitution as a social institution was portrayed as the supreme metaphor for the exploitation inherent in wage labor (Marx [1844] 1978; Engels [1884] 1978; Simmel [1907]

Figure 7-1 In recent years, sexual commerce has expanded to encompass a broad range of sexual products and services, as this Web advertisement for a San Francisco sex emporium illustrates.

1971). In the late twentieth century, however, with the shift from a production-based to a consumption-based economy, the focus of moral critique and political reform is gradually being displaced: The prostitute is normalized as either "victim" or "sex-worker,"[7] while attention and sanction is directed away from labor practices and toward consumer behavior.

In what follows, I first sketch a brief genealogy of the academic and political discourses surrounding male sexual desire and consumer demand that have developed over the past century. I next take the reader to a variety of settings in which commercial sexual consumption takes place and to the smaller subset of arenas in which the state forcefully intervenes to redirect or contain it, in order to explore the meanings and motivations that contemporary clients ascribe to their own activities. In the final section, I contrast these framings with recent attempts by state agencies to reshape demand in the wake of a booming and diversifying sexual marketplace. My discussion throughout is based upon 15 in-depth interviews with male sexual consumers, 40 in-depth interviews with male and female sex-workers, a review of local sex newspapers and other print and electronic media, and ethnographic fieldwork in sexual markets carried out in six northern California and Western European cities over the course of five years.

Explaining Commercial Sexual Demand

Like social policy, the scholarly literature on prostitution has typically grasped the varied phenomena of sexual commerce through a narrow focus on the etiology, treatment, and social symbolism of the female prostitute. Although the purity crusaders in the late nineteenth-century United States sought to problematize male sexuality, their campaign to replace the prevailing double standard with a single female standard that would be encoded into state policy met with little success (Luker 1998). After the Progressive Era, far less social or scholarly attention was paid to prostitution as functionalism and psychoanalysis reinscribed the double standard and rendered prostitution not only unproblematic for the male clientele, but structurally integral to the institution of marriage (Davis 1937; Greenwald 1958). In the 1970s and 1980s, both the sociology of deviance and feminist theory saw the prostitute (but not the client) as a symbolically laden precipitate of larger social currents. Although some second-wave feminists critiqued the lack of attention to male clients (McIntosh 1978; Hobson 1990; Høigård and Finstad 1986), as well as the sexual double standard that underpinned it, it is only during the last decade that a body of empirical literature has emerged with a sustained focus on male sexual clients.

In the past 15 years, a small but growing number of qualitative studies of client behavior have been undertaken by a new generation of feminist social researchers.[8] Meanwhile, building on Kinsey's influential—if methodologically flawed—work (1948), as well as heeding feminist calls to render male sexual clients visible, quantitative researchers have begun to correlate men's proclivity to visit prostitutes with other sociodemographic patterns. Analyzing data from the 1993 University of Chicago National Health and Social Life Survey, researchers Elliot Sullivan and William Simon found factors such as age cohort, military experience, education, and racial and ethnic background to be statistically significant predictors of commercial sexual purchase (Sullivan and Simon 1998). Commercial sexual proclivity has been shown to vary systematically with a variety of attitudinal dispositions, including "socio-emotional problems," as measured by reported feelings of emotional and physical dissatisfaction, feeling unwanted and sexually unsatisfied, and, most interestingly, by "not hav[ing] sex as an expression of love" (Sullivan and Simon 1998, 152). It has also been correlated with a "commodified" view of sexuality, as measured by number of sexual partners, use of pornography, and the belief that one needs to have sex immediately when aroused (Monto 2000).

Finally, client behavior has increasingly been featured as a key component of broader qualitative studies on commercial sexual exchange (Høigård and Finstad 1986; McKeganey and Barnard 1996; Flowers 1998; O'Connell Davidson 1998). Drawing upon field data and interviews, these scholars have generated typologies of clients and consumer motivations. Whereas research on female prostitutes has been driven by questions of etiology (how did she get that way, why would a woman do that?), this research highlights differences between men, but typically takes their status as purchasers for granted. The primary motivations identified by these authors include clients' desire for sexual variation, sexual access to partners with preferred ages, racialized features and physiques, the appeal of an emotion-free and clandestine sexual encounter, loneliness, marital problems, the quest for power and control, the desire to be dominated or to engage in exotic sex acts, and the thrill of violating taboos. While provocative and insightful, this literature has often failed to explain client motives with any degree of historical specificity, or to link these motives to social and economic institutions that might themselves structure the relations of gender domination implied by many of the explanatory categories mentioned previously. In general, typologies are presented as if based on distinct attributes of a transhistorical and unwavering masculinity. Two exceptions to this tendency are recent works on client behavior by anthropologist Anne Allison (1994) and sociologist Monica Prasad (1999).

In *Nightwork*, an ethnography of a Tokyo hostess club where beautiful young women serve businessmen drinks and light their cigarettes, keep the banter flirtatious, and make their bodies available for groping, all at corporate expense, Allison draws on Frankfurt-school theory to argue that "the convergence of play and work and player and worker, supposed and presupposed by the institution of company-paid entertainment, is a feature of any society progressing through the late stages of capitalism" (1994, 23). According to Allison, the nightly participation of Japanese businessmen in the *mizu shobai*, or erotic nightlife, as well as their emotional distance from their wives and families, epitomizes this historical trend. Meanwhile, in "The Morality of Market Exchange," an article based on phone interviews with male sexual customers that engages the classic distinction articulated by Karl Polanyi and Marshall Sahlins between market and premarket societies, Prasad argues that the prostitution exchange contains within itself a form of morality specific to mass-market societies. Her interviews reveal that

> [c]ustomers conduct the prostitution exchange in ways that are not very different from how most market exchanges are conducted today: information about prostitution is not restricted to an elite but is widely available; social settings frame the interpretation of this information; the criminalization of prostitution does not particularly hinder the exchange; and whether the exchange continues is often dictated by how well the business was conducted. In short, according to these respondents, in late-capitalist America, sex is exchanged almost like any other commodity. (1999, 188)

Noting that her interviewees "praise 'market exchange' of sex for lacking the ambiguity, status-dependence, and potential hypocrisy that they see in the 'gift exchange' of sex characteristic of romantic relationships," Prasad goes on to conclude that, in the "fervently free-market 1980s and 1990s, romantic love might sometimes be subordinated to, and judged unfavorably with, the more neutral, more cleanly exchangeable pleasures of eroticism" (1999, 181, 206).

Unlike many treatments of sexual clients, the contributions of Allison and Prasad situate sexual consumption within the context of an expanded and normalized field of commercial sexual practices. Their analyses begin to reveal a shift from a relational to a *recreational* model of sexual behavior, a reconfiguration of erotic life in which the pursuit of sexual intimacy is not hindered but facilitated by its location in the marketplace.[9]

The Subjective Contours of Market Intimacy

> I'm by myself a lot, used to it, but sometimes I crave physical contact. I'd rather get it from someone I don't know because someone I do will want more. You get lonely. There's this girl right now I'm seeing. I like the attention. But that's it, in a nutshell. I find [prostitution] exciting, kind of fun. It's amazing that it's there. More people would participate if it weren't illegal. A lot of frustration in both sexes could be eliminated.
> Don, 47, house painter

> I feel guilty every time I cheat on my wife. I'm not a psychopath. I try to hide it as much as possible. I had a nonprofessional affair once. It was

nice, and intimate, and I didn't have to pay! But I felt more guilty about that, messing with someone else's life, even though she knew I was married. You don't ever have to worry about that when you pay for it. I'm conservative by nature, but I believe in freedom of choice. If a woman wants to do it, more power to her! She's providing a service. I'm not exploiting her. Exploitation would be finding some hot 25-year-old who doesn't know any better and taking her to lunches, then to bed.

Steve, 35, insurance manager

My wife has never understood my desire to do this. I have no problem with my wife. We have a good sexual relationship. There's a Vietnamese restaurant on 6th and Market that I love, but I don't want to eat there every day. . . .

Rick, 61, data processor

I started seeing escorts during a time when I didn't have many venues to meet women. I felt isolated. My friends had moved away, and I was lacking motivation. It's more real and human than jacking off alone. My first preference was to pick up women for casual sex. Since that wasn't happening, I got into the habit. It was so easy.

Dan, 36, research analyst

Amid the disparate themes that animate the accounts clients gave me of their motivations for purchasing sexual services runs one counterintuitive thread. As Monica Prasad and Anne Allison found, for increasing numbers of men, erotic expression and the ethos of the marketplace are by no means antithetical. Indeed, contemporary client narratives of sexual consumption challenge the key cultural opposition between public and private that has anchored modern industrial capitalism.

Theorists of gender have sometimes regarded the recent growth of the commercial sex industry as a reactionary reassertion of male dominance in response to the gains of second-wave feminism (O'Connell Davidson 1998) or as compensation for men's economic disempowerment in the postindustrial public sphere (Kimmel 2000). In such scenarios, the role of commercial sex is to provide the male client with a fantasy world of sexual subservience and consumer abundance that corrects for the real power deficits he experiences in his daily life. While not disputing such accounts, I would like to suggest that men's quest for market-mediated sexual intimacy is guided by an additional set of historical transformations.

Compensatory arguments of the sort put forth by O'Connell Davidson, Kimmel, and others rest upon the implicit premise that commercial sex caters to needs that would more preferably and fulfillingly be satisfied within an intimate relationship in the private sphere of the home. Yet for many sexual clients, the market is experienced as enhancing and facilitating desired forms of non-domestic sexual activity. This is true whether what the client desires is a genuine but emotionally bounded intimate encounter, the experience of being pampered and "serviced," participation in a wide variety of brief sexual liaisons, or an erotic interlude that is "more real and human" than would be satisfying oneself alone. The platitudinous view that sexuality has been "commodified"—and by implication, diminished—like everything else in late capitalism (e.g., Lasch 1979) does not do justice to the myriad ways in which the spheres of public and private, intimacy and commerce, have interpenetrated one another and thereby been mutually transformed, making the postindustrial consumer marketplace a prime arena for securing varieties of interpersonal connection that circumvent this duality.

For many clients, one of the chief virtues of commercial sexual exchange is the clear and bounded nature of the encounter. In prior historical epochs, this bounded quality may have provided men with an unproblematic and readily available sexual outlet to supplement the existence of a pure and asexual wife in the domestic sphere. What is unique to contemporary client narratives is the explicitly stated *preference* for this type of bounded intimate engagement over other relational forms. Paid sex is neither a sad substitute for something that one would ideally choose to obtain in a noncommodified romantic relationship, nor the inevitable outcome of a traditionalist Madonna/whore double standard. Don, a 47-year-old, never-married man from Santa Rosa, California, described the virtues of the paid sexual encounter this way:

> I really like women a lot, but they're always trying to force a relationship on me. I'm a nice guy, and I feel this crushing thing happen. Right now, I know a woman; she's pretty, nice, but if I make love to her, she'll want a relationship. But I'm really used to living by myself. I go and come when I want, clean when I want. I love women, enjoy them; they feel comfortable around me. I've always had a lot of women friends. I flirt and talk to them, but I don't usually take the next step, because it leads to trouble!

Much is lost if we try to subsume Don's statements under pop-psychologizing diagnoses such as "fear of intimacy," or even a more covertly moralistic social-psychological descriptor like "techniques of neutralization" (Sykes and Matza 1957). In Don's preference for a life constructed around living alone, intimacy through close friendships, and paid-for, safely contained sexual encounters, we also see evidence of a disembedding of the (male) individual from the sex-romance nexus of the privatized nuclear family. This is a concrete example of the profound reorganization of personal life that diverse social analysts (Swidler 1980; Giddens 1992; Hochschild 1997) have noticed occurring during the last 30 or so years.[10] Demographic transformations such as a decline in marriage rates, a doubling in the divorce rate, and a 60 percent increase in the number of single-person households during this period have spawned a new set of erotic dispositions, ones which the market is well poised to satisfy.[11]

An additional advantage of market-mediated sexual encounters was articulated by Steve, a married, 35-year-old insurance manager from a middle-class California suburb. Frustrated that sexual relations with his wife had been relatively infrequent since the birth of their child, Steve had decided to look for sex elsewhere. Although elements of Steve's story invoke the sexual double standard of eras past, his reasoning during our interview betrayed a decidedly new twist. For Steve, the market-mediated sexual encounter is morally and emotionally preferable to the "nonprofessional affair" because of the clarifying effect of payment. Though he characterized himself as "conservative by nature," Steve had incorporated a fair amount of sex-worker rights rhetoric into his own discourse, describing the professional choice of his paid service providers with tangible awe. Having grappled with feminist critiques of male sexual indulgence as exploitative, he concluded that true exploitation resided in the emotional dishonesty of the premarket paradigm of seduction, rather than in the clean cash-for-sex market transactions that he participated in.

Other clients were insistent that their patronage of the commercial sexual economy did not in any way result from problems or deficits in their primary sexual relationships. Rick, a 61-year-old data processor from San Francisco, emphasized that his sexual relationship with his wife was just fine, and likened his desire to pay different women for sex to other, less socially problematic consumer experiences: "There's a Vietnamese restaurant . . . that I love, but I don't want to eat there every day." Rick's statement may be read as a variant of the classic argument that prostitution is an expression of the male "natural appetite"—a perspective which, like Steve's, is of course premised upon a notion of the sexual double standard. As Carole Pateman (1988, 198) points out, in such arguments, "the comparison is invariably made between prostitution and the provision of food." Significantly, however, Rick's explicit justification for patronizing prostitutes is less one of essential, biological drives than it is one of simple consumer choice. Rick's stated preference for variety presumes an underlying model of sexuality in which sexual expression bears no necessary connection to intimate relationship, and in which a diversity of sexual partners and experiences is not merely substitutive but desirable in its own right.

In the same vein, Stephen, a 55-year-old writer from San Francisco, described an exciting and sexually adventurous life at home with his female domestic partner of eight years. He chose to supplement this with once-a-month, paid sexual encounters involving female exotic dancers and transgender prostitutes that were "fun" and "intriguing." "Sometimes it's a really nice contact, how they touch me, how they move, but it's not for something I can't get at home," he explained. Stephen went on to elaborate upon some of his motivations for patronizing prostitutes:

> When I grew up, I was younger and shorter than everyone else, convinced I wasn't sexually desirable to anyone. I was two years ahead in school, a total nerd. The notion that these glamorous women want to persuade me to have sex with them is incredible. I understand that it's not because of my looks. I could never get this many women who are this gorgeous to be sexual with me if I didn't pay.

Interviewees like Stephen and Rick challenge the second-wave feminist presupposition that prostitution exists chiefly to satisfy sexual demands that nonprofessional women find unpleasant or feel inhibited to participate in (Rosen 1982, 97). If commercial sex is compensation for anything, it is not for something lacking in men's primary domestic relationships. Rather, it is for the access to multiple attractive partners that, in the wake of the historical shift from the family-based good provider role to the unfettered, consumeristic Playboy philosophy many male sexual clients feel they are entitled to (Ehrenreich 1983). Within the terms of this new cultural logic of male dominance, clients conjure the sexual marketplace as the great social equalizer, where consumer capitalism democratizes access to goods and services that in an earlier era would have been the exclusive province of a restricted elite.[12]

Here is another man's account of his commercial sexual activity, this time from an Internet chat room for patrons of strip clubs:

> I finally got to spend some quality time in the city by the Bay, compliments of my employer, who decided that I needed to attend a conference there last week. So, armed with a vast array of knowledge regarding the local spots, I embarked on a week of fun and frolicking. Unfortunately, I ended up spending too much time with conferencegoers so I only made three trips to clubs. I had an absolutely incredible time at both places . . . .
>
> At the first club, I adjourned to the Patpong Room with Jenny, who asked me what I was interested in. I said that a couple of nude lap dances were on the agenda and I inquired as to her price: $60 each. Okay, no problem. I forked over the cash. After the two long dances she offered me a blowjob for another $120. I said that that would be heavenly and handed her the money . . . It was an absolutely fabulous experience. I spent $30 on cover charges, $10 on tips, $240 with Jenny, and $300 with another girl named Tanya for a total of $580. Not bad for just

over two hours of illicit fun. I'm used to paying that for decent outcall so this was a nice change of pace.[13]

Like Rick and Stephen, this man is unselfconscious about depicting his experience as a form of light and unproblematic commercial consumption ("two hours of illicit fun," "a nice change of pace"). For this client, prostitution is primarily a pampering diversion financed by and casually sandwiched in between a week's worth of requisite, and presumably less pleasurable, professional activities.

Yet the paid sexual encounter may also represent to clients something more than just an ephemeral consumer indulgence. In their 1982 article, "The Phenomenology of Being a John," Holzman and Pines (1982) argued that it was the *fantasy* of a mutually desired, special, or even romantic sexual encounter that clients were purchasing in the prostitution transaction—something notably distinct both from a purely mechanical sex act and from an unbounded, private-sphere romantic entanglement. They observed that the clients in their study emphasized the warmth and friendliness of the sex-worker as characteristics that were at least as important to them as the particulars of physical appearance. The clients I interviewed were also likely to express variants of the statement that "If her treatment is cold or perfunctory, then I'm not interested." In Web-based client guides to commercial sexual services such as "The World Sex Guide," reviewers are similarly critical of sex-workers who are "clock watchers," "too rushed and pushy," who "don't want to hug and kiss," or who "ask for a tip mid-sex-act."

Although patrons of different market sectors expressed variants of these sentiments, those who frequented indoor venues enjoyed the benefit of an arrangement that was structured to more effectively provide them with the semblance of genuine erotic connection. For example, interactions with escorts as opposed to streetwalkers are typically more sustained (averaging an hour as opposed to 15 minutes), more likely to occur in comfortable settings (an apartment or hotel room, rather than a car), and more likely to include conversation as well as a diversity of sexual activities (vaginal intercourse, bodily caresses, genital touching, and cunnilingus, rather than simply fellatio) (E. Bernstein 1999; Lever and Dolnick 2000). The fact that street prostitution now constitutes a marginal and declining sector of the sex trade means a transaction that has been associated with quick, impersonal sexual release is increasingly being superseded by one which is configured to encourage the fantasy of sensuous reciprocity, a fantasy safely contained by the bestowal of payment.

In recent years, one of the most sought after features in the prostitution encounter has become the "Girlfriend Experience," or *GFE*. In contrast to commercial transactions premised upon the straightforward exchange of money for orgasm, clients describe the GFE as proceeding "much more like a nonpaid encounter between two lovers," with the possibility of unhurried foreplay, reciprocal cuddling, and passionate kisses (see Figure 7-2). As with other forms of service work, successful commercial sexual transactions are ones in which the market basis of the exchange serves a crucial delimiting function (Hochschild 1983; Leidner 1993) that can also be temporarily subordinated to the client's fantasy of authentic interpersonal connection, as the following client's description of an encounter in a commercial sex club illustrates:

> At the club, I had a memorable experience with a light-skinned black girl named Luscious . . . we adjourned to the backstage area for one full-service session during the course of my visits. This time I brought my condoms. We began with the usual touchy-feely . . . I could feel she was just soaking, an indication her moans were not faked. Several minutes later I shot my load and used the conveniently located Kleenex dispenser to wash up. The most unusual aspect of this encounter is that Luscious didn't ask for money up front, which is a first for a place of this type. I tipped her $60.

Even when the encounter lasts only minutes, from the client's perspective it may represent a meaningful and authentic form of interpersonal exchange. Clients are indeed seeking a real and reciprocal erotic connection, but a precisely limited one. For these men, what is (at least ideally) being purchased is a sexual connection that is premised upon *bounded authenticity.* As with the previous client's invocation of the physical tangibility of Luscious's desire, other clients boasted of their ability to give sex-workers genuine sexual pleasure, insisted that the sex-workers they patronized liked them enough to offer them freebies or to invite them home for dinner, and proudly proclaimed they had at times even dated or befriended the sex-workers they were seeing.

The repeated claims about authentic interpersonal connection are particularly striking to consider in light of the fact that the vast majority of sex-workers I spoke with imposed very rigid emotional boundaries between their customers and their nonprofessional lovers. For sex-workers, the former almost always constituted a thoroughly de-eroticized category of identity that was rarely if ever transgressed. One of the few sex-workers I spoke with who admitted to occasionally looking for lovers among her client pool said that she had given up the practice of offering her preferred clients bargain rates or unpaid sexual arrangements because it inevitably met with dire results:

> They pretend to be flattered, but they never come back! If you offer them anything but sex for money they flee. There was one client I had who was so sexy, a tai chi practitioner, and really fun to fuck. Since good

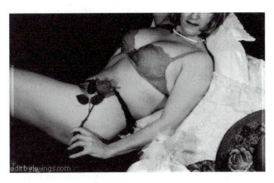

Girlfriend For Hire!

So, you've been thinking that you're working too hard, and enjoying it less. You'd have a girlfriend if only you had time. You want someone presentable, fun loving, toned and oh so naughty. I'm like that exquisite condo in Hawaii. Beautiful and serene. Just the person to make you feel like a KING. I provide great memories well after the retreat.

Outcalls available. Serving peninsula and Silicon Valley Incalls by appt. Reduced rates for extended assignments. **Especially yours, xxx**

(650) xxx-xxxx or email **xxxx@aol.com**

Figure 7-2 Advertisement from Bay Area Web site. This advertisement both democratizes access to servile women and promises the "bounded authenticity" that clients seek.

sex is a rare thing, I told him I'd see him for $20 (my normal rate is $250). Another guy, he was so sexy, I told him "come for free." Both of them freaked out and never returned. The men want an emotional connection, but they don't want any obligations. They don't believe they can have no-strings-attached sex, which is why they pay. They'd rather pay than get it for free.

Christopher, a male sex-worker who had also once tried to redefine his relationship with a client, recounted similarly: "I called a trick once because I wanted to have sex with him again . . . we agreed in advance that it was just going to be sex for sex's sake, not for pay, and that was the last time I ever heard from him!" Critics of commercialized sex may misconstrue clients' desire for bounded authenticity if their implicit point of reference is the modernist paradigm of romantic love, premised upon monogamous domesticity and intertwined life trajectories. Thus, Carole Pateman (1988, 199) asks why, if not for the sake of pure domination, would "15 to 25 percent of the customers of the Birmingham prostitutes demand what is known in the trade as 'hand relief,'" something which could presumably be self-administered. Yet, as one client insisted, after explaining to me that he studied and worked all the time, and consequently didn't have much opportunity to even meet women, let alone to pursue a romantic relationship, "it's more real and human than jacking off alone." This client reveals an underlying sexual paradigm that is not relational but recreational, compatible with the rhythms of his individually oriented daily life, and increasingly, with those of other men with similar white, middle-class sociodemographic profiles.

The State and the Redirection of Desire

It's 9 A.M. on a Saturday morning. In one of the only occupied rooms of the San Francisco Hall of Justice, I am seated in the back row of "John School," the city's pretrial diversion program for men who have been arrested for soliciting prostitutes. The city is proud of its program and boasts a low recidivism rate of less than one percent for first-time arrestees, who, for a mere $500, can have their records cleared. There are approximately 50 to 60 men in the room this morning, of diverse class and ethnic backgrounds (three of the men around me are accompanied by translators: one Spanish, one Arabic, one Cantonese).

More striking still is that there are nearly equal numbers of arrested johns and media people in the room. By the end of the first hour, I have been introduced to journalists from TV-20, the London Times, *and* Self *Magazine. "There are representatives from different media organizations here each month," announces Evelyn, the program's feisty director, to the men. "I never do this class without media coverage." In stark contrast to the johns, the media people are predominantly 30-something, stylish, educated women, acutely and evidently fascinated by the spectacle of so many sheepish and docile men before them, and by the feminist fantasy of having the gender tables turned (now these men are quiet and still, and, at least until 5 P.M. this evening, they will be forced to remain that way and listen). Although I am perhaps more conscious than they that it is as much class advantage as feminist victory that permits this witnessing, I notice too the superficial similarity between these women and me.*

Yet according to the johns I chat with during the coffee breaks, very few are passively absorbing the information presented to them, and they are far from being persuaded of the error of their ways. The men say that John School is even worse than Traffic School—an all-day ordeal in a stuffy room with a whole procession of equally stuffy speakers. "This is bullshit." "I was trapped." "These people are so hypocritical." "Prostitution should be legalized." "They act like it's something special, but all men do it . . . Men and women just think differently. Men will fuck sheep, boys, anything. They are dogs."

The first presentation is led by an assistant district attorney and is entitled "Prostitution Law and Street Facts." Although John School is officially available to all men arrested for soliciting a prostitute, the structure of the program demonstrates that those who do get arrested comprise only a small and special subgroup. This program is clearly geared for heterosexual men who shop the streets. During his presentation, the DA, trying to get the group to engage, asks, "How many of you were picked up in the Tenderloin? How many of you were picked up in the Mission?"(two of San Francisco's historically low-income and newly gentrifying neighborhoods where street prostitution is concentrated). He does not bother to ask how many were picked up at the local erotic theater, or with an escort, or while cruising for a sex-worker online, or even on Polk Street (where male and transgender street prostitutes work).

The DA's objective is to scare the men out of their established patterns of behavior by gruesomely cataloguing the potential legal repercussions of what they are doing—what it's like to get booked, to be herded into the paddywagon, to spend the night in jail, or to be forced to take an HIV test—all likely consequences of a second arrest. He shows the class a brief video reviewing the laws. I am at first confused by the last image in the sequence: the captionless depiction of a man hunched over a computer screen. The DA's final words to the men are even more remarkable: "Next time you're thinking of going out on the street, do like this guy: Go on the Internet if you have to—but stay away from minors!"

The final presentation before the lunch break features a former street prostitute and ex-heroin addict who now runs a program to help prostitute women transform their lives and get off the streets. Seated beside her is a panel of three other former homeless and drug-addicted streetwalkers. Now clean and sober, well scrubbed, well fed, and conservatively attired, their appearances are not much different from other 30- to 40-year-old professional women. Only their scathing and effusively expressed anger betrays a difference.

For the men, this is no doubt the most riveting panel of the day. At last, their attention is focused, as they sit tense and upright in their chairs. From their facial expressions and inclining postures, some even seem to be vaguely aroused. The rhetorical tactic employed by the women is a combination of shock therapy and a firm reassertion of the primacy of marital domesticity. "Most of the women I have worked with started turning tricks as children or teens," says one woman in a harsh, accusatory voice. "I learned a long time ago that it's not pedophiles involved *in that, but the men that sit here in this room." Through teary eyes and clenched teeth, another panelist tells the men her own story of early sexual abuse, addiction, and rape. Her tale, gripping and theatrical, ends with the following admonition:*

> *Once, I remember being crusty and dope sick, wearing yellow shorts, and walking around with blood caked on my thighs for two days. No one asked me what was wrong. I felt like a fallen woman that God, society, and my family would never forgive . . . . We're not out there because we like to suck dick, and you're not out there because you like us. You're the cause of our suffering, and you can become statistics yourselves. Try and realize, if you have to go back out—these women were hurt! A lot of you men are husbands, fathers, and grandfathers. What did you tell your significant others today? Hopefully, someday soon you'll learn how to have healthy relationships—with your wives.*

In the afternoon, there are three additional presentations: one featuring representatives from organized neighborhood and merchant groups, another with a sergeant from the vice squad on the dynamics of pimping, and the final presentation by a therapist on "Sexual Compulsivity and Intimacy Issues." The neighborhood groups are represented by two men and a woman, white residents and small shopkeepers from the Tenderloin district. Together with the Vice cop, they paint the johns as aggressors against family, community, and—rather ironically—business.[14] The harms that the johns are held responsible for are both symbolic and material. "Do you have sex in front of your children?" they ask. "Little boys in my neighborhood blow up condoms like balloons! You hear about victimless crimes, but our whole neighborhood is a victim! Fifteen-year-old girls turn tricks and 20 minutes later deliver babies. Millions of dollars pass through these girls, but at the end of the day they have nothing. All the way through this business, there are victims."

The final session, led by a licensed marriage and family counselor, relies upon a 12-step sexual addiction model of client behavior. The counselor is a white, middle-class, casually dressed man in his late thirties, an exemplar of northern California therapeutic culture and soft-spoken masculinity. He begins his presentation with a definition: "Sex addicts have trouble thinking of sex and love together, in the same relationship. They say, 'I love my wife, but I have sex with a prostitute.' The challenge is to do them together, to learn how to nurture relationships. This is not just a woman's job." After distributing a "Sexual Addiction Screening Test" (see Table 7-1) to the members of the class (with questions such as "Do you often find yourself preoccupied with sexual thoughts?" and "Has your sexual activity interfered with your family life?"), the therapist tries to enlist them in a discussion about why men visit prostitutes. "Stress," volunteers one man. "Curiosity," says another. "Anger? Loneliness?" offers the therapist, and some of the men agree. Finally, one john rouses himself out of boredom to protest. "Come on

TABLE 7-1 The Sexual Addiction Screening Test, distributed at the San Francisco First Offender Program. Originally printed in Carnest (1989). The SAST is designed to assist in the assessment of sexually compulsive or addictive behavior. Developed in cooperation with hospitals, treatment programs, private therapists, and community groups, the SAST provides a profile of responses which help to discriminate between addictive and nonaddictive behavior. To complete the test, answer each question by placing a check in the appropriate column.

_ yes _ no 1. Were you sexually abused as a child or adolescent?

_ yes _ no 2. Have you subscribed or regularly purchased sexually explicit magazines, such as *Playboy* or *Penthouse*?

_ yes _ no 3. Did your parents have trouble with sexual behavior?

_ yes _ no 4. Do you often find yourself preoccupied with sexual thoughts?

_ yes _ no 5. Do you feel that your sexual behavior is not normal?

_ yes _ no 6. Does your spouse [or significant other(s)] ever worry or complain about your sexual behavior?

_ yes _ no 7. Do you have trouble stopping your sexual behavior when you know it is inappropriate?

_ yes _ no 8. Do you ever feel bad about your sexual behavior?

_ yes _ no 9. Has your sexual behavior ever created problems for your family?

_ yes _ no 10. Have you ever sought help for sexual behavior you did not like?

_ yes _ no 11. Have you ever worried about people finding out about your sexual activities?

_ yes _ no 12. Has anyone been hurt emotionally because of your sexual behavior?

_ yes _ no 13. Are any of your sexual activities against the law?

_ yes _ no 14. Have you made promises to yourself to quit some aspect of your sexual behavior?

_ yes _ no 15. Have you made efforts to quit a type of sexual activity and failed?

_ yes _ no 16. Do you have to hide some of your sexual behavior from others?

_ yes _ no 17. Have you attempted to stop some parts of your sexual activity?

_ yes _ no 18. Have you ever felt degraded by your sexual behavior?

_ yes _ no 19. Has sex been a way for you to escape your problems?

_ yes _ no 20. When you have sex, do you feel depressed afterwards?

_ yes _ no 21. Have you felt the need to discontinue a certain form of sexual activity?

_ yes _ no 22. Has your sexual activity interfered with your family life?

_ yes _ no 23. Have you been sexual with minors?

_ yes _ no 24. Do you feel controlled by your sexual desire?

_ yes _ no 25. Do you ever think your sexual desire is stronger than you are?

already! It should just be legalized! Guys need a place to get relief." The police officer who is seated to my left leans over to me and whispers in my ear: "I agree. Anyway, I bet most of these men will now just go indoors, where they don't have to worry about any of this."

[Fieldnotes, San Francisco, May 1999]

Feminists have bemoaned, but also taken for granted, the sexual double standard in the treatment of prostitution by the criminal justice system. As recently as 1993, the scholar and prostitutes' rights activist Gail Pheterson (1993, 44) could righteously argue that

> [o]f course, the customer is also party to prostitution transactions and in countries where sex commerce is illegal; he is equally guilty of a crime. But such laws are not equally applied to customer and prostitute . . . Nowhere is equal punishment enforced, however, partly because law officials are either customers themselves or they identify with customers. Prostitutes have numerous stories of the sexual demands of police, lawyers, judges, and other male authorities.

Pheterson and other critics would never have predicted that, by the mid-1990s, municipal and national governments might actually intervene to challenge and reconfigure patterns of male heterosexual consumption, and even mobilize feminist arguments in the service of such interventions. Nor did they foresee that, despite a shared gender and sexual identification with customers, male authorities would be beholden to other social forces and political interests that might lead them to curtail the prerogatives of heterosexual desire. And they did not anticipate how programs such as "John School" and the expanding and diversifying market in commercial sexual services might represent what only seem to be paradoxical facets of interconnected social trends.

During the last five years, John Schools, First Offender Programs, and Client Re-education Projects have sprung up in American cities as diverse as San Francisco and Fresno (California), Portland (Oregon), Las Vegas (Nevada), Buffalo (New York), Kansas City (Kansas), and Nashville (Tennessee), as well as in Toronto and Edmonton (Canada), and Leeds (United Kingdom). Numerous other cities throughout the U.S. and Western Europe are currently considering implementing similar programs.[15] After decriminalizing prostitution in the late 1960s, in 1998 Sweden became the first national government to unilaterally criminalize the purchase of sexual services by male customers (E. Bernstein 2001). In the U.S., although sporadic and fleeting gestures toward the arrest of male clients date back to the 1970s, contemporary client re-education programs must be seen as part of a new strategy of state intervention in male sexual behavior.

In both Oklahoma City and Kansas City, for example, city officials have begun to broadcast the photos and names of male clients arrested by police for prostitution-related offenses on cable television (Hamilton 1999; Weitzer 2000b). In Huntington Woods, Michigan, the police have released the names of 16,000 alleged prostitution customers on CD-ROM ("Names" 1999; "Suburban Detroit" 1999). Police in various municipalities have also arranged for the names of arrested clients to be published in local newspapers, including *The Hartford Courant* in Connecticut, *The Brockton Enterprise* in Massachusetts, and *The Kentucky Post* in Kentucky (Lewis 1999). Perhaps the most provocative (though not state-run) recent example of john "outing" is "Webjohn," an online database organized by concerned community members, featuring johns caught on video picking up or communicating with a known prostitute. The site's mission statement notably posits johns, not prostitutes, as vectors of disease, and declares two official aims: "to deny johns their anonymity" and "to offer any residential or business communities in North America a cost-free and law suit-free mechanism to suppress street-level prostitution in their area." Taken together with a revision of legal codes to facilitate client arrests and to stiffen criminal penalties, "public outings" in the mass media, vehicle impoundment, and revocation of driver's licenses, as well as stricter prohibitions against the patronage of child prostitutes and the possession of child pornography, the new spate of social policies that seek to regulate male heterosexual behavior is historically unprecedented (Lefler 1999; Weitzer 2000b).

Allison, Prasad, and other sociologists such as Castells (1996) and Kempadoo and Doezema (1998) have rightly pointed to the burgeoning demand for commercial sexual services as paradigmatic of various key features of late capitalism: the merging of public and private, the extension in depth and breadth of the service sector, the individualization of sex, the preference for the neatly bounded commodity over the messy diffuseness of nonmarket exchange. Missing from these accounts is a recognition that commercial sexual consumption is simultaneously being *normalized* and *problematized*, and that these two phenomena are linked. Underlying the lack of attention to the recent criminalization of consumer behavior is the neglect of some other key features of late capitalist society: the relationship between postindustrial poverty and gentrification, as well as the normative push on the part of some feminists to retain a modernist model of relationally bound sexual intimacy.

John schools are the outcome of an alliance between feminist antiprostitution activists, organized groups of predominantly lower-middle-class community residents and small-scale merchants, and politicians and big businesses with interests in gentrifying neighborhoods such as San Francisco's Tenderloin and Mission districts—neighborhoods that are home to the city's principal streetwalking strolls and the most socially marginal sectors of the commercial sex trade, yet close to the business district and highly valuable real estate. Although the three groups indicated have disparate ideological and material agendas, they have joined forces to target the male patrons of prostitution's most publicly visible domain. In contrast to the moral wars of a century ago, contemporary campaigns against prostitution are chiefly concerned with cleaning up the gritty underbelly of an industry that is basically left alone so long as it remains behind closed doors, or, more preferably still, online (Weitzer 2000b). Attempts to eradicate the most "problematic" segments of the industry implicitly serve to legitimize the *unproblematic* parts that remain.

The district attorney's advice to the attendees of John School to get out of their cars and turn on their computers can in this way be rendered decipherable as an important step toward cleaner streets and gentrified neighborhoods. Thus, in 1994, when the San Francisco Board of Supervisors assembled a Task Force to investigate revisions to the city's prostitution policy, the primary and explicitly stated impetus was community and merchants' objections to disruptions on their streets (San Francisco Task Force on Prostitution 1994). In its *Final Report*, the Task Force noted that

> Despite their concerns about noise, traffic, etc., most residents [of the Tenderloin and Mission districts] supported decriminalization or legalization of prostitution . . . Residents' valid concerns about quality of life, yet support for decriminalization, was a conflict more apparent than real. The conflict could be resolved by focusing on the complaints: not against prostitution itself, but by the perceived fallout or side effects of street prostitution. (San Francisco Task Force on Prostitution 1996, 27, 29)

Although police representatives and municipal politicians continue to frame their street-focused enforcement strategy as being in accordance with the preponderance of citizens' complaints, the effect of their policies is clearly to divert sex-workers and customers into indoor and online commercial sex markets.

The new social policies targeting male sexual conduct and commercial consumption are not, however, completely absent of moral focus or content. The various strands of the ideological agenda behind programs such as John School, like the interest groups behind it, are multiple but interweaving. Many contemporary feminist activists, like their feminist forerunners, are keen upon challenging the male half of the sexual double standard. Given the emergence of the sexually consumeristic *Playboy* ideal in the 1960s (Ehrenreich 1983), the deregulation and normalization of pornography in the 1970s (Juffer 1998), and other predominantly male benefits of the sexual revolution, the reassertion of sexual domesticity and marital fidelity is experienced as particularly crucial. Responding to a similar constellation of concerns, lower-middle-class residents and small-scale merchants can be seen as participating in both a material and a symbolic "crusade" against the incursion of market forces into a longed-for protected sphere of family, neighborhood, and community.

Conclusion

The two historically unique and contradictory tendencies that I have documented here, namely burgeoning consumption and increasing state intervention, should be understood within a broad array of economic and cultural transformations that have unfolded over the last 30 years. The pursuit of *bounded authenticity* that is encapsulated in the demand for sexual commerce has been augmented by the shift from a relational to a recreational model of sexual intimacy, by the symbiotic relationship between the information economy and commercial sexual consumption, by the ways in which tourism and business travel facilitate the insertion of men into the commercial sexual marketplace, and, more generally, by the myriad mergings and inversions of public and private life that are characteristic of our era.

At the same time, the corresponding phenomena of postindustrial poverty and the gentrification of the inner city have led to an overlapping of ambitions between municipal politicians, developers, and feminist antiprostitution activists who are jointly interested in "cleaning up" the male desires that contribute to the sullying of city streets. John Schools, as well as other measures that penalize a subgroup of the male clients of commercial sex-workers, have emerged out of the confluence of these disparate political agendas. The recent crackdowns on johns and the normalization of other forms of commercial sex go hand in hand because state regulatory strategies around prostitution are deeply embedded in struggles over the allocation of urban space. Both the state policing of the street-level sex trade and the normalization of the sex business reveal a shared set of underlying economic and cultural interests: the excision of class and racial Others from gentrifying inner cities, the facilitation of the postindustrial service sector, and the creation of clean and shiny urban spaces in which middle-class men can safely indulge in recreational commercial sexual consumption.

Notes

1. I am grateful to Kerwin Kaye, Laurie Schaffner, Loïc Wacquant, Kristin Luker, Paul Willis, Lucinda Ramberg, Will Rountree, Lawrence Cohen, and Myra Marx Feree for their support, comments, and suggestions. An earlier version of this piece appeared in *Ethnography* in September 2001. Reprinted by permission of Sage Publications.

2. All of the names and identifying details of individuals and specific commercial venues have been changed or omitted to protect their anonymity. Geographical locations, when included, have been left unmodified in order to respect the locational specificity of the events I describe.

3. My focus is on heterosexual male desire and consumption patterns—increasingly the primary, if not the exclusive, commercial sex market in which the state intervenes. In touristic urban centers, heterosexual prostitution is estimated to comprise approximately two-thirds of the overall market, while paid encounters between men constitute approximately one-third (Leigh 1994). Although there is a growing literature on the emergence of women as consumers of pornographic images (Juffer 1998), and on the recent phenomenon of female sex tourism to the Caribbean (O'Connell Davidson and Sánchez Taylor, this volume), there is scant evidence that any significant number of female clients of prostitutes—either lesbian or heterosexual—exists domestically. I have thus not sought to include any female sexual clients in my sample. The lack of such a market reveals a great deal about the persistently gendered nature of commercial sexual consumption.

4. The first arrests of clients in the U.S. (which were intermittent and few in number) followed a 1975 ruling brought by the American Civil Liberties Union before a California State Court, which noted "the plain unvarnished fact . . . that men and women engaged in proscribed sexual behavior are not treated equally" (MacDonald 1978). On the increase in client arrest rates in mid-1990s San Francisco, see Marinucci (1995a) (describing a 25% increase in client arrest rates) and Marinucci (1995b) (quoting SFPD statistics indicating a dramatic surge in prostitution-related arrests of male clients to 1,000 of 4,900 total). On the emergence of a similar phenomenon in New York City as part of Mayor Rudolph Giuliani's "Quality of Life" campaigns, see Pierre-Pierre (1994) and Nieves (1999).

5. As Eric Schlosser (1997, 141) has pointed out, "most of the profits being generated by porn today are being earned by business not traditionally associated with the sex industry—by mom and pop video stores; by long-distance carriers like AT&T; by cable companies like Time Warner and Tele-Communications, Inc.; and by hotel chains like Marriott, Hyatt, and Holiday Inn that now reportedly earn millions of dollars each year supplying adult films to their guests."

6. Despite the fact that male prostitution was also prevalent in urban centers during this period, male prostitutes were typically subsumed under the new and more socially salient banner of "homosexuals" in scholarly, medical-psychological, and political discourses (Weeks, [1981] 1997).

7. It is ironic that prostitutes' rights movements have sought legitimacy under the banner of "sex-work" (Jenness 1993), considering that, for Marx and other early socialist critics, what was wrong with wage labor as work was precisely that it resembled prostitution (Marx [1844] 1978, 103).

8. The relevant studies include Mansson 1988, Prieur and Taksdahl 1993, Hart 1994, Allison 1994, Prasad 1999, and Frank 2002.

9. In the *Social Organization of Sexuality*, Laumann et al. use the terms *relational* and *recreational* to designate distinct normative orientations toward sexual behavior (1994). I use the terms both to distinguish between different normative models and to indicate successive, historically specific configurations of sexual and emotional life. Social historians have linked the relational model (also referred to as "amative" or "companionate") to the rise of modern romance and the nuclear family under capitalism, contrasting it with the prototypically *procreative* orientation of pre-industrial society (Fass 1977; D'Emilio 1983a; Luker 1984). Some social theorists have pointed to an emergent second shift in paradigms of sexuality, occurring roughly around the 1970s, in which sexuality derives its primary meanings from pleas-

ure and sensation, and is no longer the exclusive province of marital or even durable relationships. This second shift to what I am calling a *recreational* paradigm of sexuality has been variously described as the "normalization" of sex (Castells 1996), "unbounded eros" (Seidman 1991), "the postmodern erotic revolution" (Bauman 1998), and the "fun ethic" (Bourdieu 1984). In contrasting recreational sexuality with relational sexuality, I seek to distinguish the former from the romantic residues and extrasexual associations that typically accompany the notion of a relationship, but I do not mean to suggest that it must lack a meaningful intersubjective component.

10. Giddens's *Transformation of Intimacy* (1992) employs a compensatory model of men's participation in commercial sex, while also describing more general reconfigurations in late-capitalist paradigms of intimacy. Giddens introduces the term "plastic sexuality" to refer to a new paradigm of eroticism that is nonreproductive, in principle reciprocal and egalitarian, and subjectively experienced as a property of the self. Plastic sexuality is the erotic counterpart of the pure relationship, a relationship entered into for the sake of the intimacy it affords both partners. Unlike the model of recreational sex that I present here, Giddens's plastic sexuality is still essentially connected to a notion of private sphere, durable romantic relationships. Giddens uses the term "episodic sexuality" to refer to what for him is a less significant, if more troubling, cultural offshoot. Episodic sexuality is gendered masculine, compulsive in nature, and aims to neutralize the anxieties that are stimulated by the threat of intimacy contained in the pure relationship and the relative emancipation of women. As such, episodic sexuality typically finds expression in practices of commodified sex such as the consumption of pornography.

11. By 1988, nearly a third of American households consisted of a single individual. In Western European countries, single-person households have been the most rapidly growing household type since the 1960s, with from 25 percent (in the United Kingdom) to 36 percent (in Sweden) of the population living alone. In the U.S., the percentage of unmarried adults rose from 28 percent to 37 percent between 1970 and 1988 (for a fuller account of recent changes in U.S. and Western European social demography, see U.S. Bureau of the Census 1989, 1992, 2000; Sorrentino 1990; and Kellogg and Mintz 1993).

12. Marx was the first to note the ironic leveling capacity of market transactions, though in lament rather than celebration: "That which is for me through the medium of *money*—that for which I can pay (i.e., which money can buy) that am *I*, the possessor of the money. The extent of the power of money is my power. Money's properties are my properties and essential powers—the properties and powers of its possessor. Thus, what I *am* and *am capable of* is by no means determined by my individuality. I am ugly, but I can buy for myself the most *beautiful* of women" (Marx [1844] 1978, 103).

13. Although prostitution (i.e., genital-oral or genital-genital contact in exchange for payment, which are criminal acts under California state law) has been well documented in San Francisco's legal sex clubs by the clients and sex-workers I interviewed, by clients in online chat rooms, and by the local press, the clubs officially deny that illegal activities take place on their premises (Brook 1998).

14. Ruth Rosen observed a similar split between the interests of large and small-scale business owners earlier in the century, when large-scale business interests (real estate agents, landlords, and owners of saloons and breweries) supported organized brothel prostitution, whereas small shopkeepers opposed it (Rosen 1982).

15. See, for example, Marinucci 1995a and b, Kilman and Smyth 1998, Symbaluk and Jones 1998, Lefler 1999, Monto 2000, Nieves 1999, and Weitzer 2000b.

3
The Regulation of Childhood and Gendered "Innocence"

CHAPTER 8

Child Welfare as Social Defense Against Sexuality:
A Norwegian Example

KJERSTI ERICSSON

From its philanthropic beginnings, child welfare has played a role in the social regulation of sexuality in Norway. Philanthropic agencies possessed considerable powers to define good and bad motherhood, and good and bad ways to rear children. Mothers were scrutinized both for their morals and their ability to take care of and control their young. Children and adolescents were assessed for their conformity to Norwegian norms of respectability.

When child welfare became a state responsibility at the end of the nineteenth century, the power to define and intervene was then supported by legislation. Society gave child welfare the task of patrolling the borders between acceptable and unacceptable socialization of children, and between acceptable and unacceptable behavior among the young themselves. This also implied patrolling the borders between acceptable and unacceptable sexuality.

The first Norwegian Child Welfare Act was passed in 1896 and implemented in 1900. The act was part of a reform in criminal law. Behind the reform lay both humanistic concerns and a sense of danger to society. On the one hand, reformers wanted to remove "crying children" from prisons. On the other hand, these same stakeholders saw the need to erect a social defense against the depraved children of the poor. The determination of criminal liability was raised from 10 to 14 years of age. Delinquent children were no longer to be imprisoned; rather, they were to be cared for, educated, and brought up in institutions specifically designed for this purpose. There were separate institutions for girls and for boys. The authority to commit children to these institutions rested with newly created Child Welfare Boards.

Bernhard Getz, the "father" of the Child Welfare Act in Norway and its attendant system of reformatories, wanted to target both delinquent boys and girls. Reformatories were instituted not only to stem the tide of thievery among young boys, but also to prevent young girls from sliding into prostitution and to restore in them the virtues of "true womanhood" consistent with the dominant gender norms of the era.

The institutions that sprang up toward the end of the nineteenth century and the first years of the twentieth century were to endure until the 1980s. Changes in educational ideologies, therapeutic fashions, legislation, and administrative authorities impacted the manner in which these institutions were run. However, central aspects of the institutional regimes have shown an impressive longevity.

In this chapter, I analyze records from Bjerketun, a Norwegian institution for young girls in the 1950s, to exemplify child welfare as an agent of the state's regulation of sexuality. Bjerketun was called a "protective school" for girls considered delinquent. Bjerketun constituted the core of a wider network of social control, which encompassed schools, child welfare boards, other social agencies, and the police. The institution was founded in 1900 as part of the child welfare system of reformatories. My study is based on a sample of case records from 1951 to 1961 (Ericsson 1997). During the period of study, approximately 200 passed through the institution. The majority of the girls were between 14 and 18 years of age, with some as young as 10, and others as old as 20. In most cases, the length of their stay was approximately one year, though some stayed much longer—as long as seven years. Following their year at Bjerketun, the girls were usually under the authority of the institution for an additional year. During this period, they often worked as domestic servants in families chosen by the institution. Some were sent to boarding schools.

The main task of this chapter is to describe and discuss the evidence in the case records that constructed the Bjerketun girls as a social danger to society. The 1950s were a decade when the virtuous and dedicated housewife held a practically unchallenged position as the ideal of femininity in Norway. However, the construction of the girls as a danger to society has long, historical roots as well as persistence into the present. More specifically, the Bjerketun case illustrates the following three points: one, that child welfare has been deployed as a social defense by the state to control female sexuality among the poor; two, that girls were subjected to what I have come to term a gendered process of mortification; and three, that Norwegian social stereotypes lie at the basis of the state's regulation of sexuality—as seen through the Bjerketun girls.

In addition, this chapter will discuss the manner in which developments in child welfare discourse on sexuality changed from the 1950s to the 1990s.

A Social Defense Against Sexuality

In the Bjerketun case records, sexualized interpretations of girls predominate. This is in accordance with several studies, which show that delinquency has been conceptualized along gender-specific lines. Authors from a variety of nations and time periods have pointed out that girls and boys are considered deviant and placed in institutions for different reasons.[1] The main difference can be expressed in this simple formula: A delinquent boy is criminally active; a delinquent girl is sexually active. The placement of most children in institutions by Norwegian Child Welfare, at least in the first 60 or 70 years of its existence, conformed to this formula. However, it was the way children's lives were interpreted that conformed to the formula. Crime was central in the discourse on boys; sexuality was central in the discourse on girls.

In the Bjerketun case records from the period 1951 to 1961, it was customary to find the girls described in the following manner:

> Our impression is that she is capable of giving herself to any man, without considering the consequences. She is unreliable, with strong erotic urges . . . .
>
> A striking trait in the development of the patient was a strong hypersexualization that manifested itself not only in relation to the opposite sex, but also in relation to her own sex . . . .
>
> At times she is highly sexually aroused. She undoubtedly masturbates quite often. Artifacts that resemble penises have been found among her things. Their worn appearance indicates frequent use. (Ericsson 1997)

Girls' apparent lack of sexual inhibitions was emphasized. An attitude toward open sexuality was understood as an eruption of instincts and urges, which broke through weak or almost nonexistent inhibitions and moral concepts.

Through the case records, events that led to girls' institutionalization may be traced: Some hung out on street corners, were interested in boys, went dancing or to the movies, and got home late at night or early in the morning. Some ran away from home. Others visited boats in the harbor and kept company with sailors. Finally, there are those who today would be defined as victims of incest or other forms of sexual crimes. One example of this was from the account of a 12-year-old girl who was enticed with candy into having intercourse with a 70-year-old man. Frequently, the agents of formal social control struck more harshly against the victims than against the offenders.

What meaning did the girls themselves attach to behaviors such as hanging out late at night, going with boys, dancing, drinking, or partying with sailors? Possibly they saw them as fun activities, perhaps in pursuit of feelings of freedom. From the perspective of the control network, these girls constituted a sexual threat to the dominant order. Illegitimate, unwanted, and inferior children, venereal diseases, and prostitution were seen as dangers following in these girls' wake. In addition, authorities felt that the girls also should be locked up in order to protect men from seduction. This is well illustrated by the following excerpt from a conversation between a doctor and a psychologist at Bjerketun, as recorded in the psychologist's diary:

> How can you, as a doctor, permit a girl of 15 to be kept isolated, day after day, for months?
> —I don't like it myself. But, what am I to do when the staff refuses to have her in the ward? She'll run away instantly.
> Then let her run away! That would be far better than this. She's bound to be permanently damaged by such a long period of isolation.
> —There are others that also have to be taken into consideration. She pretends to be 18 or 19 years of age, and she looks it, too. Look at the documents in her case, they make an impressive pile. It's full of legal documents from cases brought against men for unlawful sexual intercourse with a minor. (Gunvald 1967, 29)

The social defense against unauthorized sexuality and its dangerous consequences included sterilization. After a long discussion where eugenic concerns played a prominent role, the Norwegian law on sterilization was passed in 1934. The law legalized forced sterilization if the person in question was insane or seriously mentally retarded, or

> ... if there is no hope of recovery or substantial improvement, and there is reason to believe that the person in question will be unable to support him- or herself and his or her offspring by his or her own work; if a serious pathological mental condition or bodily defect might be transmitted by inheritance to his or her offspring; if there is a danger that the person in question, because of abnormal sexual urges, will commit sexual crimes. (Berner 1937, 166)

If the person in question was, mildly, not seriously, mentally retarded, he or she had to consent to be operated on. In terms of IQ, the line between mentally retarded and seriously mentally retarded was drawn at IQ 50.

The spokesman for the 1934 Sterilization Act in the Norwegian Parliament was an ardent supporter of eugenic measures. In his speech, he compared eugenics to the sound management of a farm: "On the one hand, we are striving to secure a strong, fertile, and productive stock, on the other hand, we want to remove parasites and weeds" (Aasen 1989, 21). The Act was passed with only one dissenting vote.

Five years of German occupation and the deeply shocking disclosures about eugenics as practiced by the Nazi regime lay between the passing of the Sterilization Act in 1934 and its use on some of the Bjerketun girls in the 1950s. The question of sterilization was raised in 14 case sheets from Bjerketun from 1951 to 1961. The number of girls who were actually sterilized is not clear. What is quite clear, however, is that the motives behind efforts to have girls sterilized made up a rather unsavory mixture by contemporary liberal standards: contempt for "indecent" lower-class girls, diluted eugenic ideas, moral outrage, and concerns about potential social security spending. Often, authorities from the girls' home districts were more eager for surgery than Bjerketun officials. Following is an example of the way in which local representatives campaigned to have girls sterilized. In a letter to relevant authorities, one representative wrote:

> She is still devoid of all serious interests, speaking only of clothes and dresses, taking part in silly pranks, violating rules and regulations in the institution. She is absorbed with her looks and body. Repeatedly, she stands in front of a large mirror wearing only a bathing suit or panties. When travelling by bus or tram, she stares shamelessly at every male. She is still unreliable . . . As several generations have had low IQs, one has strong reasons to expect that a pregnancy would result in even more trouble and expenses for society. . . . Her mother and uncle are also quite inferior, and according to what I have heard about the father, he is of a similar kind. The mother has four children with three different fathers. 'Well, I finally managed to get married to one of them,' she told me. I have information that her sister is not unknown to the police. The husband of the mother is unemployed, and their home did not make a good impression when I visited, it was rather unattractive. Noise and rows are common. (Ericsson 1997, 65)

The Bjerketun girls seldom met the criteria of being seriously mentally retarded, which was a prerequisite for sterilization without consent. Consequently, the institution tried to talk them into having the operation. Some girls successfully resisted; others finally succumbed. One of the girls who finally gave in was named Gro. She was placed at Bjerketun because of "serious problems of adjustment" (Ericsson 1997, 70). According to Gro's records, she was "cross, difficult, and hanging out a lot." On intelligence tests, her results varied from IQ 46 to IQ 74.

While still under the authority of Bjerketun, Gro was permitted to stay at home. During this period, the institution received a letter from a woman in

Gro's hometown; there were rumors that Gro was pregnant. Bjerketun responded by writing a letter to the local Child Welfare Board suggesting that the board approach the medical health officer so that he might apply for an abortion and "simultaneously have Gro sterilized." The leader of the Child Welfare Board responded:

> Gro is now six months pregnant. It is too late for an abortion. However, there is every reason to have her sterilized immediately after the birth, while she is still at the birth clinic. I will send an application to the Central Health Authorities. The family must not be told. If they know about this, Gro will probably not enter the birth clinic. (Ericsson 1997, 70)

State agents planned to have Gro sterilized without her knowledge and consent, but the Central Health Authorities turned down their application. Bjerketun officials commented on this in a letter to the Child Welfare Board in Gro's hometown:

> It is a pity that we did not succeed in having Gro sterilized. As I understood it, the Central Health Authorities require an application signed by Gro and her mother—and that, unfortunately, we will never get. (Ericsson 1997, 70)

Despite Bjerketun authorities' early pessimism, both Gro and her mother were finally persuaded. A glimpse of the reason for this may be seen in another letter, written by the headmistress of Bjerketun to the Ministry of Social Affairs:

> Shortly after the birth, Gro escaped from the maternity home and went back to her mother. The Child Welfare Board immediately decided that she should return to Bjerketun and remain here until the question of sterilization was settled. Gro, her mother, and her guardian signed the new application, which was now accepted. Gro and her parents request that she be allowed to go directly from the hospital to her home. Bjerketun had no objections to this. We assume that the Child Welfare Board agreed, as the purpose of returning her to Bjerketun was now fulfilled. (Ericsson 1997, 71)

Following the operation, Gro was allowed to go straight back to her parents. It appears that sterilization was the price Gro had to pay to be discharged from Bjerketun.

Child Protection and Social Defense is the title of a book analyzing the social forces shaping the first Norwegian Child Welfare Act in 1896. The author, Tove Stang Dahl (1978), focuses on the Act in relation to delinquent boys and the wish to mount a campaign of social defense against crime. The Bjerketun study illustrates that crime was not the only danger that child welfare was called upon to combat. To gain a comprehensive understanding of child welfare as a social defense, sexuality has to be included.

The efforts to combine protection and social defense are not restricted to Norway. Constance A. Nathanson (1991) and Carol Smart (1992) both point to the last half of the nineteenth century as a crucial period in the shaping of new forms of control of sexuality, both in the U.S. (Nathanson) and in the U.K. (Smart). According to Nathanson, the period between puberty and marriage was regarded as especially dangerous for young girls. Nathanson identifies three main strategies for monitoring their sexuality: (1) to protect unmarried girls from a loss of sexual status and reputation; (2) to restore the status and reputation if it were lost; and (3) if restoration were seen as impossible, to place the girls literally or symbolically outside society (Nathanson 1991). A central assumption behind these strategies was that sexual or reproductive transgressions (for example, extramarital pregnancy) had intense significance for the identity and future prospects for girls. Sexual or reproductive transgressions were acts that defined her totally; she would not be a woman who happened to fall, but a fallen woman. Rehabilitation to respectable sexual status required a sort of conversion where the young woman repented her former acts and accepted the definition of her conduct that was offered by the controlling authorities.

Social defense in the U.K., according to Smart, consisted of legal, medical, and early social science discourses interwoven to picture women as basically having a problematic and unruly body—a body, according to these discourses, whose sexuality and reproduction was in need of constant surveillance and regulation (Smart 1992). This unruly body constituted a threat to the moral and social order: promiscuous women spreading venereal diseases, dangerous working-class mothers reproducing misery, and delinquency through neglect and immorality.

The issues of protection and social defense, focusing sexuality and the norms for respectable womanhood, have continued to inform the conception of female delinquency. An example is Tappan's (1947) description of the Wayward Minor Court of New York. According to Tappan, the main task of this court was to control the sexual conduct of unmarried, adolescent girls. Forty years later, Figueira-McDonough (1987) analyzes the U.S. Juvenile Courts' handling of cases involving girls. She finds that young girls are subjected to treatment and punishment basically for deviating from what is considered proper feminine behavior.

The examples from the Bjerketun case records show that the girls were constituted as dangerous and unruly bodies. They threatened the moral order through their promiscuity and by seducing married men. They threatened the social order by becoming unwed and neglectful mothers, producing a new generation of delinquent children. The threat emanating from these bodies was strengthened by the prevailing ideas of the era that biological inferiority was one of the causes of crime, immorality, and social misery. Against this threat, the ultimate defense posed was sterilization. Some of the Bjerketun girls fell victim to such measures.

A Gendered Mortification Process

In his work on total institutions, Erving Goffman (1961) analyzes the social situation of mental patients and other inmates. He pictures a process where the patient is first stripped of his or her old identity and social roles. Then a new identity is built, in accordance with the rules and goals of the institution. Goffman termed this induction a "mortification process" (1961, 16).

Bjerketun was what Goffman would have labeled a "total institution" (1961). As part of the admission process and the internee's introduction into the routines of the institutional regime, he or she was deprived of all material and symbolic support linked to his or her identity and life outside the institution. In this process, the new internee is bathed, and all traces of the outside world are cleansed away. The effect breaks down the personality.

Bjerketun had its own version of these procedures, which I came to call a gendered mortification process. Upon arrival and upon return after escapes, which were frequent, girls were routinely subjected to gynecological examinations to check for venereal diseases. In addition, girls returning after an escape were isolated. Both the gynecological examination and the use of isolation may be understood as part of this gendered process. The gynecological examination was a "cleansing" to remove impurity directly linked to girls' deviance. Accordingly, the symbolic impact was far stronger than the baths described by Goffman. Many girls must have experienced the examination in a manner similar to what nineteenth-century feminist Josephine Butler called "instrumental rape" (see Jackson 1989). In several instances, police escorts were used to bring the girls to the examination.

One case sheet contained the following paradoxical episode. A young girl named Tove had been expelled from her local school because of unacceptable relations with boys. In his statement, the headmaster wrote:

> Tove must be designated as a source of infection, spreading moral disease. This situation is known to all the boys. They are well aware of the fact that anyone may ask Tove to undress, to do whatever they want with her. (Notes from Bjerketun files, Ericsson 1997, 56)

The following ominous note from the first institution where Tove was placed was included in her case sheet: "The examination for venereal disease could not be carried out, as the girl was too shy to undress" (Ericsson 1997, 56). One may only guess what had happened to Tove prior to this incident.

When placed in isolation, several girls were deprived of their clothes. The case records record a number of episodes where the girls are forcibly undressed, with men present: the Bjerketun janitor, the groundskeeper, or policemen. The men either helped to hold the girls, or assisted in undressing. The process in which girls were forcibly undressed with the assistance of men highlights the gendered aspect of the mortification process.

In Goffman's description of total institutions, the mortification process is only the first part of the institutions' work on their inmates. The next step is building a "new" person with a new identity in accordance with the rules and goals of the institution. At Bjerketun, this process was also highly gendered; it consisted of reform through domestic work.

Official documents show that Bjerketun was a "Protective School for Young Girls." The main curriculum, however, did not consist of the usual school subjects. The school's timetable was filled with domestic work. The institution had a farm attached to it. The girls were taught to prepare all kinds of products from the farm: meat, vegetables, fruits, and berries. They made hams, sausages and meat puddings, jam, and juice. For the Norwegian Christmas, the girls learned to bake the traditional 12 kinds of cookies. They learned the correct way to clean and wash; they knitted stockings; they wove and sewed towels, sheets, tablecloths, and mats for the floors. The goal was to educate capable housewives and domestic servants.

The teaching of domestic work may, however, be interpreted not only as a transmission of skills, but also of values, habits, emotions, and ways of thinking associated with "true womanhood" in accordance with the dominant gender norms of the era. Domestic work was constituted to possess certain moral qualities: As it involved ministering to the needs of others, it inculcated a gendered ethic of caring in the girls. Also, it placed women safely in the private, as opposed to the public, sphere. Young women in public places could signal the possibility of the danger of moral corruption. Many of the Bjerketun girls had run away from home and spent their time in the streets prior to their institutionalization. They needed to be reminded of the strong connection between domesticity and virtuousness.

To domesticate deviant and dangerous femininity through domestic work had been a common denominator for most institutions committed to reforming, treating, or punishing women, from lunatic asylums in Victorian England (Showalter 1987) to women's prisons in contemporary Norway (Vegheim 1995).[2] Nathanson has described the central position of domestic work in reformatories for girls in the last part of the nineteenth and first part of the twentieth centuries (1991). She found that the literature on education gave the impression that doing domestic work was not only seen as a preparation for the girls' "natural" position as housewives in their own homes, but also as domestic servants. The leaders of reformatories regarded girls' lack of respect for, and disinterest in, domestic work as one of the causes of female delinquency. To teach respect for domestic work would, according to this logic, contribute to rehabilitation. Through strict domesticity the girls would be transformed into virtuous women. This line of thought was easily recognizable in the Bjerketun material.

Social Stereotypes at the Base of State Regulation of Sexuality

Two ideas central to the discourse regarding Bjerketun girls held sway in the control network: One was the blurring between the notions of physical and moral contagion; the other was the conception of nature as "good" and "evil."

Seen in light of physical and moral contagion, the Bjerketun girls were regarded as doubly dangerous. They offered both physical as well as moral contamination in the form of disgusting diseases and moral corruption that flowed from their all-too-available vaginas. The girls were seen as infringing on norms of decency and threatening the sexual order. Society was charged with the task of purging the filthiness emanating from the girls (both moral and physical).

Evident in these texts is the idea that women's nature has two aspects: "good" nature and "evil" nature. A woman who acts in accordance with "good nature" fulfills the role prescribed for her in the natural order: She is an instinctively loving mother, domestic housekeeper, and subservient wife. Good nature is what emerges when the natural is set against the unnatural. However, this thinking goes, when nature is set against culture, a woman takes on an evil nature with a dark and dangerous sexuality that threatens the very order of civilization. Not only does she herself lack the light of reason, she also threatens to extinguish it in men.

In Bjerketun's case records, the girls were often described in a vocabulary that invoked the nature/culture dichotomy: They were framed as being driven by "the lowest forms of sexual passion" (Ericsson 1997, 33). The representatives of the institution seemed to regard themselves as engaged in civilizing work. They believed their job was to bring the girls under the influence of culture and moral inhibition as they sought to combat evil nature.

Traditionally, racist discourses have drawn upon the nature/culture dichotomy as well. Throughout Europe and the West, labels such as "wild," "primitive," or "uninhibited" were used to describe people of African origin or people with darker skin. The Bjerketun girls were white, as the Norwegian population in the 1950s was practically uniformly of Caucasian descent. With few exceptions, they were from low- or no-income families. In the Norwegian context, the trope of class, rather than race, actualized efforts to civilize girls. However, discourses tinged with racism were present or had impact. The vocabulary of evil nature was used with extra vehemence in the description of girls from "tinker" families. Tinkers were folks who travelled through the nation and earned their living through barter and odd jobs. Children raised in migrant, low-income families were not able to attend school regularly and learn Norwegian mainstream values. The child welfare authorities of the time used tough measures to combat the travelling lifestyle of the tinkers. Many children were forcefully removed from their families and placed in orphanages. By confiscating the children of the tinkers, one hoped to root out their traditional way of life. The tinker was positioned in Norwegian family welfare literature as the dark and dangerous Other, confronting and threatening to undermine a society based on residence and discipline. Ideas of the wild and uninhibited sexuality of the tinkers were part of this picture. These ideas are manifest in the descriptions of tinker girls in the Bjerketun case records.

Bjerketun girls embodied gender and class in ways that did not obey the rules and restrictions that made middle-class women seem less carnal. These unruly bodies signaled availability and immorality. With their uninhibited sexuality, they also signaled the dangers that lie in a far too fertile underclass that poured out from the cellars of the city, creating in the minds and hearts of mainstream Norwegians the fear of riots, crime, uncontrollable growth in social spending, and the deterioration of human stock, all in one confused mixture. These fears persist today in Norway behind unspoken notions of "incessantly breeding, dark-skinned immigrant women" and the "ticking population bomb of the South."

Late-Modern Developments in Child Welfare's Discourse on Sexuality

Does the social defense against sexuality remain one of the functions of the Norwegian child welfare system? Even though the Bjerketun girls were seen as sexual agents, they were framed as sexually delinquent perpetrators, not victims. In the course of the 1960s, however, the explicit sexual discourse in child welfare seemed to fade away. It was no longer openly stated that it was the task of child welfare to "contain sexuality" as one prominent child welfare official had stated in 1946 (Tjensvoll 1946). However, girls were still being sent to institutions for running away from home, staying out late at night, and keeping company with older boys. The language of institutional case records was at times still reminiscent of the Bjerketun style. Eva Nordland's 1971 study of Norwegian children institutionalized for "adjustment problems" exemplifies this. Nordland presents excerpts from Haldis's story, as it unfolds in the institution's case records:

Haldis (14 years of age) has led an unstable existence. She was raised by her mother and father until the mother died. At that time, Haldis was six years [old]. The mother was sickly, and had a mania for cleanliness. Haldis was not allowed to stay in the apartment before bedtime. She was outdoors all day, sometimes even after dark, so that she did not dirty the apartment. The father was also very strict with the girl from a very young age.

When her mother died, the girl lived with foster parents for some time. The foster parents explain that Haldis was a very difficult child, and had to be treated severely. They often used corporal punishment, because Haldis refused to be obedient. When Haldis was 12 years old, her father decided that he could no longer afford to pay the foster parents, and Haldis moved in with her father.

When Haldis returned, the father continued his "demanding and harsh treatment" of the girl. It says in the papers that Haldis has been subjected to brutal corporal punishment, both by the foster parents and by her father. It also says in the papers that the father has been behaving "indecently" toward Haldis's elder sister. To the Child Welfare Board, relatives have claimed that an "unhealthy erotic relationship" has existed between Haldis and her father. For this reason, the relatives wanted Haldis removed from her home as soon as possible.

The family has had problems with Haldis's aggressive behavior from [when] she was quite small. If things did not instantly go her way, she reacted with fits of rage. She beat and kicked her father on several occasions. The father sometimes responded with spanking, sometimes with indifference.

In school, Haldis has shown weak aptitudes. Her standing is low in all subjects, and she is unable to concentrate. She dislikes everything that has to do with school. The child shows very poor adjustment. When at school, she repeatedly violates rules and regulations by smoking, leaving the schoolyard without permission, and by truancy. She has run away from town several times. She is shameless, impudent and untruthful, aggressive, sadistic, [and] domineering in relation to her fellow pupils, the school reports. Some of the other children find her exciting; others are terrorized by her.

Haldis prefers morally weak friends. It is the opinion of the school that she has "infected" several of her fellow pupils with her "impudent, unreliable, and untruthful behavior." Haldis takes on a hardened attitude, especially in the presence of other children. A special problem is her "sexual deviance" and "attraction to grown men." (Nordland 1971, 105)

The picture of Haldis contains elements of both victim and perpetrator. However, the incest theme is downplayed rather than emphasized. Kaye (this volume) shows in his chapter that in the U.S. the sexual abuse of children was not of scholarly interest until the early 1980s. This seems to be the case in Norway, as well. In the general child welfare discourse at the time Nordland published Haldis's story (1971), sexual abuse was not a common topic. Girls' main problems were not seen as "sexual delinquency" anymore, or "sexual victimization" yet, but as something else—drug use, for example. If a girl slept with several boys, it was interpreted as a more or less explicit exchange: Sexual access to the body of the girl was traded for drugs. When the topic of female adolescent sexuality reemerged as an explicit discourse in child welfare in the early 1980s, it was in the form of incest: Girls were no longer seen as perpetrators and seductresses, but as victims of sexual abuse from grown-up men—fathers and stepfathers. Even prostitution was framed in this 1980s discourse as one of the many harmful consequences of being an incest victim. Kaye (this volume) points out how, at the time, "incest victim" was transformed into a diagnostic category.

However, changes at the discursive level may be more distinct than changes in the way girls' problems are treated at the practical level. The brutality exhibited toward girls by authorities from the Bjerketun period has fallen out of fashion and is seen as unacceptable today. Nonetheless, "problematic" sexuality still seems to reside in girls. The sexual behavior of boys is seldom made an issue in contemporary child welfare institutions. A girl in such an institution who is quoted in a recent study, has listened her way through the therapeutic jargon and found the essential message: "No boys are placed in institutions because they like to sleep with a lot of girls. Girls, however, are sent here because they sleep with a lot of boys" (Hennum 1997, 68).

Conclusion

Norwegian child welfare was born with the double face of Janus. With one face, it looked benevolently on misbehaving children, wanting to rescue them from the horrors of prison and punishment. With the other face, it stared sternly at the same children, wanting to protect society from the danger they constituted. This danger was gendered, and with child welfare the state erected a social defense, not only against crime, but also against sexuality. Institutionalization, isolation, and in some instances sterilization were the weapons used in the battle to keep "wild," "uninhibited," "immoral" young girls at bay. This struggle was informed by age-old social stereotypes, in which the girls were cast as having an "evil nature" and spreading a filthy mixture of physical and moral contagion.

In the 1980s, the incestuous adult man replaced the sexually active young girl as the main sexual danger in the Norwegian child welfare discourse. However, child welfare has far less power over incestuous adult men than over young girls. It can neither remove the men from their families nor can it institutionalize them, as it can, and does, with girls. Power is also gendered.

The rhetoric of social defense against dangerous female sexuality has receded in favor of the rhetoric of protection. This does not apply only to victims of incest. Sexuality is a central concern in relation to young girls even today. The sexual behavior of girls and boys is still measured by different yardsticks. A young girl who is more sexually active than average may be regarded with worry, and child welfare may be called upon to protect her from being sexually exploited. The wish to protect girls from sexual exploitation may be justified. It is, however, problematic when control efforts are focused solely on girls, while the sexual behavior of boys is not made an issue. Despite the change in perspective and rhetoric, in practice, a "problem sexuality" still resides in girls, even if now they are framed as more in need of protection than punishment.

Notes

1. See Smith 1978; Jonsson 1980; Figueira-McDonough 1987; Kersten 1989; Hennum 1993.
2. See also Agustín, this volume.

CHAPTER 9

Sexual Abuse Victims and the Wholesome Family:
Feminist, Psychological, and State Discourses

KERWIN KAYE[1]

The first U.S. federal acknowledgement that sexual abuse occurred within the family came in 1974 with the passage of the Child Abuse Prevention and Treatment Act (CAPTA 1974). Official recognition for victims marked a major break with earlier psychological discourses that emphasized the culpability of sexually abused children. Notably, this legislative change occurred only after feminist activism had drawn significant public attention to the topic. Indeed, the initial version of CAPTA focused entirely upon the physical abuse of children and did not include sexual abuse within its purview; lawmakers added sexual abuse to the bill as something of an afterthought (Nelson 1984). A dramatic rise in reports of sexual abuse soon followed the passage of CAPTA, surprising both lawmakers and the child protection agencies who were required by the legislation to investigate each claim.[2] The adoption of CAPTA and the resulting rise in reported cases of sexual abuse gave feminists a degree of state legitimation as they struggled to reveal the pervasive and painful nature of sexual victimization within the family. In some cases, feminist ties with the state were direct, as many of the early feminist writers and activists held positions within the rapidly expanding child protection agencies. These positions placed them in contact with many sexual abuse cases and also conferred something of an expert status upon them. Although feminist activists certainly did not receive

143

federal funding in support of their work, the feminist victory in securing state recognition established a context of relatively strong ambient support for their ideas.

Nevertheless, feminist perspectives on sexual abuse remained marginal within both state discourse concerning abuse and within the overall field of psychology. Although feminist activism gained state recognition of sexual abuse and was also successful in pushing psychology toward acknowledging and addressing the issue, neither the state nor clinical psychology became decidedly feminist as a result. Within the dominant streams of psychology, for example, analysis of male power within the family is generally infrequent and poorly elaborated, and critical analysis of societal reactions to survivors (including their treatment within the legal system) is virtually nonexistent. Although a number of important exceptions exist within the field, clinical psychology typically pays little attention to the connections between what survivors of sexual abuse experience and the social structures that both facilitate the abuse and shape survivors' postabuse experiences.[3] Instead, the individualizing approaches favored within the dominant trends of clinical psychology work to divide survivors' experience of sexual victimization from broader questions of power and sexuality. Psychological authorities advise survivors that they are not alone in their suffering, yet the therapeutic community that survivors are invited to participate in generally focuses upon interpersonal support, not political challenge (Armstrong 1994).

Furthermore, clinical psychology's apparent lack of engagement with the sociopolitical realm conceals a politically conservative project that reinforces the privileged status of nuclear families. By focusing upon the presumed deviance of survivors, psychological accounts move to contain public narrations of abuse within a framework that does not threaten the prevailing idea of family "wholesomeness." Survivors of abuse are thus encouraged to return to the same familial configurations that produced their initial maltreatment, neatly curtailing the radical potential for actual political and structural change generated by a shared recognition of collective suffering.

This chapter provides a critical genealogical assessment of the portrayal of incestuous abuse through the lenses of four competing discourses: prefeminist narratives, early second-wave feminism, postfeminist psychology, and finally contemporary state discourse as represented in U.S. Supreme Court rulings. I begin with a brief discussion of the prefeminist narrative of child sexual abuse as a "Lolita" fable. Feminists in the 1970s attempted, with some success, to undermine this narrative and to reconstitute child sexual abuse as a political problem of male dominance and of the subjugation of women within patriarchal families. Postfeminist psychology largely accepted feminist critiques of the seductive child, but within an apolitical framework that focused upon individual deviance rather than systemic power imbalances, and which furthermore presented sexual abuse as something to cure in the individual. Last, I examine the concerns of the state as represented in the language from various twentieth-century Supreme Court rulings that have shaped the regulation of sexual abuse within the family. I argue that the relationships among dominant discourses within psychology and the policy-making level of the state serve to reform but defend the "wholesomeness" of the male-dominated nuclear family, ensuring its long-term survival in the face of a crisis caused by the rebellion of those oppressed within its structures.

Mirroring the contemporary literature on sexual abuse, this chapter focuses upon the portrayal of sexual abuse victims, and like the literature, it therefore concentrates more upon female than male survivors.[4] Arguably, it is this very fixation upon survivors that is most problematic: The psychological state of victims is pathologized and regulated while the emotional and relational patterns of offenders are normalized and subject to significantly less scrutiny (McKinnon 1995, 32). Yet by investigating the relationship between trends in the representation of sexual abuse victims, it becomes possible to discern differing political projects implicit within the distinct formulations of feminists, psychologists, and policy makers. This task is particularly necessary in relation to psychological and state discourses, where apparent and overt support for victims masks gender and familial ideologies that disempower victims and others who might be at risk of abuse. Yet feminist activism should not limit itself to discursive objectives. This chapter therefore concludes with some brief suggestions for the creation of familial structures that would mitigate against abuse by empowering the people within them.

Historical Definitions: The "Seductive" Child

A number of conceptions regarding the specific harms of incest emerged in the early twentieth century. These proposals typically revolved around a set of concerns that had little to do with potential injury to the child. Hegemonic discourses regularly treated children as active instigators rather than as victims whose suffering lay at the center of concern. For example, during English parliamentary debates in 1908, proponents of the Punishment of Incest Act focused on the possibility that a deformed or illegitimate offspring would result from such a union, or the danger that a sexualized parent-child bond would foster rivalries within the family.[5] This formulation essentially treated incest as a form of adultery, and situated sexual abuse survivors in terms of the danger they posed for the reproductive success and emotional stability of the "normal" family unit. Abuse victims were identified as willing partners, sexual deviants who needed to be controlled.

Although a feminist campaign against carnal abuse within the family occurred from the 1870s to 1930s, it had little success in changing this aspect of the public debate (Gordon 1989; Hooper 1992). Some lawmakers did align themselves with the feminist campaign against sexual abuse, speaking in favor of guarding children (especially girls) from emotional suffering, but even this objective was frequently framed in relation to "the strengthening of the fabric of the family" (Bell 1993, 136), rather than in terms of promoting the well-being of children. In sharp contrast to present-day representations, comments regarding children's suffering were notably brief, and little elaboration was offered as to the nature of the pain these children might experience. The voice of victims was, in fact, nowhere present in these early debates.

The view within medical psychiatry and clinical psychology reinforced these themes. Freud's famous revision concerning sexual abuse—in which he first proposed that women developed psychological disorders as a result of "sexual shock" from a caretaker's "seduction" (1896, quoted in Ward 1985, 104–6; see also Rush 1980, 87–8), and then later argued that women's Oedipal desires caused them to imagine that they were seduced (1900, quoted in Ward 1985, 110–14; see also Rush 1980, 93–6; Masson 1984)—undermined abuse victims' credibility. In this context, Bender and Blau's 1937 comment, which would be favorably cited in the professional literature for the next 35 years, is not surprising:

> [F]requently we considered the possibility that the child might have been the actual seducer rather than the one innocently seduced. . . . The experience offers an opportunity for the child to test out in reality, an infantile fantasy; it [sic] probably finds the consequences less severe, and in fact actually gratifying to a pleasure sense. The emotional balance is thus in favor of contentment. (quoted in Ward 1985, 90)

From Freud until the feminist challenge of the 1970s, psychological wisdom generally focused upon the presumed "closeness of the external event to the unconscious fantasy" (Lewis and Sarrel 1969, 618, quoted in Ward 1985, 146). Like state narratives, psychology of the mid-twentieth century portrayed the survivor of sexual abuse as an oversexed and delinquent "Lolita" who actively (though perhaps unconsciously) seduced her abuser. At the same time, psychologists followed Freud in claiming that actual (as opposed to imagined) seduction was not a very common occurrence, perhaps "one in a million" (Weinberg 1955, quoted in Gordon 1988, 60), an opinion cited as recently as 1975 (by Freedman et al. 1975, quoted in Russell 1986, 388).[6]

By the time second-wave feminists began to seriously engage with the issue, the movement for sexual liberation had inspired a few psychologists to take this line of thinking toward its logical conclusion. This minority forged a "pro-incest" position, one which argued that incest could be "educative" for children and encouraged "mild forms of sex play" between parents and children

(Constantine and Constantine 1973).[7] The second-wave feminist identification of incest as sexual abuse arose within and against this social environment.

Second-Wave Feminism: Establishing Incest as Abuse

Second-wave feminists were forced to counter prior portrayals of children as seducers in their attempt to establish that incest was a form of abuse. Significantly, feminist discussion concerning childhood sexual abuse began within the movement opposing sexual assault. Feminist women began speaking out publicly against rape, and the attitudes and silences that serve to perpetuate it, in the mid- to late-1960s. By the mid-1970s, the sexual abuse of girls was increasingly mentioned within these speakouts as an all-too-common aspect of women's overall sexual victimization (Rush 1974; Dinsmore 1991, 13; Jenkins, 1998, 125–8). The historical emergence of incest as a topic within the broader context of sexual assault definitively shaped the feminist challenge to psychological and state orthodoxies.

Feminist analysis of sexual assault challenged a legitimizing ideology similar to that found within the incest literature. The dominant ideology concerning rape presumed that if a woman was not entirely chaste, she must be a "whore" who wanted sex at all times and therefore could not be violated.[8] For example, in one instance, a prominent lawyer began a rape trial by spinning a bottle and showing the jury how difficult it was to insert a pencil into this "resisting" orifice, thereby suggesting that the woman had consented to the assault (Margolin 1972, quoted in Donat and D'Emilio 1998). Thus, in cases of stranger rape, as in cases of incestuous abuse, the fact of the sexual assault might itself be used as evidence against the woman's character, with the mere accomplishment of the sexual act placing the woman into the whore category (Herman 1981, 187; Ward 1985, 159). To counter this virgin/whore dichotomy, feminists emphasized the intensely unwanted and traumatic nature of rape, establishing that the event was not pleasurably sexual for the victim, and instead linking it to other types of aggressive attack through such terms as "sexual violence" and "sexual assault."

The parallels between stranger rape and incestuous abuse—the fact that men are overwhelmingly the perpetrators and the justification that the victims "wanted the sex"—lead early second-wave feminists to emphasize the similarities between the events, or even to subsume one within the other. Incest became a form of rape, as in Susan Brownmiller's early discussion of "father rape" (1975, 271–82). The resultant terminology effectively precluded victim-blaming, as in Butler's comment that "[A]ggressors . . . sexually assault their own children" (1978, 10). Such a claim would have been difficult to make within the seduction-oriented terminology that was provided by the prior experts on incest.

While clarifying questions of force and coercion, the process of renaming linked the experience of child incest victims with adults who were assaulted by strangers in less interpersonally and psychodynamically complex situations. Brownmiller's phrase "father rape," for example, is revealing on this point in that the word "father" is an adjective, suggesting that the unmodified term "rape" retained its primary meaning in relation to rape from a stranger. The phrase thereby placed the abuse of children within a category that emphasized a vastly different set of circumstances. Elizabeth Ward likewise titled her book *Father-Daughter Rape* and argued, "I believe that the sexual use of a child's body/being is the same as the phenomenon of adult rape. Terms like 'sexual abuse,' 'molestation' and 'interference' are diminuations of 'rape': They imply that something *less* than rape occurred" (emphasis in original 1985, 79). The definitional inclusion of sexual abuse as a form of rape redefined the notion of what constituted sexual assault in relation to a broader set of circumstances, yet it also utilized the earlier meanings associated with stranger rape to politically situate the child as an unwilling victim rather than addressing the possibility of any form of collusion (with all of the additional forms of suffering, confusion, and guilt that such collusion typically brings). Although feminists at times acknowledged differences between "stranger rape" and "father rape" (e.g., Ward 1985, 99–100), the need to proclaim the child's status as victim generally took precedence over these considerations in labeling and framing the experience of sexual abuse.[9]

Framing the issue of incestuous abuse in relation to stranger rape could make it difficult to fully incorporate the experiences of abused children. Feminists often discounted questions of children's agency within abusive situations, specifically undertheorizing the surface-level participation of some victims in order to counter prior victim-blaming interpretations. As more recent feminist examinations have shown, victims display a variety of means of resistance or accommodation in abusive situations. For example, in some instances, a victim may actively initiate specific sexual episodes, particularly once a pattern has been established (Wilson 1993, 93–4, 103–8; see also Scott 1988, 96). Other victims may begin to use sex "as a bargaining point in order to obtain the rewards of 'affection,' 'the right to stay up late,' or 'a bit more freedom'" (Kitzinger 1997, 172). In these cases, the abusive dynamic offers victims some small modicum of power within the family (Herman and Hirschman 1977, 748). Still other victims may allow themselves to get caught up in whatever sexual pleasure is available as a means to avoid unpleasant emotional feelings (Dinsmore 1991, 25). Although most contemporary perspectives would nevertheless emphasize the facts of parental/adult power and responsibility (see Finkelhor 1979; Russell 1984, 266–8), during the early 1970s, ruminations upon such possibilities ran the risk of being taken as admissions of culpability.

Rather than focusing on the significance of a child's potential pleasure or desire (whether affectional, sensual, or sexual), early second-wave feminists tended to emphasize the unequivocally oppositional or "unknowing" state of the victims in order to avoid enabling others in more hegemonic positions to claim that children offered "consent." Elizabeth Ward, for example, speaks only of the "powerlessness (which is read as passivity) of the girl victims" (1985, 99). She similarly identifies any potential pleasure as a "likely genital reaction" deriving from a "mind-split" (152), a formulation that carefully avoids the suggestion that the child's subjectivity might in some way be engaged. Ward's conclusion—that "Passivity (being coerced) can thus co-exist with the experience of pleasure" (153)—crucially depends upon the elimination of all subjective elements of pleasure within the context of abuse.

Sandra Butler's solo work similarly discounts the possibility of conscious involvement on the part of victims, though her framework grants that there might be some abusive situations in which a child more actively participates. Butler's reasoning focuses upon the sexual knowledge of the child:

> [A] child . . . is unable to alter or understand the adult's behavior because of his or her powerlessness in the family and early stage of psychological development. This type of incest is nonconsensual because the child has not yet developed an understanding of sexuality that allows him or her to make a free and fully conscious response to the adult's behavior. (1978, 4–5)

Butler's focus upon a presumed lack of sexual knowledge does not require that victims find abusive sexual interchange entirely repulsive. It is supplemented, however, by an understanding in which a victim's potentially positive (or conflicted) feelings can exist only in relation to a "child's inability to make or understand sexual decisions" (1978, 30). However true this might be in any given case, the act of requiring a victim's ignorance in order to define the event as "abuse" effectively repudiates the possibility that a girl might "knowingly" participate in her abuse in any manner, and thus limits possible subjectivities that a victim might claim while still maintaining a guiltless status.

There were, however, ruptures within this theoretical narrative, particularly within the first-person accounts that actually constituted the greater part of many texts (Armstrong 1978; Butler 1978; Brady 1979; and to a lesser extent, Ward 1985). Attention to the victims' perspectives was needed to counter the claim that incest was "relatively harmless" (as per Bender and Blau, above), and to act "as a political tool for giving voice to women's real experiences" of incest over and against the prior silencing myths (Armstrong 1994, 24). Questions of childhood agency were frequently raised in much more direct ways within these first-person accounts than within the feminist theory that surrounded and contextualized them. Although many of the survivors told of situations that indeed fit the framework of forced and thoroughly unwanted sex, others described situations involving various forms of abuser deception, manipulation, or emotional bribery that in one way or another coerced cooperation from the victims.

Stories from those who experienced some degree of pleasure or desire within the abuse were, in fact, not deeply hidden within the feminist texts. In the first few pages of her book, for example, Elizabeth Ward quotes extensively from a woman who felt affection toward her abusing father, and who additionally reports sometimes enjoying the sex. Nor are these facts insignificant details within this victim's account, as it was the presence of physical pleasure that gave cause for a deeply discrediting perception of self: "I did start to come, I did have orgasms. I remember now, I did start to come because that's where the guilt came from: I started to look forward to it" (Ward 1985, 10). Significantly, it was precisely this woman's subjective pleasure and sense of agency, the very elements that the early theoretical frameworks attempted to elide, that generated the most internal conflict:

> The conflict was knowing it was wrong, knowing he was my father . . .
> and at the same time, enjoying sex. And knowing that he'd love me if I
> did this. I felt guilt for a long time. I can now accept that it *was* rape . . .
> but I still can't help feeling that I'm responsible . . . why didn't I get out,
> otherwise? And because I enjoyed it sometimes. (ellipses and emphasis
> in original, Ward 1985, 13)

The ambivalence this girl felt complicated her relationship with her father, making her sense of unease that much more difficult to resolve. Having a sense of agency in the situation felt deeply implicating, despite a recognition that she ultimately did not have power in the situation ("it was rape").

Although the denial of children's agency may have been a political necessity, it made it difficult to theorize the relationship between a child's ability to act (however narrowly exercised) and the nature and impact of the abuse. Ward's analysis, for example, leads her to misidentify the sources of shame that some victims experience. She argues that "The Daughters, in expressing shame, are speaking of *what has been done to them*. They are speaking of humiliation, of powerlessness. They are speaking of the effect of having a Father use and abuse their very bodies against their will" (emphasis in original, 1985, 151). This formulation holds well when considering some of the stories that Ward presents, cases in which the sex was thoroughly unwanted, but it ignores situations in which the shame results from a sense of (limited) power and chosen (although coerced) involvement in the situation. Because feminist theoretical frameworks created space for guiltlessness only in relation to a victim's undiscerning agreement or simple acquiescence to power, it left crucial aspects of the victim-blaming paradigm untouched. The possibility of a child's conscious complicity was simply repudiated at a theoretical level, rather than acknowledged and addressed. The stance implicitly forced survivors who had lived through such situations to either deny their experience of agency or to internalize an unaddressed (and, most probably, intense) sense of self-blame.

Not all early second-wave feminists relied upon analyses that displayed this shortcoming. Feminist psychiatrist Judith Herman developed a framework that more completely emphasized the overwhelming power parents have over their children, a formulation that enables her to more fully examine the occasional participation of survivors. Herman argues:

> Because a child is powerless in relation to an adult, she is not free to refuse a sexual advance. Therefore, any sexual relationship between the two must necessarily take on some of the coercive characteristics of a rape, even if, as is usually the case, the adult uses positive enticements rather than force to establish the relationship. This is particularly true of incest between a parent and child: it is a rape in the sense that it is a coerced sexual relationship. The question of whether force is involved is largely irrelevant, since force is rarely necessary to obtain compliance. The parent's authority over the child is usually sufficient to compel obedience. Similarly, the question of a child's "consent" is irrelevant. Because the child does not have the power to withhold consent, she does not have the power to grant it. (Herman 1981, 27; see also Finkelhor 1979)

By emphasizing the overwhelming coercive power of the family environment, Herman is able to address abusive situations that extend beyond directly coerced sex, to include the possibility of a victim's more active awareness and sexual participation.[10]

But although Herman's emphasis on structural inequality offers possibilities for the recognition of divergent survivor subjectivities, it still does not permit those survivors who participated in their abuse to fully acknowledge their own experience. Herman's text informs victims that they are not to blame, yet they are not given a means with which to deal with their own potential ambivalences, to take credit (or responsibility) for any real choices they have made. The need to resituate blame onto the offender again appears through the assertion that children should not be seen as participating in acts that are fundamentally coercive, yet little attempt is made to grapple with the subjective engagements that can arise within such situations. Through this reactive process, the previous portrayal of incest survivors as seductresses (and of rape victims as sluts) continued to shape the portrayal of survivors, leading early feminists away from examining a full range of survivor subjectivities.

A contrast with a more contemporary feminist analysis of sexual abuse is instructive. Feminist psychologist Sharon Lamb, for example, comments provocatively upon the relationship between perceived agency and self-blame that many victims experience:

> [S]elf-blame sometimes is healing, and in some part appropriate . . . Victims' sense of overresponsibility, though sometimes harmful and other times pathological, should not be dismissed. At its core are real moments of responsibility, times when they made poor choices, foolish decisions. Almost every victim, except those of the most horrendous crimes, will speak of these moments. It is crucial in working with victims to tease out the accurate level of responsibility. (1996, 179–80)

Lamb notes the importance of careful reflection upon the numerous social constraints that frequently present victims with "choiceless choices" within their families (1996, 37). Nevertheless, Lamb emphasizes that victims do indeed make decisions, a perspective that allows survivors to more deeply assess the meaning of their own actions and possible involvement. Although this type of self-examination is indeed challenging, it continues to undercut the unrestricted sense of responsibility generated within the victim-blaming framework. Indeed, Lamb's formulation rests upon the assumption that a victim is basically not to blame for any abuse: Abusers are fully responsible for their own actions, whatever decisions a victim might make.

Lamb's intervention is important, however, because it challenges other difficulties that are latent within Herman's analysis that focuses upon the coercive capacity of adults (Herman 1981). Although it is an important corrective, it nevertheless simplified analyses of family dynamics by claiming that children have no power whatsoever. Herman's framework is thus compatible with other formulations that conceive of childhood as being entirely free from the stain of sex, formulations that naturalize children's "innocent" lack of power and circumvent any recognition of the socially mediated inequities that exist within male-female and adult-child relations. Although we must continue to emphasize establishing adult (male) blame for abuse, we must not ignore a victim's control, however partial, over her or his own behavior. As will be seen, many clinical psychologists have adopted this seemingly more flexible definition of sexual abuse in a manner that pushes the analysis toward a simplistic (and falsely apolitical) focus upon "age appropriateness" and "sexual innocence," and away from questions of power and coercion.

Early second-wave feminist texts clearly work against any sort of apolitical focus upon children. Typical is Rush, who speaks of abuse survivors as "victims of the family structure, they are also victims of the utter dependency of children—economically, physically, socially, legally, and of the violent nexus between power and sex, the instrument of rape, by which women and girl-children are controlled in a male supremacist society" (1984, 95). Far from idealizing the male-dominated nuclear family, feminists tended toward the view that "incest is integral to 'normal family life'" and that the family "is in fact one of the most dangerous places female children (and women) can be" (Anonymous 1985). Yet despite a universal emphasis on political critique within the texts, the pictorial representations on the covers of the early books frequently reflected a contrary preoccupation with themes of childlike innocence and familial bliss (see Figure 9-1). Publishers, who presumably chose the images, apparently thought it easier to market an image of "ruptured domestic bliss" than to develop a cover that reflected the actual analysis within the books: that abuse resulted from the very form of normative (i.e., male-dominant) domesticity idealized on the book cover.

Although the texts identified the isolated, male-dominated family as a primary source of danger for children, especially girls, the cover art promoted a

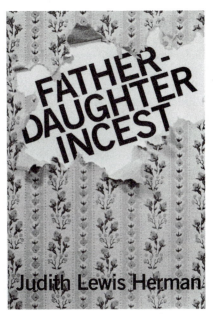

Figure 9-1 Book covers from two early feminist texts on the sexual abuse of children (Rush 1980; Herman 1981). Rush's cover features a haphazardly abandoned teddy bear (perhaps suggesting that the victim had been playing with the stuffed animal immediately prior to the abuse, which occurs off-camera). On Herman's book, the words "Father-Daughter Incest" violently tear apart picturesque wallpaper that seems to invoke conventional idealized notions of domesticity. These photos achieve impact through their disruption to notions of familial bliss (Kitzinger similarly examined book covers for these themes, 1997).

view that idealized childhood as being properly nested within a protective (and implicitly patriarchal) family.

Ethical claims emphasizing the improper violation of a virginal sphere, and hence deemphasizing imbalanced power relations between victims and abusers, are, not surprisingly, rare within the early feminist writings. An atypical comment by Butler to the effect that "The most devastating result of the imposition of adult sexuality upon a child unable to determine the appropriateness of his or her response is *the irretrievable loss of the child's inviolability* and trust in the adults in his or her life" (emphasis added, 1978, 5) is, in fact, an anomaly within the literature. What the early second-wave feminist framings share with later psychological accounts, however, is an analysis that denies the relevance of a survivor's agency. Although this emphasis is useful in establishing adult (male) blame for the abuse, it tends to ignore a victim's control, however limited and partial, over her or his own behavior. Denying the relevance of children's ability to act within abusive situations, even in limited ways, enabled latter commentators to claim a feminist stance while covertly inserting more familialist discourses into their accounts. These new discourses similarly denied the possibility of childhood agency, but did so in a way that reified patriarchal power, as will be seen below.

Clinical Psychology: "Innocence Lost" as Sexual Stain

With the advent of state funding, child protection agencies were given a primary role in defining the issue of sexual abuse and the needs of victims. Earlier psychoanalytic interpretations were rapidly pushed aside in favor of feminist-influenced frameworks that acknowledged the frequent occurrence and generally traumatic effects of sexual abuse. Although the notion of child victimization was incorporated into the literature, however, other feminist insights regarding the determining influence of male power were pushed aside. Most clinicians instead began to search for the causes of incestuous abuse in "dysfunctional family dynamics." By spreading the focus upon the entire family dynamic, this family-systems approach tended to redirect therapeutic attention away from the male perpetrator and toward the "collusive" mother, whose sexual and emotional distance was often said to "cause" the husband to seek out sexual comfort in his daughter (or son). The child victim also received a good deal of blame within these approaches as earlier Freudian-inspired theories of Oedipal seductiveness continued to hold sway (Armstrong 1990, 1994; McKinnon 1995). At present, ongoing feminist criticism has lead the majority of psychologists to distance themselves from the most egregious types of victim and mother blaming, and they have increasingly acknowledged and emphasized the male perpetrator's responsibility for his own behavior (see Sturkie 1986). Nevertheless, the majority of clinical approaches remain committed to a search for "dysfunctional behavior." By arguing that sexual abuse results from faulty interpersonal dynamics, psychological discourse individualizes the problem, effectively ignoring the propensity for abuse that lies within conventional (i.e., male-dominant) family forms.

The impact this political allegiance has on the representation of victims is significant. Even when psychologists adopt a feminist perspective regarding the blamelessness of children (and mothers), they frequently do not frame the violation in terms of sexual coercion. Whereas earlier feminists had portrayed sexual abuse survivors as victims of a male power structure, clinical psychologists more frequently portray survivors in relation to the "betrayal of trust" experienced when an adult caretaker abuses a victim. Without denying that a child may indeed experience a tremendous sense of betrayal when a parent mistreats her or him, it is important to note the manner in which this framework highlights a violation of parental norms—norms that remain nonproblematic—rather than repudiating abuse as a not-too-surprising outcome of excessive parental (and especially paternal) power. The power of men within families is thus subjected to critique only in its "abusive" manifestations, while its day-to-day workings are rendered invisible.

For example, Summit speaks of the "betrayal . . . by someone who is ordinarily idealized as a protective, altruistic, loving, parental figure," without specifying that the social source for this idealized image lies in hetero- and family-normative culture (1983, 184). Similarly, he suggests that a child idealizes her parents because to do otherwise "is tantamount to abandonment and annihilation" (1983, 184), a formulation that fails to examine the social sources of juvenile dependency: the relative isolation of children within nuclear families, the lack of economic and social options for runaway children, and the existence of cultural and legal systems that identify children as parental property. The possibility for less stratified power relations within the family is never raised, effectively naturalizing parental (and paternal) power. A primary focus upon the "betrayal" of children stands in implicit contrast to modernist images of domestic bliss, a vision that is heavily gendered in favor of male power. Disapproval of abusive fathers here focuses upon their failure to uphold their role within the arrangement, rather than upon the failings of the arrangement itself.

The other source of trauma frequently identified within the clinical literature is the presumed loss of "childhood innocence" that occurs with the abuse. With titles such as Betrayal of Innocence (Forward and Buck 1981), "Shattered Innocence" (Kohn 1987), The Right to Innocence (Engel 1991), Innocence Destroyed (Renovoize 1993), Shattered Innocence (Weiner and Kurpius 1995), and Stolen Innocence (Toldson 1997), many clinical psychologists took what existed as an aberrant concept within the feminist literature and developed it into a primary axis of concentration. Though the issue of coercion is sometimes mentioned in these clinical texts, the primary source of trauma is often identified as "an abnormal event interrupting the normal development process" (Berliner and Stevens 1982), "an intrusion into presexual person-hood" (Hancock and Mains 1987, 32), or being "prematurely introduced to sexuality" (Sgroi 1982, 114). Within much of the clinical literature, the emphasis shifts decidedly toward themes of lost childhood innocence, invoking images of formerly "pure" victims whose loss is permanent and total. Emphasizing the inappropriateness of sex beneath a certain age again removes the focus on coercion, this time placing it on the idea of "underage sex." Sexual abuse is here framed as a genderless imposition by an individually deviant adult (who just happens to more frequently be male) upon a child (who just happens to more frequently be female).

Although the image of asexual innocence seems to support the blameless status of children, in practice it continues to stigmatize those children who do not appear to be "pure." This is a key point, as many children who are sexually abused gain early sexual knowledge and act in sexual ways that are not deemed appropriate by the virginal standards of innocence. As noted by feminist sociologist Jenny Kitzinger, the imagery of childhood innocence can thereby cause great harm to the survivors of sexual abuse. Kitzinger writes:

> [I]nnocence is a double-edged sword in the fight against sexual abuse because it stigmatizes the "knowing" child. The romanticization of childhood innocence excludes those who do not conform to the ideal . . . This penalizes the child who sexually responds to the abuse or who appears flirtatious and sexually aware. (1997, 168; see also Kitzinger 1988; Alcoff 1996, 130–1; Kincaid 1998)

The notion of childhood innocence thus functions in a way that closely parallels cultural ideals of female virginity. Within this frame, the no-longer-virginal child becomes "damaged goods" and no longer merits the limited protections offered by claims of innocence. As Kitzinger notes, "If the violation of innocence is the criterion against which the act of sexual abuse is judged, then violating a 'knowing' child becomes a lesser offense than violating an 'innocent' child. . . . Indeed, a child who is known to be a victim of sexual abuse is often a target of further exploitation" (1997, 168–9).[11]

The notion of sexual abuse as "lost innocence" finds further expression in the idea that victims necessarily share common characteristics, exhibiting what has been called a "sexual abuse syndrome" (Summit 1983). The idea that all abuse is in some sense "the same" decontextualizes the events from their distinctive social environment and encourages an approach that does not examine the particularities of an individual's experience. Within this unitary definitional structure, sexual abuse is seen as a form of sexual staining, one that leaves its victims unable to achieve a normative heterosexuality. The phrase "sexual abuse victim" here ceases to be a descriptive categorical grouping and instead takes on qualities of a diagnostic term, one that purports to explain all manner of (sexual) deviance. Sexual abuse thus gains salience within a wide variety of sexual contexts, standing equally well as an explanation for prostitution, lesbianism, heterosexual "promiscuity," or abstinence. Holding these diverse outcomes together is a framework that identifies a sexual abuse survivor as someone who has been violated and thereby forever placed outside of the virginal, sexually innocent "norm." In contrast, although early feminist writers focused upon the overall structures of male dominance that generated abuse, they did not assume any uniformity of response from the victims. Far from generating a singular list of effects or "symptoms," early feminist works are characterized by the wide variety of situations and reactions that were presented (if not fully theorized).

The focus upon sexual abuse as a sexual offense, rather than as an abuse of power, is most noticeably seen in the way in which psychologists often devote a great deal of attention to the purported sexual deviance of abuse survivors. "In fact," suggest Herman and Hirschman in their early review, "failure to marry or promiscuity seems to be the only criterion generally accepted in the literature as conclusive evidence that the victim has been harmed" (1977, 739). While the contemporary research is more extensive and describes some emotional states that may well present difficulties for many survivors—confusion about sexual identity, negative reactions to sexual arousal and activity—implicit judgments are made in these discussions regarding the value of particular forms of sexual being and expression: "Confused" identities are not "healthy," nor are negative associations with sex. And as Herman and Hirschman noted, psychological writings frequently continue to problematize sexual "excess" at either end of the spectrum. Social patterns such as promiscuity or asexuality are thus rendered as symptoms in need of treatment, primarily because of their incompatibility with the conventional sexual and familial structures that the dominant forms of psychology assume to be necessary for personal fulfillment. Finkelhor and Browne, for example, list "promiscuity" and "prostitution," as well as "difficulty in arousal" and "avoidance of or phobic reactions to sexual intimacy" in their table of "Traumagenic Dynamics in the Impact of Child Sexual Abuse" (1986, 186). Presumably, an individual who slept with three different people in a week would be labeled "promiscuous," while an individual who slept with the same partner seven times during the same week would not. Similarly, a person who masturbates regularly may be reproached for "avoiding sexual intimacy," while a person who has infrequent sex with a partner is less likely to be so labeled. Thus, by pathologizing both abstinence and licentiousness, many psychologists covertly reinforce ideologies that sanction only normative, monogamous sexual relations. As Saunders argues in a slightly different context (this volume), aspects of a survivor's personality that are simply nonnormative—and that may in fact be highly adaptive—are understood through this process to be "tragic" results of abuse.

The implicit understanding that defines sexual abuse as a form of sexual staining and loss of innocence also reveals itself in the assumption that all sexual abuse victims are inescapably and permanently damaged. Totalizing comments to the effect that victims are filled with "magical expectations" (Sgroi 1982, 126), are "inwardly seething with anger and hostility" (Porter, et al. 1982), "have unusual and dysfunctional needs to control or dominate" (Finkelhor and Browne 1986, 193), or are inevitably "the dominant females" (James and Nasjleti 1983, 6) are common and establish survivors as deviants against whom normalcy can be measured. Similarly, universal declarations such as "[R]egardless of its form and the child's response, incest is a devastating experience and leaves a devastating mark on its victim" (Dinsmore 1991, 21), or blanket assertions to the effect that "Incest is a traumatic event that leaves its victims scarred into adulthood" (Lindberg and Distad 1985, 334) reinforce a sense that sexual abuse causes a stigma that irrevocably attaches itself to the victim. Lengthy lists detailing the "effects" of sexual abuse (for example, Hall and Lloyd 1993, 67; Finkelhor and Browne 1986, 186–7) likewise frame sexual abuse victims as necessarily having problems that need to be resolved. This focus upon deviance establishes sexual abuse survivors as separate Others; they are in some sense "damaged goods" whose worth has been decreased by the fact of having been assaulted (Haaken 1998, 77; McKinnon 1995; Kitzinger 1997, 168–9). The therapeutic treatment of sexual abuse can thus become another means of policing the sexual behavior of survivors (a process that can extend into institutionalization, as seen in some of the instances presented by Ericcson; this volume).

Admittedly, victims of abuse may at times be attracted toward labels of psychological disease precisely because they postulate survivor deviance. Pathological designations offer a targeted, unitary explanation for all social suffering as well as an implicit promise to ease the distress once the problem is diagnosed. "Healing from the abuse" becomes the goal within this work, but it is important to examine the kind of social world that is being theorized in such formulations. As noted previously, clinical psychology frequently operates under an assumption that the effects of the "dysfunctional" past must be exorcised for the survivor to properly adjust to an implicitly "functional" present. Adult survivors must therefore perform a tremendous amount of emotional labor in order to successfully enact the very sexual and relational scripts that caused their initial suffering. Survivors are deemed "well-adjusted" precisely to the extent that their behavior conforms to models that take no account of their experiences.

Christine Dinsmore's integration of feminist principles within her therapeutic work leads to an alternate approach. Within her perspective, suffering is not automatically positioned as something to be overcome or "worked through." Her model instead suggests that some of the lessons learned through coping with abuse may be useful, although others may not:

> In my work with incest survivors, we examine survival behaviors and attempt to determine which of these skills, if any, may in fact still be useful. . . . In other words, we do not assume that all survival skills acquired as a result of an abusive childhood are debilitating and need to be eradicated. Just as children need to learn skills to survive their childhoods, women need to learn to survive the patriarchy. (1991, 24; see also Hall and Lloyd 1993, 92–3)

Rather than narrowly scrutinizing the disposition and behavior of survivors for evidence of "dysfunctional" behavior, suffering becomes an investigatory tool that might be used to shed light on normative social practices. The perceptions and practices of survivors become potentially visionary tools forged in opposition to abusive patterns that have deep social roots.

As these comments suggest, challenging the presumed deviance of sexual abuse victims requires reexamining the presumed normalcy of society. Such an investigation must necessarily situate abuse within a larger social and political context, and examine the ways in which sexual abuse is structured into the most commonplace and mundane patterns of male dominance. This approach therefore questions the very salience of the survivor/nonsurvivor distinction, invoking the categories in a much more qualified and contingent sense, rather than automatically assuming complete dissimilarity between victims and "nonvictims." The category "sexual abuse survivor" instead becomes useful to invoke at some times (when emphasizing patterns unique to families in which coercive sexualities are enacted) and useful to deconstruct at others (when highlighting the diversity of abusive situations, or when emphasizing the commonalties between abusive situations and other sexist patterns that are generally taken for granted).

To be clear, nothing within my analysis is intended as a commentary upon the efficacy of counseling for particular individuals. While clinical psychology tends to presume that the power differentials between women and men arise out of localized interpersonal dynamics—thereby ignoring the impact of systemic, societywide oppressions upon families—it is of course true that many sexual abuse victims benefit from counseling, including the most individualized and depoliticized variants. For some survivors, therapy may provide them their only opportunity to speak about their experiences, an opportunity to reformulate their history in an environment where it is strongly emphasized that they are not to blame for their victimization. For others, the widespread encouragement psychology offers for setting boundaries and for identifying and pursuing one's desires may prove extremely beneficial, even life-altering, offering a much-needed challenge to the effects of gender, sexual, and antichild oppression manifested in both the abuse and in the broader society. By supporting a model of behavior in which individuals are encouraged to identify and pursue their own interests, clinical psychology can help to undermine certain elements of status-based hierarchical arrangements (male over female, adult over child) that have proven dangerous for victims, even as it works to support other aspects of these hierarchies (the nuclear family).

Sexual Abuse and the State

With the passage of CAPTA in 1974, the federal government threatened to significantly cut funding for human services to any state that did not possess a mandatory reporting law, essentially forcing states to adopt such legislation. CAPTA similarly required the states to investigate these reports and to protect children who were deemed to be living in abusive situations. As documented in Barbara Nelson's historical study, Making an Issue of Child Abuse (1984), the inclusion of sexual abuse within CAPTA resulted most immediately from last-minute lobbying pressure from child welfare agencies that pushed for a more inclusive definition of child abuse.[12] As noted previously, none of the legislative actors who initiated and passed CAPTA expected the tremendously large number of reports that would rapidly follow. Far from being a legislative priority, lawmakers essentially stumbled into a situation in which much more governmental activity concerning sexual abuse (and child abuse more generally) was generated than was ever expected. Notably, these augmented levels of state intervention have not been welcome among all quarters. CAPTA itself was nearly allowed to expire at the beginning of the Reagan presidency in 1982. Instead, funds to child welfare agencies, along with nearly all other health and human service agencies, were cut by 30 percent (Krugman 1997).

The tentative status of sexual abuse as a state concern can be seen in other ways as well. U.S. Supreme Court rulings with precedents extending to the 1920s have consistently ruled in favor of the relatively unrestricted rights of parents to control their children. As the court itself noted in a 1979 decision, "Our jurisprudence historically has reflected Western civilization concepts of the family as a unit with broad parental authority over minor children" (*Parham v. J.R.* 1979). These rulings were reaffirmed as recently as 2000 in *Troxel v. Granville*, in which the Court ruled "the interests of parents in the care, custody, and control of their children . . . is perhaps the oldest of the fundamental liberties recognized by this court." This history of legal precedent strongly supports "the sanctity of a man's home and the privacies of life" (*Boyd v. United States* 1886) and establishes a "private realm of family life which the state cannot enter" (*Prince v. Massachusetts* 1944).

This right to familial privacy is not absolute. U.S. law recognizes the state's power to interfere with parents' control over their children, "particularly where the children need to be protected from their own parents" (Croft 1997). However, the history of legal support for the "privacy" of family life raises the legal standards for state intervention in cases of abuse, significantly attenuating the state's willingness to intercede on behalf of children. The primacy of the family reveals itself through the disparity with which the state treats incestuous sexual abuse and nonfamilial sexual abuse: Incestuous offenders are generally dealt with by social service agencies or in civic court, although nonfamilial offenders are handled through the criminal justice system (Fisher 1998; see also Armstrong 1994). Indeed, child victims are frequently left in the custody of their abusers, placing them in further danger (Berliner 1993). Legislators have also proven willing to back down to minimally organized pressure from those seeking to protect the familialist order, both in relation to those who claim that false memories of sexual abuse are regularly "implanted" by therapeutic suggestion and in relation to those who argue that sexual abuse accusations are frequently falsified during custody disputes (Armstrong 1994; Myers 1994).

At best, then, the state has shown contradictory tendencies in relation to sexual abuse. On the one hand, it has supported intervention into the family through mandatory reporting laws and funding for social service agencies, creating through this process a base of professionals who are generally committed to strong legislative action on these issues. On the other hand, the state has proven reluctant to extend its mandate too far into the realm of family life. As might be expected, the result of these tensions has been far heavier state intervention against poor families than among those who are better able to mobilize legal protections (Armstrong 1994). While the effects of this situation clearly offer victims many advantages over the previous judicial regime that failed to identify sexual abuse, it clearly does not represent a complete break with the patriarchal norms of the past. Within the context of a society that advantages men, the right to familial privacy most directly limits any "undue interference" men might otherwise encounter in controlling their families.

State discourse concerning sexual abuse survivors further reveals the interests at play in governance over families. Before considering state discourses more fully, however, it must first be acknowledged that in many ways the language of the state *is* the language of clinical psychology. Given that the state directly funds the work of many social workers, psychologists, and psychiatrists, and given the way in which these professionals frequently exercise legal authority in their role as child welfare advocates of various sorts, the dominant views within psychology must indeed be seen as a significant part of the state apparatus. Indeed, the hegemony of psychological perspectives in discussions of sexual abuse is in no small part due to this state support and the role of psychology within the state. All the same, it is interesting to note that in those relatively limited instances when policy makers are directly called upon to describe sexual abuse survivors, the portrayals typically invoke even more stigmatizing representations of victims than are present within most clinical psychological imagery. For example, in a 1982 case referring to the making of child pornography, the U.S. Supreme Court cited several psychiatric studies of victims of child pornography, and of familial sexual abuse more generally, concluding flatly that "sexually exploited children are unable to develop healthy, affectionate relationships in later life, have sexual dysfunction, and have a tendency to become sexual abusers as adults" (*New York v. Ferber* 1982). This definitive and overarching conclusion was reiterated in a declaration by the U.S. Congress in 1999 (HR 107 1999).

Examining the views of psychologists and those of most upper-level policy makers suggests further contrasts between the two groups. Not only do policy makers tend to hold opinions that stigmatize survivors to a greater degree, but they also situate the issue of sexual abuse within a set of concerns that are different from those that prevail within psychology. While clinicians tend to assume that normative familial arrangements are necessary for personal fulfillment, the U.S. Supreme Court has ruled that "the best interests of the child" do not constitute a sufficient reason for the state to intervene into the private life of the family (*Troxel v. Granville* 2000). Instead, the Court held that the sanctity of family life requires a higher standard be satisfied in authorizing state action—that of social reproduction. As the Court comments, "A democratic society rests, for its continuance, upon the healthy, well-rounded growth of young people into full maturity as citizens, with all that implies. It may secure this against impeding restraints and dangers, within a broad range of selection" (*Prince v. Massachusetts* 1944). As noted previously, the 1982 case of *New York v. Ferber* argued that sexual abuse threatens the ability of children to later develop "healthy, affectionate" relationships, to carry on a "functional" sex life rather than a "dysfunctional" one, and to not become abusive (and, presumably, thereby injure others' ability to carry out either of the former activities). It is thus the threat to the family, to "healthy, functional" relationships, that triggers state intervention, and not simply a threat to a victim's personal safety or well-being.

The social and physical perpetuation of society through the family unit has been at issue even since the 1908 Punishment of Incest Act in Great Britain, which showed a similar concern. There are, however, two important differences between the Victorian legislation and contemporary dialogues: (1) the discourse of concern has shifted from physical to social reproduction, and (2) the child is no longer viewed as a sexual competitor for the father's affection, and is instead seen as an innocent victim, someone whose sexual innocence defines the abhorrent nature of the crime. Although contemporary state discourse places more emphasis on the suffering of children, it does so only within the framework of promoting the well-being of "democratic society," for which familial and sexual "normalcy" are apparent prerequisites.[13]

By emphasizing the absolute deviance of survivors, the state justifies its regulation of family life through county agencies such as Child Protective Services as well as the simultaneous freedom it gives to "functional" families (particularly when they are white and nonpoor). But although the state is clearly concerned with maintaining the relative independence of familial units (which typically amounts to freedom for the men within such units), its basic willingness to intervene in at least some cases of abuse shows it has an interest in limiting the enactment of power within the familial hierarchy. Actions that are judged to cause problems in relation to the future social and physical reproduction of society are deemed unacceptable and labeled as abusive, not just by psychologists, but by the full power of the state. As with the literature within clinical psychology, the Supreme Court's decisions move beyond an expression of concern for victims toward a prescription of healthy relationships and functional sex lives, that is to say, toward the reproduction of the modern family. Although interventions by the therapeutic state indeed undermine male familial authority in certain limited ways, they offer discourses that obfuscate male-dominant gender relations, and that discipline victims in ways that support the recreation of the very same familial and sexual structures that enabled the initial abuse. Action against abuse is thus best seen as a reformist attempt to restrict the harm caused by the patriarchal family in order to better reassure its ongoing continuance.

Conclusion

Remedying this situation clearly requires challenging state-therapeutic discourses. Yet such activism should not limit itself to discursive objectives. As Linda Gordon argues,

> Probably the most important single contribution to the prevention of incest would be the strengthening of mothers. By increasing their ability to support themselves and their social and psychological self-esteem, allowing them to choose independence if that is necessary to protect themselves and their daughters, men's sexual exploitation could be checked. (1988, 62)

Numerous feminist commentators have noted a connection between women's ability to challenge wife abuse and their financial situation (see Brandwein 1999, for example), and it seems only reasonable to presume that similar dynamics exist in relation to sexual abuse. Strengthening the welfare system, instituting a more progressive tax structure, or introducing the idea of comparable worth are all difficult but eminently practical actions that would enable many poor mothers to prevent the abuse of their children. Increasing children's material opportunities outside the familial home, by providing better quality alternative and foster care, supporting shelter and food programs for runaways, and allowing teenagers to economically support themselves would similarly disrupt both male and parental power. Recognizing ways in which psychological and state discourses reinscribe the normative, male-dominant, heterosexual family should lead to action against not only the discursive manifestations of this dangerous inequity, but its material foundations as well.

Notes

1. I would like to thank Clare Corcoran, Astrea Davidson, Ali Luterman, Penelope Saunders, Ali Miller, and most especially Laurie Schaffner and Elizabeth Bernstein for their tireless work in helping me to produce this essay, from thinking through the initial ideas to editing the final text.

2. The rise in reports of sexual abuse was much more sudden than the rise in reports of child abuse as a whole. For example, from 1976 to 1983, reports of sexual abuse in the U.S. increased nearly tenfold (from 7,559 to 71,961), while reports including all forms of abuse during approximately the same time period increased by 150 percent (Berrick and Gilbert 1991). Similarly, from 1980 to 1986, reports of sexual abuse more than tripled (resulting in approximately 155,000 reports of sexual abuse), while reports of physical abuse and neglect rose by 58 percent (National Center on Child Abuse and Neglect 1988).

3. For key exceptions, see, for example, MacLeod and Saraga 1988; Dinsmore 1991; Wilson 1993; Lamb 1996, 1999; Haaken 1998, 1999.

4. A slightly different analysis arises when male survivors are considered; Haaken 1999, 23–6.

5. See Hooper 1992, 60; Bell 1993, 126–49; see also Bailey and Blackburn 1979; Jackson 2000, 46–50, 120–2.

6. For feminist reviews of this literature, see Rush 1980, 97–103; Ward 1985, 139–61; Breines and Gordon 1983; Masson 1988; Summit 1988; Costin 1992; Olafson et al. 1993; McKinnon 1995.

7. See also DeMott 1980; "Attacking the Last Taboo" 1980; Leo 1981. For critiques, see Finkelhor 1979; Rush 1980; Janus 1981; Russell 1984, 1986; Armstrong 1994.

8. See, for example, Connell and Wilson 1974, 128–30; Brownmiller 1975, 220, 370–1, 385; Butler 1978, 165–8; Griffin 1979, 10–17.

9. Herman and Hirschman were extremely critical of Brownmiller on this point, and their comments merit quoting at length:
   Stressing the coercive aspect of the situation, she [Brownmiller] calls it "father rape." To label it thus is to understate the complexity of the relationship. The father's sexual approach is clearly an abuse of power and authority, and the daughter almost always understands it as such. But, unlike rape, it occurs in the context of a caring relationship. The victim feels overwhelmed by her father's superior power and unable to resist him; she may feel disgust, loathing, and shame. But at the same time she often feels that this is the only kind of love she can get, and prefers it to no love at all. The daughter is not raped, but seduced.
   In fact, to describe what occurs as a rape is to minimize the harm to the child, for what is involved here is not simply an assault, it is a betrayal. A woman who has been raped can cope with the experience in the same way that she would react to any other intentionally cruel and harmful attack. She is not socially or psychologically dependent upon the rapist. She is free to hate him. But the daughter who has been molested is dependent on her father for protection and care . . . . She must endure it and find what compensations she can. (1977, 748)
   Herman and Hirschman's observations are quite astute, and foreshadow some of the analysis that follows in this essay. Unfortunately, while these comments appear in their jointly authored essay in *Signs*, Herman chooses not to include these remarks in her booklength monograph where she instead argues that "it is a rape in the sense that it is a coerced sexual relationship" (1981, 27). More generally as well, the above views formed a decidedly minoritarian opinion among most feminists writing on the topic.

10. Herman's earlier work with Hirschman (1977) is even more explicit in noting the agency of victims in responding to abuse, albeit from within a very narrowed range of options. Arguing that a victim "must endure it [the abuse], and find in it what compensations she can" (748), Herman and Hirschman utilize language which portrays victims as extremely active in negotiating the terms of their abuse with whatever resources they may have at their disposal. They note, for example, that
    Many of the daughters effectively replaced their mothers and became their fathers' surrogate wives. They were also deputy mothers to the younger children and were generally given some authority over them. While they resented being exploited and robbed of the freedom ordinarily granted to dependent children, they did gain some feeling of value and importance from the role they were given. (748)
    While making clear that results such as these do not represent attractive bargains for victims, such an analysis incorporates a sense of a victim's agency into the overall approach.

11. As Schaffner points out (this volume), the protections of "childhood" are also applied disparately with regard to both race and gender. To the extent that the image of childhood innocence offers any sense of protection at all, it is severely mitigated in relation to girls who are not white and (at least) middle class. While innocence is applied somewhat ambivalently to even these girls, as seen previously, whiteness and class respectability nevertheless seem to be prerequisites for any of innocence's shield. See also Wilson (1993).

12. This information is somewhat buried in Nelson's discussion but can be gathered by examining the differing definitions of abuse within the initial legislation passed by the Senate in 1973 and the final legislation as signed into law in 1974 (106–7, 114–7). For an additional historical treatment of the passage of CAPTA, see Weisberg 1984.

13. It is notable, in this regard, that the Supreme Court originally ruled that homosexuality did not merit constitutional protection precisely because "No connection between family, marriage, or procreation on the one hand and homosexual activity on the other [was] demonstrated" (*Bowers v. Hardwick* 1986). In overturning this decision (*Lawrence v. Texas* 2003), the Court held that the right to privacy extended *beyond* the realm of the family, further noting favorably that the case "does not involve whether the government must give formal recognition to any relationship that homosexual persons seek to enter." Thus, while engaging in homosexuality is now recognized as a legal right, the court does not yet find that same-sex partnerships could constitute a family as such. Given that same-sex couples are not defined as part of that which helps to uphold democratic society, but are merely allowed to exist within the private sphere, it follows that the state is allowed to promote and reward heterosexual marriages while denying benefits to homosexual partnerships. Similarly, while *Lawrence* permits sexual practices to exist within the private sphere, it leaves untouched the notion that families are to have greater access to privacy than are nonfamilies. While the content of such a distinction is unclear, the state could theoretically decide to establish a lower threshold of intervention into the lives of children living with same-sex couples than for those living with heterosexual parents. It could, for example, decide that living with a same-sex couple constitutes a threat to a child's ability to later form a proper family—therefore removing the child from its home—even while holding that homosexuality itself would not be prosecuted. However unlikely this scenario, the distinction between familial and nonfamilial rights to privacy must be noted.

CHAPTER 10

From Identity to Acronym:
How "Child Prostitution" Became "CSEC"

PENELOPE SAUNDERS

The Second World Congress Against Commercial Sexual Exploitation of Children (CSEC) held in December 2001 constituted an international reunion of key stakeholders concerned with ending child prostitution and similar abuses of children in the global sexual marketplace. The themes of the Congress regarding child protection, law enforcement, and the nature of the sex exploiter represent more than two decades of engagement of nongovernmental organizations (NGOs) with children's rights reflecting the aim of preventing commercialized sexual activity.[1] Documents produced at the World Congresses have allowed the NGO sector to pressure nation-states to change their conceptualizations of the commercial sexual abuse of children and rewrite local legislation and policy to reflect these new human rights concerns. This chapter traces the emergence of CSEC as the framework encompassing phenomena that are known individually as child prostitution, child pornography, and trafficking in children. A primary goal of this chapter is to consider how NGO practice, research, report writing, and dissemination of information in various media, have fashioned images of the victims of CSEC that not only bolster public sympathy for their cause, but also for a particular formulation of children's rights.

Anthropological and historical research reveal that childhood and what constitutes the child itself are socially constructed (Nieuwenhuys 1996). The notion that children are fundamentally distinct from adults and should be protected from spheres of commerce and sexual activity is pivotal to NGO constructions of the problem of CSEC. Social constructionist viewpoints and pleas from anthropologists for cultural sensitivity in regard to child labor have therefore been viewed with suspicion by many NGO practitioners in the field of child protection. Yet, as the following sections illustrate, anti-CSEC campaigners have themselves facilitated a significant revision of the ways in which children and youth engaging in sex for remuneration are described. The individuals affected by CSEC are rewritten as child victims rather than street children, runaways, throwaways, or juvenile delinquents, as they were once known.[2] The move from stigmatized identity, for example, from child prostitute to this protective, neutral acronym has created some possibilities for youth to speak in different modes about their sexual experiences, including the experience of exploitation. In current parlance, such youth are considered change agents and are encouraged to participate in program design and campaigns to end CSEC (Muntarbhorn 2001). However, not all youth perspectives are afforded status as acceptable voices for change. A second goal of this chapter is to examine the ways in which nonconforming youth are pathologized and ultimately silenced by the framework of CSEC.

The fact that the majority of this chapter is about the representation of an issue should not obscure the reality of the sexual abuse of children by adults. It is clear that tragic events ensue when youth and children are the objects of the sexual activities of adults, whether this occurs through information technology or physical contact. For example, the discovery in Belgium of the murder of two 8-year-old girls along with the abduction, sexual abuse, and torture of two teens, shortly before the First World Congress Against Commercial Sexual Exploitation in 1996, provided further impetus for the NGO sector to stop abusers like Marc Dutroux and his associates (McCulloch 2001, 20). In the following analysis of the rise of CSEC as a way of framing these and other events, it is not my intent to dismiss the pain and suffering experienced by children, youth, and their families and communities when confronted by horrendous crimes or when facing abuse. Rather, I wish to consider the outcomes, both predicted and unexpected, of the campaigns that have brought such concerns into the human rights arena.

Definitions and elements of CSEC are enshrined in the *Convention on the Rights of the Child* (United Nations 1989), in documents produced by the United Nations Special Rapporteur on the Sale of Children, and via a number of other international human rights instruments (Ennew et al. 1996; Van Bueren 2001). The impetus for this acknowledgement in the U.N. system is the direct result of campaigns by activist NGOs concerned with preventing child prostitution and pedophile activities.[3] The following sections will examine trends in the NGO response to child prostitution, commercial sexual exploitation of children and youth, child pornography, and trafficking in children in order to interpret current definitions of CSEC present in international human rights law.

Sex Tourism and "Foreign Pedophiles"

High-profile campaigns to end child prostitution are not a recent phenomenon, and historical analyses have considered the importance of class, gender
and the invocation of sexual innocence in their formulation.[4] The current
campaign distinguishing child prostitution as an international issue emerged,
in the 1970s and flowed throughout the decade in which the *Convention on the
Rights of the Child* was drafted.[5] From the outset, NGO documentation located
the cause of CSEC in relationships of inequality and exploitation between nations and regions. One early publication by the NGO Terre des Hommes drew
attention to First World "pedophile tourism" to Sri Lanka (Bond 1980). This
report was unusual in that it described the prostitution of boys, whereas most
concern has focused on girls and young women. For example, material from
Southeast Asia dominated the literature during this period, elaborating the
harms of tourism to girls and young women in Thailand and the Philippines
(Health Action Information Network 1987; Heyzer 1986; Crick 1989, 324).
The presence of foreign military bases was also implicated in fueling the market for child prostitution. Father Shay Cullen of the People's Recovery,
Development and Assistance Foundation critiqued one U.S. military base in
Olongapo City, the Philippines, saying, "It is the poor and most vulnerable of
society who . . . have to offer themselves up to satisfy the lust of the tourists
and sailors that are here only because of the bases and the industry that caters
to them" (Cullen 1990; see also Enloe 1989). As the *Convention on the Rights
of the Child* neared completion, estimates of the scope of the problem of child
prostitution skyrocketed. In 1989 Norwegian Save the Children published a
comprehensive report, *The Sexual Exploitation of Children in Developing
Countries*, producing the often-quoted figure of "100 million child prostitutes
in Asia" (Narvesen 1989).

In 1990, the NGO that became the most successful strategist and lobbyist,
End Child Prostitution in Asian Tourism (ECPAT), was established in
Thailand. ECPAT publications and activities encapsulated the way in which the
problem of commercial sexual exploitation was framed by NGOs in this period. Concern centered on sex tourism that catered to the tastes of pedophiles
from countries in Europe, North America, Australia, and Asia. In the words of
INTERPOL, the problem of child sex tourism was "the growing numbers of pedophiles, pretending to be tourists, who travel from Western countries to developing countries [and] whose aim [it] is to engage in illicit sexual activity
with easily available and cheap, young, prostituted children" (INTERPOL 1996,
87). Specialty sex tours for foreign men gained special notoriety in the media.
Press coverage of the bar, massage parlor, and nightclub life of certain locales
such as Bangkok and Manila, as well as the presence of young girls in the sex
industry in Thailand and the Philippines, were transmitted to ever-eager documentary news-hour shows in the U.S., Europe, and Australia.

Significantly, accounts by journalists and documentary makers about these issues unerringly followed a template (Ennew et al. 1996). A typical report would focus on a very young girl who had been forced or duped into working in a brothel, serving scores of customers each evening. The language used to tell her story would be emotive, and her youth would be repeatedly emphasized. The girl would be described as receiving little or nothing in return for her suffering because a brothel owner kept almost all the money she earned. The report would imply through narrative or images that it was the demand from Western men driving the need for young prostitutes. Impressions of the entertainment industry would be included via representations of nightclubs, alcohol use, crowds, and neon lights. The narrative would reveal that the girl's plight became known when she was rescued by a welfare agency. Ultimately, she would be sent back to her village where a medical practitioner, or some other health official, announces that she is HIV-positive and will shortly die. The girl's village would almost always be represented in daylight accompanied by stylistic portrayals of the countryside, including depictions of agriculture, rudimentary housing, and slow-paced community life.

These formulaic representations operated on a number of axes to construct the child prostitute as "a potent symbol of touristic excess: the ultimate commodification of humanity in its most vulnerable and innocent form" (Black 1995, 13). Despite early reports of the sexual exploitation of young boys, femininity and victim status were central in this process. Those harmed were constructed as female, young, and powerless, while perpetrators were male, privileged, and unfettered.[7] Violation was depicted as occurring in urban zones associated with commercialized pleasure clearly demarcated from the sphere of family, tradition, and community life. Girls, lured out of the safety of home and village, fell from sexual innocence when bought and consumed by drunken, depraved foreigners in locales specifically designed to fulfill their appetites without sanction. Thus, sex tourism became a powerful metaphor for the inequalities between North and South, recalling other analyses of colonialism and neocolonialism (Crick 1989, 332). Significantly, representations of sex tourism and child prostitution fortified the importance of the NGO sector in helping girls and in publicizing the problem that governments had assiduously chosen to ignore. Help was framed in terms of dramatic interventions, unfortunately too late or insufficient to fully redeem lost innocence.

Local Demand

As campaigns to prevent child prostitution and exploitation matured, several agencies, including ECPAT, began to publicize that not all problems could be attributed to debauched outside influences. For example, beginning in 1990, reports from Thailand estimated that Western tourists made up a very small fraction of the clientele of the sex industry and revealed that many tourists patronized women above age 18. The majority of the demand for prostitutes of all kinds, including young girls, came from local men (Skrobanek 1990). NGOs needed to develop more sophisticated analyses of what had previously been portrayed as a foreign pedophile problem.

The lives of street children emerged as a theme in the literature in the late 1980s. This concern originated in the Latin American region where hundreds of thousands of children were thought to be living on the streets turning to prostitution to survive (Rocha 1991, 5). Local demand for young sexual partners of either gender was viewed as the problem for these young people rather than necessarily the demands of foreign tourists. The children and youth involved in prostitution on the street came to symbolize other societal discontents matching responses to concern about sex tourism and influence of the West on developing countries. Young street children selling flowers, candy, and, by implication, their bodies were described as "disposable children,"[8] a sad indictment on societies fragmented by military violence and families in disorder due to structural adjustment fiascos. The complicity of local actors, including corrupt officials, the military, and the police, was central to analyses of the existence of the phenomenon of street children and their engagement in prostitution (Dimenstein 1991; Treguear and Carro 1994). For example, paramilitaries and police in Latin America punished street children for property crimes, such as theft of food from local merchants, forcing them to rely on the sale of sex in order to survive. NGO materials provide the following quote from a Brazilian teenager illustrating his decisions based on limited options available on the street:

> I started living on the street when I was seven years old, when I lost my mother and couldn't survive . . . I used to take drugs and start stealing again, and then get arrested and beaten . . . When I got fed up with being beaten [by the police], I went back to being a prostitute but then the bastards slapped me around if I didn't want to have sex with them. If I was to tell that to the policemen, they would just put me in jail and beat me up again. (Dimenstein 1991, 22)

NGO concern was also fueled by numerous reports of abduction and murder of street children by authorities and paramilitaries (e.g., Castilho 1995). International organizations, such as Amnesty International, effectively publicized the dehumanizing logic of the perpetrators building on the theme of disposable children.

NGOs working in the field often took a pragmatic approach, researching the needs of street children and then providing services. One study into the lives of 143 street children in Guatemala City carried out by Casa Alianza found that commercial sex was a reality for almost all of these young people as a form of survival (Harris 1996). Street children were found to be taking drugs, using glue and other substances as inhalants, and such behaviors were interpreted as methods to block out the harsh realities of life on the street (Rocha 1991, 2). Practical programs to assist this subset of child prostitutes included outreach programs, drop-in centers, and alternative education (e.g., Longo 1998). HIV prevention strategies shaped much service provision, and NGOs working with such issues constituted a different sector than groups concerned with sex tourism or street children. In order to carry out effective HIV prevention work, these NGOs acknowledged the need to build trust with youth and similar hard-to-reach populations, and constructed them as potential peer educators, active in reducing violence and unsafe sex (e.g., Swaminathan et al. 1991). Sexual activity was considered a risk factor in the spread of HIV but not necessarily a cause of corruption or loss of innocence per se. Some programs, for example, included a workshop on "sexuality, health, and citizenship" in which generalizations about the experience of street youth were questioned (Pereira et al. 1992). Thus, by the early 1990s, NGO concern about the commercial sexual exploitation of children had diverged in two directions. One strand of NGOs continued to develop notions of harm to children drawing on concerns about corruption of sexual innocence and began speaking openly about local complicity and demand. The other strand began to question the utility of broad symbolic frameworks formulated around idealistic notions of childhood, especially during attempts to prevent the spread of HIV.

Trafficking in Children

More recently, NGOs have placed much less emphasis on the problem of sex tourism, and although numerous programs assisting street children around the world continue in their service work, the problem most likely to receive attention is "trafficking in children."[9] This trend is best represented by the 1997 name change of ECPAT from "End Child Prostitution in Asian Tourism" to "End Child Prostitution, Child Pornography and the Trafficking of Children for Sexual Purposes." The emergence of the shift in concern from child prostitution toward sexual trafficking of children can be traced to several key reports during the 1990s that drew international attention to the issue.

Trafficking in human beings, whether children or adults, is a concept that developed definitionally in two planes. First, trafficking was defined in various U.N. declarations and documents. One well-known attempt to define trafficking can be located in the *Optional Protocol to Prevent, Suppress, and Punish Trafficking in Persons, Especially Women and Children* (2000). Second, many NGOs understand trafficking to merge concerns about prostitution with the forced movement of persons, including abduction, kidnapping, and sale of individuals. The phrase "trafficking in children" is sometimes used interchangeably with the term "sexual trafficking in children." Many of the documents and studies that consider the problem of trafficking encompass the transportation of children from one place to another without necessarily crossing borders. Well-publicized cases include instances where young Brazilian women have been taken to remote villages in the Amazonian mining districts to work in canteens and bars and provide sexual services for local laborers (Beyer 1996). Human rights organizations have documented many cases of international trafficking involving the transport of minors across borders. One of the most well-known human rights reports documented situations in young Burmese women and girls who were sold by their parents to traffickers who then took them to work in Thai brothels (Asia Watch 1993).

NGO publications typically describe two ways in which children and youth come to be trafficked. First, parents facing poverty or social disruption (e.g., famine, war) sell their children to recruiters (Asia Watch 1993). Second, children leave home voluntarily, attracted by economic possibilities elsewhere, as in the following account:

> Maria reluctantly left the desperation of her devastated post-Hurricane Mitch family shack in Tegucigalpa and headed out. She did not know she would be trafficked out of Honduras. She did not know she would be overly charged several hundred dollars for the land transportation to Mexico, and she was beaten into understanding that she had to pay the money back through sex. (Harris 2001)

Here, we can observe a possible connection to the discourse on street children where children and youth may be viewed as having some agency to leave home to escape abuse or poverty, only to find themselves in a worse situation on the street. However, portrayals of trafficking in children firmly reinforce youth, innocence, and vulnerability that negate any suggestion of agency. For example, Maria from the previous example, is introduced as "[t]he pretty little bronzed skinned girl [sitting] there with empty eyes and a blank stare as she answered our questions about her recent past" and at "barely 14 years old . . . she is a slave" (Harris 2001).

Documentary descriptions of trafficking in children, most notably the film *The Selling of Innocents* (Gupta 1996), resonate with earlier portrayals of sex tourism and the influence of foreign pedophiles. *The Selling of Innocence* conveys several instances of young women rescued from brothels in Bombay. The film recounts the story of one young woman who was placed in the care of an NGO where she is said to be safe in a shelter. The director of the NGO discusses the young woman's time in prostitution, her eventual liberation, and her HIV-positive status. The NGO director assumes, in a similar fashion to journalistic accounts of sex tourism, the inevitable demise of her charge and narrates the comfort to be provided to her in her last days. The discourse on trafficking in children is, then, tightly linked to the original conceptualization of commercial sexual exploitation that posited unredeemable sexual violation as a metaphor for global inequalities.

Current concerns about trafficking update the issue, drawing on more recent interpretations of the changes wrought by globalization that lead to displacement and clandestine circulation of human beings for profit. The perpetrators are no longer pedophiles or tourists who leave their countries to seek illicit pleasure abroad. Rather, they are businessmen and transnational criminals who show no compunction in tearing children and youth from their families and communities in order to transport them to far distant locales and profit from their sexual exploitation. The divergent interpretations of agency and meanings of sexual activity that emerged in relation to the concept of street children are not possible in discussions of trafficking where the child victim is subject to the overwhelming powers of highly organized criminal networks.

Intersections Between NGO Work and Human Rights

As the previous sections illustrate, perspectives on the commercial sexual exploitation of children derive from both direct service provision with populations affected and from broader social critiques implicating gender, sexuality, and global inequities. The inclusion of some of these ideas within the world of human rights has been a protracted process during years of development of key children's human rights documents. The majority of NGOs working against CSEC, especially those providing direct services, has fairly limited contact with the U.N. system and with the formal construction of human rights discourse.

Significantly, during the drafting of the *Convention on the Rights of the Child,* a section of the NGO community honed lobbying skills and found effective ways to influence these processes (Detrick 1992, 24). NGOs were directly responsible for key articles regarding child prostitution and CSEC, including Article 32 (Protection from economic exploitation), Article 34 (Protection from sexual exploitation), and Article 35 (Prevention of abduction, sale, or traffic in children). Furthermore, some NGOs have been highly successful in pushing for the creation of extraterritorial laws to convict sex tourists who formerly evaded law enforcement because of limits due to national sovereignty.[10] These interventions indicated a growing engagement of the NGO sector in the formalization of CSEC as a human rights tool.

The event that highlights the extent to which the NGO sector has lead in establishing the CSEC framework was the World Congress Against Commercial Sexual Exploitation of Children held in Stockholm in 1996. ECPAT proposed the conference in 1994 as part of a new program of action to promote direct involvement of governments in ending the commercial sexual exploitation of children (ECPAT 1994). Conference planning was overseen by ECPAT, UNICEF, and the Geneva-based NGO Group for the *Convention on the Rights of the Child*, representing a further 41 nongovernmental bodies working in the area of children's rights. The First World Congress was certainly successful in achieving government delegation attendance and in raising the issue in the media.[11] NGO participation was integrated into the Congress, rather than segregated into an NGO Forum or alternate conference typically held at world conferences.

The Congress unanimously adopted a Declaration and Agenda for Action, highlighting governments' commitment "to a global partnership against the commercial sexual exploitation of children." The 1996 document defined CSEC as

> . . . a fundamental violation of children's rights. It comprises sexual abuse by the adult and remuneration in cash or kind to the child or a third person or persons. The child is treated as a sexual object and as a commercial object. The commercial sexual exploitation of children constitutes a form of coercion and violence against children, and amounts to forced labor and a contemporary form of slavery. (*Stockholm Declaration and Agenda for Action* 1996, Paragraph 5)

NGO efforts, then, brought together the threads of U.N. work on child prostitution, child pornography, and trafficking in children to create a widely accepted definition of CSEC and a monitored agenda for action.

Even though the *Declaration and Agenda for Action* are not legally binding documents, this preemptive action on behalf of the nongovernment sector was strategic given the extremely drawn-out process of creating additional documents in the U.N. system.[12] Furthermore, NGOs were provided with the impetus to lobby their home countries for policy reform because the *Declaration and Agenda* urged countries to create national plans of action to end CSEC. In this sense, NGOs instrumented significant reconsideration of juvenile justice and sexuality at the level of the state by bringing children's rights discourses into local discourses. Other results of the conference were somewhat less tangible, but equally important for the NGO sector. NGOs formed an Advisory Group to the U.N. Special Rapporteur on the Sale of Children, Child Prostitution, and Child Pornography. ECPAT took a key position in monitoring the actions of governments, NGOs, and intergovernmental organizations (IGOs) in the area of child prostitution, child pornography, and the trafficking of children for sexual purposes. Since 1996, ECPAT's reporting on CSEC has professionalized considerably[13] and, to date, the ECPAT network has expanded from four groups (all in Asia) prior to the World Congress in 1996 to 60 groups in 50 different countries by 2001.

The Second World Congress on CSEC, held in 2001, continued many of the plans set out in 1996 and did not result in a new statement about CSEC. Rather, delegates reaffirmed commitment to the *Stockholm Declaration and Agenda for Action* and strengthened their engagement in ongoing processes to develop national agendas and action plans (Yokohama Global Commitment 2001). Even though the conference did not significantly alter interpretations of the core elements of CSEC, several issues were emphasized. New technologies were spotlighted—in particular, child pornography on the Internet. One workshop discussed the "misuse of mobile phones for CSEC not only by means of telephone calls but also electronic messages via mobile phones" (Muntarbhorn 2001). Curbing the demand for CSEC was emphasized throughout the conference, resulting in discussions of the nature of the sex exploiter, and examinations of patterns of behavior that allow men to perpetrate crimes against children. Finally, exclusionary practices critiqued at the first meeting in 1996 were addressed by public calls to prioritize the inclusion of youth with personal experience of CSEC, often described as "experiential persons," in processes of concern to them, including the development of policy, program design and implementation, and media representation of the issue.[14]

Loose Ends That May Trouble CSEC

✗ "I am turned away by prostitute agencies, I am turned away by the gay community, I am turned away by my friends and family because I am not only selling my body, I am gay and selling my body to guys." (Youth quoted in the *Declaration and Agenda for Action of Sexually Exploited Children and Youth* 1998, 8)

CSEC describes a set of behaviors perpetrated against children and youth, defines these actions clearly as human rights violations, and locates volition as well as blame in the actions of abusers. Activists have transformed older conceptualizations of juvenile delinquency that stigmatized children into a new protective understanding of children and youth as casualties of adult sexual misconduct. Similar rethinking of the nature of the child has also taken place in psychology and other social welfare programs: The changes observed in the global concept of CSEC reflect a more general shift that has played out at national and local levels (see chapters by Ericcson, Kaye, and Schaffner, this volume).

While in numerous ways this approach is superior to preexisting frameworks, it flounders when confronted with youth who do not consider themselves victims or who do not view the harms done to them in the same way as the NGO advocates who intend to help them. Advocates of a human rights approach to CSEC have endeavored to describe nonconforming youth who engage in sexual activities with adults for remuneration, such as Japanese teenagers who date older men in exchange for costly consumer goods, as sexually exploited. Further, some youth, as the previous quote suggests, who have been harmed from their reliance on sex for survival are excluded from assistance because they do not conform with a nonsexual configuration of child-victim status. The remainder of this chapter will examine these challenges using a social constructionist human rights viewpoint that consciously examines "rights work (standards creation, advocacy, documentation, and other interventions) for its role in production, repression, construction or liberation of sexuality, and the idea of the human" (Miller 1999, 291).

As noted previously, some NGOs, specifically those working to prevent HIV/AIDS, have questioned the utility of CSEC as a result of their interactions with street youth. My reason for choosing this area to open a discussion of the loose ends that trouble CSEC is due to my personal experience in NGOs of this kind. In 1995 and 1996, I coordinated a research project about sexual risks faced by homeless youth in Adelaide, South Australia. Our research team members were all drawn from the HIV/AIDS advocacy sector in Australia, including an agency dedicated to the issues of concern to gay and lesbian youth, a youth training project, and a sex-worker health and rights agency.[15] The research project had a broad HIV prevention goal as well as specific responses to several social issues. Some local youth health agencies in South Australia were very concerned that young homeless people were being abused by pedophiles, selling sex to survive on the streets, and that a child prostitution ring operated in inner-city Adelaide. However, the team, due to geographic isolation and the placement of the research as part of the HIV sector (as opposed to being framed as a human rights endeavor), had no connection with groups working on CSEC or with the preparation for the First World Congress that proceeded at that time.

Sex for Favors

In order to examine the nature and extent of the child prostitution problem in South Australia, 106 young people aged 12 to 23 years were interviewed regarding their possible engagement in sex for gain or remuneration of any sort.[16] During preparation of the research project, many researchers and youth workers expressed the opinion that youth would simply not talk about sensitive issues surrounding sex for gain with adults. In order to counteract this, a self-assessment survey was designed to go with the interview that allowed participants a way of indicating whether or not they had exchanged sex for accommodation, food, clothing, safety, drugs, or transport.[17] A variety of efforts were made to encourage young people to describe themselves and to reveal what their needs were, rather than imposing external frameworks. Eventually, the research team came to describe these exchanges as "sex for favors" since this term encompassed the behaviors and attitudes of young people interviewed and was acceptable to youth program workers, whom we ultimately wished to train about the issue. The research revealed that one-third of the young people interviewed had exchanged sex for favors and another 10% said they would consider doing so in the future.

An important element that emerged was that young people who engaged in sexual exchanges almost never defined themselves as prostitutes or linked their activities to prostitution per se. In qualitative interviews, youth talked in very circumspect ways about what they did when needing money, replying with ambiguous statements including "liv[ing] off the town for a while" or "go[ing] in to the city to get some." Similar elliptical speech about sexual exchanges has been observed in other populations. In a case study of a village next to a tourist resort in Thailand, Heather Montgomery (1998) noted that children and young people who engaged in what could be termed prostitution with tourists as a way of supporting their families, considered it an insult to be called a child prostitute. They would refer to their activities in more ambiguous language such as "having guests" or "meeting with foreigners" (Montgomery 1998, 145).

Sexuality and the Street

The second theme that emerged from the Adelaide research was the wide variety of sexual experience on the street involving both heterosex and homosex, significantly among young men. Some research has found that a disproportionate number of street youth who engage in prostitution also report homosexual or bisexual identifications (Yates et al. 1991, 547). More recently other qualitative research has complicated the issue by examining both the ways in which sexual exchanges for remuneration have multiple meanings and how youth actively employ particular readings of their behavior in order to protect themselves from discriminatory attitudes towards homosexuality. Caceres's (1998) study of *fleteo,* or sale of homosex, in Lima, Peru, provides detailed analysis of the interaction between sexual behavior and identity present in exchanges. Young men who identify as *fletes* engage in sex with other men for money or some other kind of remuneration. Some of these young men strongly identify as heterosexual and deny that they are sexually interested in their clients or homosexuality. However, other young men in this study commented that *fleteo* allowed them to engage in homosex without necessarily having to assume an unambiguous homosexual identity (Caceres and Rosasco 1999, 269).

Some acknowledgement of the importance of sexuality and sexual meaning has emerged in connection to CSEC. For example, a theme paper prepared for the First World Congress on CSEC observed that the activities of boys on the street are poorly understood and that the behaviors in which they engage belong within "an entirely different complex of social ideas [from female prostitution], which does not seem to have been researched in depth" (Ennew et al. 1996). While in general the Adelaide research echoes this sentiment, it may be methodologically useful to frame the concern differently. Research about the varieties of sexual experience of young people of any gender who engage in sexual exchanges tends to be limited. Innovative NGO-based research with street youth in Tanzania found that exchanges that can be clearly labeled as prostitution account for perhaps less than 5% of all sexual encounters among these youth (Rajani and Kudrati 1996, 307). A great deal of sexual interaction occurs between peers on the street, exchanges that may or may not be easily negotiated safely by young women (Farquhar 1995). Information about young women and their sexuality is very scarce in the literature, perhaps due to research methods that may not ask the correct questions or do not allow young women sufficient time to disclose their behaviors. Young women are more likely to reveal their sexual orientation and discuss their behavior during longer-term studies with researchers they have come to trust (e.g., Pfeffer 1997, 6).

Age Matters

Our sample included young people aged 12 to 23 years old and it was clear that the experience of life on the street was significantly different for very young interviewees. For example, some very young people interviewed had not had sex yet but knew about opportunities to exchange sex for favors and considered it something they might do in the future. Clearly, the health and education needs of these young people differed from older teenagers who were already involved in sex for favors. Thus, I urge us to target interventions in an age-appropriate fashion and to provide young people with information about sexual risk that will help them protect themselves. In short, research has taught us that age matters.

The fact that our research did not uncover any very young people having sex with adults for favors was disappointing to many media representatives interested in our findings. The desire to provide simple summaries for maximum "reader impact" is strong, but it is essential to be clear about the ages of study participants or clients who are served by NGO programs. Frequently, individuals at risk are not as young as press reports would have us believe. The 1996 International Labor Organization report on child workers in the hotel, tourism, and catering industries in the Philippines, Sri Lanka, Kenya, and Mexico concluded from this four-country study that most child prostitutes are in fact better described as youth or young people (Black 1996). The report found no individual who sold sex on a regular basis was younger than 15 nor had any interviewee begun this work younger than 14 years old. Findings such as these <u>do not mean that abuse of very young or prepubescent children never occurs</u>. All too sadly, it does. However, it clearly is desirable when reporting about the lives of children and young people that terms are employed that accurately and sensitively describe their lives and reflect what they might say about themselves.

The Advantages and Limits to CSEC

The change from constituting sexual practices, choices, and behaviors of children as identities to renaming them as an experience bodes well for the potential to address many concerns. Social justice issues such as helping young people heal and mature, organizing for change, and challenging stereotypes and inequities can be seen in a new light because they reject older notions of the child as inherently at fault and build new formulations of the child as a human rights subject. Key to this new idea is the representation of the child as a highly sympathetic subject, vulnerable to the actions of adults and to the unrestrained forces of the global marketplace. Furthermore, this new analysis emerged not so much from policy makers but from grassroots service providers who could claim to know the lived reality of the children in question. Thus, the sympathetic portrait of the child at risk in this formulation has an unassailable claim to truth. Aspects of the framework that did emerge from the U.N. bureaucracy had the advantage of growing from the *Convention on the Rights of the Child* with its new vision of children as persons with rights, including an emphasis on their participation in the creation of a society that would both value and listen to them. CSEC provides a potential escape from the problematic term "child prostitute," so vehemently rejected by many young people that agencies concerned with prostitution seek to help. Commercial sexual exploitation is an activity perpetrated by others, rather than an identity somehow inherent to "delinquent children" who may never fully be redeemed.

Yet the concept of CSEC is curiously limited and seemingly unable to fully embrace the experience of persons who do not fit into the traditional vision of the exploited or prostituted child. Silence almost always reigns about the realities of life for gay, lesbian, bisexual, and transgender youth. CSEC does not seem to include youth who may be sexually active on their own terms while at the same time experiencing sexual abuse and exploitation in other arenas of their lives. Youth who no longer look or act like small, frightened children but wish to speak out about their own lives and construct their own futures, which may not include marriage, the nuclear family, and sober middle-class values are not fully invited into the "participatory framework."

For example, First World Congress materials proudly trumpet the presence of a "youth delegation." Yet closer consideration reveals that of some 47 youth participants, only a few were actively engaged in the process. Of those youth in attendance, only three "self identified as having personal experience with commercial sexual exploitation—one having known someone, and the two others having been involved in the sex trade."[18] The fact that youth were seen but not heard at the First World Congress, and that the majority of youth invited were not experiential, prompted one of the two experiential youth at the 1996 conference to organize the Out from the Shadows International Summit of Sexually Exploited Youth. This conference, held in Canada in 1998, included 55 delegates with experience as sexually exploited children and youth from across the Americas. The *Declaration and Agenda for Action* from the Out from the Shadows Conference rejected older frameworks declaring "that the term child or youth prostitute can no longer be used" and reiterated the importance of CSEC as the most desirable terminology (*Declaration and Agenda for Action of Sexually Exploited Children and Youth* 1998, 3). The document prioritized peer-led programs, including male, female, and transgender youth from a diversity of sexual orientations.

The presence of experiential children and youth who represent and situate themselves within the framework of CSEC creates the potential for reshaping current approaches. The Second World Congress, as a result of pressure from these young activists, included many more experiential youth and explicitly noted the importance of these persons as change agents in agendas and programs for change. However, participants—especially those with personal experience of CSEC—have been critical of how significant these responses have been in actuality. Youth at the Second World Congress arrived to find that their participation would be limited to prestructured "youth activities" that separated them from decision making at the main Congress.[19] Furthermore, issues of sexual orientation and gender identity raised in the Out from the Shadows Agenda were given very little attention.[20]

Youth who speak from a number of different experiential positions should be included in meaningful ways as the CSEC framework matures and attracts more resources. But closer examination of the makeup of the revisioned "child victim" and other sexuality and gender tropes in play suggests that barriers to a participatory framework may be greater than simply a lack of money and time. First, while CSEC does offer a way to end the use of terms that have marginalized youth in other ways, it remains an approach that carefully undermines the agency of children of any kind. CSEC's strength (that is, something that is always done to passive children's bodies) is also its weakness. Resistance displayed by children and youth to heteronormative, age-based societies is, in this formulation, unimaginable. Furthermore, CSEC in its present state does not consider the experiences of transgender youth. The commercial sexual exploitation of transgender youth in the U.S., Canada, and Mexico was closely examined, producing three pages of tables and multiple definitions (Estes and

Weiner 2001). The report is unusual in the genre because it includes more than a passing comment on transgender individuals affected by CSEC. The authors note that numerous, if as yet unquantified, numbers of transgender youth are homeless, engage in some form of prostitution, and can thus be said to be "commercially sexually exploited." These youth seem to demonstrate a good deal of agency:

> The espoused goal of many transgender youth is to raise sufficient money through pornography and prostitution to finance their hormone therapy and, in time, gender transformation surgeries. However, the investigators never encountered a single youth who was able to raise sufficient funds to pay for the latter. (Estes and Weiner 2001, 72)

Yet transgender youths' volition must be negated in order for them to fit as commercially sexually exploited children. Apparently, transgender youth are rarely successful in their attempts to transform their bodies. When individuals by some chance are successful, their stories are collapsed into a tragic narrative. The following case study included in the Estes and Weiner report illustrates the way in which such narratives proceed:[21]

> Of Hawaiian and Samoan descent, Cathy was born male, to a poor family in Hawaii. From earliest memory, her father, brothers, and uncles sexually assaulted her. Her family allowed, even promoted, other family members and strangers to use her sexually. When Cathy did not cooperate with this sexual exploitation, she was locked in a closet. At age 12, Cathy ran away and began doing street prostitution as a female. She attended school as a boy during the day and worked in Chinatown as a female at night. Amazingly Cathy managed to graduate intermediate high schools even though she was homeless—staying with tricks, drug dealers, and a prostitute. No one at school knew her secret life.
>
> During the summer of her junior year at age 16, and using a fake ID, Cathy went to New York, prostituted, and had an underground sex change operation. She returned to Hawaii and completed her senior year of high school as a female. Cathy remained a prostitute and became seriously addicted to drugs. She was arrested on drug charges at age 32 and sentenced to Drug Court. Cathy was diagnosed with multiple personality disorder, borderline personality, and homicidal impulses. She is under the care of a psychiatrist and has been sober for up to one year at a time. She has been able to maintain legitimate employment and is able to function "normally" when she takes her psychiatric medications. (Estes and Weiner 2001, 73)

Cathy's story is not unlike that of other youth who decide to leave home in order to escape sexual abuse, or because their families accept with difficulty children who act outside dominant gender norms.[22] Youth who make a decision to leave home and survive alone display a great deal of strength and agency. They may form friendships or relationships on the street that are ultimately harmful or they may find themselves subjected to abuse by people who initially appeared to offer them further independence. However, even though they face risks, they continue to challenge heteronormativity, the mandate to create nuclear families, and other mainstream constructions of gender and sexuality in order to live differently. The idea of commercial sexual exploitation is, in these cases, not necessarily conducive to uncovering these individuals' own strengths and putting them to use to change their communities and their lives. In fact, in the previous example, transgender youth are effectively positioned as beyond help because they are portrayed as permanently physically and mentally harmed. The pathologization of these youth, the notion that they are inherently defective because of their gender difference, also places them outside the world of children's rights. In Estes and Weiner's previous narrative, Cathy can never be fully redeemed because she was never, and never can be, normal, thus innocent.

Concluding Comments: From Identity to Acronym to Social Justice

At several points throughout this chapter, I have explored narratives in which children and youth fall from sexual innocence to face death or to suffer permanent damage. These narratives highlight human rights abuses associated with CSEC by positioning sexuality as a dangerous perversion and by constructing the child as innocent, separated from society, commerce, and of course sexual activity. The persistence of stories of "childhood innocence lost" in NGO practice is not an accident or the result of the foibles of a few NGO executive directors.[23] These narratives endure because the drama of purity besmirched at the hands of adults plays neatly into cultural notions of the sacred nature of childhood, where the child must necessarily be preserved in a state of innocence outside of the realm of economics and sexuality (Zelizer 1985; Levesque 1999, 46, 47). Such stories are not new and resonate well with liberal social rhetoric, hence their continued reiteration each decade in a slightly altered format.[24]

The pitfalls of employing appealing images of children in peril may not immediately be apparent to all those dedicated to creating a world in which children and youth can live in safety and with justice. Primarily, this is because from time to time very young children are victims of CSEC. Such examples have driven many agendas for change both locally and internationally. However, practitioners working in service provision for children and youth, and indeed youth themselves, recognize that the majority of abuses occur to individuals who are not innocent, not very young, and not unknowing of sexual activity and the world of work. Increasingly advocates note that by exclusively focusing world attention on extreme forms of CSEC, more pervasive forms of injustice may be obscured (Mahler 1998, 83). Other contributors to this volume have revealed further difficulties in attributing blame for sexual abuse, assigning punishment, and constructing victim narratives. Kaye (this volume) reveals the conundrum faced by feminist theorizing of familial sexual abuse that both repudiates children's agency and inadvertently instills self-blame among victims. Schaffner (this volume) cautions that state approaches to youth sexuality and criminality continue to be illogical, racist, and gender stereotyped, imposing punishment on young men for their "adult" behavior and controlling young women through their perceived sexual vulnerability. State responses may have more to do with policing what is "normal" and "healthy," ensuring social reproduction, and limiting dissent and diversity (Kaye, this volume; Ericsson, this volume). How can advocates both protect children and avoid playing into these traps that ultimately undermine children's rights?

Ideally, human-rights-based conceptualizations should prevent children and youth from facing legal sanctions for sexual activity, end vigilante actions against youth deemed to be acting inappropriately, and afford commercially sexually exploited children and youth the full range of rights protections accorded under the *Convention on the Rights of the Child*. In order to move beyond the limitations of CSEC, the notion of children developing self-determination must be part of any protective framework. This includes acknowledging and fostering the ability of children to participate in their growth as human beings as well as in their own development as sexual persons as they mature. Such an approach is in stark contrast to current formulations that rely on abstract notions of sexual purity and construct the dangers of commercial sexual exploitation to children for that reason only. A full children's rights agenda would locate ways of including the various perspectives of youth who have experienced commercial sexual exploitation regardless of sexual and gender orientation, presumed sexual innocence, and current or future lifestyle. Opening the discussion to include youth who find the agenda of CSEC useful in interpreting their experience, as well as to those who do not describe themselves as sexually exploited, will be a positive step in developing a more comprehensive framework. Finally, fruitful discussions could also be had between child rights advocates who have worked to expand access to information about sexuality, HIV prevention, and similar issues and those who wish to protect children from potential abuse. Advocates who wish to alter state responses to youth sexuality and abuse have much to gain from embracing diversity and new formulations of childhood that inspire inclusion, justice, and rights.

The commercialization of child sexual abuse, sex for favors, young people who work in the sex industry, and the forced trafficking in children and youth across state and national lines present us with a plethora of health and legal concerns. Currently, one approach, CSEC, provides the framework for understanding these concerns in both the NGO sector and the world of human rights. While this approach may allow us to dispense with outdated terms, it has not been subjected to scrutiny for its uncritical reliance on narratives of lost childhood innocence. While some youth activists have begun to lobby for change within this framework, others seem to be permanently negated by it. Youth who do not follow paths to narrow forms of redemption (leaving the streets, ending drug use, cutting all ties with sex for gain, forming heterosexual nuclear families, and living in "respectable," correctly gendered ways) are not likely to become poster children for campaigns against CSEC.

Notes

1. The six themes of the Congress were (1) the Prevention, Protection, and Recovery of Children from Sexual Exploitation; (2) the Profile of the Sex Exploiter; (3) the Role and Involvement of the Private Sector; (4) Legislation and Law Enforcement; (5) Trafficking in Children; and (6) Child Pornography (Muntarbhorn 2001).
2. Notions of juvenile delinquency have historically been highly gendered, intersecting with contemporary notions of sexuality (see Ericsson, this volume). Girls and young women were more likely to be prosecuted for sexual transgressions and boys and young men for property crimes or violence (see Schaffner, this volume). Schlossman and Wallach note that young women during the Progressive Era received tougher penalties than boys because their sexual activity was leading them on the "road to ruin" to prostitution (1978).
3. NGO influence on the *Convention on the Rights of the Child* is considered "without parallel in the history of drafting international instruments" (Detrick 1992, 24).
4. Perhaps the most well-known analysis is Judith Walkowitz's chronicling of nineteenth-century campaigns to end the sex trade in working-class girls where protagonists "set out to expose a conspiracy of privileged men" and represent "sexual perversion as an expression of corrupt male power" (1992, 118).
5. The process of developing a children's rights document began in 1978 when a draft was tabled by the government of Poland. The United Nations *Convention on the Rights of the Child* was completed and opened for signature in 1989 and came into force in 1990.
6. Schaffner (this volume) observes that boys are less likely to be described as vulnerable to sexual predation. She concludes that under the contemporary gender system in the U.S. "girls are vulnerable and boys agentic, in relationship to both sexuality and crime." If concern about boys is expressed, it is most commonly done in relation to fears about male homosexuality and its purported link to pedophile activity.
7. For a discussion of sex tourism in which gender and privilege do not neatly align, see O'Connell Davidson and Sánchez Taylor (this volume).
8. For example, the May/June 1995 edition of *NACLA Report on the Americas* was entitled "Disposable Children: The Hazards of Growing Up Poor in Latin America." The report opened with the following: "The drama unfolded before one of the NACLA editors as she was sipping coffee at an outdoor café in Cochabamba, Bolivia, several years ago. A little girl, no more than six, was crying forlornly at the perimeter of the tables. An older girl, perhaps 10 or 12, whom she took to be the child's sister, was cajoling the youngster: *you must do it! go ahead!* The little girl wept, and shook her head. The older girl would not relent and gave her sister a shove. The little girl, her cheeks still wet with tears, approached the table. Her eyes cast to the floor in shame, she put out cupped hands, and asked for some coins."
9. For example, the pamphlet, "Commercial Sexual Exploitation of Children: Youth Involved in Prostitution, Pornography and Sex Trafficking," mentions sex tourism as a concern but the pamphlet focuses clearly on a broader definition of CSEC, most notably trafficking in children (Barnitz 1998, 5).
10. People charged with sex offenses perpetrated while overseas may be able to avoid culpability if they leave the country where the offenses had occurred. Their country of residence may be reluctant to return them to face charges, and countries of residence may not have the jurisdiction to prosecute their own citizens for crimes committed overseas. Pressure from NGOs, most notably ECPAT-Australia, led to the adoption of the Australian Crimes (Child Sex Tourism) Amendment Act of 1994, which enables prosecution of its citizens for crimes against children even if they are committed outside of the country. Other countries have enacted similar legislation: Belgium, Amendment to Penal Code (1995); New Zealand, Crimes Amendment Act (1995); Austria, Amendment Act (1996); Ireland, Sexual Offences (Jurisdiction) Act (1996); U.K., Sexual Offenders Bill (1997); Canada, Bill C27 (1997).
11. Five hundred media representatives reported on the event, and 718 government officials representing 122 countries attended along with 105 representatives from the United Nations and intergovernmental organizations (ECPAT, nd).
12. For example, the *Optional Protocol to the Convention on the Rights of the Child on the Sale of Children, Child Prostitution and Child Pornography* was more than six years in the making, before finally being adopted and opened for signature by the U.N. General Assembly in May 2000.

13. ECPAT's first publication, *The Child and the Tourist* (O'Grady 1992), is a journalistic account containing no original research. The organization's most recent monitoring report (ECPAT 2001) is well referenced and almost completely devoid of unsubstantiated commentary on child prostitution.

14. For example, Cherry Kingsley, a young woman who lived on the streets in Canada from ages 14 to 22 and who has been an outspoken activist for the rights of commercially sexually exploited youth, was a keynote speaker (Kingsley 2001).

15. The "On the Job" research team was a collaboration between Youth Sector Training Council/COPE, Second Story Youth Health Service, and the Sex Industry Network, a program area of the AIDS Council of South Australia.

16. The following material is drawn from the final report of the project published by Tschirren et al., 1996.

17. The self-assessment survey included numerous reasons for having sex, such as "I have sex because I need someone to hug" and "I have sex because I want to be like everyone else," interspersed with material exchanges such as "I have sex because I need cigarettes" and "I have sex because I need a bed for the night."

18. Planning document for the "Out from the Shadows International Youth Summit," 1997, Ottawa, Canada, www.sen.parl.gc.ca/lpearson/1-shadows.html

19. Personal communication with Kelly Hill, Founder of SOS, Hawaii (May 19, 2003).

20. Personal communication with Mia Spangenburg, formerly of ECPAT-NY (May 22, 2003).

21. Case summary prepared by P. Vessels and J. Bopp of the Life Foundation (Honolulu, HI) and cited in Estes and Weiner, 2001.

22. Schaffner (1997) observed that young women seem to pursue sexual and romantic relationships as one of the few avenues available to them to reach autonomy and perhaps flee sexual predators.

23. Publicity materials produced by NGOs continue to reproduce the notion of the commercial sexual exploitation of very young children and the most horrific events even after the concerted efforts of the Out from the Shadows participants. O'Connell Davidson (2001a) comments on the use of particular images: "broken rose buds, discarded toys, small children being led away by large, shadowy male figures." During a preview in 1999 of ECPAT Australia's commercials to help Australian tourists think globally about child abuse, I observed similar tropes. ECPAT describes the Public Service Announcements saying: "The first ad is set in a local school yard. Three girls are eating their lunch. Two girls giggle innocently about a first kiss, while the third, Katie, sitting next to them, recalls far more painful memories—of abuse. The second television announcement involves a conservatively dressed man at his office computer late one night swapping images of child pornography. The third advertisement is set on a beach in Thailand where a young Asian boy is happily playing Frisbee with a tourist. When the tourist summons the boy, the young boy's expression changes to despair." ECPAT 1999.

24. Moral panics in the United States surrounding the White Slave Trade during the Progressive Era were facilitated by similar discourses about a "loss of innocence" (Grittner 1990).

CHAPTER 11

Capacity, Consent, and the Construction of Adulthood

LAURIE SCHAFFNER[1]

Adulthood is a legal designation conferred by the state. Socially, majority status represents an age of reason, rights, and responsibilities. United States citizens earn most measures of majority on their eighteenth birthdays when they are bestowed new statutory gains and freedoms. However, codes of permission, consent, privacy, and culpability vary by age across jurisdictions. Laws regarding juveniles' free movement are unevenly apportioned. For example, in certain jurisdictions, young people may not purchase alcohol until their twenty-first birthday, or may be vulnerable plaintiffs in a statutory rape case at 17 years of age, yet may be sentenced to death for crimes committed at age 15 (Cothern 2000; Snyder and Sickmund 1999).[2]

A juvenile waiver to an adult court and statutory rape present two competing examples of laws regulating contemporary U.S. legal constructions of adulthood. Although these two statutes are distinct in their focus and purpose, both are based on assessments of the constitution of juveniles' abilities to make decisions for themselves and to reason as adults, as well as to receive benefits from and be responsible to a larger community.

In this chapter, I compare two bodies of law that govern differing domains of behavior, and both lead to legal conclusions about when youths are capable of reason and intent. The first concerns the finding of capacity or intent when youth commit certain crimes, a finding that may lead to prosecution in adult criminal court. The second body of statutes surrounds the age of heterosexual

189

sexual consent—that is, granting youth the legal status to decide at what age they may legally engage in sexual activity. Although comparing statutes that govern two different dimensions of behavior may seem illogical, the paradox before us here is where these two domains meet—in the sociolegal arena of consent and culpability. Ultimately, it is an "age of reason" that the state scrutinizes, as if in hopes of designating an age when children may be assigned legal responsibility for their acts.

Driven by historically situated narratives about when adolescents develop their decision-making capabilities, both bodies of law construct as they control the transition to adulthood. Both statutes regarding the protection and punishment of minors are purportedly gender and race neutral. However, over the last 30 years, states have lowered the age of capacity for certain offenses, resulting in the punishment of boys as adults at younger ages. Over the same time period, many states have raised the age of sexual consent, resulting in a prolongation of childhood for girls and ultimately disarming them of their capacity to make adult (sexual) decisions. These conflicting sets of statutes have resulted in a racialized skew as well. As this chapter details, the majority of boys sent to adult court are boys of color, and many cases of statutory rape are prosecuted to "protect" white girls.

Legal chauvinism is not a surprising or new development. What is new is this recent presentation of it. The trend to try more and younger children in adult court places the state in the position of reaching opposite conclusions about adolescent development and the construction of adulthood in children of exactly the same age, depending on their gender. Why is it that these laws regarding capable decision-making develop in converse, gendered, age-graded trends? The foundational concepts of adulthood and consent upon which statutory rape laws are currently based challenge the logic of capacity in waiving juveniles to adult court. Surveying the changes over time in the ages of consent and emancipation and the legal language in the codes, I reveal contradictions resulting in clearly constructed, hierarchical gender and racial biases in the discourses surrounding these two bodies of statutes. I find that, although they are neutral in word, ultimately they result in the deployment of gender ideologies to control sexual and criminal behavior and thus construct a gendered and sexualized legal definition of adulthood.

I argue that two complementary notions are at work in these legal codes: the idea of the difference between boys and girls and the notion that agency and action derive from an uncomplicated rational choice. "Different genders" are enshrined and enforced as gender norms are created through regulatory directives. For example, the dominant presentation of juvenile male violent offenders posits them pulling triggers as cold, calculating adults. Girls, by consent laws, however, are postulated to be too young, immature, and naive to choose to have sex.

The only specific federal age of adulthood for all adolescent behavior is a nationally recognized law by all states regarding the attainment of majority status (that includes, for example, the right to vote in federal elections) at 18 years of age. In actuality, juvenile law regarding permission to participate in an array of activities remains dependent on the specific behavior as well as the jurisdiction (see Table 11-1). Age limits for these behaviors can be set, approved, or disapproved by varying bodies of state apparatus, from local city councils to the federal Supreme Court, resulting in differences not only in the definitions of adulthood or delinquency, but also in experiential outcomes during childhood.

As Table 11-1 indicates, statutory regulations determine the activities in which U.S. youth are allowed to participate, as well as punishments for which they are eligible. As shown, minors in many jurisdictions may not sign a legal document (such as a lease or deed of sale for real property), marry, open a bank account on their own, or be outside after 10:00 P.M. before the age of 18. Although statutes that affect young people may vary by state and local mandate, clear gender contradictions emerge when we examine regulations concerning sexual and criminal behavior side by side.

Sexual vs. Criminal Law

In adulthood, sexuality and criminality are often seen as two unrelated and separate spheres of human endeavor and of jurisprudence. Whatever the

Table 11-1 Legal Capacity for Selected Behaviors, by Age*

Age (Years)	Legal Capacity
10	May be housed in a juvenile detention facility
13	Is eligible to be tried as a felon
15	Is eligible for capital punishment
15 ¹/₂	May obtain a driving permit
16	May operate a motor vehicle
16	May work for pay in a public establishment
16	May marry without parental or court permission
16	May observe public curfew
17	Emancipated generally (sign contractual agreements)
18	May vote
18	May serve in the armed services
18	May purchase cigarettes
18	May inherit wealth and assets
18	May consent to sexual intercourse
21	May purchase alcohol

*Ages vary by jurisdiction.

Source: Adapted from Schaffner 1999.

emotional, religious, or cultural geography of the experience, the move to engage in sexual behavior is considered a normative, expected, and eventually encouraged social achievement for young adults. According to current dominant norms in the United States, most parents hope that their children will eventually experience a healthy and happy adult sexuality in their lifetime, albeit for many, preferably in a religiously and legally sanctioned heterosexual long-term monogamous relationship that would lead directly to childbearing.

Criminality, on the other hand, entails a different set of social responses. The "decision" to commit a crime is nowhere held to be normative or encouraged behavior at any age. Gender scholars argue that norms for masculinity may explain many forms of aggression or criminality (Messerschmidt 1993; Newburn and Stanko 1994), and that learning to be masculine includes manifestations of violence against other men (Kaufman 1987). However, felonious crime-committing is hardly considered a "natural" or normatively encouraged developmental stage in growing up. Despite this fact, ever-younger boys are increasingly represented in criminal courtrooms as rational and capable felons.

These disparate constructions of adolescent decision-making and state responses to them share three common dimensions. First, in the manner that the state currently regulates youth behavior, these discourses both share paradigmatic conventional gendered assumptions: that girls are vulnerable to victimization, whereas the boys are willful and agentic, in relationship to both sexuality and crime. For example, although boys are technically protected by child abuse laws, it was not until an explosion in 2002 of (re)allegations of sexual abuse of boys by Catholic priests that boys were framed in popular myth as potential victims who might be vulnerable to sexual predators. When young men engage in sexual activity with slightly older women, prosecutors have historically looked the other way and framed it as "just getting lucky" (Shoop 1999). Psychological and legal literature reveals many more studies of girls' precocious sexuality and its effects, and boys' aggression and violence, than the reverse.[3]

Second, both domains (sexuality and criminality) are frequently represented in public discourse and debate. Adolescent sexuality and adolescent crime present potent battlegrounds for fierce debates about urban poverty, family values, community violence, welfare reform, and the "decline of morality" in society. Scholars, advocates, and public intellectuals debate causes and consequences of "teen pregnancy" or "youth violence" more often than adversarial discussions focus on, say, how old children need to be before they can drive a car. The latter topic will not typically raise a moral panic in national editorial pages or courtrooms.

Last, both sets of statutes form key components in the legal construction of adulthood. Along with granting capacity to work for pay in a public establishment, consume alcoholic beverages, be excused from mandatory education, or roam freely in public at certain hours, giving consent to participate in sexual behavior and assigning culpability in law-offending behaviors sit at the core of the state's paradigm of the rights and responsibilities assumed at the age of majority. The quantity of changes over time and the existence of a much larger body of law in these two areas than in other areas governing majority indicates the centrality of these concepts to the state's framing of rights to adulthood. Thus, unlike other age-graded areas of life, the sexual and criminal practices of young people are not only problematic, but are considered by some commentators to be markers of adulthood, the actions that themselves transform children into adults.

The following sections of this chapter detail the legal construction of adulthood as follows: Part One presents a brief genealogy of legal criteria for adult waiver. These criteria of *mens rea* allow us to explore the logic of the trend that lowered the age of culpability laws over time, as do aggregate data that reflect the resultant gendered and racialized skew of juveniles processed as adults. Part Two provides a parallel genealogy of statutory rape codes, focusing specifically upon the language of the statutes, a key Supreme Court ruling in this area, and what little we can empirically validate about the demographics of case outcomes. By comparing the language of the law and the empirical outcomes, the paradox of the legal construction of adulthood can be seen within notions of empowerment and protection in childhood. I thus make the case that inconsistencies behind the rationale for protecting children from their own capability to consent to certain acts contradicts the logic of assigning them capacity of intent for other acts. This discussion raises a formidable legal paradox: Which (violent) children do we treat like adults and which (sexual) adults do we treat like children?

Part One: Adult Waiver

The decision to prosecute juveniles in adult court is variously referred to throughout the United States as "automatic waiver," "transfer to criminal court," "criminal waiver," "adult waiver," "criminal transfer," or "adult transfer." The process of moving juveniles to adult court may also be referred to as "legislative exclusion" and "prosecutorial direct file." The terms surrounding adjudicative competence are important. The language of the juvenile court purposively differentiates between "delinquents" and "criminals," "adjudication" versus "prosecution," and "detention" versus "prison." One of the key doctrines of reforming the U.S. criminal justice system when the juvenile court was established in 1899 was precisely to separate children from adults (McNamee 1999). Today, such decisions around the use of a waiver accomplish the opposite: They blur and reverse jurisdictional distinctions between juveniles and adults, as well as between delinquents and criminals.

Despite a profound decrease in overall rates of juvenile crime in the 1990s, the decade witnessed an unprecedented change in juvenile corrections systems' approaches to handling serious, habitual, or violent crime by transferring children to adult courts (Bonnie and Grisso 2000). From 1992 through 1997, all but six states enacted or expanded transfer provisions (Snyder and Sickmund 1999). Due to the lack of a unifying federal juvenile court system, we confront an array of terms, standards, codes, statutes, decisions—and data collection— that vary by jurisdictions, often at the county or even city level. The stakes, however, are high. One report found that about two-thirds of juvenile felony defendants waived to adult court and convicted of violent offenses were sentenced to prison (DeFrances and Strom 1997). In criminal court, juveniles (64 percent) were more likely to be charged with a violent felony than were adults (24 percent) (Rainville and Smith 2003). Each year in the last decade of the twentieth century, between 5,000 and 6,000 minors were sent to adult prisons (Bradsher 1999). Minors are transferred to adult court mainly for two reasons: drug sales and serious violent crime, such as forcible rape or homicide.

Table 11-2 displays the outcomes of trends in the latter part of the twentieth century that swept through state legislatures and judges' benches to lower age limits so that juveniles could be transferred from delinquency courts to adult courts. The legal minimum age for juvenile offenders to be transferred to adult courts was lowered generally in a nationwide trend during the 1980s and 1990s: Kansas and Vermont currently allow 10-year-olds to be waived to adult court. Twenty-three other states prefer not to detail a specific lower age limit, leaving it open to interpretation and discretion by a wide array of state actors.

Various statutory provisions offer descriptions of the categories of minors considered young enough to be treated as children, that is, "fit and proper subjects to be dealt with under the juvenile court law" (Griffin, Torbet, and Szymanski 1998). Varying by jurisdiction, these statutory codes provide strict and complex criteria to be met before a minor may be or must be transferred to adult court, with several categories of waiver, depending on jurisdiction.

The notion that children are in essence no different than adults predates the contemporary juvenile corrections system. Ancient and medieval images represented children as mini-adults, laboring without mandatory schooling or other protections (Aries 1962; DeMause 1976). Enlightenment philosophers were the first to introduce innocence and naiveté as the hallmark of "childhood," a term which only became a socially meaningful concept in the nineteenth century. The premise of a juvenile court separating children from adults was revolutionary at the time, declaring that children should be regarded differently from adults. The concept of rehabilitation and training guided the early courts, reflecting the values of some sectors of society who believed in the notion that youthful miscreants could be corrected.

Table 11-2 Lowest Legal Age for Juvenile Waiver to Adult Court, by Jurisdiction, 1997

State	Adult Waiver	State	Adult Waiver
AK	NS*	MT	12
AL	14	NC	13
AR	14	ND	14
AZ	NS*	NE	NS*
CA	14	NH	13
CO	12	NJ	14
CT	14	NM	15
DC	NS*	NV	NS*
DE	NS*	NY	13
FL	NS*	OH	14
GA	NS*	OK	NS*
HI	NS*	OR	NS*
IA	14	PA	NS*
ID	NS*	RI	NS*
IL	13	SC	NS*
IN	NS*	SD	NS*
KS	10	TN	NS*
KY	14	TX	14
LA	14	UT	14
MA	14	VA	14
MD	NS*	VT	10
ME	NS*	WA	NS*
MI	14	WI	NS*
MN	14	WV	NS*
MO	12	WY	13
MS	13		

*"NS" indicates "none specified," because no lower age is in the statute; therefore, transfer into criminal court depends upon prosecutors', judges', or lawmakers' discretion.

Source: Griffin, Torbet, and Szymanski 1998.

Proponents of rehabilitation continue to argue for a supplemental, reworked, and invigorated "jurisprudence of capacity" for the twenty-first century safeguarding of minors' rights and responsibilities (DiMatteo 1995). What is interesting about the current and widespread move against this, the drive to lower the age of responsibility for crimes committed by youth, is that it belies the foundations upon which the reform movement to build a juvenile justice system was built in the first place, turning the clock back toward a pre-Enlightenment notion of children as no different from adults in intention. This swing backward also contradicts the findings of developmental psychologists who have argued throughout the last century that children most certainly are not adults, and that their capacity for judgment is variant (Steinberg and Cauffman 1996; Scott 2000).

The trend toward criminal waiver stems from a belief that pulling the trigger in and of itself has the potential to make a child into an adult. By the mid-1980s, in a panicked response to a purported rise in juvenile violent crime, "reforms" waiving juveniles into the adult system were initiated (Heilbrun et al. 1997). Several political, legal, and cultural factors coalesced during the same time period. Children became victims of or involved in an inordinate amount of community violence (Davis 1999) and guns became readily available to young people (Males 1999). Illegal pharmaceuticals poured into depressed communities (Bourgois 1995). Afterschool programs closed and "zero tolerance for school violence" policies were adopted across the nation (Ayers, Dohrn, and Ayers 2001). Parents worked longer hours, many at two jobs (Hochschild 1997). Newspaper and television reports about rising youth violence, "drive-by shootings," and youth gang crime saturated communities. With more young people left to fend for themselves, and experiencing less adult interaction except with law enforcement, juvenile arrest rates rose. Policing and detention replaced education and family as key socialization agents for increasing numbers of young people, particularly disadvantaged children of color. "Children" were reconstituted as "criminals."

Before a child may be sent to adult court, a determination must be made that he or she is "fit." Fitness is a term denoting a body of specific legal criteria that determine a person's competency to stand trial as a sane adult, or whether he or she can still be rehabilitated in juvenile court. In the following example from California, fitness is determined at a special hearing that draws from testimony on the following five criteria from the *California Welfare and Institutions Codes*, Section 707(a)(1), (West Group 2003):

1. The degree of the criminal sophistication of the minor
2. Whether the minor can be rehabilitated prior to the expiration of juvenile court jurisdiction
3. Previous delinquent history of the minor
4. Success of previous attempts to rehabilitate
5. The circumstances and the gravity of the current offense alleged in the petition

Although these waiver criteria do not articulate gender as a factor in transfer decisions, the results are distinctly skewed by both race and gender. In the eyes of many prosecutors and judges, the implicit profile of the "serious habitual offender" is male. Recent national studies confirm that only a small percentage of juvenile transfer cases are girls (Austin, Johnson, and Gregoriou

2000). Only 5% of the cases waived to adult court nationally in 1997 had female defendant minors (Puzzanchera 2000). In the one year surveyed, less than 6% of adult transfer cases in Illinois involved girls as defendants (Kooy 2002). Adult waiver statutes exacerbate the disproportionate representation of boys—and boys of color in particular—in adult penal systems.

The racialized roots of the trend towards delinquent waiver to criminal court are clearly demarcated in the 1999 national report on the disproportionate representation of minorities in the juvenile legal system (OJJDP 1999). One sociological study details the processes by which African American boys were already "adultified" in public schools and, as such, punished more harshly than "little boys" might have been (Ferguson 2000). Another ethnography in a school setting found that, although most educators claimed to be "color-blind," almost every boy of African American descent in one school had been considered a "troublemaker" at some point by his teachers and administrators (Lewis 2003). Adult waiver statutes, like school "zero-tolerance" policies and death penalty laws, remain race-neutral in wording yet produce overwhelmingly racially skewed outcomes.[4] For example, in Cook County, Illinois, one of the largest juvenile jurisdictions in the nation, less than 1% of cases in a recent study of adult transfers involved "Caucasian" defendants, while over 99% of cases had defendants of African American and Latino heritage (Kooy 2002).

The ironic backdrop to adult waiver is that even before jurisdictions lowered their age limits, actual juvenile violent crime rates were on the decline. The tragic charade of this racially and gender-skewed legal definition of adulthood becomes even more apparent when placed in relief with another set of statutes that regulate capacity: the age of sexual consent.

Part Two: Sexual Consent

No nationally agreed-upon minimum age signals the legal capacity to consent to sexual intercourse. "Statutory rape" is the term for sexual contact with a minor; it originated in the Western medieval notion that girls' chastity represented their chance to be marriageable (girls' "virtue" constituted their survival mechanism). Despite social, economic, political, and cultural shifts in gender norms since the seventeenth and eighteenth centuries, sexual consent laws have persisted into the present (Odem 1995).[5] According to guidelines presented by the United States Department of Justice, current consent laws have several purposes, which include protecting minors from sexual intercourse, protecting minors from exploitation by older predators, preventing and reducing teen pregnancy, reducing the number of young mothers on welfare, and encouraging responsibility in sexuality and parenting (Davis and Twombly 2000). Many commentators agree that some degree of gendered state intervention is sorely needed: The risk of being sexually assaulted is 170 percent greater for children than adults, and girls are abused, assaulted, and raped at higher rates than boys (Finkelhor 1994; Crimes Against Children Research Center 2001).

Originally, limits on the legal age of sexual consent were organized explicitly by gender. In terms of age of consent to marry, general practice in fourteenth-century Europe accepted that girls could consent to marriage at age 12, although boys could consent at age 14 (Olsen 1984; Andre-Clark 1992; Phipps 1997). The gendering of sexual and marital consent laws persisted well into the nineteenth century (Larson 1997). During the twentieth century, almost all states equalized the codes for girls and boys, and by the year 2000, only two states retained gendered differences in the ages at which boys and girls could consent to marry. Table 11-3 displays changes in the legal age of sexual consent

TABLE 11-3 Changes in Lowest Legal Age for Heterosexual Consent, 1885 and 1996

State	1885	1996	State	1885	1996
AK	n/a*	16	MT	10	16
AL	10	16	NC	10	13
AR	12	16	ND	10	15
AZ	10	18	NE	10	16
CA	10	18	NH	10	13
CO	10	15	NJ	10	13
CT	10	16	NM	10	13
DC	12	16	NV	12	16
DE	7	16	OH	10	13
FL	10	18	OK	n/a*	16
GA	10	16	OR	n/a*	18
HI	n/a*	14	PA	10	14
IA	10	16	RI	10	16
ID	10	16	SC	10	14
IL	10	18	SD	10	16
IN	n/a*	14	TN	10	18
KS	10	16	TX	10	17
KY	12	16	UT	10	16
LA	12	17	VA	12	13
MA	10	16	VT	10	16
ME	10	16	WA	12	18
MI	10	13	WI	10	18
MN	10	13	WV	12	16
MO	12	14	WY	10	16
MS	10	14			

*Not available.

Sources: Odem 1995; Eskridge and Hunter 1997.

laws by state jurisdictions in the United States from 1895 to 1996. As the table indicates, the age of heterosexual consent has gradually risen in the last 100 years in every state in the nation.

Although it is outside the scope of this chapter to explore in detail the implications of the fact that statutory rape codes encompass only heterosexual congress, it is important to note that current understandings of statutory rape consider it almost exclusively in heterosexual terms. Legally constituting statutory rape as a primarily heterosexual offense creates another set of inequalities where the state deploys gender to control sexual behavior. "First consensual sexual activity" is generally assumed to mean heterosexual penetrative intercourse. Despite the fact that the 2003 Supreme Court ruling *Lawrence v. Texas* outlawed discrimination based on sexual orientation, it is unlikely that many cases of statutory rape have been or will soon be vigorously prosecuted with the intent to protect lesbian, gay, bisexual, or transgender adolescents.

In its 1985 *Model Penal Code,* the American Law Institute (ALI) proposed language for jurisdictions to adopt in an effort to standardize laws for statutory rape. However, the ALI assumed that statutory rape, child sexual abuse, and criminal sexual assault were heterosexual crimes. The authors indicated that the prevailing pattern was to deal with "imposition upon males" in a separate statute (American Law Institute 1985). Normative heterosexuality was also made explicit in the statutes when, for example, the authors referred to a choice between either "heterosexual relations with a female under the age of 10" or "deviate sexual intercourse with any *person* less than 10 years old" (American Law Institute 1985) (emphasis added).

The sculptors of the *Model Penal Code* noted that the age of consent for "deviate sexual intercourse" (meaning homosexuality) was set for 18 years of age because the "emotional instability" of adolescence is more prolonged for males than for females. Thus, they argued, it was justified and desirable to "extend protection against homosexual seduction of both males and females through the normal years of secondary education" (American Law Institute 1985, 380). Herein lies the key sociolegal debate regarding the legal age of responsibility: In the context of a waiver to adult court, boys are regarded as more mature. But the *Model Penal Code* asserts that, because boys mature later than girls, they should be protected from "homosexual seduction" through high school. These contradictions, crucial to the adolescent legal experience, are rarely considered in the courtroom.

As befits the gendered intent of the law, statutory rape laws are also gender-specific in practice. In general, the state focuses upon prosecuting older men for sexual intercourse with young women and does not address the gender-specific experiences of statutory rape for boys by women (Nelson and Oliver 1998). In 2000, the first year that California tracked the gender of statutory rape defendants, fewer than 100 of 2,500 cases had female defendants (Levine

2003). In the 1970s, California law explicitly defined unlawful sexual intercourse as any "act of sexual intercourse accomplished with a female not the wife of the perpetrator, where the female is under 18 years of age" (*Michael M. v. Sonoma* 1981).

A 1981 case tested this statute before the U.S. Supreme Court. Michael M., a 17-year-old white boy, was charged with having sexual intercourse with Sharon, a 16-year-old white girl. Sharon met Michael M. at a bus stop and went to a nearby park to drink and socialize with him. After kissing and touching each other, Sharon pleaded with Michael M. to desist, but he forced the completion of sexual intercourse with Sharon against her will. Found guilty of violating California's statutory rape law, Michael M. challenged the constitutionality of the law regarding the vagueness of consent. Not only did the Court uphold the California conviction, but its decision hinged specifically upon the gendered language of the statute. The U.S. Supreme Court defended this gender-responsive language, citing that "young men and young women are not similarly situated with respect to the problems and the risks of sexual intercourse" (*Michael M. v. Sonoma* 1981).

Most likely due to feminist legal advocacy on behalf of children, almost all states recrafted their consent laws to be gender-neutral. For example, the altered language in the California statute now reads that it is unlawful to engage in sexual intercourse that is " . . . accomplished with a person who is not the spouse of the perpetrator, if the person is under the age of 18 years" (West Group 2003). In other states such as Illinois, the term "statutory rape" has been further degendered into the more symbolically neutral language of "criminal sexual assault against a minor" (Illinois Compiled Statutes 2003). Yet despite the gender-neutral language, evidence suggests that a majority of prosecutions concern sexual relations between minor girls and adult men.[6] This concern was reflected in the sample of one major study by the American Bar Association, as noted in the title, "Sexual Relationships Between Adult Males and Young Teen Girls" (Elstein and Davis 1997).

Among the feminists and legal scholars who work in this area of law, it is not unusual to find contradictory arguments about discrepancies between the gender-, race-, and sexual orientation-neutral de facto language of the law and the decidedly skewed de jure outcomes. On one hand, girls need protection from predatory men.[7] On the other hand, young women's sexual and romantic relationships may serve as pathways to autonomy, the filling of a need for attachment and protection that they perceive as missing in their families, or even as a way to get away from sexual predators.[8] Controversial discussions among life-course theorists debate whether sexual contact between children and adults might at times be deemed "sexual transition" instead of "sexual trauma."[9] Finally, the promotion of the idea of protecting "innocence" is a form of infantalizing girls that Western culture does not impose on boys. Given the amount of sexual activity extant among youth, statutory rape laws are not only selectively prosecuted but in most cases essentially unenforceable (Hollenberg 1999; Oberman 2000). In a 2003 national report, 56 percent of respondents aged 15 to 17 confided that they had "been with someone in an intimate or sexual way" (The Kaiser Family Foundation 2003).

Furthermore, in the language of the *Handbook* issued by the American Bar Association, there appears to be an intentional conflation of adolescent sexuality with victimization, pregnancy, promiscuity, dependency, and forcible rape, and a blurring of important distinctions among these incidents (Davis and Twombly 2000). Merging adolescent sexuality, unwed teenage pregnancy, and criminal sexual assault against children suggests that the state's age-based consent and capacity laws have high political stakes. For example, in the late 1980s and early 1990s, in response to a nationwide moral panic over unwed teenage pregnancies and single mothers on welfare, the U.S. Department of Justice allocated funds to revitalize statutory rape units in states' attorneys' offices (Lynch 1998; Hollenberg 1999). California funded counties with high rates of unmarried teenage births to form "Statutory Rape Vertical Prosecution" (SRVP) units. By 1997, former California Governor Pete Wilson had dedicated $8.4 million dollars to these programs (Elton 1997), particularly focusing upon older men who impregnated young girls (Hallinan 1998). From 1995 to 1997, 43% of the cases filed for prosecution in California involved a pregnancy (Hollenberg 1999). The state appeared more motivated to find "somebody" to pay for these pregnancies rather than to acknowledge that forcible rape and child sexual abuse was occurring, or, more importantly, that young women were possibly capable of consenting. As one California government report made clear, a chief goal of its Statutory Rape Vertical Prosecution (SVRP) program was "to seek paternity determination and enforce child support and obligation" (SRVP 2002).

In the eyes of the state, statutory rape leads to pregnancy, which leads to welfare: hence, the need for revitalized prosecutory units.[10] However, many prosecutors were themselves suspicious of this argument. In one study, even though 74% of Kansas City state attorneys "believed in aggressive enforcement" of statutory rape, only 24% believed enforcement would reduce adolescent pregnancy (Miller and Miller 1998). Research has shown that even successful enforcement of statutory rape laws is unlikely to lead to substantial reductions in teen childbearing (Elo, King, and Furstenberg 1999).

Federal collection sites for data regarding statutory rape prosecutions by race, ethnicity, gender identity, sexual orientation, age, and relationship between plaintiff and defendant are nonexistent, so it is difficult to determine precisely the demographics of victims and perpetrators. However, we do know that the number of reported arrests for unlawful sexual intercourse with a minor doubled from 1992 to 1999 in California (California Department of

Justice 2001). California data clearly demonstrates that the law is overwhelmingly applied against males: In 1999, for example, there were arrests of 1,280 males versus 117 females (California Department of Justice 2001). Because demographic case-by-case data is not available, the disparity among instances of statutory rape, arrests, and the selective prosecutions of these incidents in accordance with the victims' and perpetrators' racial and ethnic backgrounds is not known. Possible regulatory inequities demand improved public scrutiny.

Conclusion

Discussions of childhood, sexuality, and youth crime persist in stimulating virulent morality battles in the contemporary United States. The lowering age of puberty and the declining age of first consensual sex have been important contributors to changes in sociosexual mores (The Alan Guttmacher Institute 1994; Brumberg 1997). Girls, in particular, engage in sexual experimentation at earlier ages now than their counterparts 100 years ago (The Kaiser Family Foundation 2003). This, coupled with an increase in the amount of unwanted, unsolicited, and nonconsensual sexual attention that young women receive, has led some advocates who work with victimized girls to argue for their increased protection and to regard the expansion of statutory rape codes and the stepped-up enforcement of child protection standards as reasonable legal solutions.

On the other hand, for most teens in the United States the very human decision to proceed with sexual relations is not a matter of if, but when. The infantalizing and protectionist tendencies inherent in age-of-consent laws may hinder or even harm children as they grow into adulthood. Some scholars have suggested that child-adult sex may someday become more normalized in Western societies, akin to trends that anthropologists have documented in non-Western contexts (Bleibtreu-Ehrenberg 1991; Herdt 1997). In an equally explosive debate within psychology, researchers challenged certain conventional understandings of child sexual abuse, such as that it always causes harm and that the experience is just as negative for boys as it is for girls (Rind et al. 1998). Their "meta-analytic" review of studies sought to demonstrate that the long-term impact of child sexual abuse was not necessarily traumatic. They suggested renaming "child sexual abuse" with a more morally neutral term such as "adult-child sex" (Rind et al. 1998). Response to this position was rapid and severe: Other researchers, as well as the American Psychological Association, distanced themselves from it and sought to discredit this research.[11] Yet the fact that this debate occurred at all suggests the possibility that current ideas about childhood sexuality may eventually become anachronisms like the miscegenation ordinances of eras past.

Meanwhile, parallel disputes over the legal trend to prosecute minors in adult court are waged in popular and legal arenas. Proponents argue that, given changes in cultural and social mores regarding children, the juvenile court should be abandoned altogether (Feld 1999; Bradshaw 1995; Howell 1997). "Three strikes and you're out" laws and "zero tolerance" policies have been adopted around the nation (Ayers et al. 2001). Media representations of children depict them as simply much too violent to be protected from punishment anymore. Yet critics note in horror that children who committed their crimes before the age of 18 can be and are put to death (Males 1999). The tug-of-war over whether children *should* grow up fast or *already* have grown up fast continues.[12]

The history of state responses to adolescent sexuality and adolescent delinquency reveals that the state actually constructs gendered categories of adulthood as it moves to protect, control, and punish youth. In the two areas of law discussed in this chapter, girls are represented as in need of protection, and boys in need of punishment. Whereas young girls are seen as not having the capability to make adult decisions (i.e., sexual choices), young boys are increasingly regarded as capable of clear, logical, informed adult decision making (to engage in criminal conduct). Boys of color are disproportionately represented in the juvenile court system and form the majority of children transferred to adult facilities. This provokes a disturbing paradox: Must the state continue to safeguard minors' rights, or have we exhausted our current juvenile system for the protection and amelioration it promised?

The mission of this chapter has not been so much to resolve the conflicts regarding the value of statutory rape laws, or to determine definitively whether or not children are adult enough to be put to death for their crimes, but rather to reframe these questions in the light of the actual sociological purposes toward which these laws are utilized. Racialized, heterosexualized, and gendered patterns of protectionism emerge when compared with opposing trends towards culpability that operate in relation to serious juvenile offending. Young boys of color need and deserve as much protection as girls. Mature young women should be afforded the same respect for their "decisions" as young boys, yet rationales regarding the two bodies of law that regulate these behaviors reflect the opposite.

Reviewing the underlying reasoning and political discourses that surround these laws leads me to make the following four recommendations. First, statutory rape laws are archaic, unenforceable, and should be dispensed with. Eliminating "statutory" rape gets the state out of the social business of overseeing the activities in teenagers' beds. Phasing out "statutory" rape laws challenges states to unify criminal sexual assault statutes with extant child sexual abuse codes so that sexual intercourse between adults and children is captured as criminal and "regular" forcible rape laws (i.e., not statutory rape laws) capture all other instances of forcible sexual assault. All states have laws regarding the criminal sexual assault of children. State by state, statutory consent laws should be abandoned and child sexual abuse, sexual assault, and rape laws unified and strengthened federally. Forcible rape should be punished as a federal hate crime against humanity—no matter the age, gender identity, sexual orientation, racial or ethnic heritage, or any other demographic factor of the victim or perpetrator.

Second, the Justice Department and state governments must drop their pursuit, through prosecution of statutory rape, of unrelated and competing goals such as unwed teen pregnancy and welfare dependency. Studies show that these social problems are better addressed outside the courtroom (Roberts 2001). The juvenile legal system must not continue to inherit adult-made problems derived from failed social, political, and economic policies.

Third, juvenile waiver to an adult court, according to any criteria, should be completely abandoned as a judicial policy. Children are better served in juvenile court. If problems with juvenile court exist, we must focus our attention on solving them, not on disbanding the court. If a review of the adolescent psychological literature tells us one thing, it is that children are not adults. The way out of our current prosecutorial standoff to constituting adulthood logically is through a shift in adult thinking, not more strictly limiting children's behaviors. Delinquency courts could become revitalized locations of peer education, peer juries, family education, community resources, and public health campaigns.

Solutions to social problems of youth violence and adolescent pregnancy are not simple, inexpensive, or fast. Indeed, they are complex, expensive, and time-consuming. Case by case, each child deserves to have his or her life's circumstances sorted out with care and innovation. We must move off the stalemate produced by the question, "How old is an adult?" and move to the real issue, "How do adults model adult behavior and dispense adult power?" Discussions about sexual education; frank discussions about the meanings of sexuality; conversations about anger, violence, and guns; rehabilitating violent offenders all take time, money, and energy. This leads me to my last recommendation.

The *United Nations Convention on the Rights of the Child* sets as an international standard that a child is any person under the age of 18 years. This international agreement affords children protections they require, including the protection from the state to impose upon them adult punishment. As was the unanimous international demand at the 2002 World Congress of the Child, the United States must adopt and enforce the provisions of the *Convention*. As we enter a new century, we witness an increased sexualization of young girls, along with the overcrowding of adult prisons with boys of color. The absurdity of putting children in adult prisons with one set of laws, as we prolong their childhood with another, becomes clear when the sexual and criminal codes are placed side by side. The central dilemma we are left with is not to come up with magic numbers to represent variant "ages of reason" for adulthood, but to notice how the state deploys gender to control sex. How the state moves to equalize these trends will have great consequences for our nation's children.

Notes

1. For research assistance, intellectual support, and critical readings, I would like to thank Elizabeth Bernstein, Lorena Diaz de Leon, Bernadine Dohrn, Elena Gutierrez, Sara Hall, Kerwin Kaye, Mindie Lazarus-Black, Kay Levine, Amanda Lewis, Greg Matoesian, Gayatri Reddy, Penelope Saunders, and Beth Richie.
2. *Black's Law Dictionary* suggests that legal usage of the term "minor" usually refers to children who have not achieved the status of the age of majority, and advocates usage of the term "juvenile" to refer to minors being adjudicated as delinquent offenders (Black 1991). In this chapter, I use the terms "children," "youth," "juveniles," and "minors" interchangeably.
3. Kaye (this volume) provides a feminist and historical critique of child sexual abuse. He notes that although the issue is often presented as genderless, the phenomenon is deeply gendered in both discourse and practice.
4. Zero-tolerance policies were adopted by schools across the United States in response to saturating nationwide media coverage of school shootings in the 1990s. The policies recommend zero tolerance for any kind of indication of violence, including threatening violence or bringing in sharp objects that could be used as weapons.
5. Ericsson (this volume) suggests that a parallel trend can be traced in Norway.
6. Excellent presentations of this argument can be found in Davis and Twombly (2000), Leitenberg and Saltzman (2000), Nezlek (2002), and Levine (2003).
7. Variations of this are well argued in Higginson (1999), Phillips (1999), and Oberman (2000).
8. See Musick (1993), Jacobs (1994), Schaffner (1997), and Oliveri (2000).
9. See discussions in Browning and Laumann (1997), Levesque (2000), and Levine (2002).
10. See also Donovan (1997).
11. See Erickson (2000) and Tavris (2000).
12. For interesting versions of this argument see Elkind (1981), Postman (1983), Winn (1993), and Hymowitz (1999).

4
Beyond Regulation:
Towards Sexual Justice

CHAPTER **12**

How Libertine Is the Netherlands?
Exploring Contemporary Dutch Sexual Cultures

GERT HEKMA

Some years ago, I conducted research on gay men and lesbian women in organized sports in the Netherlands. The government wanted to know about discrimination and racism in sports, as well as about discrimination against gays and lesbians. The results were both comforting and disturbing. They were comforting because there was little discrimination, but they were disturbing because of the reason: Gays and lesbians in general kept silent about their preferences. Discrimination occurred only in the most brazenly lesbian sport: women's soccer. Most incidents of violent and verbal abuse happened precisely in the sport where lesbians prevail, so much so that some soccer clubs even refused to have women's teams. The conclusions were clear: If gays and lesbians were to come out of the closet and begin to speak as freely as straight athletes did about their sexual interests, they would undoubtedly face discrimination. At the time of our research, violence and abuse were absent because homosexual interests and preferences were silenced (Hekma 1994).

This research led me to wonder about Dutch liberalism, particularly because half of our respondents lived in Amsterdam, which is reputed to be an international gay capital (Hekma 1999). Yet the situation for gay men and lesbian women has not been as rosy as the popular media image of the Netherlands suggests. Not surprisingly, the government used only the positive findings from my research, in order to point to a lack of discrimination. What was quickly passed over was the reason for gays' and lesbians' continued silence: the

209

persistent fear of displaying homosexual desire in a straight world. This chapter seeks to explain the meanings of the gap between the libertine reputation and conservative practices of the Dutch.

The argument of the chapter runs as follows. First, I discuss the discrepancy between liberal Dutch sexual attitudes and conservative sexual practices. Second, I seek to explain this discrepancy by pointing to a one-sided sexual ideology that privileges nature over culture, male over female, love over sex, and private over public, while insisting upon the absolute antagonism between sex and violence. This is an ideology that stems from the eighteenth-century Enlightenment, one that has been altered little by the various sexual revolutions that have occurred since that time. In the conclusion to this chapter, I suggest that the ideological apparatus that surrounds sex in the Netherlands ought to be expanded to create a greater variety of erotic possibilities and choices for individuals.

Contemporary Sexualities in the Netherlands

Paradoxes abound when it comes to sexuality in the Netherlands, and not only with regard to the gap between homosexual practices and identities. Another paradox exists between tolerant sexual attitudes, on one hand, and the actual amount of sexual experimentation on the other. Explicit sexual imagery is pervasive in the media, and many people seem to enjoy this. But, in general, very few people ever do what they see depicted in these images, according to national sex surveys (Zessen and Sandfort 1991).

After the sexual revolution of the 1960s, some commentators predicted an explosion of sexual freedom. According to all recent sex surveys, this did not happen. What did happen, according to sociologists, was that mainstream attitudes caught up with long-term changes in sexual practices. People had long been doing what they "should not" do. Before the 1960s, people were already participating in the acts that, after the sexual revolution, they would perform with less shame and less secrecy (Schnabel 1990). Before the 1960s, morality and practice diverged, but in the 1960s, the Dutch began to accept their own behaviors. Morality and practice came into agreement, and then morality got ahead of practice. Since the 1960s, fewer men have homosexual sex, although more men define themselves as gay. Although the Dutch have become more accepting in many areas of sexuality (with the notable exception of children's sexuality), practices lag behind.

The general template for contemporary Dutch sexual practices can be summarized as follows: serial monogamy with a limited promiscuity at the beginning of sexual careers, and faithfulness in relationships. The normal sex act is coital with some oral foreplay, and other forms of sex are infrequent. Coital sex is so normalized that government campaigns tend to see a choice only between sex with a condom and no sex at all, as if most sexual practices were unsafe without a condom. Prostitution is now on the decline, both for sexual initiation and for extramarital sex. Less than 3% of Dutch men report having experience with prostitutes (Zessen and Sandfort 1991, 92).

To keep desire alive inside sexual relations, the consumption of soft pornography is on the rise. The Dutch use twice as much pornography as do U.S. citizens (Zessen and Sandfort 1991, 121; Laumann et al. 1994, 135). In the Netherlands, more men say they are gay than in Britain or in the U.S., but fewer men participate in homosexual acts (Zessen and Sandfort 1991, 80–81; Wellings et al. 1994, 182–189; Laumann et al. 1994, 293–294). Homosexual behavior is becoming confined to a small minority, while the traditional sexual border traffic between gay and heterosexual men, between "queen" and "trade," is disappearing (Hekma 1992; Chauncey 1994). Meanwhile, self-stimulation is on the rise for both men and women (Zessen and Sandfort 1991, 128–129). One could argue that with individualization comes onanization. Feelings of guilt about masturbation are slowly disappearing, more quickly in Holland than in the U.S. (Zessen and Sandfort 1991, 130; Laumann et al. 1994, 85).

Since the 1970s, the Netherlands has been among the nations with the most open-minded attitudes toward abortion, contraception, premarital sex, pornography, prostitution, and homosexuality (Zessen and Sandfort 1991, 102–103). Because of the strong commitment to relations premised upon love, extramarital sex is becoming less tolerated. This belief in love and equal relations is the basis for the wide acceptance among the Dutch of gay and lesbian marriage. An exception to Dutch tolerance is everything that is connected to child sexuality, from incest to child pornography to sex play among children. After discussions of the sexual abuse of children emerged in the late 1970s, intergenerational sex has become coterminous with abuse (Rossen 1989). In 2001, the government raised the age of consent from 12 to 16 years, and raised the legal age for working in pornography or prostitution from 16 to 18. The law passed Parliament with a very rare unanimous vote (*De Nieuwe Sekstant* 2002).

Shifts in Dutch social attitudes have been reflected in other legal changes as well. Statutes regarding abortion, pornography, public sex, and homosexuality have become less strict (Melai 1980; Moerings and Swier 1997). Earning money from prostitution was legalized in October 2000. Prostitution is now considered to be normal labor for all parties concerned and regulated at the level of the city. Today, sex-workers have their own organizations, and streetwalkers have been provided with safe zones (called "tippelzones") where they can solicit clients under the protection of the police (*NRC Handelsblad* 1999). However, the social acceptance of prostitution lags behind legal improvements, as it continues to be seen by most Dutch citizens as an abject profession.

For gays and lesbians, additional important changes have transpired in the last 30 years. Since 1974, they have been allowed entry into the armed forces

(Ketting and Soesbeek 1992, 6). Since the 1980s, gay cruising areas are no longer raided, but rather are protected by the police (Lieshout 1995). The Dutch Army and the police specifically advertise for gay and lesbian soldiers and officers. Since April of 2001, legal marriage has been available to same-sex couples and has included full social and financial rights, including adoption (Velde 2001).

The sexual policies of the Netherlands, which seem on the surface to make sex more easily and widely available, in practice have not had this effect. To the contrary, legally protected forms of sex, such as homosexuality and prostitution, are even on the decline. It is my contention that the main explanation for this is to be found in another field of sexual politics. Today, men and women alike restrict their sexual pleasures to stable relationships, in a sense realizing the vision of Friedrich Engels (1883, 511), who argued that under socialism, not only women, but men, too, would be monogamous. The Netherlands has become a sexual-social democracy, premised upon equal and monogamous partnerships. Outside of the context of stable relationships, both men and women have difficulty finding pleasure.

I offer the following explanations of why the Dutch, notwithstanding their liberal reputation, still have a sexual culture that remains highly restricted. These restrictions have remained in place despite the fact that in other fields of consumption, social differentiation has developed far more quickly. The points I am making are not specific to the Dutch, but pertain largely if in different ways to other Western countries. My examples will be, however, mainly from Holland.

My questions are: Why didn't the sexual revolution bring about a revolution of erotic practices? Why was a fuller range of sexual freedom not realized? What obstacles keep tolerant attitudes from becoming libertine practices? One could argue with Foucault (1978) that experienced freedoms are also expressions of power effects, and the repression of sexualities a side effect of their production. With certain feminists, one could argue that, under conditions of male dominance, men's sexual freedom and women's sexual subjection are merely two faces of the same coin (MacKinnon 1989). Or with Bataille (1957), one could argue that Eros and Thanatos (the sex and death drives) are closely linked. While acknowledging the merits of these arguments, in this chapter I will investigate a series of additional obstacles to sexual expression in contemporary Western societies.

I have identified five major obstacles to sexual freedom that prevail in Western ways of thinking. The first is the sexual-gender division; the second is the view that sex and sexuality belong to nature; the third is that sex and love should be combined; the fourth is that sex is a private affair; and the fifth is that sex should be nonviolent.

1. *Sex is a male affair.* In sexual surveys, men confess to engaging in more sex than do women in nearly all domains: heterosexual and homosexual acts, masturbation, and the use of pornography (Zessen and Sandfort 1991; Spira et al. 1993; Wellings et al. 1994; Laumann et al. 1994). Men define themselves in sexual terms more frequently than do women. Women answer affirmatively in higher percentages than men only in response to questions of sexual abuse and the desire to be dominated (Zessen and Sandfort 1991, 125; Laumann et al. 1994, 336). The gender division is even clearer in the world of prostitution. Prostitution transactions consist almost exclusively of men buying the services of women, and when men sell their bodies, they do so primarily to other men (Visser and Oomens 2000; Pheterson 1996). Although some male sex-workers cater to women (O'Connell Davidson and Sánchez Taylor, this volume), this is a small minority of the sex trade in most locations. A rather intriguing new trend, the presence of male-to-female transsexuals, transgender persons, and transvestites among female prostitutes, seems to interrupt the gender dichotomy, but it also strengthens the male sexual position as a consumer of prostitution, with men and former men offering sexual services alongside women to so-called heterosexual men (Bast 1997).

Gender differences are also very clearly in evidence among gays and lesbians. Although dozens of gay institutions exist in Amsterdam, as in other "gay capitals," the number of lesbian venues is less than a dozen. Gay spaces offer access to sex in dark rooms, saunas, and public cruising areas, whereas the few endeavors to organize public sex spaces for lesbians have failed (Kooten Niekerk and Wijmer 1985; Nijboer 1994; Hekma 1992 and 1999).

Admittedly, the range of sexual practices that women participate in has expanded a great deal in recent decades. Women now attend sex parties, participate in sadomasochism (S/M), fetish, and exhibitionist groups (Rubin 1991; Squires 1993), and have even broached the topic of female pedophilia (Sax and Deckwitz 1992). But the women who do so are a tiny minority, in much smaller proportions than men. The only dark room for heterosexuals in Amsterdam attracts many more men than women. The gender disparity is further revealed by the fact that women or heterosexual couples who go to parties and discos do not have to pay for entry, although men alone or in groups are charged an entrance fee.

The sexual-gender division is very clear: Since the late-eighteenth century, women have been considered in Western thought to be asexual or love-oriented, and sex has primarily been a male privilege. Until the eighteenth century, women were believed to become prostitutes out of lust; in the nineteenth century the explanation was more often found in socioeconomic conditions, especially poverty. Since that time, men have been believed to desire sex, and women to desire love (Pol 1996; Laqueur 1990; Kraakman 1997). Although the modern sexual-gender system has come under criticism, its broad parameters are still intact. Gender differences may be slowly disappearing in many areas in the Netherlands, but the erotic field remains resistant to change.

In the Netherlands, the state actively perpetuates the sexual-gender divide that is produced in families and peer groups. As part of feminist sexual policy, the government fights against the sexual oppression of women. It is very active in the struggle against sexual abuse and the trafficking of women. Accordingly, public school sex education and commercials produced by the government instruct girls and women to say "no" to the sexual advances of boys and men, and instruct boys and men to accept that girls and women say "no." The presumption of this kind of education is both sexist and heterosexist. Teaching children only how to civilly decline heterosexual sex does not help children of either gender to explore their sexual preferences, or to enjoy sex in all its diversity. Teaching kids to say yes to sex might more effectively instill a healthy sexuality, because once they had learned to say yes to what they desired, they would also know to say no to specific undesired or destructive sexual propositions.

2. *Sex is natural.* Sexuality is defined by the state, public education, and science as a drive—an instinct that resides in genes and hormones. Sexual preference is presumed to be founded in bodily structures such as genes, brains, or chromosomes. Most research on sexual preference is on the physiology of gay men's sexual choices, as if the sexual preferences of heterosexuals and lesbians were blank spots (LeVay 1993). Sex education, in most cases, is confined to physiology and partnership: discussions about the physiology of genital organs, making relationships work, and some information about pregnancy and venereal disease. It rarely addresses courtship, seduction, sexual acts, bodily functioning, or the culture and history of sex. Masturbation is not considered something you have to learn; supposedly, it comes naturally. Sex education is about the prevention of disaster, not about the production of pleasure.

The overwhelming message is that sex is natural. There is a strange refusal to acknowledge the cultural sides of sex. This is all the more problematic given prevailing levels of sexual harassment and abuse. The belief in the naturalness of sex offers a ready excuse to men who perpetrate sexual abuse—they say that they could not "help it," because their hormones forced them to do what they should not do. Yet the last thing authorities consider is education about sexual etiquette, styles, and cultures, because they generally believe sexuality is natural and flows unmediated from genes and hormones. Although most contemporary social theorists believe that sex is culturally constructed, very few people outside this discipline or academia share that viewpoint.

The contemporary idea of the nature of sex has been handed down from the eighteenth century, as physical nature replaced divine nature. During the Enlightenment, religious explanations were replaced by biological and physiological explanations. The nineteenth-century Darwinian theory of evolution and early sexology spread and strengthened the idea that sexuality was founded in nature, but philosophers such as Lamettrie and Sade had come up with the idea a century earlier (Hekma 1987, 30; Stockinger 1979). Since the late nineteenth century, sexual preference, especially male homosexuality, has been considered to be innate (Wettley 1959; Lanteri-Laura 1979; Hekma 1987; Bullough 1994; Oosterhuis 2000). Since the 1980s, ideas about the nature of sex have been strengthened even more (Fausto-Sterling 2000). The Dutch government promotes this message in its propaganda, in media campaigns and on billboards. Yet what Western societies most need is not the naturalization of desires, but sexual culture, or the cultivation of sexuality.

3. *Sex is love.* From sexual and social surveys, it appears that most Dutch people strongly endorse the idea that sex should be confined to love or marital relations. A large majority of the youth endorse the idea of sexual fidelity (Vogels and Vliet 1990, 80–82). The vast majority of heterosexual and lesbian people want to be faithful to their partners. Only among gay men is it quite common to separate love and sex, although the emergence of gay marriage has inclined many gay men away from promiscuity. Few people accept extramarital sex. Jealousy is very much an artifact of the present time, however outdated the concept may seem.

Remarkably, throughout most of Western history, love was defined in opposition to sex. In medieval courtly love, sexual acts were excluded. Spiritual love was ascetic. Even the romantic love tradition was platonic—that is to say, nonsexual (Paz 1993; compare Goodrich 1996). Until the twentieth century, marital relations expressed primarily economic or social necessities, rather than an ideal of egalitarian or democratic loving relations. Marriage was a contract between families, not between individuals who had fallen in love. Only very recently has the idea that sex and love should be combined become general practice and ideology.

Yet combining love and sex may pose severe problems both for love and for sex. Kinsey (1948, 226–227) noted that the sexual output of men diminished in their twenties, and he argued that this was to be explained by male sexual physiology. Later Dannecker and Reiche (1974, 200–203) reanalyzed this decline not as a biological fact but as a result of sexual boredom in marital relations. They found that the gay population who did not combine sex and love continued to have a high sexual output until their late thirties, and that sexual activity declined only after age 40, due to the fetishism of youth in gay culture.[1] A recent American survey analyzed sexual adaptation in couples and came to the conclusion that basing sex in love is unrealistic because it is highly improbable that people who suit each other in love, also suit one another sexually (Laumann et. al., 1994, 161–71). Often, people divorce one another when sexual desire is extinguished. Nevertheless, because marriage is culturally defined as the major road to both sex and love, most people will seek the fulfillment of their sexual desires and loving relations inside this institution.

4. *Sex is private.* One of the strongest ideas concerning sex relates to privacy. The liberal argument is that the state and the citizen each have their own realm: The state is responsible for public affairs, and the citizen for his or her private affairs. The state should not touch upon the privacy of the citizen unless there is good reason to do so. Sexuality belongs to the private realm. This social order came about with the Enlightenment and the French Revolution. Before that time, sex was a public affair of families, villages, churches, and the king. Showing the bloodstained sheets after the first wedding night was a custom that made sex a public affair. The French Revolution brought with it a complete change in making sex a private affair. It introduced penal laws against public indecency, forbidding all sex that was performed in public. This law replaced older laws that forbade nonmarital and nonprocreative sex, especially laws against lewdness and sodomy (Hekma 1987, 31–37).

Under the new regime, the private world was male and heterosexual. It was a world of respectability. All forms of sex that did not fit this model were driven into public, where they were liable to persecution under public decency laws. In the Netherlands in the nineteenth century, public decency laws were mainly used against same-sex acts between men. At the end of the century, the new category of exhibitionism was added, although heterosexual sex rarely was persecuted. When it was, punishments were much less severe than for homosexual and exhibitionist cases (Hekma 1987, 109). Only one case of lesbianism was prosecuted under this law in nineteenth-century Amsterdam, which even figured in the Dutch translation of Krafft-Ebing's *Psychopathia Sexualis* (1897, 111) because of its rarity. There was, however, one main exception to the relegation of sex to the private world, and that was prostitution. Its public nature was reflected in terms such as "public women" and "public lewdness." Prostitution offered a safety valve against roaming male desires on urban streets, in order to protect the respectability of bourgeois women.

If the idea of privacy was central to liberal thinking, and later also to socialist thinking, it did not mean that private sex was protected. In the first place, private and public carry quite diverse and sometimes even opposing meanings. In legal cases in Holland, "public" was defined as what was visible from a public place, and there was discussion over whether privacy could be claimed in all kinds of semipublic places, such as army barracks, hospital wards, public toilets, or parks that were closed for the night. In general, opinion held that such places were public. In 1886, with the new penal law, public indecency came to include offenses that took place in private but in the presence of nonconsenting others (Smidt 1882, 275*ff.*).[2] In addition, sex acts with minors under 12, or assaults in private were considered criminal, and thereby public, offenses.

Marital rape, however, remained legal until very recently: In private, the husband had the right to do with his wife whatever he wished (Moerings and Swier 1997, 14).[3]

Meanwhile, citizens have been cut off more and more from public life over the last two centuries and have relegated its control to state bureaucracies such as the police. The street that has always been an extension of private life has been lost to the citizen and left to the police and other officials. The increasing political apathy of citizens could well be explained by the gradual loss of public space for private uses. The idea of sexual privacy is deeply ingrained in Western cultures and makes all signs of sexuality in public highly problematic, from sex acts to sex education to erotic imagery on the streets and in the media.

A prime example of the difficulties of making sex public is the "coming out" of gay men and lesbian women, as well as others with predilections once classified as "perversions." Such individuals are caught in a double bind: Their preferences are considered to be a private matter, yet they have public consequences. In my research on sports and homosexuality, this double bind was clear; in Holland gay men and lesbian women hold stricter to their privacy than in the United States, and in general do not want to be considered part of a gay and lesbian community.[4] The lesser extent of homophobia in the Netherlands might explain this reluctance on the part both of gays and lesbians and of heterosexuals to acknowledge the existence of specific gay and lesbian demands for public space and other facilities.

What is the public side of sex? Let me give some examples. For many people, sexual desire is stimulated by public sex. Some people like to make love in parks, forests, or dark alleys; others simply have sex while leaving the door ajar or the windows open. Still other people make their sex life known through the sounds that they make. Couples in love show their excitement in full public view in squares and markets or in more secret lovers' lanes.[5] Sex is also made public by the media, politics, education, and other social institutions. Marriage, for example, is a public institution that regulates sex. However much or little is said in schools about sex, education has a sexual side (that is to say, whether you speak about sex or not, *not speaking* sends as clear a message as does speaking about sexuality in the classroom). Laws and law enforcement agencies deal regularly with forbidden forms of sexual desire. And finally, prime examples of a continuous stream of public sexual representations are those institutions that often try to hinder them: media and politics. Thanks to former U.S. President Bill Clinton and the media, the vaginal play with cigars has received worldwide exposure.

The rejection of claims to space by gays, lesbians, and others with alternative sexual interests makes public space into a heterosexual, respectable sphere that confirms the heterosexism of Dutch society. After a recent visit to Amsterdam, American sociologist and queer theorist Steven Seidman asked where homosexuality was visible in public life (Seidman 1994). His own implied answer to the question was quite clear: nearly nowhere. Indeed, very few signs of gay and lesbian life can be seen even in Amsterdam's public spaces. The Homomonument and gay and lesbian couples holding hands are the most manifest and renowned examples, but even those couples remain rare in the inner city. Other signs are only visible to cultural insiders, such as the rainbow or leather pride flags that indicate gay and lesbian venues. The most obvious sexual cultures in Amsterdam, and in some other Dutch cities, are the red-light districts, but they are closely controlled and curtailed. In the mental map of the Dutch, these places are off-limits. They may attract foreign tourists, but most respectable Dutch have the feeling that prostitution is a necessary evil that should be relegated to a place where they will never venture.

At present, there is a feeling among many people in Holland that the sexual revolution has gone too far, and that we are witnessing a process of *verloedering* (filthification) of public culture. Signs of this filthiness are considered to be drug addicts, erotic postcards, sexual advertising, the offensive eroticism of the red-light districts, the sale of child and bestial porn, sex in the media, and ostentatious homosexuality. City authorities have, in turn, recently forbidden the public display of erotic postcards, arrested illegal prostitutes, and closed down bordellos where these women worked (Chorus 1995). Recently, right-wing groups tried to mobilize a popular sense of "decency" to combat the presence of erotic advertisements in public. A quite academic poster of Andres Serrano showing a female urinating on a male as well as advertisements for pizzas and clothing exhibiting scantily clothed women have aroused the wrath of Dutch conservatives (Lamoree 1997; Brendel 1997). Broadcasters have promised not to show any violent or sexual imagery on Dutch television before 10 o'clock in the evening (Boogaard 1998). The major battlefield in the Netherlands might well become the sexual use of public space and the diversification of sexual cultures. In the late 1990s, the city government of Amsterdam began to crack down on all kinds of hedonistic celebrations in public spaces, furthering the transfer of the street as an extension of private life, the domain of the citizen, to a public space controlled and regulated by state authorities. The police have set strict rules for gay and lesbian parades, closed down certain sex shops and a gay cinema because of the presumed availability of child pornography, and restrained gay cruising in several areas through building projects or the creation of new bicycle lanes (Hekma 1996; Maatman and Meijer 1992). In an ostentatious raid in a small alley in the red-light district, the police tried to show they were in control of this district and that they were able to stand up to the major, mafia-like criminal networks that were presumed to have invaded it (Fijnaut and Bovenkerk 1996). Yet the big fish were not arrested, but rather the petty criminals and illegal transsexual prostitutes who often are themselves victims of the mafia. Were it not for tradition, we might question why it is that Dutch people object so much to public sex and not to eating, smoking, or practicing religion in public, all activities which are arguably as private as sexual ones, and some much more dangerous to other people. This crackdown is a marker of a process of deliberalization going on in the Netherlands, as well as elsewhere in Europe.

5. *Sex is nonviolent.* A discussion of sexual violence and conflict are in order, so that my perspective does not seem too idealistic. Violence and conflict also belong to the sexual domain, as they are a component of all social relations. In the 1960s, the slogan "Make love, not war" emerged, expressing the vision that sex and love could pave the way toward a utopian world. But to imagine that love and peace can be equated is to presume that love and sexuality can be easily disentangled from conflict and violence.

Expectations that the sexual revolution would pave the way for a more peaceful world were shattered when second-wave feminists opened up a cloaca of rape and abuse. In the 1970s, men's desire for heterosexual sex came under attack because it often involved force and exploitation. In the 1980s, sexual ideals were once more shattered by the rise of venereal diseases, and especially by the then-fatal disease, AIDS. In the same years, the terminology of abuse was extended in both feminist and popular discourses, so that even voluntary intimate acts could be defined as abusive if they transpired between children or between social unequals.[6] Western culture's traditionally widespread and diffuse fear of sex transformed itself into a fear of dangerous intimate acts.

Violence inheres in sexual relations in a number of ways. The emotional pressures on sexual relationships make them conflictual and potentially violent. Because violence is inherent in all social relations (political, economic, or otherwise), it would be surprising if sexual connections were free of it. Feminist scholars have rightly criticized the idea of the home as "a haven in a heartless world" (Lasch 1979), and suggestions that the private world, where sexuality is generally located, is a space where violence and conflict do not exist. Yet violence and sexual desire may be intertwined in other ways as well. Many people have preferences for sadomasochism (S/M), and others who have no such explicit fantasies may harbor dreams about forced sex. The ideal of sexual equality or democracy runs counter to existing social inequalities and may even be counterproductive for sexual pleasures that can be stimulated by various contrasts, such as gender, bodily aesthetics, power, age, class, color, and so forth. Difference, like disgust, is a frequent companion to desire.

The notion of consent, conceived of as absolute and essential, is another component of the denial of the conflict and violence that inhere in sex. Ironically, theories about sexual relations promoted in sex education curricula are frequently premised upon a notion of informed consent, even if most forms of education are compulsory—children typically learn language, and other requisite life skills, without their consent, and will be grateful later to have been obliged to achieve such capabilities. Only in the field of sexuality is consent considered to be pivotal. In keeping with the belief that sex is natural, erotic techniques are not formally taught to children. They do not learn, not even in the Netherlands, to discuss sexuality frankly and openly (Paans 2002).

If sexual socialization were compulsory, like other forms of education, it might more adequately prepare children for their erotic lives. Most early sexual experiences are confusing for children, and often they are abusive. The provision of a controlled environment for early sexual training is a sensible solution for sex education in a highly sexualized society. Children are becoming sexual beings at about age 12, according to biologists and child psychologists (Graaf and Rademakers 2003; see also Schaffner, this volume). It thus seems self-evident to start with sexual education before that age, to prepare children to be sexually autonomous and to make meaningful sexual choices.

The concept of consent that is used in many theories of sexual ethics is highly problematic because of its voluntaristic and individualistic presuppositions. It neglects a social context in which most people consent to whatever sexual norms societies produce. It also neglects to address fluctuations in feelings about consent. People often consent to acts that, in afterthought, they assess as abusive and nonconsensual. This contradiction can reflect a mismatch between desires and values. Conversely, people may oppose most vehemently that which they might like best.

Violence is central to sexual pleasures, ethics, and relations. Any theory that denies the centrality of violence in its negative aspects, like harassment and abuse, and in its positive aspects, like introduction to pleasure, is necessarily incomplete. The denial of violence leads to the social production of sexual victims who are not enabled to overcome feelings of violation and mistreatment because they have only learned that sexuality should be nonviolent and nonabusive (Kaye, this volume). The representation of violence as the "bad" side of sexuality hinders a practical approach to sexual pleasure. Sex is indeed dangerous, but people should be prepared for such dangers, not avoid them. Instead of using a vocabulary of consent and choice, it would be better to create a sexual infrastructure that offered young and old people alike chances to invent new forms of relationships, pleasures, and ethics (a point that I shall elaborate upon in the following section).

How Libertine Are the Dutch?

The sexual liberalism of the Dutch is a surface phenomenon only. Beneath this veneer, the Dutch are nearly as restricted in their notions of sexual pleasure as the Americans, Russians, or English. Despite the commercial appropriation of some forms of sexual relations (E. Bernstein, this volume), consumer capitalism has failed to influence sexual worlds and to expand sexual possibilities to the same extent for sex as it has for cars, vacations, and electronic media. That somewhat more acceptance of sexual diversity exists in the Netherlands than in other Western countries might be explained by Dutch pragmatism and by a rather limited respect for minorities.

The Netherlands is an overorganized country with established rules for everything, from the color of houses to the use of any square meter of its small surface. Strong state controls, combined with a dense population and lack of space, contribute to the fact that officials will quite often stumble on sexual topics. Leftover spaces, ruins, or untouched nature resorts are very rare, which makes space for public sexual adventures limited. The strong "cowboy" individualism that is typical of U.S. culture had no chance to develop in the Netherlands. Struggles over public space for sports, nature, transportation, highways, housing, and so forth are coming to the fore, and in such fights sex is always at the losing end.

The sexual ideology of most Dutch, and of Westerners in general, is one-sided. It needs to be amended. It is not my intention to promote another one-sided ideology (polymorphous hedonism, as opposed to heterosexual monogamy), but to open up the traditional sexual ideology as outlined previously to more options. Among the many forms of citizenship, sexual citizenship deserves a place in political debates (Bell and Binnie 2000). Sexual desire has become a central feature of private and public life and deserves the frankness and openness of debate and action that is pivotal to democracy.

Others have begun to craft proposals for the development of more diverse sexual cultures (Wal 1995; Vermeulen 1997). Returning to the research on sports that I began this chapter with, I could say that such cultures would have everything sports have: spaces, clubs, training, rules, referees, and libraries. A sexual infrastructure could be put in place for people who want to use it, and education might point the way for those who wish to learn more about their sexual interests and possibilities. Such a sexual infrastructure would be a safe, public place, controlled and protected by its users—probably safer than the private bedroom where intimacies take place without witnesses. It would offer a learning experience for people who wish to "have a look" before indulging themselves in such pleasures. It would offer educational material for young people to learn about sexual variety and responsibility. It would also offer examples for parents and teachers to broach sexual topics. Such public space is as essential for the cultivation of sexuality as it is for athletic activities.

Holland may appear to be liberal, but it is only to a limited degree. That other countries consider Holland to be so tolerant demonstrates the relative lack of sexual tolerance in Western cultures more generally. This lack increasingly influences Dutch policies because of processes of globalization and integration.

The Dutch are caught up in a European Union that remains sexually conservative and is strongly influenced by U.S. politics, media, and scholarship, which mirrors the sexual fundamentalism of American society (Altman 2001). These processes endanger the small kernel of sexual liberalism that is present in the Netherlands. Although the Netherlands is developing into a multicultural society, I argue that, unfortunately, this society is not becoming multisexual.

Notes

1. An interesting comparative case could be gleaned by research into the gay leather scene, where this adoration of youth is less important, and gay men remain sexually active into their sixties.

2. English law goes further still, in which any sex act, including more than two people, is by definition public. This point of view was recently endorsed by the European Court of Human Rights in the so-called British Spanner case, which involved consensual S/M acts between gay men (Thompson 1994).

3. Donzelot (1979) has demonstrated the ways in which the French state could also selectively intrude into the private world of citizens for reasons of public health or social welfare, thus undermining its own philosophy of privacy. He has analyzed how the retreat of the state from the private sphere with the French Revolution changed direction during the nineteenth century, when more and more social institutions of the civil state reclaimed the right to intrude into the protected private world of the home, for reasons ranging from health promotion to the prevention of child abuse.

4. Henk Krol, the editor of the principle gay journal of the Netherlands, *De Gay Krant*, has insisted that his journal is only needed as long as the goal of integration of gays in Dutch society has not been reached. The media consider him to be the spokesperson for the gay movement (Pinedo 2003).

5. See general discussions of public sex in Bell and Valentine (1995), Dangerous Bedfellows (1996), and Leap (1999); for discussions of public sex in the Netherlands, see Maatman and Meijer (1992) and van Lieshout (1995).

6. The rules on sexual harassment at the University of Amsterdam define touching another person on a shoulder or speaking sexually explicit language as possible forms of sexual harassment. Sexual expression between children has become sufficiently suspect that even the children's game of "playing doctor" has led to criminal investigations (Koinos 2000).

CHAPTER 13

From Outsider to Citizen

STEVEN SEIDMAN[1]

Sex laws and policies are guided by a norm of the good sexual citizen. By criminalizing and disenfranchising certain sexual acts, identities, or intimate arrangements, the state helps to create a sexual hierarchy. Some acts or identities are tolerated but barely, others are not tolerated at all, and still other sexual expressions are deemed so intolerable that those who engage in them are scandalized as "bad sexual citizens"—immoral and dangerous to society. Bad sexual citizens become the targets of social control, which may include public stereotyping, harassment, violence, criminalization, and disenfranchisement. In the early decades of the twentieth century, women who had children out of wedlock, sexually active youths, adults who sexually desired youths, and individuals who engaged in interracial sex were often labeled bad sexual citizens.

The good sexual citizen was most definitely heterosexual. However, it was only after World War II that homosexuals became perhaps the personification of the bad sexual citizen. As they took on the role of a social and moral menace, a network of controls evolved that had the effect of creating the closet. And the closet clearly marked gays as outsiders—as moral, social, and political aliens.

As the closet became the defining reality for many gay Americans, a political movement took shape that challenged this condition. This movement was and still is divided between, roughly speaking, a "liberationist" and an "assimilationist" ideology and agenda.

If assimilationists aim to broaden the notion of the good sexual citizen to include homosexuals, liberationists challenge this ideal. If the norm of the good sexual citizen defines sex exclusively as a private act, liberationists defend public forms of sexuality (for example, sex in parks, tea rooms, or bath houses); if the ideal sexual citizen is gender-conventional, liberationists aim to scramble gender norms such that being active or passive, aggressive or submissive, is not coded as masculine or feminine; if the good sexual citizen tightly binds sex to love or intimacy, liberationists relax the bond, allowing for legitimate sex within and outside intimacy; and if the ideal sexual citizen is married, liberationists advocate either the end of state regulation of adult intimate relationships or state recognition of a diversity of families. In short, assimilationists want homosexuals to be recognized and accepted as good sexual citizens; liberationists challenge the sexual norms associated with this ideal.

Liberationist politics emerged after the Stonewall rebellions in 1969.[2] Liberationists opposed the system of compulsory heterosexuality that produced the closet. They were also critical of the assimilationist politics of organizations like the Matdachine Society and the Daughters of Bilitis, which, they argued, left heterosexual domination in place.

Gay liberationism arose during a time of extraordinary social turmoil. The protests against the Vietnam War and the rise of militant, in-your-face movements for racial and gender justice stirred hopes of revolutionary change. Liberationists absorbed the spirit of radical feminism, lesbian feminism, and black liberation. Gays were not just the targets of prejudice and discrimination but were oppressed by a heterosexual dictatorship. Writes one liberationist,

> One is oppressed as a homosexual every minute of every day, inasmuch as one is restrained from acting in ways that would seem normal to a heterosexual. Every time one refrains from an act of public affection with a lover—in the park, in the movie line—one dies a little. And gay people, of course, die a little every day. . . . Everything in society—every movie, every billboard, everything . . . reminds the gay person that what he or she is is unnatural, abnormal. (Byron [1972] 1992, 58)

Liberation required dismantling the "system." The fight for gay justice was viewed as inseparable from struggles to transform gender roles, the institution of marriage and the family, and the political economy of capitalism and imperialism.[3] Challenging gay oppression meant changing America, from top to bottom.

The early 1970s were the heroic years for gay liberationism. Groups such as the Gay Liberation Front, the Fairies, the Furies, and Radicalesbians created their own political organizations, published newspapers, newsletters, and books, and forged distinctive cultures with their own ideologies. They marched, organized sit-ins, met with newspaper editors, appeared on television, published manifestos, and formed alliances with other movements. Their militancy and almost swaggering sense of pride and confidence was for many individuals a welcome departure from the subdued, cautious politics of assimilationism that had dominated the 1950s and 1960s. For a moment it looked as if liberationism would become the chief political and cultural force in gay life.

This did not happen. By the mid-1970s, gay liberationism virtually disappeared as an organized political movement. Many liberationist groups dissolved or were greatly weakened by the incessant battles over ideology and strategy. Their Marxist or radical feminist rhetoric, which portrayed America as fundamentally corrupt and in need of a revolution, alienated many gays who gravitated toward reform-minded groups such as the Gay Activist Alliance. In the end, liberationism proved more effective in shifting gay politics away from the cautious assimilationism of the previous decades than at mobilizing mass support for its own radical vision and agenda.

Liberationists never managed more than a marginal presence in organized gay politics after the mid-1970s. Yet artists, writers, activists, and academics have sustained its critical spirit. And, in response to AIDS and organized anti-gay politics from the late 1970s onward, a broadly liberationist political agenda surfaced in the organized politics of ACT UP, Queer Nation, Lesbian Avengers, and Sex Panic![4] Except perhaps for ACT UP, none of these groups managed more than a short-lived organizational life. Liberationism lives on primarily as a cultural sensibility.

An assimilationist agenda has been and still is the driving force of the gay movement.[5] Although differences can be identified among assimilationists, they share an agenda aimed at bringing the homosexual into the circle of sexual citizenship. These reformers do not wish to change America beyond altering the status of gays from outsider to citizen. An assimilationist agenda does not necessarily protest the dominant status of heterosexuality; it's about minority rights, not toppling the majority. Nor do these reformers wish to challenge the broader spectrum of sexual-intimate norms that govern behavior, such as the norm of marriage, monogamy, or gender norms of sexuality. Assimilationists press America to live up to its promise of equal treatment for all of its citizens; they wish to be a part of what is considered a basically good nation. This requires reform, not revolution.

In the initial wave of political organizing in the 1950s, the focus of assimilationist politics was to end the harassment and persecution of homosexuals that was sanctioned and often initiated by the state. The key political organizations of the time were the male-oriented Mattachine Society and female-organized Daughters of Bilitis (D'Emilio 1983b; Marotta 1981). Without much public fanfare, these organizations cautiously but courageously, given the times, challenged state-driven discrimination. They protested the firing of homosexuals by government agencies and their persecution by the random enforcement of laws such as those prohibiting loitering, solicitation, lewdness, or cross-dressing. However, because they believed that the source of prejudice is ignorance or a misinformed view of homosexuals as different and dangerous, their chief political strategy was public education. Through sponsoring public talks, promoting research, and encouraging positive public role models to step forward, these organizations sought to persuade the public that homosexuals are no different from heterosexuals. The Mattachine Society declared that its chief task was to "dispel the idea that the sex variant is unique, 'queer' or unusual, but is instead a human being with the same capacities of feelings, thinking and accomplishment as any other human being" ("Editorial" 1962, 2). The ultimate purpose was to end legal discrimination and public stereotyping; social integration would mean the end of the homosexual as a separate identity and subculture.

As the 1950s gave way to the 1960s, a gay movement pursuing an assimilationist agenda grew more confident. Appealing to constitutional principles of privacy, due process, and basic rights of free speech and association, municipalities were taken to court to end street harassment and police entrapment, to halt bar raids and unnecessary search and seizure, and to stop government actions that shut down businesses catering to gays. For example, the California State Supreme Court and legislature took giant steps in deregulating consensual same-sex adult behavior by narrowing the meaning of public decency, lewdness, and vagrancy statutes so that they could no longer be used to persecute homosexuals. Most impressively, invoking recent judicial rulings, gay organizations successfully challenged obscenity laws that were used to censor gay public speech (for example, in gay magazines, newsletters, books, art, and pornography) (D'Emilio 1983b).

By the mid-1970s, provoked and inspired by the defiant spirit of liberationism, a more assertive rights-oriented gay movement challenged laws that criminalized homosexuality. In the aftermath of Supreme Court decisions such as *Griswold v. Connecticut* (1965), *Eisenstadt v. Baird* (1972), and *Stanley v. Georgia* (1969), gay rights advocates argued that acknowledging the fundamental role of sexuality in personal liberty, which was at the heart of cases that extended privacy rights to adult private consensual sex, should apply to homosexuals as well.[6] Appealing to a constitutional right to privacy and equal treatment, state laws that criminalized sodomy were challenged. By 1983, 25 states had decriminalized consensual sodomy, while 11 states reduced sodomy to a misdemeanor. In the 1990s, many states and cities banned anti-gay discrimination in state employment. And, although Congress has continued to block federal civil rights legislation that would include sexual orientation, the Civil Service Commission and ultimately an executive order by President Clinton, ended legal job discrimination in all federal agencies.

Strategies aimed at decriminalizing homosexuality were supplemented by deliberate efforts at gaining equal civil rights. From the mid-1970s on, the gay movement turned its attention and resources to gaining positive rights. In small towns and large cities across the country, organizations dedicated to enacting gay rights ordinances were formed. And well-financed, professional national organizations such as the Lambda Legal Defense, the National Lesbian and Gay Task Force, and the Human Rights Campaign made gaining equal civil rights the chief aim of a national gay movement. The intent of so-called gay rights laws is to get the state to recognize lesbians and gay men as citizens deserving the same positive liberties and protections as any other citizen. In the course of the 1970s, there were few victories—only 40 communities passed gay rights. However, by 2000 the number had swelled to well over 300. Moreover, gay rights laws are no longer confined to urban centers but have been passed in small towns and suburban communities, and not just in the Northeast and West, but in the South, Midwest, and Northwest. The wave of domestic partnership law beginning in the mid-1990s is indicative of moderate but real success at legal integration. By the late 1990s, 421 cities and states, and over 3,500 businesses or institutions of higher education offered some form of domestic partner benefit.[7]

William Eskridge summarizes the considerable gains toward legal and social integration during this period:

> The gay rights movement had won many successes by 1981—judicial nullification or legislative repeal of laws criminalizing consensual sodomy in most jurisdictions, of almost all state criminal laws targeting same-sex intimacy, and municipal cross-dressing ordinances, of the immigration and citizenship exclusions, of all censorship laws targeting same-sex eroticism, of almost all laws or regulations prohibiting bars from becoming congregating places for gay people, and of exclusions of gay people from public employment in most jurisdictions . . . . Since 1981 an increasing number of states and cities have adopted laws affirmatively protecting gay people against private discrimination and violence, recognizing gay families as domestic partnerships, and allowing second-parent adoption by a parent's same-sex partner. (Eskridge 1999, 139)

This wave of legal reform made possible a "post-closeted regime where openly gay people could participate in the public culture" (Eskridge 1999, 124).

Legal reform has brought gays into the national community, but not as equal citizens. The battle over the meaning of legal and social equality has become the chief focus of the gay movement today.

Tolerated but Not Equal

The legal and social integration of gay Americans has not been an unqualified story of success, to say the least. A majority of cities and states lack laws that protect gay people from housing and job discrimination. The Federal Gay and Lesbian Civil Rights Bill, introduced in Congress in 1975, has virtually no hope of passage. The more modest Employment Non-Discrimination Act (ENDA), introduced in 1994, has few realistic prospects of passage at this time. The result: The jobs and homes of the overwhelming majority of gays and lesbians are not legally protected by any local, state, or federal laws. Moreover, anti-gay legislative proposals, at the local and state levels, may very well have exceeded positive legislative efforts in the 1990s. One analyst counts 472 cases of proposed anti-gay legislation (Walters 2001, 9). And government policies such as "Don't ask, don't tell" and the Defense of Marriage Act and judicial decisions like *Bowers v. Hardwick* (1986) and *The Boy Scouts of America and Monmouth Council et al. v. James Dale* (2000) underscore gays' second-class citizenship status. Many Americans stand opposed to the social integration of gays. They would like to reinstate the conditions of the closet or at least to maintain gays' status as outsiders.

Surveys document continued widespread moral disapproval. Polls through the early 1990s indicate that an overwhelming majority of Americans believed that homosexuality is wrong or immoral (Lewis and Edelson 2000, 195). Summarizing data from 13 surveys between 1973 and 1991, two political scientists conclude, "Between 67 percent and 75 percent of respondents said that 'sexual relations between two adults of the same sex' were 'always wrong.'" However, researchers document a dramatic and unexpected shift in moral attitudes in the mid-1990s. "Surprisingly, given almost 20 years of stability, the percentage saying 'always wrong' dropped 15 percent between 1991 and 1996 [to 56 percent], suggesting the first major decline in disapproval."[8]

Moreover, as survey questions shift from abstract moral beliefs about homosexuality to the morality of discrimination, the trend toward social tolerance is even clearer. A majority of Americans—and in the late 1990s the support has climbed to around 70 to 80%—support a wide range of rights for gays. Assessing the available survey data, two researchers conclude, "Americans increasingly support civil liberties for gay people. Between 1973 and 1996, the percentages saying that 'a man who admits he is a homosexual' should 'be allowed to teach in a college' and 'to make a speech in your community' and who would not favor taking 'a book he wrote in favor of homosexuality . . . out of your public library' rose steadily by 28, 20, and 15 percent, respectively. By 1996, substantial majorities (75 percent, 81 percent, and 69 percent, respectively) supported each of these rights. Between 1977 and 1996, the percentage saying 'homosexuals should . . . have equal rights in terms of job opportunities' rose 27 percent (to 83 percent)" (Lewis and Edelson 2000; Yang 1997).

The battleground of gay politics is shifting away from whether or not gays should be socially integrated to the meaning of gay citizenship. The politics of the closet is hardly history; still, public anti-gay campaigns are increasingly local rather than national and are spearheaded by ad hoc groups that lack the backing of the state and often major cultural elites (for example, newspaper editors, television commentators, and national political and public figures). Indeed, the absence of anti-gay politics in the last Republican primary and the distancing of the Bush administration from the anti-gay politics of the Christian Right underscore just how marginal such politics have become, even within the conservative wing of the Republican party. Legal and social integration is the chief trend, no matter how uneven, across different regions and populations. Today, the question of whether gays' integration means tolerance or equality is at the center of social conflict.

It is telling that gays' greatest successes have been in weakening the twin supports of the closet. Many laws criminalizing homosexuality have been repealed or today go unenforced, and though homophobic representations are still a part of American public life they are now often criticized as a form of bigotry and prejudice. Gays are increasingly being viewed as fully human and as part of the American community. This is a significant change. It makes it possible for many gays and lesbians to exercise greater personal choice and to conduct lives of integrity. However, as the gay political agenda shifts from the struggle for toleration to establishing real social equality, resistance has stiffened.

The push for equal citizenship has exposed the limits of state liberalization. The refusals to grant gays the right to marry and serve in the military stand as telling statements of the government's denial of gays' status as first-class citizens. This opposition may at first glance seem puzzling. After all, heterosexual dominance is hardly in jeopardy if equal rights are extended to a small minority, so what's the big deal?

I think part of the explanation lies in the connection between the issues of gay equality and national identity. First, blacks challenged a white-defined America, Latinos and other people of color followed, and then women protested a masculine understanding of national identity. Establishing gay equality would challenge another core feature of American national identity. It would effectively mean, as some members of the Supreme Court understood in *Bowers v. Hardwick* (1986), ending or weakening the historical association of nationhood with heterosexuality. It was Chief Justice White who explicitly repudiated any association of homosexuality with American nationality: "Proscriptions against that conduct [homosexual sodomy] have ancient roots. Sodomy was a criminal offense at common law and was forbidden by the laws of the original 13 states when they ratified the Bill of Rights . . . In fact, until 1961, all 50 states in the Union outlawed sodomy . . . Against this background, to claim that a right to engage in such conduct is 'deeply rooted in this nation's history and tradition' . . . is, at best, facetious" (Eskridge and Hunter 1997, 46).

The sexual politics of national identity are at the heart of the conflict over gays in the military and gay marriage. If gays were to openly serve in the military and to marry, this would be a major challenge to the national ideal of the heterosexual citizen.[9]

From this perspective, the military policy of "Don't ask, don't tell" is a striking sign of gays' unequal status and their ambivalent status as not quite outsiders or citizens. The military is not an institution like, say, a bank or a hospital, but it is symbolically linked to Americans' core sense of nationhood. As many scholars remind us, citizenship is not just a legal reality but is symbolic—something we have an idea and ideals about (Anderson 1983; Greenfeld 1992; Spillman 1997). Serving in the military or being eligible to serve are key markers of being a good American. The strong tie between the military and the nation is captured in the memorializing of soldiers and national wars in the nation's capital and in a popular culture that celebrates military triumphs and heroes. For a fully abled adult to be excluded from military service because of his or her race, national origin, or sexual identity publicly marks the individual as an outsider.

The institution of marriage is equally invested with national significance in American culture. Whether it's the legal restriction of marriage to heterosexuals, the state privileging of heterosexual marriage over all other intimate unions, or the idealization of marriage in popular culture and commerce (for example, the wedding industry), the ideal national citizen is married (Ingraham 1997). Americans may be more tolerant today toward individuals who choose to be single or cohabitate, but these choices occupy a lesser status than marriage. For this reason, the struggle to extend marital rights to gays is as much about symbolic struggles over national identity as about the politics of equality (Smith 2001; Westervelt 2001; Mohr 1994).

The issue of whether the state should, as a matter of morality or law, recognize gay relationships has bounced around the courts for some time (Eskridge 1996; 2002). However, in the last decade or so, as lesbians and gay men have been creating stable, long-term families, and as the question of intimate rights became an urgent healthcare issue because of the AIDS crisis, the gay movement has made the legal recognition of gay relationships *a priority*. Although some individuals in the gay community oppose gay marriage because it legitimates the state's regulation of intimate life and devalues all nonmarital intimate arrangements, most gays and lesbians consider the denial of the right to marry as compromising their goal of achieving social equality. Gay marriage became a national issue after the Hawaii State Supreme Court, in *Baehr v. Lewin* (1993), ruled that not allowing gays to marry was a form of gender discrimination. However, even before the courts could resolve the issue, the Hawaii legislature acted in 1994 to restrict marriage to heterosexuality. Other states quickly followed suit, and in 1996 the U.S. Congress passed, with the overwhelming support of the Democrats and President Clinton, the Defense of Marriage Act. This reaffirmed a national ideal that defines marriage as an exclusively heterosexual institution.

To summarize, in the last decade or so the gay movement has shifted its focus from tolerance to social equality. Gays want to be equal citizens. We already have the same obligations and duties; we want the same rights, opportunities, and respect as any other American citizen. And although the state and other institutions have retreated significantly from the repressive practices that produced the closet, they have also refused to grant gays equal citizenship. Gays' continued unequal status reflects a public that is still divided over the moral status of homosexuality; it reflects, as well, a public that worries that gay equality means the end of heterosexual privilege and the ideal of a heterosexual national identity.

The declining social significance of the closet can only have the effect of intensifying demands for equality. Gays will not be satisfied with tolerance. As many of us approach being gay as an ordinary and good status, as we live outside the closet, and as our lives have individual integrity and purpose, we will demand full social inclusion and first-class citizenship. There is no turning back to the days of the closet. Efforts to reinstate the closet are a losing cause. And activists who interpret every anti-gay action as evidence of the still-dominant reality of a homophobic, repressive heterosexual dictatorship are no less stuck in the past than anti-gay crusaders. With the decline of the closet, the battleground shifts: from the politics of coming out, pride, and visibility to equality—before the law and across social institutions.

Beyond Assimilation and Liberation

As a civil rights agenda has come to dominate the gay movement, some gays have raised doubts about its politics. No one questions that equal rights are a condition of personal freedom and political democracy. However, critics rightly ask, would gaining equal rights establish social equality? Would gaining rights bring about social respect, equal treatment, and full social integration? Can and should the pursuit of social equality be separated from a wider agenda of sexual and social justice?

The current debate over the politics of sexual citizenship expresses a longstanding division between the civil rights or assimilationist and the liberationist ideologies. At the heart of this political division are contrasting images of America.

Generally speaking, rights advocates view America as a fundamentally good society. America is faulted for incompletely realizing its promise of delivering individual freedom, equality, and happiness. Rights advocates expect America to live up to its ideals, to include gays in the circle of full citizenship. By contrast, liberationists tend to see America as deeply flawed; this nation is said to have betrayed its promise of freedom and equality, and not only to gays. For liberationists, a rights-oriented agenda amounts to a wish to be integrated into a flawed, repressive society. Real social progress requires something like a social revolution.

It's time to get past these polarizing positions. Liberationism emerged during the heyday of the making of the closet. This period is passing. Gays have gained considerable personal freedom and are being incorporated into American life. This change undercuts a liberationist view of a seamless world of homosexual hatred and repression.

My own preference is to take a rights-based agenda as the starting point. The view of America as incompletely realizing the promise of a good society is compelling both as a social perspective and as a political strategy. However, I share liberationist criticisms that the rights agenda assumes a thin sociological understanding of heterosexual dominance and a one-sided view of social change.

I intend to sketch a view of the politics of sexual citizenship that blends a rights-oriented and a liberationist approach. This "third way" brings together the forward-looking, reform-minded politics of rights activists and the deep sociology and broad political vision of liberationists.[10]

Consider the strengths and weaknesses of the most serious theoretical defense of rights-oriented politics. In *Virtually Normal*, the well-known writer and political commentator Andrew Sullivan defends a movement oriented to establishing gays' equal civil and political rights (Sullivan 1996). He offers an elegant, if minimal, liberal defense of gay equality. Sullivan maintains that the cornerstone of liberalism is the idea of a separation between the public and private spheres. The guiding principle of the public or political sphere is the formal or legal equality of its citizens. All individuals who are citizens are bearers of the same rights and duties. By contrast, the guiding principle of the private or civil sphere is personal freedom and social diversity.

From this liberal standpoint, America's gay citizens suffer a glaring injustice. "Gay citizens vote for their own government, pay for it with their own taxes, and have an equal right to participate in it in the same manner as any other citizen. Their unequal treatment by their own state is a fundamental abrogation of fundamental rights" (Sullivan 1996, 216). The focus of the gay movement should be, according to Sullivan, establishing gays' legal political equality. "This politics affirms a simple and limited principle: that all public . . . discrimination against homosexuals be ended and that every right and responsibility that heterosexuals enjoy as public citizens be extended to [homosexuals]. And that is all. No cures or re-educations, no wrenching private litigation, no political imposition of tolerance; merely a political attempt to enshrine formal public equality" (Sullivan 1996, 170).

Sullivan recognizes that inequalities exist in the private or civil sphere as well. Growing up gay, he encountered the shame, isolation, and prejudicial treatment that many gays still experience. However, he maintains that the state should not be used to remedy civil inequalities, for example, through such policies as affirmative action, quotas, hate-crime legislation, and antidiscrimination policies in the workplace. This would violate the core liberal principle of the separation of the public and the private spheres. Enlisting the state to remedy these social injustices might advance the cause of equality but at the potential cost of our individual freedom. Of course, individuals can privately organize to challenge inequalities in the private sphere. "While I would passionately support Microsoft's adoption of antidiscriminatory regulations, I would passionately oppose the government's attempt to impose them" (Sullivan 1996, 216).

Sullivan's ideas reveal many of the strengths of a rights agenda. In particular, I would recommend the following: a view of America's core institutions and culture as partially realizing positive types of freedom, social diversity, and a democratic public life; a principled defense of political equality; an uncompromising conviction that rights are the basis of individual freedom, democracy, and justice; and a healthy suspicion of agendas of top-down, state-based social reform.

The underlying weakness of Sullivan's argument, which is indicative of rights-oriented politics in general, is its thin sociology. Sullivan is not naive. He understands that disrespect and discrimination toward gays are pervasive in private and civil life. He believes, however, that a movement focused on establishing legal political equality would go a long way toward bringing about real social equality. If gays were recognized as equal citizens, they would be more likely to be open and visible, and as straight Americans routinely encountered gays as fellow citizens—for example, in the workplace, in the army barracks, and as neighbors—discrimination would diminish as gays were seen as "virtually normal." Sullivan's faith in the positive effects of an agenda of equal citizenship rights is forcefully expressed in the significance he attaches to establishing equal marital rights. "If nothing else was done at all, and gay marriage was legalized, 90 percent of the political work necessary to achieve gay and lesbian equality would have been achieved" (Sullivan 1996, 185). Gay marriage, Sullivan believes, would encourage gays to be more open, as they would feel a stronger sense of integrity and social belonging, and it would encourage straight Americans to view gays as like themselves, and therefore worthy of respect and integration.

But Sullivan offers no evidence or reason to believe that formal political equality would gradually translate into social equality. He relies on the hope that gays' increased social visibility and social integration will weaken prejudice and stigma. If the examples of people of color, women, or the disabled are at all telling, however, there is little reason to be sanguine; these groups remain social unequals despite their legal equality and social visibility. Just as most social scientists understand white racial privilege and men's dominance as built into American social structure and culture, heterosexual dominance must also be understood as deeply rooted in social life, not just a product of law or individual prejudice.[11] The strength of the liberationist tradition is precisely its sociological understanding of heterosexual dominance.

From early statements by lesbian feminists and gay liberationists to contemporary queer perspectives, liberationists hold that heterosexual dominance is maintained less by unjust laws and individual prejudice than by the very social structure and organization of American life. For example, many liberationists assert a tight fit between gender norms and heterosexual dominance.[12] America is said to be a society organized around dichotomous norms of gender. From birth, individuals are expected to exhibit a consistency in their self-presentation and behavior between their assigned sex identity as male or female and their gender identity as man or woman. Institutions from the family to schools and the mass media impose expectations that individuals should adopt masculine or feminine gender roles reflecting their status as males or females. These contrasting gender identities and roles are said to reflect the complementary physical and psychological nature of men and women. From this point of view, heterosexuality is understood as expressing the natural fit of gendered bodies, psyches, and social roles. Men and women form a natural unity, each attracted to the other and each finding fulfillment in the other.

Individuals who deviate significantly from gender norms are stigmatized as homosexual. For example, women who are masculine, aggressive, or erotically assertive may be called whores, but also dykes; men who are passive or too emotional or feminine in their self-presentation are labeled sissies, fags, or queers. These disparaging labels aim to enforce a binary gender order that also assumes the normality and rightness of heterosexuality. So long as binary gender norms continue, there will be heterosexual dominance. There is little evidence that extending rights to gays weakens dichotomous gender norms (see Currah and Minter, this volume). This is so because gender norms are not primarily upheld by laws but by institutions (for example, family, economic institutions, military, schools) and by culture—that is, the media, advertisements, popular music, television, film, scientific and medical knowledge, and the daily customs and practices in families and peer groups.

A rights agenda cannot stand alone. Legal equality easily coexists with social inequality. Gays' equal status will only be achieved when heterosexual dominance is ended, and that requires challenging its deep cultural and institutional supports. Urvashi Vaid has stated this position sharply and forcefully:

> Civil rights strategies do not challenge the moral and antisexual underpinnings of homophobia, because homophobia does not originate in

our lack of full civil equality. Rather, homophobia arises from the nature and construction of the political, legal, economic, sexual, racial, and family systems within which we live. As long as the rights-oriented movement refuses to address these social institutions and cultural forces, we cannot eradicate homophobic prejudice. (Vaid 1995, 183)

A rights-oriented political agenda should be broadened in at least three ways. First, equality is about more than political equality or equal rights; it's about social equality across the spectrum of national institutions from the government to the workplace, schools, familiec, and welfare and healthcare institutions. And no matter how important it is to gain equal rights, opportunities, and protections, equality is also about respect and representation. Gays may have the right to vote and hold office, but we remain unequal citizens if our interests and points of view are not respected and are not represented in political agencies. For example, if we don't have spokespeople in political parties or if public officials do not promote our social interests or agendas, equal political rights will not translate into social equality. Rights without respect and representation in the institutions that make up social life are only the shell of social equality.

Second, equality is not only about becoming equal citizens and participants in social life, but also about a right to be heard and to have our interests taken seriously. Equality is not about extending equal rights to gays but only on the condition that we conform to dominant gender, sexual, familial, and social norms. Equality is about institutions encouraging dialogues in which gays participate as equals in shaping the social norms and conventions of our institutions. In other words, equality means encouraging the distinctive voices of gays to be heard and to potentially shape social life.

A third problem can be identified with a rights agenda: It severs any tie between the pursuit of gay equality and broader issues of sexual and social justice. Consider the politics of citizenship from a sexual justice perspective. Rights activists fight for gays to become first-class citizens. Becoming a citizen is understood as being integrated into a network of rights, duties, and state protections. But citizenship is not only about rights and duties. Citizenship also involves an ideal of the citizen or a notion of the kind of personal traits and behaviors that a nation values and would like to see in its individual members. In other words, citizenship involves a norm of "the good citizen."

In contemporary America, the good sexual citizen, roughly speaking, is an individual whose sexual behavior conforms to traditional gender norms, who links sex to intimacy, love, monogamy, and preferably marriage, and who restricts sex to private acts that exhibit romantic or caring qualities. Although rights advocates protest unequal citizenship rights, they have not challenged the sexual norms associated with the good sexual citizen. Accordingly, gays might gain equal rights, but those who deviate from norms of the good citizen would still be considered outsiders. For example, women who are sexually aggressive and dominant, individuals who choose to be single or enjoy commercial sex or are coupled but nonmonogamous, or individuals who like rough consensual sex might have formal rights but their sexual-intimate choices would be disrespected and perhaps be targets of social control. Although it may be the case, as some rights advocates claim, that a majority of gays support all of the sexual norms associated with the good sexual citizen, surely some don't. What's crucial is that the very issue of the legitimacy of these sexual norms is not even part of a civil rights political discussion.

A narrow rights agenda ignores the way ideas of sexual citizenship establish social boundaries between insiders (good citizens) and outsiders (bad citizens). And, although same- or opposite-gender preference is surely one boundary issue, many other dimensions of sexuality are used to separate the good and bad sexual citizen, such as gender norms, the age of the sex partners, whether sex is private or public, commercial or not, casual or intimate, monogamous or not, gentle or rough. In particular, a rights-oriented movement does not challenge forms of social control that create sexual victims and outsiders of individuals whose sexual preferences are between consenting adults. By narrowing its agenda to gaining equality and integration, a rights-oriented movement leaves the dominant sexual norms, other than gender preference, in place and removed from political debate.

The strength of a liberationist perspective is its understanding of heterosexual dominance as being deeply rooted in social life and as part of a broader pattern of sexual and social inequality. Liberationists argue that the struggle for gay equality should be linked to other battles for sexual-intimate and social justice. There will be, of course, disagreements about which norms beyond compulsory heterosexuality are unjust and which regulations are defensible. The point, though, is that a rights agenda can't avoid being implicated in broader patterns of sexual and social inequality; it should, then, be blended with a liberationist politic.

Rights and Justice: The Debate over Gay Marriage

To illustrate something of what a blend of rights and liberationist politics might look like, I briefly consider the debate over gay marriage. This debate has been polarized between a rights-based defense of gay marriage and a liberationist critique.[13]

Rights advocates defend gay marriage as a matter of establishing equal rights and a respected social status. There can be no equality without the right to marry. In America, marriage is a marker of first-class citizenship and carries an assortment of economic and social benefits. Furthermore, to the extent that gays are excluded from marriage, their intimate relationships will be viewed as inferior; they will be less stable and solid. And, because of the centrality of intimate love to personal happiness in American society, lacking marital rights translates into diminished prospects for self-fulfillment.

Liberationists offer two key criticisms. First, marriage has been and still is a male-dominated, repressive institution. The gay movement should challenge marriage, not endorse and participate in it. Second, as a state-recognized institution, marriage imposes a narrow and uniform norm of intimacy that has the effect of symbolically and materially devaluing all nonmarital intimacies, which has particularly bad effects on the poor and people of color, who are less likely to marry. Also, supporting a norm of marriage contradicts the values of erotic freedom and variation that have been at the heart of gay culture. The gay movement should focus on either ending the state's regulation of intimate life (long-term goal) or extending state recognition to a multiplicity of intimate arrangements (short-term goal).

At the root of these polarizing positions are two contrasting views of the institution of marriage and its effect on gays. Rights advocates emphasize the benefits of marriage; it will enhance personal happiness, bring stability to gay relationships, and advance their full integration into what is considered a basically good society. By contrast, liberationists criticize marriage as a chief source of male dominance and compulsory heterosexuality; it reinforces a repressive society. Moreover, marriage domesticates sexuality and has been part of an ideology of "familialism" that has been hostile to a playful, erotic culture that values choice, experimentation, and variation. Marriage will benefit a small slice of gay America while leaving in place the privileged status of men and heterosexuality.

Differences in values and social perspectives between rights advocates and liberationists cannot simply be smoothed over. However, it's useful, I think, to try to stake out a less polarizing position.[14] Defenders of gay marriage make a compelling, and to my mind winning, point: To the extent that marriage in the United States is associated with first-class citizenship, including social respect, being denied this right is a pointed public statement of the disrespected and socially inferior status of gays. Lacking marital rights positions gays as outsiders, denies us a host of crucial material benefits and rights, devalues our relationships, and reduces our chances for personal well-being and a meaningful sense of social and civic belonging. These are real effects of being denied marital rights. Accordingly, no matter how compelling critics' arguments against marriage, there is no credible evidence and no reason to believe that Americans would even consider ending the state sanctioning of marriage or its material and symbolic support of marriage. Marriage is here to stay for the immediate and near future; this reality must be the starting point of any serious political discussion.

Yet liberationist criticisms of marriage should not be dismissed. Marriage has been and still is organized by gender roles that reinforce male dominance;

this is not an incidental part of this institution. It's not merely a fact of the past; it must still be reckoned with. However, contrary to what some liberationists seem to assume, it is not a fixed part of marriage. Evidence exists that the gender ordering of marriage has weakened significantly and, at a minimum, has lost considerable cultural authority.[15] Moreover, there is little reason to believe that gays would adopt gender roles if permitted to marry; in fact, the evidence strongly suggests that gender roles do not have much impact on patterns of gay intimacy.[16]

So, whereas rights advocates miss the broader significance of the politics of marriage by narrowing the issue into one solely of equal rights, liberationists often collapse this politics into one of sexual and gender repression. However, approaching marriage as an institution worth defending but in need of reform suggests an alternative political standpoint: Gay marriage should be defended —not only on the basis of equal rights arguments, but as part of the defense of an institution that promises intimacy between equals. This approach would connect the struggle for equal marital rights to a struggle over the very social meaning of marriage. In other words, gays should make the case for same-sex marriage but in the context of arguing for a view of marriage as an intimate union of equals. The defense of marriage would then be connected to a critique of the male-dominated organization of this institution.

But what about the liberationist point that state-sanctioned marriage devalues nonmarital arrangements, deprives the poor and especially minority populations of much-needed benefits and resources, and betrays a gay culture that has valued erotic experimentation? Here, too, I think that marriage can be defended but not in a narrowly individualistic and legalistic language. Rights advocates often rationalize the marginalizing effects of marriage by appealing to a language of individual choice. The right to marry, they say, merely gives gays a choice that they presently lack; it doesn't preclude individuals from choosing to not marry, and it doesn't necessarily devalue other intimate arrangements. Individuals choose intimate arrangements that reflect their specific wants, needs, and values; the point, they say, is to give gays the range of options available to straight citizens.

This argument is sociologically naive. If the poor or people of color marry less than other Americans, it is not merely a "lifestyle" choice; it relates to social factors such as job insecurity, low income, transient living conditions, racism, or high rates of unemployment and incarceration among men. And, contrary to what rights advocates seem to think, a nonmarital status is a social, economic, and cultural disadvantage. Marriage establishes a privileged status (rights, resources, benefits, prestige) in relation to being single and to being in nonmarital intimate arrangements. The state enforces this hierarchy.

Liberationists understand well the politics of marriage. As a state-sanctioned institution, it creates a social hierarchy among intimate choices. But opposition to marriage doesn't necessarily follow. Although marriage is a socially privileged type of intimate arrangement, there does not have to be a huge gap in terms of status, rights, and benefits relative to nonmarital arrangements. The fact that more Americans are choosing cohabitation, are divorcing, or are remaining single for longer periods of time suggests that marriage is losing its "normalizing" status or its role as a marker of respectability. And nonmarital arrangements such as civil unions, common-law relationships, cohabitation, and domestic partnerships are gaining many of the rights once restricted to marriage. So the hierarchy is being weakened from both sides—marriage is less exulted, and nonmarital arrangements are gaining respectability and rights.[17]

Instead of raging against marriage, a more politically effective strategy would be to argue for enhanced state recognition and support of nonmarital arrangements (in the short term) and to make the case for uncoupling basic healthcare and social security benefits from marriage (in the long term).[18] These strategies would have the effect of further diminishing the normative status of marriage while equalizing intimate choices—symbolically and materially. Such strategies would also have the added political benefit of avoiding opposing an institution that remains a fundamental type of value commitment for the vast majority of Americans.

Beyond the Politics of Tolerance

The closet has been at the center of gay politics in the United States since at least the 1950s. At the root of the closet has been a culture that views gays as not only different in basic ways from heterosexuals, but inferior and threatening—to children, families, and to the nation's moral and military security. Accordingly, the dismantling of the closet has meant persuading Americans that gays are just ordinary people, who like heterosexuals, can be disciplined, productive, loyal, and loving. If homosexuality is understood as a natural or ordinary human trait, the closet would be judged unfair. Gays would be welcomed into the community of Americans.

Gays are winning this cultural battle, even if some of our enemies remain resolute and the social landscape is littered with the victims of a terrorizing hatred of homosexuals. Whether we look at television, the movies, literature, art, book publishing, newspapers and magazines, science, or elite opinion (expressed in editorials and political party platforms, for example), images of gays as just people or as fully human are steadily gaining ground. Public expression of homophobia, though by no means rare, is more and more being challenged as a form of bigotry or as a marker of being unenlightened in a global, multicultural world that values a cosmopolitan respect for social diversity.

As gays are viewed as fully human and as deserving to be citizens, there is pressure for institutions to be accommodating. This has not always gone smoothly. Battles are being waged in virtually every institution. In general, institutions that cultivate a cosmopolitan outlook such as big corporations and unions, colleges and universities, and health and civil service bureaucracies are more welcoming than small businesses, secondary schools, and churches that are highly responsive to local and parochial interests and sentiments. The major exception to this rule is the military, whose resistance, I've suggested, is perhaps explained by its powerful symbolic association with American nationalism.

The public integration of gays has created new sources of tension. In particular, conflicts have surfaced around whether integration involves tolerance or equality. To date, tolerance has been the dominant type of social accommodation. Tolerance entails decriminalization and the delegitimation of blatant homophobic behavior. Gays are to be acknowledged as part of America, but not necessarily accepted or valued as equals. It is hard, however, to draw the line at tolerance. Once homophobic practices are criticized as hateful and hurtful, there is an implicit acknowledgment that gays are ordinary folk deserving of respect and equal treatment. The tension between the cultural legitimation of gays and their continuing institutional inequality is at the core of contemporary lesbian and gay politics.

It is not only that America's public culture is becoming more respectful and welcoming toward gays. More and more gay people accept themselves, define being gay as a good part of themselves, and feel a sense of entitlement—to be treated respectfully by all other Americans. This sense of personal integrity drives the political struggle for equality into every institution. Yes, equality before the law is important, but so is equality in our schools, healthcare and welfare agencies, in our churches and political parties, in our local YMCAs and American Legion clubs. The struggle for social equality across the institutional spectrum pushes a rights agenda to the left, to a more expansive understanding of equality and a broadening of its political strategies.

These escalating expectations for inclusion, respect, and equality in a context of continued resistance, indeed sometimes spirited opposition, have spurred the renewal of the spirit of liberationism. In particular, the AIDS epidemic, which simultaneously exposed a reality of intolerance as well as growing mainstream support for gay integration, was especially important in pressuring a rights agenda to edge toward the left. This radical spirit expresses something of the sense of integrity and entitlement that many of us who are living beyond the closet feel; it also exposes the real limitations of a rights agenda by grasping heterosexual dominance as rooted in our institutions and culture, not just in laws, attitudes, and ignorance.

However, as in the past, liberationism has largely failed to find a solid organizational footing in gay political culture. No doubt there are many reasons for this. My own sense is that liberationism alienates many gays to the extent that its social vision is wedded to a romantic rejection of America. Many liberationists seem temperamentally unable to see in the present anything more than repression, exclusion, marginalization, and domination. Rights are discounted as benefiting only middle-class whites, integration and legal equality is said to reinforce a repressive social order, and culturally respectful images are "exposed" as assimilationist or exclusionary. In short, a good America can only be imagined as a future possibility. This sort of romanticism, which parades as left politics, must be abandoned. But the heart and soul of liberationism is its understanding of the social roots of heterosexual dominance and a political vision that connects rights and equality to social justice. This should also be the heart and soul of the gay movement.

Notes

1. An earlier version of this chapter appeared in Steven Seidman (2002). Reprinted with permission.
2. For overviews of liberationist politics, see Engel (2001), Adam (1995), Epstein (1999), Humphreys (1972), Duberman (1993), Echols (1989), Taylor and Rupp (1993), and Kissack (1995).
3. See the essays by the Red Butterfly Collective, Wittman, Jay and Young, Third World Gay Revolution and Gay Liberation Front (Chicago), Woman-Identified Woman, and Martha Shelley in Jay and Young (1992 [1972]).
4. On the renewal of gay liberationist politics, see Vaid (1995), Warner (1993), Fraser (1966), and Crimp and Rolston (1990).
5. For overviews of rights-oriented gay politics of the 1980s and 1990s, see Rimmerman, Wald, and Wilcox (2000), Bull and Gallagher (1998), Deitcher (1995), Rayside (1998), and Button, Rienzo, and Wald (1997).
6. For a fuller discussion of these cases, see Seidman 2002.
7. For an overview of gains and losses through the mid-1990s, see National Gay and Lesbian Task Force Policy Institute (1997); see also Schroedel and Fiber (2000) and Button et al. (2000).
8. Researchers have documented a dramatic and unexpected shift in moral attitudes in the mid-1990s. See Loftus (2001), Yang (1997), and Dumenco (2001).
9. On nationalism and sexual identity, see Alexander (1994), Mosse (1985), Puri (2002), Berlant and Freeman (1993), and Stychin (1998).
10. A number of scholars have recently made similar arguments. See, for example, Calhoun (2000), Eskridge (2001), and Kaplan (1997).
11. On the way race organizes social institutions and culture, see Omi and Winant (1986), Feagin and Vera (1995), and Oliver and Shapiro (1995). On gender as organizing social structure, see Connell (1987), Epstein (1988), and MacKinnon (1989).
12. There is substantial theoretical and research literature on the role of gender in shaping patterns of sexual identification and dynamics of the closet and coming out. The literature of gay liberationism and lesbian feminism is crucial. On the tradition of lesbian feminism, see Myron and Bunch (1975). For gay liberationism, see Jay and Young (1992 [1972]). For more recent theoretical and empirical statements, see Butler (1990), Martin (1994), Ingraham (1996), Sanday (1990), Williams and Stein (2002), and Weston (1996).
13. For the defense of gay marriage, see Stoddard (1993), Sullivan (1996), and Hunter (1991). For arguments against gay marriage, see Ettelbrick (1993) and Warner (2000).
14. For similar arguments, see Calhoun (2000) and Eskridge (2002).
15. Virtually all researchers document a considerable weakening of "traditional" gender roles in the organization of heterosexual families since the 1960s. There is much less agreement regarding the extent and meaning of this change and the role of factors such as women's earning power as well as bearing and caring for children in shaping the gendered character of heterosexual intimacy. For some recent overviews of this research, see the work of the following sociologists: Bianchi et al. (2000), Coltrane (1998) and (1996), and Waite (2000).
16. See Weeks, Heaphy, and Donovan (2001); Carrington (1999); and Lewin (1998).

17. I have drawn considerably here on arguments developed by Eskridge (2002). The historian Nancy Cott has also commented on the historical weakening of the "normalizing" and normative status of marriage. "It could be contended, then, that by the 1980s the states and the nation had let go their grip on the institution of marriage along with their previous understanding of it. States' willingness to prosecute marital rape and wife abuse formed the most recent items in a trail of evidence, including the unchaining of morality from formal monogamy, the demise of the fiction of marital unity, and the institution of no-fault divorce. State legislatures and courts . . . resuscitated their much earlier willingness to treat couples 'living together' as if they were married, at least in economic terms. The families of unmarried couples are treated as families in courts. Parents' rights over children do not diminish . . . just because of birth out of wedlock." Cott speaks of a "public willingness to see marriage-like relationships as marriage" (Cott 2000, 212; see also Rountree, this volume). Despite what Cott calls the "disestablishment" between marriage and the state, the 1990s saw a renewal of the preeminence of marriage in the face of new challenges such as extending marriage to gays or the "flaunting" of the severance of marriage from monogamy in the Clinton-Lewinsky affair.

18. For persuasive arguments to uncouple a range of basic material benefits from marriage, see Calhoun (2000) and Warner (2000).

CHAPTER 14

Sex and Freedom

JANET R. JAKOBSEN AND ELIZABETH LAPOVSKY KENNEDY

Virtually any contemporary social movement faces deep contradictions in the effort to turn social movement into social policy. These are the contradictions of dealing with the liberal state, contradictions that are intensifying at the current moment as neoliberalism takes over the globe (at least in its imagination of itself, and a very powerful imagination it is).[1] These contradictions are particularly acute when it comes to sexuality.

The United States government presents itself as a guiding light in promoting freedom, a freedom ensured and protected by human rights, but the U.S. has at best a contradictory record with regard to human rights, particularly in relation to issues of gender and sexuality. For example, in its role of promoting freedom and protecting human rights, the U.S. has recently granted asylum in a number of cases, some promoted with a particularly high profile, in which those applying for asylum did so on the basis of threats against their person in the form of "genital mutilation" or "gender violence."[2] Without the same high profile, the U.S. has also begun granting asylum in some cases based on the persecution of sexual minorities. At the same time, the U.S. maintains a number of regressive policies on these same issues. The U.S. refuses to ratify the United Nations treaty on women's rights and continues to have trouble fighting domestic violence against women, trouble that was certainly not alleviated by the 2000 Supreme Court decision vitiating part of the Violence Against Women Act (see *U.S. v. Morrison,* "Supreme Court Strikes Down Violence Against Women Act" 2000). Moreover, in 1996 the federal government passed a ban on same-sex marriages despite the fact that at the time no state allowed such marriages. With the Supreme Court's 2003 *Lawrence v. Texas* decision that de-criminalized sodomy, legislators began mobilizing again to prevent gay mar-riage, suggesting even the possibility of a constitutional amendment to define marriage as "between one man and one woman." Nor is the U.S. free from the threat of extralegal violence that has been the basis for some of the asylum cases, a fact that was brought home in a series of well-publicized murders linked to hate crimes in 1998, including the killing of Dr. Barnett Slepian in Buffalo, NY, because his medical practice included the provision of abortion, and the murder of gay college student Matthew Shepard. It is clear that the United States regulates and controls sexuality as much as it defends sexual human rights or freedom.

In trying to address such contradictory state policies, social movements face potential contradictions in their own positions. Feminist movements and movements for lesbian, gay, bisexual, and transgender rights often adopt posi-tions that advocate state support in matters of sexuality, while these same movements must simultaneously resist state regulation and control. Over the last three decades of the twentieth century, feminists actively sought state sup-port in addressing sexual harassment and violence, while they opposed state control over women's sexuality and reproduction. The persistence of debates over such issues as what constitutes sexual harassment or whether prostitution should be illegal attest to how difficult it is to resolve the role of the state in re-lation to freedom. Similarly, advocates of lesbian and gay rights have sought state support on a number of issues from gay marriage to hate crime laws, while they have also sought to end state regulation through sodomy laws (see M. Bernstein, this volume). These issues have produced strong contests in various movements dealing with sexuality over when and how to engage with the state. Movement critics, including those who identify with queer politics, have ar-gued that both gay marriage and hate crime laws can have deleterious effects precisely because they depend in some fashion on the state regulatory appara-tus. Interactions among movements can be equally complex: Queer move-ments often reenact the sexism and racism that feminist movements and antiracist movements seek to redress, while neither feminist nor antiracist movements are free from homophobia. Each of these cases makes clear the complexities of interactions between social movements and the state on issues of sexuality.

These complexities were powerfully highlighted in 1998 and 1999 when President Clinton was impeached and tried in a case that centered on his sex-ual conduct. The trial brought sex to the front pages of newspapers, to prime time television, and to dinnertime conversation in many homes. Public reac-tion to the discussion of sex in a trial staged by the federal government was mixed: Many people felt privacy should be respected, while others felt that some sexual behavior should be regulated. Throughout the course of the impeachment proceedings different expressions of these conflicting feelings were predominant, often varying from community to community. African Americans were some of Clinton's strongest supporters. As Orlando Patterson wrote in an editorial essay in *The New York Times*, so much of African-American history has been one long violation of privacy, and of sexual privacy in particular, that many African Americans were more concerned about the investigations' violation of Clinton's privacy than about Clinton's violation of his marriage vows (Patterson 1998). Moreover, the conflict within a public dedicated to both privacy and some forms of sexual regulation was mirrored in confusions over sexual harassment. It is clear that many people now recognize sexual harassment exists and should be stopped, but the relation between stopping sexual harassment and regulating sex more generally remains fuzzy and contradictory.

How are social movements to respond to these contradictions? Whatever heightened understanding about sex that was displayed in these public perceptions was formed out of the set of social movements that marked the second half of the twentieth century in the U.S., including feminist movements' fights against sexual coercion and for sexual liberation; years of action on the part of the gay and lesbian liberation movements to bring issues of sexuality to public attention; the struggles of people of color for civil rights, and struggles over economic issues like welfare rights, particularly in regard to keeping the state from interfering in private life. For example, the welfare system in the United States has often involved punitive state interference with the private lives of those receiving benefits, beginning with "morals" checks of recipients in the nineteenth century. Those who have fought for basic economic sustenance as a right have always argued that poor people should be granted the same rights to privacy as the middle classes.

Despite the efforts of these social movements, there are obvious limits to the public and governmental understanding of sex in the United States. Although there was some public defense of the president in terms of privacy, sexual freedom was rarely incorporated into the debate. It was completely absent from the Congressional proceedings and rarely mentioned in public discussion. In this chapter we argue that liberal privacy without a concomitant notion of social freedom will prove inadequate. Moreover, we argue that it is necessary to rethink the meaning of both privacy and freedom if these terms are to prove useful for progressive social movements. The 2003 Supreme Court decision in *Lawrence v. Texas* makes this more imperative; having been granted respect for their private lives, gays and lesbians need to address the potential limits of politics organized around privacy and develop concepts that work beyond the strictures of liberalism.

Sexual freedom is not the only site of social movement that faces problems and contradictions in relation to the liberal state; a number of related issues raised by post-World War II social movements are also in tenuous condition. Throughout the 1990s the relationship of the state to various kinds of civil rights, and affirmative action in particular, has been attenuated. The Supreme Court's 2003 validation of limited forms of affirmative action in *Grutter v. Bollinger* was tentative at best. Now is the time to reformulate understandings among various movements for civil rights. Thus, in taking up the question of sexual freedom, we will also consider whether freedom could provide a connecting point among various movements. At one time, new social movements in the U.S. were recognized as "freedom movements," but now the invocation of freedom is as likely to be used against these movements as in their favor. Participants in progressive movements are either accused of being too free and encouraging social irresponsibility or they are portrayed as the enemies of freedom that enforce political correctness. In the not-too-distant past, freedom in the form of "liberation" was also a connecting point among movements. Early post-Stonewall politics were organized around names like the Gay Liberation Front to signal connections not only to U.S. movements for economic and racial justice and women's liberation, but also to worldwide anticolonial freedom movements. Gay liberation sought a freedom fundamentally associated with justice.

Now, however, in dominant public discourse, freedom seems like a word that refers only to conservative projects. Freedom means the triumph of markets over most of the globe and the concomitant individual privilege of consumption. Freedom means the extension of neocolonial dominance rather than liberation from colonialism. And freedom has become the name for U.S. militarism. When Muslims objected to the name "Infinite Justice" for the 2001 U.S. war in Afghanistan, the name was instantly changed to "Enduring Freedom." And "Operation Iraqi Freedom" was the name given to the U.S. war in Iraq in 2003. What are the implications for social movements once dedicated to liberation, when the U.S. has chosen to impose freedom through military means? Is it possible to advocate sexual freedom as a progressive policy, while the U.S. requires the world to "endure" its particular version of freedom?

Many progressive social movements are now likely to discredit freedom because of its contemporary conservative associations. It seems extremely difficult to pursue freedom and justice conjointly, and when so pressed, left-wing movements have turned to a focus on justice to the exclusion of freedom.

This chapter works to formulate future directions for sexual freedom and civil rights, addressing new dilemmas in the twenty-first century, including the question: Is it possible to appeal to the state to prevent sexual violence and harassment and to resist state interference in cases of sexual exchanges between consenting adults? How is it possible to connect understandings of, and movements for, sexual freedom to other forms of freedom and other movements for civil rights both within the U.S. and transnationally? Given the implication of freedom in the contemporary era of neoliberal dominance, this may seem like a quixotic project, but we believe that freedom is crucial to the project of "progressive" movement.

Values-Based Movement

These questions take on a particular urgency, because of shifts in the organization of American social movements in the late twentieth century. In the 1980s, the liberationist movements begun in the 1970s tended to become movements that were primarily organized by identity politics. Identity-based movements, including gay, lesbian, bisexual, and transgender movements, made some important gains, but by the 1990s they had begun to stagnate—a stagnation due both to right-wing backlash and internal problems. Identity politics was formed, in part, on the basis of criticisms of the preceding leftist, new social movements of the 1960s and 1970s that couldn't seem to deal with issues of race, gender, sexuality, or even class differences, despite their overarching critique of capitalism, "the system," and even "the man." The most radical identity politics, like that described by the Combahee River Collective (Combahee River Collective 1983) used articulations of complex identities as the basis for multi-issue politics. But often identity politics did not live up to such a radical and complex vision, and instead identity-based movement often devolved to single-issue politics that could not sustain either alliances or a broad progressive vision.

From the very beginning of the 1980s, with the publication of anthologies like *This Bridge Called My Back* (Moraga and Anzaldúa 1981), the problems as well as the benefits of identity politics were the subject of discussion and critique. Mainstream lesbian, gay, and bisexual movements have exemplified the problems of identity politics. As they gained greater recognition through the 1980s and into the 1990s, they became more focused on single issues, less able to make alliances, and ultimately more conservative. Gay Liberation's early attempts to make connections with international struggles for justice were replaced by a single-issue conservatism that reached a pinnacle with the Human Rights Campaign's endorsement of the conservative New York Senator Alfonse D'Amato over a more liberal Charles Schumer in the 1998 senatorial elections.

As early as the beginning of the 1990s, this growing conservatism had induced a new sexuality politics that was "queer" rather than identity-based. Influenced by poststructuralist critiques of identity, these movements hoped to resist the problems that accompany identity politics. Resistance to the norms of identity and to the state insofar as it enforced these norms was the watchword of these movements. Nowhere is the difference between identity politics and queer movement more apparent than with respect to the issue of gay marriage. Although gay marriage has become the primary issue for lesbian and gay politics, most queer politics eschew the type of normalizing effects entailed by the state's legitimation of marriage. With state legitimation comes regulation, and queer politics is suspicious of both.

As we move into the twenty-first century, however, the queer impulse toward resistance has begun to seem like an insufficient basis for social movements. Although queer politics provided great clarity about what progressives were fighting against, it was much harder to articulate what we were fighting for. Holding on to the importance of resistance, a number of queer theorists and critical theorists have now made a turn to ethics precisely to address the limits of resistance alone.[3]

These issues have played out differently in the women's movements and in civil rights movements for racial and economic justice, but the problems facing identity politics—right-wing backlash and an inability to recognize differences within identity categories—have persisted across movements. In each case the increasing conservatism of the U.S. public sphere and the limitations of identity politics tended to produce established movement organizations that were relatively conservative and that focused on single issues, only rarely forming alliances across movements or issues. Strong poststructuralist critiques developed in both feminist and critical race theory and politics, but like queer politics, these critiques did not lead to immediately revitalized social movements.

The tail end of the twentieth century, however, has produced some new possibilities for social movements. There is a new radicalism that seems to have emerged most visibly in the United States since the World Trade Organization (WTO) demonstrations in Seattle in the fall of 1999, followed by the actions in Washington, D.C., to challenge the World Bank and the International Monetary Fund (IMF), the week of April 9–16, 2000. The U.S. wars in Afghanistan and Iraq have also generated new peace movements, with hundreds of thousands of people in New York and other cities across the country marching to protest the invasion of Iraq. Like the resistance movements of the 1990s, these new movements tend to be focused on direct action and have been comprised of relatively autonomous, small groups that come together for larger actions. These new movements often seem defined as much by what they are against—the WTO or U.S. wars and imperialism—as by what they are for. Groups like Not in Our Name and New Yorkers Say No to War have been effective parts of the new organizing. The umbrella for antiwar organizing in New York has taken on the name of United for Peace and Justice, but its largest actions have been antiwar demonstrations.

If neither identity nor resistance is a sufficient basis for politics, how do we think beyond the negative categories, whether antiglobalization or antiwar? Do we need an affirmative program beyond an overarching commitment to peace and justice? It seems as though many of us who might call ourselves progressive have a general agreement on broad principles, and it seems that these principles might connect various movements. But we also know (a knowledge created from often bitter experience) that we will never agree on the details. Does it make a difference, beyond a commitment to social justice or to peace, which values are named as the basis for progressive movement?

A recent debate within lesbian, gay, bisexual, transgender, and queer (LGBTQ) movements both exemplifies the alternative that a values-based movement is supposed to provide to identity politics and allows us to explore further the question of values and their effectiveness. The Millennium March sponsored by the national gay and lesbian lobby group, the Human Rights Campaign (HRC), and the gay Christian Metropolitan Community Church (MCC) took place just a few short weeks after the 2000 April actions against the World Bank and IMF. The Millennium March was called by HRC and MCC without much consultation with other groups and it was originally billed under the banner of a march for "faith and family." Both the conservative slogan and the lack of consultation produced immediate controversy, as activists from various quarters took up the call for an "open process." Ultimately, the faith and family pairing proved too conservative to be sustainable, but the abandonment of the slogan did not indicate an opening for discussion of the values that might be motivating the march.

This failure to achieve an open process was the motivation behind an e-mail communication to the march organizers from a group of young activists called "FROM ISOLATION TO JUSTICE: A letter to the LGBT movement from the Next Generation." This letter articulates a set of values under the broad banner of justice and argues that the structure of the Millennium March is more likely to hamper the realization of these values than to contribute to their actualization in the world.

What Are Our Values?

> Each one of us grew up in a homophobic society that taught us to feel alone and isolated. From this isolation, we reach out to each other to build community and act together to build a movement. We are our friends' found families, the creators of new traditions and ethics. We are reinventing gender. We act up, and kiss in. We build community centers and other social service programs everywhere. When the nation was in homophobic denial, together we launched an unprecedented response to the AIDS epidemic and we created the most poetic monument in the country, the Quilt.
>
> From these experiences, the core values of our movement emerge: compassion, belief [in] and commitment to the common good, nondiscrimination, political freedom, freedom from violence and harassment, control over our own bodies, and equal opportunity.

These values are part of a larger legacy that links justice movements together. Do we believe in these values as a "Simple Matter of Justice" for all people? If we truly do, the LGBT movement must resist isolation and return wholeheartedly to this nation's struggle for justice. (E-mail Communication, February 10, 2000)

From this statement of values the letter moves on to present two contrasting possibilities: one, single-issue, identity-based politics focused only on the most narrow rendering of "lesbian and gay" issues; or two, a movement that comes out of isolation to form alliances and address the multiple interrelated issues that can build social justice in the contemporary moment. With the Next Generation we heartily endorse the latter of these two alternatives. But is this kind of statement of values adequate to the task of building broader coalitions and movements?

We also have some questions about the content and efficacy of the type of values-based movement advocated by the Next Generation. What are the values on which we might base a movement? And what is the relationship between these values and the movement shift from "isolation to justice?" It is not precisely clear, for example, how the values articulated by the Next Generation might distinguish them from the Human Rights Campaign. All of the values they name are liberal values; they are, in fact, values that it seems likely the Human Rights Campaign could adopt. They include the basic values of individual autonomy: freedom from violence and harassment and control over our own bodies. Freedom is designated as "political freedom," but social justice is configured as equal opportunity and nondiscrimination, rather than any type of structural justice. Sexual freedom is not even mentioned as one of the core values of our movement.

The Next Generation wants a movement that looks very different from the Millennium March, but the values they espouse are those that have reproduced the contradictions of liberalism time and time again.[4] Framing a movement in terms of "nondiscrimination," for example, is one of the main mechanisms in U.S. public life that set up single-issue movements. As critical race theorists like Kimberlé Crenshaw have shown, a movement focus on producing nondiscrimination law virtually forces a declaration within a single category: race or gender or, for the Human Rights Campaign, sexuality (Crenshaw 1989). The only contrasts to these expressly liberal values are the social values of compassion and the common good. These values come not from the tradition of radical social justice, however, but from the communitarian tradition that has accompanied liberalism in U.S. history. One needs only to think of George W. Bush's campaign slogan, "compassionate conservatism," as a complement to a Republican economic agenda to have grounds for doubting that dedication to compassion will produce the type of critique advocated by the Next Generation.[5]

What do we need in order to accomplish a shift away from single-issue politics and toward a complex movement for social justice? How do we connect different movements for social justice, movements that have certainly had difficulty forming alliances when operating within the liberal framework of the contemporary public sphere?

In the rest of this chapter, we will explore alternative possibilities for a values-based movement. Instead of searching for a single framework, either the framework provided by the liberal public sphere or one provided by a single movement, we are working with concepts that foster interaction among social movements and between movements and the state. We pursue two genealogies of values in order to show how it is possible to articulate the value of freedom for new social movements. We are interested in articulating freedom as a value with radical potential, but which does not require us to adopt a strictly oppositional stand in relation to liberal freedom or the liberal state. Such an articulation of values contributes to the possibility of a new social movement that is not trapped in the contradictions of the engagement with the liberal state, but can rather work these contradictions to radical ends. We will explore two interrelated genealogies: one of privacy and one of freedom. In the liberal state, freedom is protected through privacy, but privacy has proven to be a fickle protection at best. For a values-based freedom movement to develop, we must address and reconfigure the notion of privacy, and we must go beyond privacy to a complementary and more extensive understanding of freedom.

The Value of Privacy

One of the main contradictions in the structure of the contemporary liberal state is enacted around the notion of privacy. Since U.S. Supreme Court decisions in the 1960s, most notably *Griswold v. Connecticut* (1965), *Eisenstadt v. Baird* (1972), and *Roe v. Wade* (1972), popular consciousness about U.S. law understands privacy to be the protection of all kinds of freedom, including sexual freedom. Privacy has been crucial to the development of rights around issues of sex and gender, serving, for example, as the basis in the U.S. for the right to use birth control without intervention from the state, and for women's access to abortion. Most recently, privacy was the basis for the U.S. Supreme Court's decision in *Lawrence v. Texas*.[6] This decision struck down the Texas sodomy statue and also overturned the Court's own 1986 decision in *Bowers v. Hardwick* that had refused to apply the right to privacy to homosexual sodomy.[7]

And yet privacy has also proven to have extremely porous boundaries and to be extremely fickle about whom it protects. Patricia Williams argues that privacy cannot protect those without property, using the example of homeless people who are denied rights to both personal privacy and public space (Williams 1988). Privacy sometimes protects too much, laying out a zone under which various types of violence against women can take place without being treated as violence. But privacy can also protect too little. As Susan Bordo has shown, the right to bodily integrity that privacy describes is often scrupulously defended for men, even sometimes extended to male prisoners, but is loosely and squeamishly applied in relation to women (Bordo 1993; see also Kaye, this volume).

Until the *Lawrence* decision, the sexual freedom that was protected by privacy was only that of sanctified heterosexual marriage outlined in the *Griswold* decision about birth control.[8] At this time it is too soon to tell the implications of the *Lawrence* ruling, but it does raise the issue once again of whether privacy is a sufficient protection of sexual rights. The extensive limitations on access to abortion point to the ways in which Court decisions based on privacy provide protections that are tenuous at best. Both federal and state legislatures have enacted a series of restrictions on the practice of reproductive rights, such as the Partial Birth Abortion Ban Act of 2003, and many women cannot get access to an abortion in a time when many areas of the country do not even have facilities that offer the procedure.

We suggest, then, that although privacy may be necessary to the possibility of sexual freedom, it may very well not be sufficient. We will argue that rethinking the meaning of both privacy and freedom is an important step in preserving whatever protections *Lawrence* has to offer and overcoming the limits of politics based on privacy alone. In particular, based on research done by Elizabeth Kennedy, we suggest that privacy is itself a social relation that can be configured in a number of different ways. It is not simply a matter of drawing the line between the public and the private at the appropriate point. The question of privacy can be much more fruitfully pursued by asking about the various social relations within which privacy is embedded. Our two genealogies, one located in gay and lesbian history and the other in African-American freedom movements, shift our understanding about the social configuration of privacy and its relation to freedom.

The division between the public and the private has been central to the organization of gay and lesbian life in this century, as indicated by the concept of the closet. The popular or simplified model of gay and lesbian history is that before Stonewall gays and lesbians lived furtive, hidden lives, while after Stonewall they could "come out."[9] This model, however, doesn't capture the public dimensions of gay and lesbian life in the first half of the twentieth century or the complex negotiations of gays and lesbians through the private and public. Two useful moments for illuminating the various ways lesbians have forged rewarding and fulfilling lives, creatively managing the distinction between the public and private, are upper-class lesbian life in rural western New York in the 1930s and working-class lesbian life in Buffalo, New York, in the 1940s and 1950s. In neither case did lesbians live isolated, furtive lives, relegating their sexuality to a moment of individual privacy. Unlike today's military policy of "don't ask, don't tell" that assumes a clear distinction between public life and private individual sex acts, both cultures were based in communities that knowingly gave support to individual lesbians. In comparing the working-class lesbian bar experience to that of circles of upper-class lesbians, the social dimensions of sexuality, of privacy, and of sexual freedom become apparent.

Kennedy's research on Julia Boyer Reinstein and her circle of friends indicates the ways class privilege expanded the realm of the domestic or private sphere to protect sexual expression. Reinstein, who was born in 1906 to an upper-class family in rural western New York, was a teacher, and her circle of friends included teachers and other professional women—nurses, journalists, and artists. They were discreet about their sexuality, but nevertheless were active sexually as lesbians from 1924 through 1942. While teaching in Castile, Reinstein lived there by herself in a rented room during the week. On weekends she and her partner would be together in Reinstein's mother's house, where they occupied a suite that had been remodeled for them. Their weekends might be spent with family, sometimes joined by visits from lesbian friends, or sometimes traveling or visiting with lesbian friends. In the summer she and her partner went to Columbia University's Teachers College, renting an apartment together. They made new friends in New York City through one of Reinstein's lifelong lesbian friends who had taken a job as a nurse in New York City. They also were visited by other friends.

The evidence indicates this life was not furtive, governed by fear of exposure. Rather, as lesbians, Reinstein and her friends were able to create a life of sociability and fun. According to Reinstein, they all understood themselves to be lesbians and for them this meant being sexually active with women, something they knew about from literature and from medical writings. But they never, or at most rarely, talked about it with one another or with close family, and never with the outside world. Unquestionably, their lesbian lives were constructed as part of a private world, but this private world was not limited to single individuals. It included close family and friends, allowing a spatial dimension so that lesbians could thrive. For example, Reinstein and her partner lived in her mother's house, having their own space but also sharing family space. In listening to Reinstein's stories, we are most struck that these social arrangements did not seem to generate shame or self-hate in connection with being a lesbian.

What social structures made it possible for Reinstein and her friends to develop satisfactory lesbian lives in the interstices of upper-class society? First and foremost is something Kennedy calls "discretion," never publicly indicating or announcing lesbianism. There seemed to be an unstated social agreement that Reinstein and her friends would never do anything that would draw unnecessary attention to their transgressions. At least while in the towns where they worked and lived, they followed the rules of decorum for upper- and middle-class women, dressing well, attending social functions, and the like. This wasn't experienced as a restriction by Reinstein, but as a pleasure, associated with being part of upper- and middle-class circles. She loved good clothes and enjoyed attending dances and concerts, or playing cards with family and friends. At the same time, parents and their friends were part of this agreement to be discreet. They did not treat their lesbian daughters as "deviants," pressuring them to lead more conventional lives. This system of discretion seems to be modeled on the way a husband's adulterous transgressions were treated—that is, ignored if discreet. It was aided by the fact that in the nineteenth century, deep friendships between women were common. These ideas still carried over well into the first third of the twentieth century, so that the lesbian relationships of Reinstein and her friends were not immediately suspect in all circles.

Second, lesbian life could flourish in the interstices of upper-class society because families had the will, money, and prestige to protect daughters from social condemnation. If someone intended to harass these daughters, their parents would pay to quiet the troublemaker down. And in fact, in Reinstein's life there were several examples of this. Her father paid off the previous lover of Reinstein's lover who was threatening to cause trouble. More dramatically, the father of a good friend of Reinstein paid off the friend's husband when he found her in bed with a woman and threatened to expose her in the school where she taught. It was not simply money that offered protection, but also the prestige of the families, allowing them to make life miserable for people who gossiped too much.

In the situation of Reinstein and her friends, which we imagine was not unusual in the 1920s and 1930s, sexual expression is located completely in the realm of the domestic and is regulated by the family. Discretion, money, and power allow these families to expand the domestic enough to include lesbian sociability and sexuality. This system has many advantages from which we can learn. It allows Reinstein and her friends to pursue a lesbian life without much, if any, stigma. These lesbians lived as full and valued human beings even while transgressing the social norms of heterosexuality. But this system has some serious weaknesses that don't allow us to easily refurbish it for today. It is obviously not generalizable because it requires money and power that are so unevenly distributed in our society. The family must cooperate for it to work, accepting their daughters, being discreet, and actively protecting them. Although Reinstein's family did cooperate, as did those of her friends, history is clear that not all upper-class families were so inclined. Many daughters of upper-class families ended up in insane asylums with no recourse. Yet another problem with this system is that it hides abuse. The same system that protects a husband's adultery and a daughter's lesbianism also protects sexual abuse, battering, and rape. Finally, this system has very limited application in contemporary capitalism, because it requires social stability, living close to one's family and upper-class friends. If job circumstances take a person away from the circle of family and friends where discretion and protection are the norm, it becomes difficult to establish a lesbian life.

In the 1940s and 1950s, working-class butch-fem bars and house parties came to predominate as a form of lesbian social life, one that was well adapted to the mobility of industrial capitalist society. No matter what city a person was in, she could find working-class butch-fem social life by going to these bars and house parties. Most often they were racially segregated, but sometimes they were mixed. For these working-class women, coming out not only meant recognizing that one was different—gay, lesbian, butch, fem—but also searching for others like oneself and entering the gay world. Due to a lack of money and lack of social power, there was little possibility of developing a social life around one's own homes or in colleges. Working-class lesbians needed to find and build their own spaces, learning about possibilities from word of mouth through childhood friends or army buddies, from taxi drivers, or from local lore.

The bars were multipurpose gathering places. In bars, lesbians could hang out with others of their kind, tell stories, and learn about lesbian life. They also were a central place for meeting prospective lovers, giving bars an erotic dimension. Bar lesbians displayed their sexual attractiveness, dressed according to style, and flirted openly. In addition, bars were also a place where lesbians interfaced as lesbians with the heterosexual world, testing the limits of what was possible. When hostile straights came into their bars, lesbians would joke or fight to maintain their dignity. Should a bar they frequented close down, they would often help to negotiate with straight bar owners to open a new bar, or fight to take over other bars. In these bars there developed a sense of community, a consciousness of kind.

This social life was premised on the fact that there was no protection for private sexual expression, which had become abundantly clear during the 1950's McCarthy witch hunts and earlier army discharges (Berube 1990). Bars and large house parties represented lesbians taking their own lives in their hands and defending themselves. Why would working-class lesbians feel the need to build communities or at least public gathering places? Working-class lesbians who came out in the 1940s and 1950s answer this in terms of the loneliness of being the only one, the search for others like oneself, and the feeling of being home when one finds them.

When the bar experience is compared with the circles of upper-class friends, the social dimension of sexuality becomes even more apparent. Sexual desire—even desire that deviates from the social norm—is expressed in a social context. Without such sociability it is difficult to meet others and to explore one's sexuality. Upper-class society created an expanded domestic realm that protected lesbian daughters like Reinstein. Working-class lesbians created a social context for themselves in bars. Thus, bars, although definitely public space, are an unusual form of public space, one that exists to foster and support private expressions of sexuality.

The strengths and problems with this working-class bar context for lesbianism were recognized by those who participated in it. Participants describe contradictory views, often held by the same person. Bars were both wonderful and terrible places. They offered an exciting social life and involved lesbians in self-activity to build their own communities, the long-term effect of which was to put lesbianism on the social map and to begin to confirm a distinct identity. Yet by becoming public, lesbians were often stigmatized as sick and deviant, leading many to struggle with corroding forms of self-hatred.

This analysis suggests the need to refine notions of the closet, shifting our understanding of the relation between public and private. These two examples of the ways lesbianism was organized in this century demonstrate how freedom of sexual expression cannot fall back on protection that is rooted in a limited idea of individual privacy, even if that protection could be extended for all groups in society. If a fundamental aspect of sexual freedom is the right to public assembly, then the meaning of "gay rights" sought by social movements would challenge the liberal state and its understanding of sexual freedom as based on privacy. Finally, these examples suggest that rights alone are not enough. Freedom cannot simply be a negative right; it must also be a positive good. There needs to be a social value that embraces sexual variety or the stigma attached to sexual transgression will generate self-hate and loathing.

The Value of Freedom

How are we to take the notion of social privacy developed through Kennedy's genealogy and connect it to a broadly based social movement like that advocated by the Next Generation? Kennedy's genealogy shows the ways in which social possibilities for sex are related to issues of privilege and social class. To develop a model of social privacy that would not be limited to those who can assume the privilege of discretion requires access to social space, an access that is often limited by class and race. Working-class lesbians had to fight for this type of social space. We conceptualize this necessary access to social space in terms of freedom of assembly—freedom in the sense of a right to social space, regardless of one's ability to pay for it. But can these notions of freedom with regard to sexual practice and with regard to sexual assembly be connected to movements for racial and economic justice? Kennedy's analysis points to some of the ways in which these issues can overlap. Working-class lesbians sometimes built a bar life that was racially mixed, while Reinstein's circle excluded both people of color of all classes and all working-class people. Part of the success of that way of life depended on society's assumption about the refined sensibilities of upper-class white women; their close friendships were beyond scrutiny.

To think further about how to connect movements, we now turn to a second genealogy: that of freedom in African-American movements. The concept of freedom developed in African-American social movements extends some of the formulations provided by Kennedy's work on privacy. In particular, African-American movements have often articulated freedom in social rather than individualistic and private terms. Freedom has been a contested concept within and among various African-American movements; this genealogy is not a representation of some essential African-American idea, but rather an exploration of alternative meanings of freedom produced in specific movements. We also turn to this genealogy, however, because any discussion of freedom in the U.S. context must come to terms with the history of slavery. We must think about how central slavery was to the constitution of freedom in the U.S., both literally—to the production of the U.S. Constitution with its enshrined freedoms—and figuratively—to the development of a concept of freedom as the central value in U.S. social life (Patterson 1991; Morrison 1990).

Finally, we turn to this genealogy because it is particularly useful as we think about building a complex and connected movement. The question of sex and freedom is acute in relation to African-American concepts of freedom because sexuality has so often been used against African Americans. In U.S. racist discourses, African Americans have been posited as licentious and sexually irresponsible—in short, as too sexually free. Not surprisingly, sexual freedom has been a contested category within African-American movements. How do they challenge this sexualized racist discourse without reasserting the sexual regulation that is at the base of this form of racism? The project of connecting movements against domination has to struggle with the same issue. If we attempt simply to apply a concept of sexual freedom developed in predominantly white movements to African-American contexts, we may end up participating in or even extending sexualized racism, rather than resisting it.

One step in building a movement that resists sexualized racism is to pursue alternate visions of freedom to that of the dominant white society. The presumption of white capitalist freedom is that freedom means individuals will have the opportunity to pursue their own projects and desires without limits; they will be autonomous, and free from social restraints. African-American freedom movements have posed another possibility, however: movement toward an alternative, less destructive form of freedom. This alternative implies a critique—of the application of white freedom to African-American contexts, but more importantly, a critique of the predominant understanding of freedom itself.

Ethicist Katie Cannon in *Black Womanist Ethics* (1988) argues that the notion of freedom developed in the tradition of movements that she identifies as "womanist" is different than that developed in dominant white ethics. Womanist ideas of freedom are also, of course, different from those developed in other African-American movements, and in particular womanist ethics are different from those African-American movements that are closer to the dominant U.S. tradition of liberalism. Cannon argues that the dominant meaning of freedom—that of the autonomous individual with physical mobility and the ability to make choices—is one that was developed from the experience of those who have racial and economic privilege, even if it is sometimes adopted by those who do not have such privilege. This vision of freedom, like other aspects of privileged existence, was only made possible through the labor of others. In a slave economy, the labor of slaves made possible the sense of freedom experienced by privileged whites. But, even in capitalist economies, and even after emancipation, the work of wage laborers has made possible the experience of individuality, mobility, and choice that defines freedom for the privileged. What this history suggests is that any notion of sexual freedom that is to "come out of isolation and into justice" as the Next Generation suggests, requires that we not replicate the autonomous and individualistic notion of freedom that depends upon the work of others to produce a sense of freedom for some.

But this notion of freedom is not the only one possible, or even the only American understanding. Cannon describes a vision of freedom that contrasts strikingly with that of the autonomous, liberal individual. This vision, part of a womanist ethical tradition, is based in a movement that simultaneously resists gender, racial, and economic oppression. If in liberalism, the free individual is marked by choice and consent, African-American women have historically been denied choice and consent. And yet, argues Cannon, womanist ethics identify a sense of moral agency under conditions of constraint and an ideal of freedom that is not dependent on a wide range of choices. Cannon is articulating a notion of freedom that resists exploitation, whether in the form of slavery or of wage labor. Freedom under these conditions does not mean a condition free from social constraint. But freedom does provide a central value that can form the basis of social struggle:

> Throughout the various periods of their history in the United States, Black women have used their creativity to carve out "living space" within the intricate web of multilayered oppression. From the beginning, they had to contend with the ethical ambiguity of racism, sexism and other sources of fragmentation in this acclaimed land of freedom, justice and equality. The Black woman's literary tradition delineates the many ways that ordinary Black women have fashioned value patterns and ethical procedures in their own terms, as well as mastering, transcending, radicalizing and sometimes destroying pervasive, negative orientations imposed by the mores of the larger society. (1988, 76)

Rather than being marked by individualism, this womanist understanding of freedom is fundamentally relational. Moral agency is focused not on choice, but on struggle—the communal struggle for survival and the communal struggle for social change.

Historian Saidiya V. Hartman (1997) argues that one of the places slaves enacted practices of freedom was in surreptitious communal gatherings. Hartman is careful to resist the temptation to romanticize either freedom or the notion of community; rather she sees community as an ambiguous term, "an articulation of an ideal and a way of naming the networks of affiliation that exist in the context of difference, disruption, and death" (61). These communal gatherings were, however, the simultaneous articulation and enactment of possibilities for freedom. They were the enactment of freedom because they often involved "stealing away" to sites that were not completely controlled by the masters. For example, Hartman talks about the practice of sneaking away to praise meetings, which were religious meetings to praise a revolutionary God that saves in history. And this act of freedom made possible the moments in which freedom could also be articulated:

> The activities encompassed in the scope of stealing away played upon the tension between the owner's possession and the slave's dispossession and sought to redress the condition of enslavement by whatever limited means available. The most direct expression of the desire for redress was the praise meeting. The appeals made to a "God that saves in history" were overwhelmingly focused on freedom. (66)

But this combination of enactment and articulation also made the meetings subject to intense punishment. These punishments for the enactment of freedom show the depth of freedom's paradoxes. The only time the "will" of the slave was recognized was for the purposes of ascribing punishment. Thus, the African-American subject of freedom is also the African-American subject to punishment.

These paradoxes imply that freedom is not free from the contradictions and ambivalences of domination, and thus the freedom promised by the liberal state is never simply "free." As Cannon's ethics make clear, the negation of enslavement informs both white dominant and African-American notions of freedom, but this negation is taken in different directions by the different participants in the relation of freedom and domination. In liberal ethics, being free, not being a slave, meant an existence as, what Hartman terms "the unencumbered self, the citizen, the self-possessed individual, and the volitional and autonomous subject"; alternatively, African-American demands for freedom begin from "yearning to be liberated from the condition of enslavement" (p. 61). For slaves this yearning in practice produced a necessarily double meaning that does not reduce to a desire to become an "unencumbered self." On the one hand, slaves practiced "provisional ways of operating within the dominant space; local, multiple, and dispersed sites of resistance that have not been strategically codified or integrated; and the nonautonomy and pained constitution of the slave as person" (61). On the other hand, these practices took place in relation to a discourse of freedom that negated enslavement fully, requiring a revolution of social relations. This revolution would not simply "free" African Americans so as to provide them with the individual rights inherent in liberal freedom. The dominant society, its ethics and social relations, would have to change for the realization of this freedom.

Hartman identifies a radical paradox of freedom under slavery: Survival often depended upon a vision of life provided in praise meetings where to proclaim oneself the subject of freedom was also to proclaim oneself the subject of punishment and control, of unfreedom. The paradox of freedom may have changed with emancipation, but because emancipation did not offer the complete revolution envisioned in freedom's radical moment, the problem of freedom continued. Freedom remained a term through which new forms of "free" relation—such as that of sharecropping—could extend domination, even as freedom remained the sign of radical transformation. As reconstruction showed, emancipation could and would continue the problematics of freedom.

Sexual freedom is particularly complicated in relation to this history. The complexities of sexuality for African-American women have been traced by a number of writers, including Hortense Spillers (1992) and Evelynn Hammonds (1994). Hartman pursues the question through an incisive reading of Harriet Jacobs's *Incidents in the Life of a Slave Girl.* Hartman concentrates on two points that have not been emphasized in previous readings of Jacobs's narrative: first, that Jacobs is describing "incidents" in the life of a slave girl. Jacobs cannot give us a picture of life under slavery as it is wrought whole, because the contradictions of Jacobs's position mean that it is impossible simply to tell all. Second, under these conditions Jacobs is able to articulate something that is "akin to freedom" (104).

Jacobs articulates the sexual violence that is normative both in the conditions of enslavement and the different, but intertwined, violence in the white patriarchal family of her owner, Dr. Flint. Violence is normative both in the sense that it is pervasive, the normal state of things, and in the sense that it is required within the contradictory moral system that undergirds liberal values. As a result of this pervasiveness, sexual freedom is denied to African Americans in terms that are simultaneously public and private. In describing why the rape of African-American women cannot be recognized by the law during slavery, she points out that to recognize sexual violation would undercut both the "prerogatives and entitlements of the private sphere," which included the master's private ownership and control over his slaves and the "white violence requisite to preserving the public good" (101). When "good" is defined as the maintenance of slavery, all slaves must be made submissive to all whites in public as well as private. In short, changing these relations requires a different institution of freedom in both public and private relations.

Hartman succinctly summarizes the fundamentally contradictory nature of Jacobs's position in her description of Jacobs's choice to take Mr. Sands, a white man, as her lover. This choice marks for Jacobs some measure of removal from the power of Dr. Flint, but "the same act both holds out the possibility of freedom and intensifies the burdens and constraints of enslavement" (109):

> The feat of *Incidents* is not simply its representation of the normativity of the representation of sexual violence, but also the endeavor to actualize something "akin to freedom" in this context, even if it affords little more than having a lover one is thankful not to despise. (10)

Jacobs's move toward freedom is so contradictory in part precisely because it involves sexual freedom. Sexual freedom is the site of some of the most intense contradictions, in which the racialized and gendered violences of liberal freedom come to bear most intensely on the body, even as sexual freedom remains one site in which it is possible to embody an alternative reality.

On the one hand, it seems as if in the dominant moral system in which choice depends on virtue, neither the enslaved nor free African-American woman can be virtuous because she is always already presumed to be unchaste. She is without standing before the law (and hence her rape cannot be acknowledged), and she is also without standing before the moral community (and hence her moral action cannot be acknowledged). As Cannon states quite directly, African-American women are presumed to be either amoral or immoral, a presumption that is reinforced by the refusal of sexual virtue to African-American women.

On the other hand, Cannon demonstrates in her articulation of "Black Womanist Ethics" that choices and actions taken even under these conditions of deep constraint are not without moral valence. Learning to distinguish and develop values under these conditions is the product of African-American women's moral labor. The implication of this moral capability is that not all actions have the same moral meaning under conditions of constraint. "Something akin to freedom" is not the same as utter enslavement, nor is it the same as liberal autonomy. For part of Jacobs's life, the only thing "akin to freedom" was the freedom to choose a sexual partner, Dr. Sands, in resistance to the forcible sexual advances of her master. Her choice of lovers was not free from restraint, but it also resisted the most brutal practices of enslavement.

In this genealogy, then, practices of freedom are articulated in relation to, and are akin to, liberal freedom.[10] Such practices are constrained by freedom, by the liberal narrative that depends on white supremacy both in Jacobs's time and in our own. These practices are also productive of freedom, in the transitory moments of freedom that are experienced in stealing away for a praise meeting and in the vision of freedom that demands revolutionary change. This vision is not dependent upon enslavement as its opposite in the way that dominant liberal notions of freedom have been, nor is the envisioned possibility of freedom simply the opposite of liberal freedom. It is, rather, akin to, and different from, liberal freedom. The abjection of the enslaved necessary to produce the autonomous liberal subject is not necessary to the subject constituted through practices of freedom. Practices of freedom demand neither the moral purity that places the subject beyond contradiction and complication, nor the liberal autonomy that places the subject beyond the bounds of relation.

The fact that the freedom sought by African Americans is different than that offered by the liberal state has produced a complex (and contested) strategy for African-American freedom movements. Liberal freedom is certainly better than enslavement and, thus, most African-American freedom movements have sought basic civil rights. In the modern world, one cannot *not* want rights, even if such rights are flawed. We cannot simply reject rights and refuse to deal with the liberal state. Neither can we simply work on the basis of liberal notions of freedom. As Patricia Williams argues in *The Alchemy of Race and Rights* (1992), engagement with the liberal state is both necessary and complicated.

Conclusion

In sum, then, this genealogical work provides a vision of sexual freedom that is not a reenactment of liberal or capitalist versions of freedom. Freedom can be organized around struggle rather than choice. Freedom does not have to be individualistic in the liberal or capitalist sense; rather it can be relational in complicated ways. This concept of freedom requires a legal enactment that extends beyond the bounds of privacy. It needs both public and private elements, and its public enactment must include both free exercise and free assembly.[11]

This alternative sense of freedom has rather a complicated relationship to liberalism: It is neither completely free from liberalism, nor is it completely determined by it. This vision doesn't pose the liberal state as the site of freedom, nor does it pose state involvements as the opposite of freedom. As such, it allows for articulation in relation to the liberal state that is resistant without being oppositional. Movements based on this notion of freedom would be leery of strategies that simply appeal to the state in ways that contemporary gay rights groups like the Human Rights Campaign are not. It is unlikely that a movement with this notion of freedom would seek state-based gay marriage, for example, because state-sanctioned marriage would enmesh sexuality more deeply in a state that offers limited freedom at best.

Nonetheless, neither would this understanding of freedom lead movements to simply eschew engagement with the state. Shifting movement notions of freedom allows different types of negotiation vis-à-vis some of the contradictions of the liberal state. If, for example, freedom is not based on privacy, then the ways in which the boundary of privacy is both too narrow and too broad might be rearticulated. What if sexual freedom rather than sexual regulation could be the basis for resisting what is now called "domestic violence?" What if freedom of assembly and the principle of free exercise rather than privacy were to protect sexual practices?

But how is this alternative vision of freedom to be realized? Here the Next Generation's emphasis on movement is crucial: Values may be important, but they are not enough; a certain type of movement is also necessary to support those values. In the contemporary moment, such a movement needs to be based on a network of alliances that could maintain the complexity of overlapping meanings of freedom without collapsing one meaning into another. There are, for example, certain connecting points between the sense of social privacy and the social freedom of assembly described in Kennedy's lesbian genealogy and the African-American understandings of freedom described in Jakobsen's genealogy. Some of these connections can be made specifically around sexual issues. For example, in the U.S. struggle over the passage of the 1996 welfare reform bill, sexual conservatism was a driving ideological and legitimating force, but those who resisted the enactment of this policy had no strong or well-developed language through which to counter this conservatism. A language of sexual freedom might have been, and could still be, a connecting point for movements organized around gender and sexuality and for movements organized in resistance to both the racism and economic oppression of the contemporary welfare system.

Although there are these connections, Cannon and Hartman show us some of the complexities of developing connected movements. Freedom is a word of great historical import for African-American social movements, just as we have argued that freedom has at certain points been an operative concept in progressive social movement around sexuality. But the meanings of freedom in these two sets of movements are not always the same. We are suggesting that for movements to succeed these meanings need not be the same; rather, their differences need to be recognized and engaged. This engagement can be a site for working out conflicts in movement. For example, only by engaging with differences in the meaning of freedom across movements can sexual freedom develop in a manner that does not extend sexualized racism in the U.S. Thus, values alone will not build a connected movement; rather, only the practice of engagement across movements can produce values and movements that come out of isolation and into justice.

In other words, we think that the type of connected movement described by the Next Generation is better founded on and also better able to support the radical, rather than liberal, value of freedom. This shift to a radical notion of freedom is also important in dealing with some of the contradictions of the liberal state. Movements that advocate radical freedom can be articulated in a liberal public sphere, but they do not necessarily have to become immediately enmeshed in the contradictions of liberal freedom. Such movements would not have to accept liberal, individualist notions of privacy in order to protect sexual practices from government interference, nor would they have to seek protection from violence only in the terms of liberal rights. The scholarship on sexuality, social movements, and difference has exploded in the last 20 years. Let us use it to full advantage, to resist repeating old frameworks and to develop new ones that can connect movements and rethink freedom.

Notes

1. For analyses of the importance of the imagination of globalization to social processes of change, see Smith (1997) and Joseph (2002).
2. The U.S. has a very mixed record on asylum cases related to gender violence. It has granted asylum to some and denied it to others. For a roundup of some of these cases, see Sachs (1999).
3. See, for example, Warner (2000).
4. One could, of course, take the path suggested by Eisenstein (1981). She maintains that the only way to realize even these liberal values is to develop a radical movement. The letter does in its description of the movement in or out of isolation tend in this direction, but such a shift is hardly self-evident, and Eisenstein suggests not only that liberal feminism can lead to a radical movement, but also that only radical values can ultimately frame such a movement. Moreover, the contradictions of liberal values have proven to be quite powerful and difficult to escape. The sense of possibility evoked by Eisenstein's book in 1981 is much less readily available in the 2000s. Our current moment is perhaps more adequately marked by Joan Wallach Scott's 1996 appraisal of the founding moment of liberalism in revolutionary and postrevolutionary France as having "only paradoxes to offer." Scott argues that the contradictions of liberalism lead to a repetition of certain problems and paradoxes for feminists (Scott 1996).
5. The communitarian tradition asserts itself more or less vigorously at different historical moments, but it can be read, at least since de Tocqueville, as a necessary complement to liberalism. In other words, communitarianism does not necessarily present a critique of liberal individualism, but rather may be a necessary complement that creates room for managing the contradictions of liberalism. For a case study of the relations between liberal and communitarian values, see Chapter 1 of Jakobsen (1998).
6. The majority opinion in *Lawrence* found that private intimate relations between adult mutually consenting homosexuals is protected by the Due Process clause of the Fourteenth Amendment: "It is a promise of the Constitution that there is a realm of personal liberty in which the government may not enter" ("Excerpts from Supreme Court's decision Striking Down Sodomy Law" 2003).
7. According to John D'Emilio, "The lower court argued that the previous court rulings on the constitutional right to privacy involved marriage, the sanctity of the home, and family life—none of which are applicable to gay people! It rationalized the prohibition of homosexual behavior as a means of encouraging heterosexual marriage, and quoted from the Bible to support the contention that homosexuality is a form of moral delinquency not to be condoned. The Supreme Court supported this ruling without comment" (D'Emilio 1992, 193).
8. *Griswold v. Connecticut* (1965). But in fact heterosexual sex has not always been protected either. Class, race, and ethnicity have also been limiting factors. The right of women on welfare to intimate partners has been prohibited by welfare legislation and not protected by the judicial system. Even the sanctity of the family has not been always upheld by court decisions, as in cases when Native-American children were taken from their families and placed with state-run Indian Schools in order to achieve a more "appropriate" educational environment (Brant 1985).
9. In this version of the story, pre-Stonewall homosexuality was a secret that was revealed to no one but an intimate partner or perhaps a close circle of friends, not because gays thought that their private life would be protected by American culture and law, but because if no one knew, they could not be persecuted, harassed, or punished. Gay liberation transformed the furtive lives of gays by encouraging them to be out in all settings. The meaning of the term "coming out" changed from self-recognition of one's own gayness to a political strategy of letting the world know of one's sexuality (D'Emilio 1983). Steven Seidman has argued that "the closet" most accurately refers to a social formation that is the result of 1950's repression and shouldn't be applied to earlier periods. See Seidman (2002) and this volume. Kennedy's genealogy, however, raises questions about how we should think about the narrative of the closet even in the 1950s.

10. The claim that practices are akin to liberal freedom implies that practices are not wholly inscribed in the liberal paradigm. "Practices" does not refer to the daily activity that ultimately and necessarily leads to either progress in the liberal frame or revolution in the radical frame. Neither, however, are practices inscribed in a wholly local context that can be understood without reference to the discourses in which they take place, including the discourse of liberal freedom and the revolutionary discourse of a freedom that would involve an end to white supremacy and a shift in human relations so that they are not mediated by the condition of property in which the best that African Americans can expect once emancipated from slavery is to have a stake in possession of the self as one's own property.

11. Grasping the importance of public assembly, a number of commentators have suggested thinking about sexual freedom in relation to freedom of religion. There is much that is appealing and useful about this analysis, but religious freedom can be understood in either expansively or in extremely narrow and privatized terms. The efficacy of the analogy to religious freedom depends entirely upon how it is envisioned and enacted (for a full consideration of these issues, see Jakobsen and Pellegrini 2003).

References

Aasen, Henriette Sinding. 1989. *Rasehygiene og Menneskeverd.* Oslo, Norway: Institutt for Offentlig Retts Skriftserie.

Abelove, Henry, Michele Barale, and David M. Halperin, eds. 1993. *The Lesbian and Gay Studies Reader.* New York: Routledge.

Adam, Barry. 1995. *The Rise of the Gay and Lesbian Movement.* New York: Twayne Publishers.

Agustín, Laura. 2003. "A Migrant World of Services." *Social Politics* 10(3): 377–396.

Agustín, Laura. 2002a. "Challenging Place: Leaving Home for Sex." *Development* 45(1): 110–116.

Agustín, Laura. 2002b. "The (Crying) Need for Different Kinds of Research." *Research for Sex Work* 5: 30–32.

Agustín, Laura. 2001a. "Mujeres Imigrantes Ocupadas en Servicios Sexuales." In *Mujer, inmigración y trabajo,* Colectivo Ioé, ed. Madrid, Spain: IMERSO. pp. 647–716.

Agustín, Laura. 2001b. "Sex Workers and Violence against Women: Utopic Visions or Battle of the Sexes." *Development* 44(3): 107–110.

Alan Guttmacher Institute. 1994. *Sex and America's Teenagers.* Washington, DC: Author.

Alcoff, Linda Martín. 1996. "Dangerous Pleasures: Foucault and the Politics of Pedophilia." In *Feminist Interpretations of Michel Foucault,* Susan Hekman, ed. University Park, PA: Pennsylvania State University Press. pp. 99–135.

Alexander, Jacqueline. 1997. "Erotic Autonomy as Politics of Decolonialization: An Anatomy of Feminist and State Practice in the Bahamas Tourist Economy." In *Feminist Genealogies, Colonial Legacies, Democratic Futures,* Chandra Mohanty, ed. London, UK: Routledge. pp. 63–101.

Alexander, Jaqueline. 1994. "Not Just (Any) Body Can Be a Citizen: The Politics of Law, Sexuality, and Postcoloniality in Trinidad and Tobago and the Bahamas." *Feminist Review* 48 (Fall): 5–23.

Alexander, Priscilla. 1998. "Prostitution: Still a Difficult Issue." In *Sex Work: Writings by Women in the Sex Industry,* second edition, Federique Delacoste and Priscilla Alexander, eds. Pittsburgh, PA: Cleis Press. pp. 184–231.

Alexander, Priscilla. 1995. "Prostitution in Sex Work: Occupational Safety and Health." New York: North American Task Force of Prostitution.

Allison, Anne. 1994. *Nightwork: Sexuality, Pleasure, and Corporate Masculinity in a Tokyo Hostess Club.* Chicago, IL: University of Chicago Press.

Altink, Sietske. 1995. *Stolen Lives: Trading Women into Sex and Slavery.* London, UK: Scarlet Press.

Altman, Dennis. 2001. *Global Sex.* Chicago, IL: University of Chicago Press.

Amenta, Edwin, Kathleen Dunleavy, and Mary Bernstein. 1994. "Stolen Thunder? Huey Long's Share Our Wealth, Political Mediation, and the Second New Deal." *American Sociological Review* 59: 678–702.

American Civil Liberties Union. 2003. "As President Proclaims 'Marriage Protection Week,' ACLU Calls for Equal Protection for All Americans." October 9. www.aclu.org.

271

American Law Institute. 1980. *Model Penal Code and Commentaries.* "Deviate Sexual Intercourse by Force or Imposition, Comment." Code sec. 213.2. Philadelphia, PA: Author. pp. 357–376.

American Law Institute. 1955. *Model Penal Code and Commentaries.* Philadelphia, PA: Author.

American Psychiatric Association. 1994. *Diagnostic and Statistical Manual of Mental Disorders,* 4th ed. Washington, DC: Author.

Amos, Valerie, and Parmar Pratibha. 1984. "Challenging Imperial Feminism." *Feminist Review* 17: 3–19.

Anderson, Benedict. 1983. *Imagined Communities.* New York: Verso.

Anderson, Patricia, and Michael Witter. 1994. "Crisis, Adjustment and Social Change: A Case Study of Jamaica." In *Consequences of Structural Adjustment: A Review of the Jamaican Experience,* E. Le Franc, ed. Kingston, Jamaica: Canoe Press.

Andre-Clark, Alice Susan. 1992. "Whither Statutory Rape Laws: Of Michael M., the Fourteenth Amendment, and Protecting Women from Sexual Aggression." *Southern California Law Review* 65: 1933–1993.

Anonymous. 1985. "Best Kept Secret?" In *Women Against Violence Against Women,* Dusty Rhodes and Sandra McNeil, eds., London, UK: Onlywomen Press. pp. 159–164

Apasu-Gbotsu, Yao, Robert J. Arnold, Paul DiBella, Kevin Dorse, Elisa L. Fuller, Steven H. Naturman, Dung Hong Pham, and James B. Putney. 1986. "Survey on the Constitutional Right to Privacy in the Context of Homosexual Activity." *University of Miami Law Review* 40(1): 521–657.

Aries, Philippe. 1962. *Centuries of Childhood: A Social History of Family Life.* New York: Vintage Press.

Armstrong, Louise. 1994. *Rocking the Cradle of Sexual Politics: What Happened When Women Said Incest.* New York: Addison-Wesley.

Armstrong, Louise. 1990. "Making an Issue of Incest." In *The Sexual Liberals and the Attack on Feminism,* Dorchen Leidholdt and Janice Raymond, eds. New York: Teachers College Press. pp. 43–55.

Armstrong, Louise. 1978. *Kiss Daddy Goodnight.* New York: Hawthorne Books.

Armstrong, Nancy. 1987. "The Rise of the Domestic Woman." In *The Ideology of Conduct,* N. Armstrong and L. Tennenhouse, eds. New York: Methuen. pp. 96–141.

Asia Watch Women's Rights Project. 1993. "A Modern Form of Slavery: Trafficking of Burmese Women and Girls into Brothels in Thailand." New York: Human Rights Watch.

"Attacking the Last Taboo: Researchers are Lobbying Against the Ban on Incest." 1980. *Time,* April 14: 72.

Austin, James, Kelly Dedel Johnson, and Maria Gregoriou. 2000. *Juveniles in Adult Prisons and Jails: A National Assessment.* Washington, DC: U.S. Department of Justice.

Ayers, William, Bernadine Dohrn, and Rick Ayers. 2001. *Zero Tolerance: Resisting the Drive for Punishment in Our Schools.* New York: New Press.

Backer, Larry Cata. 1993. "Exposing the Perversions of Toleration: The Decriminalization of Private Sexual Conduct, the Model Penal Code, and the Oxymoron of Liberal Toleration." *Florida Law Review* 45 (5): 755–802.

Bailey, Victor, and Sheila Blackburn. 1979. "The Punishment of Incest Act 1908: A Case Study of Law Creation." *Criminal Law Review* 20: 708–718.

Barber, Elinor G. 1955. *The Bourgeoisie in 18th Century France.* Princeton, NJ: Princeton University Press.

Barnitz, Laura. 1998. "Commercial Sexual Exploitation of Children: Youth Involved in Prostitution, Pornography, and Sex Trafficking." Washington, DC: Youth Advocate Program.

Barry, Kathleen, 1995. *The Prostitution of Sexuality: The Global Exploitation of Women.* New York: New York University Press.

Barry, Kathleen. 1992. "Trafficking in Women: Serving Masculine Systems." Speech Given at the Annual Conference of the National Organization for Women, Chicago, IL.

Bast, Truska. 1997. "Elke Avond Fluisteren in Blacklight." *Het Parool,* September 19: 4.

Bataille, Georges. 1957. *L'érotisme.* Paris: Minuit.

Bauman, Zygmunt. 1998. "On Postmodern Uses of Sex." *Theory, Culture, and Society* 15(3): 19–34.

Beisel, Nicola. 1997. *Imperiled Innocents: Anthony Comstock and Family Reproduction in Victorian America.* Princeton, NJ: Princeton University Press.

Bell, David, and Jon Binnie. 2000. *The Sexual Citizenship: Queer Politics and Beyond.* Cambridge, UK: Polity.

Bell, David, and Gill Valentine, eds. 1995. *Mapping Desire: Geographies of Sexualities.* New York: Routledge.

Bell, Robert, and Michael Gordon. 1972. *The Social Dimension of Human Sexuality.* Boston, MA: Little Brown and Co.

Bell, Vikki. 1993. *Interrogating Incest: Feminism, Foucault and the Law.* New York: Routledge.

Bellah, Robert, Richard Madsen, William Sullivan, Ann Swidler, and Steve Tipton. 1985. *Habits of the Heart: Individualism and Commitment in American Life.* New York: Harper Row.

Bender, Lauretta, and Abraham Blau. 1937. "The Reactions of Children to Sexual Relations with Adults." *American Journal of Orthopsychiatry* 7: 500–518.

Benjamin, Harry. 1996. *The Transsexual Phenomenon.* New York: Julian Press.

Béraud, F. F-A. 1839. *Les Filles Publiques de Paris et la Police qui Les Régit.* Vol. I Paris: Leipzig.

Berlant, Lauren, and Elizabeth Freeman. 1993. "Queer Nationality." In *Fear of a Queer Planet: Queer Politics and Social Theory,* Michael Warner, ed. Minneapolis, MN: University of Minneapolis Press. pp. 193–229.

Berliner, Lucy. 1993. "Is Family Preservation in the Best Interest of Children?" *Journal of Interpersonal Violence* 8(4): 556–562.

Berliner, Lucy, and Doris Stevens. 1982. "Clinical Issues in Child Sexual Abuse." In *Social Work and Child Sexual Abuse: Journal of Social Work and Human Sexuality,* Vol. I n. 1/2, Conte and Shore, eds. New York: Haworth Press. pp. 556–562.

Berner, Jørgen H. 1937. "Lov Om Adgang Til Sterilisering av 1. Juni 1934." In *Social Håndbok for Norge,* Einar Storsteen, ed. Oslo, Norway: Foreningen for Sosialt Arbeid.

Bernstein, Elizabeth. 2001. *Economies of Desire: Sexual Commerce and Post-Industrial Culture.* Ph.D. Dissertation, Department of Sociology, University of California, Berkeley, CA.

Bernstein, Elizabeth. 1999. "What's Wrong with Prostitution? What's Right with Sex-Work? Comparing Markets in Female Sexual Labor." *Hastings Women's Law Journal* 10(1): 91–119.

Bernstein, Mary. 2004. "'Abominable and Detestable:' Understanding Homophobia and the Criminalization of Sodomy." In *Companion to Criminology*, Colin Sumner, ed. Oxford, UK: Blackwell Press. pp. 309–324.

Bernstein, Mary. 2003. "Nothing Ventured, Nothing Gained? Conceptualizing Social Movement 'Success' in the Lesbian and Gay Movement." *Sociological Perspectives* 46(3): 353–379.

Bernstein, Mary. 2001. "Gender, Queer Family Policies and the Limits of Law." In *Queer Families, Queer Politics: Challenging Culture and the State,* Mary Bernstein and Renate Reimann, eds. New York: Columbia University Press. pp. 420–446.

Bernstein, Mary. 1997. "Celebration and Suppression: The Strategic Uses of Identity by the Lesbian and Gay Movement." *American Journal of Sociology* 103(3): 531–565.

Berrick, Jill, and Neil Gilbert. 1991. *With the Best of Intentions: The Child Sexual Abuse Prevention Movement.* New York: The Guilford Press.

Berube, Allan. 1990. *Coming Out Under Fire: The History of Gay Men and Women in World War Two.* New York: Macmillan.

Beyer, Dorianne. 1996. "Child Prostitution in Latin America." *Forced Labor: The Prostitution of Children.* Symposium Proceedings. Washington, DC: United States Department of Labor. pp. 32–40.

Bianchi, Suzanna, Melissa A. Milkie, Liana C. Sayer, and John P. Robinson. 2000. "Is Anyone Doing the Housework? Trends in the Gender Division of Household Labor." *Social Forces* 79 (December): 191–228.

Bishop, Ryan, and Lillian Robinson. 1998. *Night Market: Sexual Cultures and the Thai Economic Miracle.* London, UK: Routledge.

Black, Henry Campbell. 1991. *Black's Law Dictionary.* St. Paul, MN: West Publishing Co.

Black, Maggie. 1995. *In the Twilight Zone: Child Workers in the Hotel, Tourism and Catering Industry.* Geneva, Switzerland: International Labor Organization.

Bleibtreu-Ehrenberg, Grisela. 1991. "Pederasty Among Primitives: Institutionalized Initiation and Cultic Prostitution." In *Male Intergenerational Intimacy: Historical, Socio-Psychological, and Legal Perspective,* Sanfort, Brongersma, and van Naerssen, eds. New York: Haworth Press. pp. 13–30.

Bond, Tim. 1980. *Boy Prostitution in Sri Lanka: The Problems, Effects and Suggested Remedies.* Colombo, Sri Lanka: Terre Des Hommes, in association with the Ministry of Planning and Information.

Bonnie, Richard, and Thomas Grisso. 2000. "Adjudicative Competence and Youthful Offenders." In *Youth on Trial: A Developmental Perspective on Juvenile Justice*, Thomas Grisso and Robert Schwartz, eds. Chicago, IL: University of Chicago Press. pp. 73–104.

van den Boogaard, Raymond. 1998. "De Grens Is Heilig." *NRC Handelsblad*, January 9.

Bordo, Susan. 1993. *Unbearable Weight: Feminism, Western Culture, and the Body*. Berkeley, CA: University of California Press.

Bourdieu, Pierre. 1984. *Distinction: A Social Critique of the Judgment of Taste*. Cambridge, MA: Harvard University Press.

Bourgois, Philippe. 1995. *In Search of Respect: Selling Crack in El Barrio*. New York: Cambridge University Press.

Bower, Lisa. 1997. "Queer Problems/Straight Solutions: The Limits of 'Official Recognition.'" In *Playing With Fire: Queer Politics, Queer Theories*, Shane Phelan, ed. New York: Routledge. pp. 267–291.

Boyden, Jo. 1997. "Childhood and the Policy Makers: A Comparative Perspective on the Globalization of Childhood." In *Constructing and Reconstructing Childhood*, Allison James and Alan Prout, eds. London, UK: Falmer Press. pp. 190–229.

"Boy Used in Smuggling Scheme Can Stay in U.S." 2001. *CNN Online*. www.cnn.com/2001/LAW/07/23/human.trafficking.

Bradshaw, Judy A. 1995. "The Juvenile Justice System: Is It Working?" *FBI Law Enforcement Bulletin* May 1995: 4–16.

Bradsher, Keith. 1999. "Fear of Crime Trumps the Fear of Lost Youth." *The New York Times*, November 21. A3.

Brady, Kathleen. 1979. *Father's Days*. New York: Seaview.

Brace, Laura, and Julia O'Connell Davidson. 1996. "Desperate Debtors and Counterfeit Love: The Hobbesian World of the Sex Tourist." *Contemporary Politics* 2(3): 55–78.

Brandwein, Ruth, ed. 1999. *Battered Women, Children, and Welfare Reform*. Thousand Oaks, CA: Sage Publications.

Brant, Beth. 1985. "A Long Story." In *Mohawk Trail*. Ithaca, NY: Firebrand Books. pp. 77–86.

Breines, Wini, and Linda Gordon. 1983. "The New Scholarship on Family Violence." *Signs* 8(3): 490–531.

Brendel, Carel. 1997. "De Oplaaiende Strijd Om de Goede Zeden." *Algemeen Dagblad* March 3.

Bronski, Michael. 1998. *The Pleasure Principle: Sex, Backlash, and the Struggle for Gay Freedom*. New York: St. Martin's Press.

Brook, Kerwin. *See* Kaye, Kerwin.

Brown, B. Bradford, Reed W. Larson, and T. S. Saraswathi, eds. 2002. *The World's Youth: Adolescence in Eight Regions of the Globe*. Cambridge, UK: Cambridge University Press.

Brown, Wendy. 1995. *States of Injury: Power and Freedom in Late Modernity*. Princeton, NJ: Princeton University Press.

Brown, Wendy, and Janet Halley, eds. 2002. *Left Legalism/Left Critique*. Durham, NC: Duke University Press.

Browning, Christopher, and Edward Laumann. 1997. "Sexual Contact Between Children and Adults: A Life Course Perspective." *American Sociological Review* 62: 540–560.

Brownmiller, Susan. 1975. *Against Our Will: Men, Women and Rape*. New York: Bantam.

Brugman, Emily. 1995. *Jeugd en Seks 95: Resultaten van het Nationale Scholierenonderzoek*. Utrecht, the Netherlands: SWP.

Brumberg, Joan Jacobs. 1997. *The Body Project: An Intimate History of American Girls*. New York: Random House.

Brussa, Licia. 2000. "Migrant Sex Workers in the Netherlands Speak Out." In *Research for Sex Work* 3: 19. Amsterdam, the Netherlands: Vrije Universiteit.

Bull, Chris, and John Gallagher. 1998. *Perfect Enemies: The Religious Right, the Gay Movement, and the Politics of the 1990s*. New York: Crown Publishers.

Bullough, Vern L. 1994. *Science in the Bedroom: A History of Sex Research*. New York: Basic Books.

Burstein, Paul. 1985. *Discrimination, Jobs, and Politics: The Struggle for Equal Employment Opportunity in the United States Since the New Deal*. Chicago, IL: University of Chicago Press.

Butler, Judith. 1990. *Gender Trouble: Feminism and the Subversion of Identity*. New York: Routledge.

Butler, Sandra. 1978. *Conspiracy of Silence: The Trauma of Incest*. San Francisco: New Glide Publications.

Button, James W., Barbara A. Rienzo, and Kenneth D. Wald. 2000. "The Politics of Gay Rights at the Local and State Level." In *The Politics of Gay Rights*, Craig Rimmerman et al., eds. Chicago, IL: University of Chicago Press.

Button, James W., Barbara A. Rienzo, and Kenneth D. Wald. 1997. *Private Lives, Public Conflicts: Battles Over Gay Rights in American Communities*. Washington, DC: Congressional Quarterly Press.

Button, James W., Barbara A. Rienzo, and Kenneth D. Wald. 1996. "The Politics of Gay Rights in American Communities: Explaining Antidiscrimination Ordinances and Policies." *American Journal of Political Science* 40(4): 1152–1178.

Byron, Stuart. [1972] 1992. "The Closet Syndrome." In *Out of the Closets: Voices of Gay Liberationism*, Karla Jay and Allen Young, eds. New York: New York University Press. pp. 58–66.

Cabezas, Amalia. 1999. "Women's Work Is Never Done: Sex Tourism in Sosúa, the Dominican Republic." In *Sun, Sex and Gold: Tourism and Sex Work in the Caribbean*. Kamala Kempadoo, ed. Oxford, UK: Rowman and Littlefield. pp. 93–124.

Caceres, Carlos, and Oscar G. Jiménez. 1998. "Fleteo in Darque Kennedy: Young Men Who Sell Sex to Men in Lima." In *Men Who Sell Sex: International Perspectives on Male Prostitution and AIDS*, Peter Aggleton ed. London, UK: University College London Press. pp. 179–195.

Caceres, Carlos, and Ana Maria Rosasco. 1999. "The Margin Has Many Sides: Diversity Among Gay and Homosexually Active Men in Lima." *Culture, Health and Sexuality* 1(3): 261–275.

Cain, Patricia A. 1998. "Stories from the Gender Garden: Transsexuals and Anti-Discrimination Law." *Denver University Law Review* 75: 1321–1359.

Calhoun, Cheshire. 2000. *Feminism, the Family, and the Politics of the Closet*. New York: Oxford University Press.

Calhoun, Craig. 1993. "'New Social Movements of the Early 19th Century." *Social Science History* 17(3): 385–427.

Califia, Pat. 1994. *Public Sex: The Culture of Radical Sex*. Pittsburgh, PA: Cleis Press.

California Department of Justice. 2001. "Criminal Justice Statistics." Sacramento, CA: Author, February.

Campbell, Shirley, Althea Perkins, and Patricia Mohammed. 1999. "Come to Jamaica and Feel All Right: Tourism and the Sex Trade." In *Sun, Sex and Gold: Tourism and Sex Work in the Caribbean*, Kamala Kempadoo, ed. Oxford, UK: Rowman and Littlefield. pp. 122–157.

Cannon, Katie G. 1988. *Black Womanist Ethics*. Atlanta, GA: Scholars Press.

Carnes, Patrick. 1989. *Contrary to Love: Helping the Sexual Addict*. Minnesota: Compcare. pp. 218–219.

Carnes, Tony. 2000. "Odd Couple Politics: Evangelicals, Feminists Make Common Cause Against Sex Trafficking." *Christianity Today Magazine*. October 16. www.christianitytoday.com.

Carrington, Christopher. 1999. *No Place Like Home: Relationships and Family Life Among Lesbians and Gay Men*. Chicago, IL: University of Chicago Press.

Case, Mary Anne C. 1995. "Disaggregating Gender from Sex and Sexual Orientation: The Effeminate Man in the Law and Feminist Jurisprudence." *Yale Law Journal* 105: 1–105.

Casert, Raf, and Paul Shepard. 2001. "Of Human Bondage." *Santa Cruz County Sentinel,* November 25. A2.

Castells, Manuel. 1996. "The Net and the Self: Working Notes for a Critical Theory of the Informational Society." *Critique of Anthropology* 16(1): 9–38.

Castilho, Carlos. "Children to the Slaughter." 1995. *The WorldPaper,* January.

CATW, 2003. Coalition Against Trafficking in Women. www.catwinternational.org/.

Chancer, Lynn S. 1992. *Sadomasochism in Everyday Life: The Dynamics of Power and Powerlessness*. New Brunswick, NJ: Rutgers University Press.

Chant, Sylvia, and Cathy McIlwaine. 1995. *Women of a Lesser Cost: Female Labour, Foreign Exchange and Philippine Development*. London, UK: Pluto.

Chapkis, Wendy. 1997. *Live Sex Acts*. New York: Routledge.

Chauncey, George. 1994. *Gay New York: Gender, Urban Culture, and the Making of the Gay Male World 1890–1940*. New York: Basic Books.

Chester, F. M. 1999. "Address at the Lexington-Fayette Urban County Meeting." In *Transgender Equality: A Handbook for Activists and Policymakers*, Paisley Currah and Shannon Minter, eds. July 1. www.ngltf.org/library/index.cfm.

Chew, Kristi. 2000. "Judge declares Vilsack Executive Order Invalid," Associated Press, State and Local Wire. December 7.

Chorus, Jutta. 1995. "Het recht op openbare seksbeleving." *NRC Handelsblad*, September 16.

Chow, Rey. 1999. "The Politics of Admittance: Female Sexual Agency, Miscegenation, and the Formation of Community in Frantz Fanon." In *Frantz Fanon: Critical Perspectives*, Anthony Alessandrini, ed. London, UK: Routledge. pp. 34–57.

Clift, Stephen, and Simon Carter, eds. 2000. *Tourism and Sex: Culture, Commerce and Coercion.* London, UK: Pinter.

Cohen, Cathy J. 1999. *The Boundaries of Blackness: AIDS and the Breakdown of Black Politics.* Chicago, IL: University of Chicago Press.

Cohn, Steven, and James Gallagher. 1984. "Gay Movements and Legal Change." *Social Problems* 23(1): 72–86.

Coltrane, Scott. 1998. *Gender and Families.* Thousand Oaks, CA: Pine Forge Press.

Coltrane, Scott. 1996. *Family Man: Fatherhood, Housework, and Gender Equity.* New York: Oxford University Press.

Combahee River Collective. 1983. "Combahee River Collective Statement." In *Home Girls: A Black Feminist Anthology*, Barbara Smith, ed. New York: Kitchen Table/Women of Color Press.

Connell, Noreen, and Cassandra Wilson, eds. 1974. *Rape: The First Sourcebook for Women by New York Radical Feminists.* New York: New American Library.

Connell, Robert. 1987. *Gender and Power: Society, the Person, and Sexual Politics.* Cambridge, UK: Polity Press.

Constantine, Larry, and Joan M. Constantine. 1973. *Group Marriage.* New York: Macmillan.

Cook, Daniel Thomas, ed. 2002. *Symbolic Childhood.* New York: Peter Lang.

Corbin, Alain. [1978] 1990. *Women for Hire: Prostitution and Sexuality in France after 1850.* Cambridge, MA: Harvard University Press.

Costin, Lela B. 1992. "Cruelty to Children: A Dormant Issue and Its Rediscovery, 1920–1960." *Social Service Review* 66(2): 177–198.

Cothern, Lynn. 2000. "Juveniles and the Death Penalty," *Coordinating Council on Juvenile Justice and Delinquency Prevention Bulletin.* Washington, DC: Office of Juvenile Justice Delinquency Prevention, November.

Cott, Nancy. 2000. *Public Vows: A History of Marriage and the Nation.* Cambridge, MA: Harvard University Press.

Crenshaw, Kimberlé. 1989. "Demarginalizing the Intersection of Race and Sex: A Black Feminist Critique of Antidiscrimination Doctrine, Feminist Theory, and Anti-Racist Politics." Chicago, IL: University of Chicago Legal Forum.

Crick, Malcolm. 1989. "Representations of International Tourism in the Social Sciences: Sun, Sex, Sights, Savings, and Servility." *Annual Review of Anthropology* 18: 307–344.

Crimes Against Children Research Center. 2001. *Fact Sheet.* Durham, New Hampshire: University of New Hampshire.

Crimp, Douglas, and Adam Rolsten. 1990. *AIDS Demo Graphics.* Seattle, WA: Bay Press.

Crossette, Barbara. 2000. "Human Trafficking Spawns Burgeoning Crime Wave." *San Francisco Examiner*, June 25. A15.

Cruz-Malave, Arnaldo, and Martin Manalansan, eds. 2002. *Queer Globalizations: Citizenship and the Afterlife of Colonialism.* New York: New York University Press.

Cullen, Father Shay. 1990. *The Social Costs of the U.S. Military Bases*, PREDA Archives, www.preda.org/archives/r9005281.htm.

Currah, Paisley. 1997. "Politics, Practices, Publics: Identity and Queer Rights." In *Playing With Fire: Queer Politics, Queer Theories*, Shane Phelan, ed. New York: Routledge. pp. 231–266.

Currah, Paisley, and Shannon Minter. 2000. *Transgender Equality: A Handbook for Activists and Policymakers.* New York: Policy Institute of the National Gay and Lesbian Task Force and the National Center for Lesbian Rights. www.ngltf.org/library/index.cfm.

Dahl, Tove Stang. 1978. *Barnevan og samfunnsvern.* Oslo, Norway: Pa forlag.

Daley, Suzanne. 2000. "French Couples Take the Plunge." *The New York Times*, April 18. A1.

Dangerous Bedfellows, eds. 1996. *Policing Public Sex: Queer Politics and the Future of AIDS Activism.* Boston, MA: South End Press.

Dannecker, Martin, and Reimut Reiche. 1974. *Der gewöhnliche Homosexuelle. Eine soziologische Untersuchung über männliche Homosexualität in der Bundesrepublik.* Frankfurt, Germany: Fischer.

Davidoff, Leonore, and Catherine Hall. 1987. *Family Fortunes: Men and Women of the English Middle Class*, 1780–1850. London, UK: Hutchinson.

Davis, Angela. 1983. *Women, Race and Class*. New York: Vintage.

Davis, Kingsley. 1937. "The Sociology of Prostitution." *American Sociological Review* 2: 744–755.

Davis, Nanette. 1999. *Youth in Crisis*. Westport, CT: Praeger.

Davis, Natalie Zemon. 1975. *Society and Culture in Early Modern France*. Stanford, CA: Stanford University Press.

Davis, Noy, and Jennifer Twombly. 2000. *State Legislators' Handbook for Statutory Rape Issues*. American Bar Association Center on Children and the Law. Rockville, MD: Office for Victims of Crime Resource Center.

"Debate over immigration." 2000. *Congressional Quarterly Research*. July 14. www.library.cgpress.com.

Declaration and Agenda for Action of Sexually Exploited Children and Youth. 1998. Ratified by the Youth Delegates of Out from the Shadows, International Summit of Sexually Exploited Youth, March 12. Victoria, BC, Canada.

DeFrances, Carol, and Kevin Strom. 1997. *Juveniles Prosecuted in State Criminal Courts*. U.S. Bureau of Justice, Statistics Report NCJ–164265. Washington, DC: U.S. Department of Justice.

Deitcher, David, ed. 1995. *The Question of Equality: Lesbian and Gay Politics Since Stonewall*. New York: Scribner.

Delacoste, Frederique, and Priscilla Alexander, eds. 1998. *Sex Work: Writings By Women in the Sex Industry*. San Francisco, CA: Cleis Press.

D'Emilio, John. 1992. *Making Trouble: Essays on Gay History, Politics, and the University*. New York: Routledge.

D'Emilio, John. 1983a. "Capitalism and Gay Identity." In *Powers of Desire: The Politics of Sexuality*, Ann Snitow, Christine Stansell, and Sharon Thompson, eds. New York: Monthly Review Press. pp. 100–117.

D'Emilio, John. 1983b. *Sexual Politics, Sexual Communities: The Making of a Homosexual Minority in the United States*, 1940–1970. Chicago, IL: University of Chicago Press.

DeMause, Lloyd. 1976. *The History of Childhood*. London, UK: Souvenir Press.

DeMott, Benjamin. 1980. "The Pro-Incest Lobby." *Psychology Today*, March. 11–16.

Detrick, Sharon. 1992. *The United Nations Convention on the Rights of the Child: A Guide to the Travaux Preparatoires*. Boston, MA: Martinus Nijhoff, Dordrecht.

DiMatteo, Larry. 1995. "Deconstructing the Myth of the 'Infancy Law Doctrine:' From Incapacity to Accountability." *Ohio Northern University Law Review* 21: 481–525.

Dimenstein, Gilberto. 1991. *Brazil: War on Children*. London, UK: Latin America Bureau.

Dinsmore, Christine. 1991. *From Surviving to Thriving: Incest, Feminism, and Recovery*. Albany, NY: State University of New York Press.

Dizon, Kristin. 1999. "City Council Faces Human Rights Vote" *Boulder Daily Camera*, July 20. C1.

Doezema, Jo. 1998. "Forced to Choose." In *Global Sex Workers*, Kamala Kempadoo and Jo Doezema, eds. New York: Routledge. pp. 34–50.

Dollimore, Jonathon, 1991. *Sexual Dissidence: Augustine to Wilde, Freud to Foucault*. Oxford, UK: Clarendon Press.

Donat, Patricia, and John D'Emilio. 1998. "A Feminist Redefinition of Rape and Sexual Assault: Historical Foundations for Change." In *Confronting Rape and Sexual Assault*, Mary Odem and Jody Clay-Warner, eds. Wilmington, DE: Scholarly Resources. pp. 35–49.

Donovan, Patricia. 1997. "Can Statutory Rape Laws be Effective in Preventing Pregnancy?" *Family Planning Perspectives* 29(1): 30–35.

Donzelot, Jacques. 1979. *The Policing of Families*. New York: Pantheon Books.

Douglas, Jack, ed. 1970. *Observations of Deviance*. New York: Random House.

Douglas, Mary. 1973. *Natural Symbols*. New York: Random House.

Duberman, Martin, ed. 1997. *A Queer World: The Center for Lesbian and Gay Studies Reader*. New York: New York University Press.

Duberman, Martin. 1993. *Stonewall*. New York: Dutton.

Duberman, Martin, Martha Vicinus, and George Chauncey, eds. 1989. *Hidden from History: Reclaiming the Gay and Lesbian Past*. New York: New American Library.

Duggan, Lisa, and Nan D. Hunter. 1995. *Sex Wars: Sexual Dissent and Political Culture*. New York: Routledge.

278 • Regulating Sex: The Politics of Intimacy and Identity

Dumenco, Simon. 2001. "They're Here, They're Queer, We're Used to It." *The New York Times,* March 5. 29–31.

Dworkin, Andrea. 1987. *Intercourse.* London, UK: Secker and Warburg.

Echols, Alice. 1989. *Daring to Be Bad: Radical Feminism in America, 1967–1975.* Minneapolis, MN: University of Minnesota Press.

ECPAT. 2001. *Five Years After Stockholm: The Fifth Report on the Implementation of the Agenda for Action Adopted at the First World Congress Against the Commercial Sexual Exploitation of Children, Stockholm, Sweden, August 28, 1996.* Bangok, Thailand: ECPAT International.

ECPAT. 1999. ECPAT *Australia Newsletter* 53: September/October.

ECPAT. 1994. www.ecpat.net

"Editorial." 1962. *Mattachine Review.* Vol. 8, November.

Ehrenreich, Barbara. 1983. *The Hearts of Men: American Dreams and the Flight from Commitment.* New York: Doubleday.

Ehrenreich, Barbara, and Arlie Russell Hochschild, eds. 2002. *Global Woman: Nannies, Maids, and Sex Workers in the New Economy.* New York: Metropolitan Books.

Eisenstein, Zillah. 2002. "Feminisms in the Aftermath of September 11th." *Social Text* 72 Fall: 79–99.

Eisenstein, Zillah. 1981. *The Radical Future of Liberal Feminism.* Boston, MA: Northeastern University Press.

Elkind, David. 1981. *The Hurried Child: Growing Up Too Fast, Too Soon.* Reading, MA: Addison-Wesley.

Elo, Irma, Rosalind Berkowitz King, and Frank Furstenberg Jr. 1999. "Adolescent Females: Their Sexual Partners and the Fathers of Their Children." *Journal of Marriage and the Family* 61: 74–84.

Elstein, Sharon, and Noy Davis. 1997. *Sexual Relationships Between Adult Males and Young Teenage Girls.* Washington, DC: American Bar Association Center on Children and the Law.

Elstein, Sharon, and Barbara Smith. 2000. "Victim-Oriented Multidisciplinary Responses to Statutory Rape: Training Guide." Washington, DC: American Bar Association.

Elton, Catherine. 1997. "Jail Baiting: Statutory Rape's Dubious Comeback." *The New Republic* 217(16): 12–14.

Engel, Beverly. 1991. *The Right to Innocence: Healing the Trauma of Childhood Sexual Abuse.* New Haven, CT: Ivy Books.

Engel, Stephen. 2001. *The Unfinished Revolution: Social Movement Theory and the Gay and Lesbian Movement.* Cambridge, UK: Cambridge University Press.

Engels, Friedrich. [1884] 1978. "The Origin of the Family, Private Property, and the State." In *The Marx-Engels Reader,* Robert Tucker, ed. New York: W.W. Norton, pp. 734–760.

Engels, Friedrich.[1845] 1958. *The Condition of the Working Class in England.* Oxford, UK: Basil Blackwell.

Enloe, Cynthia. 2000. *Maneuvers: The International Politics of Militarizing Women's Lives.* Berkeley, CA: University of California Press.

Enloe, Cynthia. 1989. *Bananas, Beaches and Bases: Making Feminist Sense of International Politics.* Berkeley, CA: University of California Press.

Ennew, Judith, Kusum Gopal, Janet Heeran, and Heather Montgomery. August 26–31, 1996. *Children and Prostitution: How Can We Measure and Monitor the Commercial Sexual Exploitation of Children?* New York: UNICEF Headquarters, Children in Especially Difficult Circumstances Section, Centre for Family Research, University of Cambridge and Childwatch International. 2nd ed., with additional material prepared for the Congress Against the Commercial Sexual Exploitation of Children, Stockholm, Sweden.

Entman, Robert M., and Andrew Rojecki. 1993. "Freezing Out the Public: Elite and Media Framing of the U.S. Anti-Nuclear Movement." *Political Communication* 10: 155–173.

Epstein, Cynthia. 1988. *Deceptive Distinctions: Sex, Gender, and the Social Order.* New Haven, CT: Yale University Press.

Epstein, Steven. 1999. "Gay and Lesbian Movements in the United States: Dilemmas of Identity, Diversity, and Political Strategy." In *The Global Emergence of Gay and Lesbian Politics: National Imprints of a Worldwide Movement,* Barry Adam, Jan Willem Duyvendak, and Andre Krouwel, eds. Philadelphia, PA: Temple University Press.

Epstein, Steven. 1998. *Impure Science: AIDS, Activism, and the Politics of Knowledge.* Berkeley, CA: University of California Press.

Epstein, Steven. 1993. "A Queer Encounter: Sociology and the Study of Sexuality." In *Queer Theory/Sociology*, Steven Seidman, ed. Oxford, UK: Blackwell Publishers. pp. 145–168.

Erickson, Julia. 2000. "Sexual Liberation's Last Frontier." *Society* 37(4): 21–25.

Erikson, Erik. 1950. *Childhood and Society*. New York: Norton.

Ericsson, Kjersti. 1997. *Drift og dyd*. Oslo: Pax Forlag.

Escoffier, Jeffrey. 1998. *American Homo: Community and Perversity*. Berkeley, CA: University of California Press.

Eskridge, Jr., William. 2002. *Equality Practice: Civil Unions and the Future of Gay Rights*. New York: Routledge.

Eskridge, Jr., William. 1999. *Gaylaw: Challenging the Apartheid of the Closet*. Cambridge, MA: Harvard University Press.

Eskridge, Jr., William. 1996. *The Case for Same-Sex Marriage: From Sexual Liberty to Civilized Commitment*. New York: Free Press.

Eskridge, Jr., William, and Nan Hunter. 1997. *Sexuality, Gender, and the Law*. Westbury, NY: The Foundation Press.

Estes, Richard J., and Neil Alan Weiner. 2001. *The Commercial Sexual Exploitation of Children in the U.S., Canada, and Mexico: Full Report of the U.S. National Study*. Philadelphia, PA: University of Pennsylvania.

Ettelbrick, Paula. 1993. "Since When Is Marriage a Path to Liberation?" In *Lesbians, Gay Men, and the Law*, William Rubenstein, ed. New York: New Press.

Evans, David. 1993. *Sexual Citizenship: The Material Construction of Sexualities*. London, UK: Routledge.

"Excerpts from Supreme Court's Decision Striking Down Sodomy Law." 2003. *New York Times*, June 27. A-18.

Fabian, Johannes. 1983. *Time and the Other: How Anthropology Makes its Object*. New York: Columbia University Press.

Farmer, Paul. 2001. *Infections and Inequalities: The Modern Plagues*. Berkeley, CA: University of California Press.

Farmer, Paul. 1993. *AIDS and Accusation: Haiti and the Geography of Blame*. Berkeley: University of California Press.

Farquhar, Stephanie Ann. 1995. "A Critical Assessment of a Street Youth Health Survey." *Cultural Anthropology Methods* 8(1): 7–9.

Fass, Paula. 1977. *The Damned and the Beautiful: American Youth in the 1920's*. Oxford, UK: Oxford University Press.

Fass, Paula, and Mary Ann Mason, eds. 2000. *Childhood in America*. New York: New York University Press.

Fausto-Sterling, Anne. 2000. *Sexing the Body: Gender Politics and the Construction of Sexuality*. New York: Basic Books.

Feagin, Joe, and Hernan Vera. 1995. *White Racism*. New York: Routledge.

Feld, Barry. 1999. *Bad Kids: Race and the Transformation of the Juvenile Court*. New York: Oxford University Press.

Feldblum, Chai. 1997. "The Moral Rhetoric of Legislation." *New York University Law Review* 72: 992–1008.

Feldblum, Chai. 1996. "Sexual Orientation, Morality, and the Law: Devlin Revisited." *University of Pittsburgh Law Review* 57: 237–335.

Fennema, Meindert, and Troetje Loewenthal. 1987. *Construccion de Raza y Nacion en Republica Dominicana*. Vol. DLXXIV. Santo Domingo: Editora Universitaia-UASD.

Ferguson, Ann Annette. 2000. *Bad Boys: Public Schools and the Making of Black Masculinity*. Ann Arbor, MI: University Press.

Ferguson, James. 1992. *Dominican Republic: Beyond the Lighthouse*. London, UK: Latin America Bureau.

Figueira-McDonough, Josefina. 1987. "Are Girls Different? Gender Discrepancies Between Delinquent Behaviour and Control." In *Toward a Feminist Approach to Child Welfare*, Lela B. Costin, ed. Washington, DC: Child Welfare League of America: 79–95.

Fijnaut, Cyrille, and Frank Bovenkerk. 1996. *Georganisserde Criminaliteit in Nederland. Een Analyse de Situatie in Amsterdam*. Den Haag: SDU.

Fine, Michelle. 1993. "Sexuality, Schooling, and Adolescent Females: The Missing Discourse of Desire." In *Beyond Silenced Voices: Class, Race, and Gender in United States Schools*, Lois Weis and Michelle Fine, eds. Albany, NY: State University of New York Press. pp. 75–99.

Finkelhor, David. 1994. "Current Information on the Scope and Nature of Child Sexual Abuse." *The Future of Children* 4: 31–53.

Finkelhor, David. 1979. "What's Wrong with Sex Between Adults and Children? Ethics and the Problem of Sexual Abuse." *American Journal of Orthopsychiatry* 49(4): 692–697.

Finkelhor, David, and Larry Baron. 1986. "Risk Factors for Child Sexual Abuse." *Journal of Interpersonal Violence* 1(43): 43–71.

Finkelhor, David, and Angela Brown. 1986. "Initial and Long-Term Effects: A Conceptual Overview." In *A Sourcebook on Child Sexual Abuse*, David Finkelhor et al. eds. Beverly Hills, CA: Sage Publications. pp. 180–98.

Fisher, Nancy. 1998. "Defending the Symbolic Boundaries of the Family: Legal Discourse on Child Sexual Abuse." Paper presented at the 93rd Annual Meeting of the American Sociological Association. San Francisco: CA.

Flowers, Amy. 1998. *The Fantasy Factory: An Insider's View of the Phone Sex Industry*. Philadelphia, PA: University of Pennsylvania Press.

Forsythe, Steven, Julia Hasbun, and Martha Butler de Lister. 1998. "Protecting Paradise: Tourism and AIDS in the Dominican Republic." *Health and Policy Planning* 13(3): 277–286.

Forward, Susan, and Craig Buck. 1981. *Betrayal of Innocence: Incest and Its Devastation*. New York: Penguin.

Foucault, Michel. 1978. *The History of Sexuality: An Introduction*. New York: Vintage Books.

Frank, Katherine. 2002. *G-Strings and Sympathy: Strip Club Regulars and Male Desire*. Durham, NC: Duke University Press.

Franke, Katherine M. 1995. "The Central Mistake of Sex Discrimination Law: The Disaggregation of Sex from Gender." *University of Pennsylvania Law Review* 144: 1–97.

Franke, Katherine M. 1999. "Current Issues in Lesbian, Gay, Bisexual, and Transgendered Law." *Fordham Urban Law Journal* 27: 379–381.

Freedman, Alfred M., H. I. Kaplan, and B. J. Sadock, eds. 1975. *Comprehensive Textbook of Psychiatry*. Baltimore: Williams & Wilkins.

Fraser, Michael. 1966. "Identity and Representation as Challenges to Social Movement Theory: A Case Study of Queer Nation." In *Mainstream(s) and Margins: Cultural Politics in the 90s*, Michael Morgan and Susan Leggett, eds. Westport, CT: Greenwood Press.

Freud, Sigmund. [1953] 1986. "The Aetiology of Hysteria." *Collected Papers of Sigmund Freud*. Vol. I. London, UK: Hogarth.

Freud, Sigmund. [1913] 1985. "Totem and Taboo." *Sigmund Freud: Collected Works*. Vol. XIII. Harmondsworth, UK: Penguin.

Gallo, Jon J., Stefan M. Mason, Louis M. Meisinger, Kenneth D. Robin, Gary D. Stabile, and Robert J. Wynne. 1966. "The Consenting Adult Homosexual and the Law: An Empirical Study of Enforcement and Administration in Los Angeles County." *UCLA Law Review* 13(3): 647–832.

Gamson, William. 1990. *The Strategy of Social Protest*. Belmont, CA: Wadsworth Publishing Company.

Garet, Ronald R. 1991. "Self-Transformability." *Southern California Law Review* 65: 121–203.

"Gays to Marry in Belgium." February 5, 2003. Chicago Free Press. A1.

"Global Alliance Against Trafficking in Women." December 14, 2003. www.thai.net/gaatw/.

Gibbs, Nancy. 2003. "A Yea for Gays: The Supreme Court Scraps Sodomy Laws, Setting Off a Hot Debate." *Time*, July 7. www.time.com.

Giddens, Anthony. 1992. *The Transformation of Intimacy: Sexuality, Love, and Eroticism in Modern Societies*. Stanford: Stanford University Press.

Giroux, Henry. 2000. *Stealing Innocence: Corporate Culture's War on Children*. New York: Palgrave.

Goffman, Erving. 1961. *Asylums*. New York: Anchor Books.

Goodrich, Peter. 1996. "The Letter of the Law." In *Recht en Liefde*, Maris, Lissenberg, and Pessers, eds. Nijmegen, the Netherlands: Ars Aequi Libri. pp. 105–118.

Gordon, Linda, ed. 1990. *Women, the State, and Welfare*. Madison, WI: University of Wisconsin Press.

Gordon, Linda. 1989. *Heroes of Their Own Lives: The Politics and History of Family Violence*. London, UK: Virago.

Gordon, Linda. 1988. "The Politics and History of Child Sexual Abuse: Notes from American History." *Feminist Review* 28: 56–64.

Gordy, Molly. 2000. "A Call to Fight Forced Labor." *Parade Magazine,* February 20.

Gould, Deborah. 2001. "Rock the Boat, Don't Rock the Boat Baby: Ambivalence and the Emergence of Militant AIDS Activism." In *Passionate Politics: Emotions and Social Movements,* Jeff Goodwin, James M. Jasper, and Francesca Polletta, eds. Chicago, IL: University of Chicago Press. pp. 135–157.

Graaf, Hanneke, and Jany Racemakers. 2003. *Seks in de Groei.* Delft, the Netherlands: Eburun.

Grahn, Judy. 1970. "Lesbians as Bogeywomen," *Women* 1 (Summer): 36–38.

Green, Jamison. 2000. "Introduction." In *Transgender Equality: A Handbook for Activists and Policymakers,* Currah and Minter, eds. www.ngltf.org/library/index.cfm.

Greenberg, David F. 1988. *The Construction of Homosexuality.* Chicago, IL: University of Chicago Press.

Greenberg, Julie A. 1999. "Defining Male and Female: Intersexuality and the Collision Between Law and Biology." *Arizona Law Review* 41: 265–328.

Greenfeld, Liah. 1992. *Nationalism: Five Roads to Modernity.* Cambridge, MA: Harvard University Press.

Greenhouse, Linda. 2003. "Justices, 6–3, Legalize Gay Sexual Conduct in Sweeping Reversal of Court's '86 Ruling." *The New York Times,* June 27. A1.

Greenhouse, Linda. 2000. "Battle on Federalism." *The New York Times,* May 17. A18.

Greenwald, Harold. 1958. *The Elegant Prostitute: A Social and Psychoanalytic Study.* New York: Ballantine Books.

Griffin, Christine. 1993. *Representations of Youth: The Study of Youth and Adolescence in Britain and America.* Cambridge, MA: Polity Press.

Griffin, Patrick, Patricia Torbet, and Linda Szymanski. 1998. *Trying Juveniles as Adults in Criminal Court: An Analysis of State Transfer Provisions.* Washington, DC: U.S. Department of Justice.

Griffin, Susan. 1979. *Rape: The Politics of Consciousness.* San Francisco: Harper and Row.

Grittner, Frederick K. 1990. *White Slavery: Myth, Ideology and American Law.* New York: Garland Publishing.

Gunvald, Gori. 1967. *Bjerketun.* Oslo: Pax Forlag.

Gupta, Ruchira. 1996. *The Selling of Innocents.* A Halpern/Jacbovici Production Malofilm Video, 96401.

Haaken, Janice. 1999. "Heretical Texts: The Courage to Heal and the Incest Survivor Movement." In *New Versions of Victims: Feminists Struggle with the Concept,* Sharon Lamb, ed. New York: New York University Press. pp. 13–41.

Haaken, Janice. 1998. *Pillar of Salt: Gender, Memory, and the Perils of Looking Back.* New Brunswick, NJ: Rutgers University Press.

Haider-Markel, Donald P., and Kenneth J. Meier. 1996. "The Politics of Gay and Lesbian Rights: Expanding the Scope of Conflict." *Journal of Politics* 58(2): 332–349.

Hall, Liz, and Siobhan Lloyd. 1993. *Surviving Child Sexual Abuse: A Handbook for Helping Women Challenge Their Past.* Washington, DC: Falmer Press.

Halley, Janet E. 1994. "Reasoning About Sodomy: Act and Identity In and After *Bowers v. Hardwick.*" *Virginia Law Review* 79: 1721–1780.

Hallinan, Terence. 1998. "Statutory Rape and Female Juvenile Delinquency." Program Training Materials, Governer's Partnership for Responsible Parenting Initiative. San Francisco, CA.

Hamilton, Arnold. 1999. "Lurid Tactics: Oklahoma City Threatens Prostitution Participants Glare of TV Publicity." *Dallas Morning News,* March 18. 33A.

Hammonds, Evelyn. 1994. "Black (W)holes and the Geometry of Black Female Sexuality." *Differences: A Journal of Feminist Cultural Studies* 6: 213, 126–145.

Hancock, Maxine, and Karen Mains. 1987. *Child Sexual Abuse: Hope for Healing.* Wheaton, IL: Harold Shaw Publishing.

Harper, Philip Brian. 1993. "Eloquence and Epitaph: Black Nationalism and the Homophobic Impulse in Responses to the Death of Max Robinson." In *Fear of a Queer Planet: Queer Politics and Social Theory,* Michael Warner, ed. Minneapolis, MN: University of Minnesota Press. pp. 239–264.

Harris, Bruce. 2001. *Show Me the Way to Go Home: The Trafficking of Children in Central America.* A Report to the International Bar Association at their Annual Conference, November 1. Cancun, Mexico.

Harris, Bruce. 1996. "All They Have Left to Sell Is Themselves: Sexual Exploitation of Children Increasing Worldwide." *One World News Service: Covenant House.* August 20.

Hart, Angie. 1994. "Missing Masculinity? Prostitutes' Clients in Alicante, Spain." In *Dislocating Masculinity: Comparative Ethnographies*, Andrea Cornwall and Nancy Lindisfarne, eds. New York: Routledge. pp. 48–66.

Hartman, Saidiya V. 1997. *Scenes of Subjection: Terror, Slavery, and Self-Making in Nineteenth-Century America*. New York: Oxford University Press.

Hawthorne, Susan, and Bronwyn Winter, eds. 2003. *After Shock: September 11, 2001: Global Feminist Perspectives*. Vancouver, BC: Raincoast Books.

Health Action Information Network. 1987. *Child and Youth Prostitution in the Philippines*. Manila.

Hecht, Tobias. 1998. *At Home in the Street: Street Children of Northeast Brazil*. Cambridge, UK: Cambridge University Press.

Heilbrun, Kirk, Cara Leheny, Lori Thomas, and Dominique Honeycutt. 1997. "A National Survey of U.S. Statutes on Juvenile Transfer: Implications for Policy and Practice." *Behavioral Sciences and the Law* 15: 25–179.

Heise, Lori L. 1997. "Violence, Sexuality, and Women's Lives." In *The Gender Sexuality Reader*, Roger Lancaster and Micaela di Leonardo, eds. New York: Routledge Press, 411–434.

Hekma, Gert. 1999. "Amsterdam." In *Queer Sites: Gay Urban Histories Since 1600*, David Higgs, ed. New York: Routledge. pp. 61–88.

Hekma, Gert. 1996. "Amsterdam moet niet moraliseren." *NRC Handelsblad*, March 23.

Hekma, Gert. 1994. "Als ze maar niet provoceren." *Discriminatie van Homoseksuele Mannen en Lesbische Vrouwen in de Sport*. Amsterdam, the Netherlands: Het Spinhuis.

Hekma, Gert. 1992. *De RozeRand van Donker Amsterdam*. Amsterdam, the Netherlands: Van Gennep.

Hekma, Gert. 1987. *Homoseksualiteit, een Medische Reputatie. De Uitdoktering van de Homoseksueel in Negentiende-Eeuws Nederland*. Amsterdam, the Netherlands: SUA.

Hennum, Nicole. 1997. *Den Komplekse Virkelighet. Krise- og Utredningsinstitusjoners Tvetydige Verden*. Oslo: Norsk Institutt for Forskning om Oppvekst, Velferd og Aldring.

Hennum, Nicole. 1993. *Det Organiserte Nederlaget*. Oslo: Barnevernets Utviklingssenter.

Henslin, James M., ed. 1971. *Studies in the Sociology of Sex*. New York: Meredith Corporation.

Herdt, Gilbert. 1997. *Same Sex/Different Cultures: Exploring Gay and Lesbian Lives*. Boulder, CO: Westview Press.

Herdt, Gilbert, ed. 1989. *Gay and Lesbian Youth*. New York: Haworth Press.

Herman, Judith. 1981. *Father-Daughter Incest*. Cambridge, MA: Harvard University Press.

Herman, Judith, and Lisa Hirschman. 1977. "Father-Daughter Incest." *Signs* 2(4): 735–756.

Herrell, Richard. 1996. "Sin, Sickness, Crime: Queer Desire and the American State." *Identities* 2(3): 273–300.

Heyzer, Noeleen. 1986. *Working Women of Southeast Asia: Development, Subordination, and Emancipation*. Milton Keynes, UK: Open University Press.

Higginson, Joanna Gregson. 1999. "Defining, Excusing, and Justifying Deviance: Teen Mothers' Accounts for Statutory Rape." *Symbolic Interactionism* 22(1): 25–46.

Hobson, Barbara. 1990. *Uneasy Virtue: The Politics of Prostitution and the American Reform Tradition*. Chicago, IL: University of Chicago Press.

Hochschild, Arlie Russell. 2003. *The Commercialization of Intimate Life: Notes from Home and Work*. Berkeley, CA: University of California Press.

Hochschild, Arlie Russell. 1997. *The Time Bind*. New York: Metropolitan Books.

Hochschild, Arlie Russell. 1983. *The Managed Heart: Commodification of Human Feeling*. Berkeley, CA: University of California Press.

Høigård, Cecilie, and Liv Finstad. 1986. *Backstreets: Prostitution, Money, and Love*. University Park, PA: Pennsylvania State University Press.

Hollenberg, Elizabeth. 1999. "The Criminalization of Teen Sex: Statutory Rape and the Politics of Motherhood." *Stanford Law and Policy Review* 10(2): 267–286.

Holt, Kristine W. 1997. "Re-evaluating Holloway: Title VII, Equal Protection, and the Evolution of a Transgender Jurisprudence." *Temple Law Review* 70: 283–319.

Holzman, Harold, and Sharon Pines. 1982. "Buying Sex: The Phenomenology of Being a John." *Deviant Behavior* 4: 89–116.

Hooper, Carol-Ann. 1992. "Child Sexual Abuse and the Regulation of Women: Variations on a Theme." In *Regulating Womanhood: Historical Essays on Marriage, Motherhood and Sexuality*, Carol Smart, ed. New York: Routledge. pp. 53–77.

Howard, David. 1999. *Dominican Republic*. London, UK: Latin America Bureau.

Howell, James. 1997. *Juvenile Justice and Youth Violence*. Thousand Oaks, CA: Sage.

Human Rights Campaign. 2003. www.hrc.org.

Humphreys, Bob. 1997. "The Poor, the Very Poor and the Poorest: Responses to Destitution after Industrialisation." *Recent Findings of Research in Economic and Social History* 24. www.ehs.org.uk.

Humphreys, Laud. 1972. *Out of the Closets: The Sociology of Homosexual Liberation*. Englewood Cliffs, NJ: Prentice Hall.

Hunt, Alan. 1990. "Rights and Social Movements: Counter-Hegemonic Strategies." *Journal of Law and Society* 17(3): 309–328.

Hunter, Nan. 1992. "Life After Hardwick." *Harvard Civil Rights-Civil Liberties Law Review* 27: 531–554.

Hunter, Nan. 1991. "Marriage, Law, and Gender: A Feminist Inquiry." *Law and Sexuality* 9.

Hyde, Sue. 1990. "Memo To: NGLTF Program Review Committee, From Sue Hyde, Director, Privacy Project, Re: Report to Program Review Committee, June 1, 1990." Collection 7301, (National Gay and Lesbian Task Force), Box 130, Folder "Privacy Project Program Review." Ithaca, NY: Cornell University Library.

Hyde, Sue. 1989a. "Memo To: NGLTF Board of Directors, From Sue Hyde, Privacy Project Director, Re: April Staff Report, May 5." Collection 7301 (National Gay and Lesbian Task Force), Box 130, Folder "Privacy Project Update." Ithaca, NY: Cornell University Library.

Hyde, Sue. 1989b. "Memo To: NGLTF Board of Directors, From Sue Hyde, Privacy Queen. Re: February Staff Report, March 7." Collection 7301 (National Gay and Lesbian Task Force), Box 130, Folder "Privacy Project Update." Ithaca, NY: Cornell University Library.

Hyde, Sue. 1987a. "Memo To: NGLTF Board of Directors, From Sue Hyde, Coordinator, Privacy Project, Re: November Staff Report, December 2, 1987." Collection 7301, (National Gay and Lesbian Task Force), Box 130, Folder "Privacy Project Program Review." Ithaca, NY: Cornell University Library.

Hyde, Sue. 1987b. "Memo To: NGLTF Board of Directors, From Sue Hyde, Coordinator, Privacy Project, Re: June Staff Report, June 30, 1987." Collection 7301, (National Gay and Lesbian Task Force), Box 130, Folder "Privacy Project Program Review." Ithaca, NY: Cornell University Library.

Hyde, Sue. 1987c. "First Draft of Update and Position Paper of Privacy Project, Sodomy Law Reform, Sexual Liberation, and the Cosmic Importance of the Individuation of Sexual Transcendence. By sh, [Sue Hyde] Privacy Queen." Collection 7301 (National Gay and Lesbian Task Force), Box 130, Folder "Privacy Project Update." Ithaca, NY: Cornell University Library.

Hyde, Sue. n.d. "Sex and Politics: Challenging the Sodomy Laws." Collection 7301 (National Gay and Lesbian Task Force). Box 130 Folder "Privacy Project Program Review." Ithaca, NY: Cornell University Library.

Hymowitz, Kay. 2000. *Ready or Not: Why Treating Children as Small Adults Endangers Their Future — and Ours*. New York: Free Press.

Ingraham, Chrys. 1999. *White Weddings: Romancing Heterosexuality in Popular Culture*. New York: Routledge.

Ingraham, Chrys. 1996. "The Heterosexual Imaginary: Feminist Sociology and Theories of Gender." In *Queer Theory/Sociology*, Steven Seidman, ed. Oxford, UK: Blackwell. pp. 168–194.

INTERPOL. 1996. "The International Law Enforcement Response, International Criminal Police Organization (INTERPOL)." In *Forced Labor: The Prostitution of Children*. Papers from a symposium cosponsored by U.S. Department of Labor, Bureau of Labor Affairs, the Women's Bureau, and the U.S. Department of State, Bureau of Democracy, Human Rights and Labor, September 29, 1995, Washington, DC.

"It's Time Illinois." May 1999. *Fourth Annual Report on Discrimination and Hate Crimes Against Transgendered People in Illinois*. www.genderadvocates.org.

Jackson, Louise. 2000. *Child Sexual Abuse in Victorian England*. New York: Routledge.

Jackson, Margaret. 1989. "Sexuality and Struggle: Feminism, Sexology and the Social Construction of Sexuality." In *Learning Our Lines: Sexuality and Control in Education*, Carol Jones and Pat Mahoney, eds. London, UK: The Women's Press. pp. 1–22.

Jackson, Stevi. 1996. "Heterosexuality and Feminist Theory." In *Theorising Heterosexuality*, Diane Richardson, ed. Buckingham, UK: Oxford University Press. pp. 21–38.

Jacobs, Janet. 1994. "Gender, Race, and Class and the Trend Toward Early Motherhood: A Feminist Analysis of Teen Mothers in Contemporary Society." *Journal of Contemporary Ethnography* 22(4): 442–462.

Jakobsen, Janet R. 2002. "Can Homosexuals End Western Civilization As We Know It? Family Values in a Global Economy." In *Queer Globalizations*, Arnaldo Cruz-Malavé and Martin Manalansan, eds. New York: New York University Press. pp. 49–71.

Jakobsen, Janet R. 1998. *Working Alliances and the Politics of Difference: Diversity and Feminist Ethics.* Bloomington, IN: Indiana University Press.

Jakobsen, Janet R., and Ann Pellegrini. 2003. *Love the Sin: Sexual Regulation and the Limits of Religious Tolerance.* New York: New York University Press.

James, Allison, and Alan Prout, eds. [1990] 1997. *Constructing and Reconstructing Childhood: Contemporary Issues in the Sociological Study of Childhood.* London, UK: Falmer Press.

James, Beverly, and Maria Nasjleti. 1983. *Treating Sexually Abused Children and Their Families.* Palo Alto, CA: Consulting Psychologists Press.

James, W. 1993. "Migration, Racism and Identity Formation: The Caribbean Experience in Britain." In *Inside Babylon: the Caribbean Diaspora in Britain*, W. James and C. Harris, eds. London, UK: Verso.

Janus, Sam. 1981. *The Death of Innocence: How Our Children Are Endangered by the New Sexual Freedom.* New York: William Morrow.

Jay, Karla, and Aleen Young, eds. [1972] 1992. *Out of the Closets: Voices of Gay Liberationism.* New York: New York University Press.

Jeffreys, Sheila. 1997. *The Idea of Prostitution.* North Melbourne, Australia: Spiniflex.

Jeffreys, Sheila. 1996. "Heterosexuality and the Desire for Gender." In *Theorising Heterosexuality*, Diane Richardson, ed. Buckingham, UK: Oxford University Press, pp. 75–90.

Jenkins, Philip. 2001. *Beyond Tolerance: Child Pornography on the Internet.* New York: New York University Press.

Jenkins, Henry, ed. 1998. *The Children's Culture Reader.* New York: New York University Press.

Jenkins, Philip. 1998. *Moral Panic: Changing Concepts of the Child Molester in Modern America.* New Haven, CT: Yale University Press.

Jenness, Valerie. 1993. *Making It Work: The Prostitutes' Rights Movement in Perspective.* New York: Aldine de Gruyter.

Jenness, Valerie, and Ryken Grattet. 1996. "The Criminalization of Hate: A Comparison of Structural and Polity Influences on the Passage of 'Bias-Crime' Legislation in the United States." *Sociological Perspectives* 39(1): 129–154.

Joffe, Carole. 1986. *The Regulation of Sexuality: Experiences of Family Planning Workers.* Philadelphia, PA: Temple University Press.

Johnson, Steve. 1998. "Transgender Rights." *Chicago Tribune*, September 2. C7.

Jonsson, Gustav. 1980. *Flickor på Glid—en Studie i Kvinnoförakt.* Stockholm, Sweden: Tidens förlag.

Joseph, Miranda. 2002. *Against the Romance of Community.* Minneapolis, MN: University of Minnesota Press.

Juffer, Jane. 1998. *At Home with Pornography: Women, Sex, and Everyday Life.* New York: New York University Press.

Kaiser Family Foundation. 2003. *National Survey of Adolescents and Young Adults: Sexual Health, Knowledge, Attitudes, and Experiences.* Menlo Park, CA: Author.

Kaplan, Morris. 1997. *Sexual Justice: Democratic Citizenship and the Politics of Desire.* New York: Routledge.

Katz, Jonathan Ned. 1995. *The Invention of Heterosexuality.* New York: Dutton.

Katz-Rothman, Barbara. 1989. *Recreating Motherhood: Ideology and Technology in a Patriarchal Society.* New York: W. W. Norton.

Kaufman, Michael. 1987. *Beyond Patriarchy: Essays by Men on Pleasure, Power and Change.* Oxford, UK: Oxford University Press.

Kaye, Kerwin. 1999. "Male Sexual Clients: Changing Images of Masculinity, Prostitution, and Deviance in the United States, 1900–1950." Unpublished manuscript on file with author.

[Kaye], Kerwin Brook. "Peep Show Pimp: San Francisco Strip Clubs May be Pushing Dancers into Prostitution." *San Francisco Bay Guardian.* February 4, 1998: 18–21.

Keller, Susan Etta. 1999. "Operations of Legal Rhetoric: Examining Transsexual and Judicial Identity." *Harvard Civil Rights-Civil Liberties Law Review* 34: 329–383.

Kellogg, Susan, and Steven Mintz. 1993. "Family Structures." In *Encyclopedia of American Social History*, Vol. III, M.C. Cayton et al., ed. New York: Scribner. pp. 1925–1941.

Kempadoo, Kamala, ed. 1999. *Sun, Sex and Gold: Tourism and Sex Work in the Caribbean*. Oxford, UK: Rowman and Littlefield.

Kempadoo, Kamala, ed. 1998. "Globalizing Sex Workers' Rights." In *Global Sex Workers*. Kamala Kempadoo and Jo Doezema, eds. New York: Routledge. pp. 1–33.

Kempadoo, Kamala, and Jo Doezema, eds. 1998. *Global Sex Workers: Rights, Resistance, and Redefinition*. New York: Routledge.

Kersten, Joachim. 1989. "The Institutional Control of Girls and Boys: An Attempt at Gender-Specific Approach." In *Growing up Good: Policing the Behaviour of Girls in Europe*, Maureen Cain, ed. London, UK: Sage Publications. pp. 129–144.

Kessler, Suzanne J., and Wendy McKenna. 1978. *Gender: An Ethnomethodological Approach*. Chicago, IL: University of Chicago Press.

Ketting, Evert, and Klaas Soesbeek. 1992. *Homoseksualiteit & Krijgsmacht*. Delft, the Netherlands: Eburon.

Kilman, Lisa, and Kate Watson-Smyth. 1998. "Kerb Crawlers Offered Aversion Therapy Course." *Independent*, August 3: 5.

Kimmel, Michael. 2000. "Fuel for Fantasy: The Ideological Construction of Male Lust." In *Male Lust: Power, Pleasure, and Transformation*, Kerwin Kay et al., eds. New York: Haworth. pp. 267–273.

Kincaid, James R. 1998. *Erotic Innocence: The Culture of Child Molesting*. Durham, NC: Duke University Press.

Kingsley, Cherry. 2001. Keynote address on behalf of the NGO Group for the Convention on the Rights of the Child. Second World Congress Against the Commercial Sexual Exploitation of Children. December 17–20. Yokohama, Japan.

Kinsey, Alfred, Wardell Pomeroy, and Clyde E. Martin. 1948. *Sexual Behavior in the Human Male*. Philadelphia, PA: W.B. Saunders Company.

Kissack, Terence. 1995. "Freaking Fag Revolutionaries: New York's Gay Liberation Front, 1969–1971." *Radical History Review* 62: 104–134.

Kitschelt, Herbert. 1986. "Political Opportunity Structures and Political Protest: Anti-Nuclear Movements in Four Democracies." *British Journal of Political Science* 16: 57–85.

Kitzinger, Jenny. 1997. "Who Are You Kidding? Children, Power, and the Struggle Against Sexual Abuse." In *Constructing and Reconstructing Childhood*, Allison James and Alan Prout, eds. Washington, DC: Falmer Press. pp. 165–189.

Kitzinger, Jenny. 1988. "Defending Innocence: Ideologies of Childhood." *Feminist Review* 28: 78–79.

Klawitter, Marieka M., and Victor Flatt. 1998. "The Effects of State and Local Antidiscrimination Policies for Sexual Orientation." *Journal of Policy Analysis and Management* 17(4): 658–686.

Knight, Robert H. 1999. "How Domestic Partnerships and 'Gay Marriage' Threaten the Family." In *Same Sex: Debating the Ethics, Science and Culture of Homosexuality*, John Corvino, ed. Lanham, MD: Rowman and Littlefield. pp. 289–304.

Kohn, Alfie. 1987. "Shattered Innocence." *Psychology Today* 21 (February): 54–58.

Koinos. 2000. Amsterdam, the Netherlands: Stichting Amikejo. pp. 26–27.

Kooten, Niekerk, Anja Van, and Sacha Wijmer. 1984. *Verkeerde Vriendschap Lesbisch Leven in de Jaren 1920–1960*. Amsterdam, the Netherlands: Sara.

Kooy, Elizabeth. 2002. "The Status of Automatic Transfers of Children to Adult Court in Cook County Illinois, October 1999 to September 2000." Juvenile Transfer Advocacy Unit, Office of the Cook County Public Defender, Chicago, IL.

Kraakman, Dorelies. 1997. *Kermis in de Hel. Vrouwen en Het Pornografisch Universum van de Enfer 1750–1850*. Amsterdam, the Netherlands: Eigen Beheer.

Kracauer, Siegfried. 1937. *Offenbach and the Paris of His Time*. London, UK: Constable.

von Krafft-Ebing, Richard. 1897. *Leerboek van de Zielsziekten van Het Geslachtsleven*. Vol. II. Amsterdam, the Netherlands: Van Klaveren.

Krugman, Richard. 1997. "Child Protection Policy." In *The Battered Child*, Mary Helfer, Ruth Kempe, and Richard Krugman, eds. Chicago, IL: University of Chicago Press. pp. 627–641.

Kymlicka, Will. 1991. "Rethinking the Family." *Philosophy and Public Affairs* 20: 77–97.

Lamb, Sharon. 2001. *The Secret Lives of Girls*. New York: Free Press.

Lamb, Sharon, ed. 1999. *New Versions of Victims: Feminists Struggle with the Concept*. New York: New York University Press.

Lamb, Sharon. 1996. *The Trouble with Blame: Victims, Perpetrators, and Responsibility*. Cambridge, MA: Harvard University Press.

Lamoree, Jhim. 1997. "Peepshow in Groningen." *Het Parool*, February 22.

Landes, Joan B. 1988. *Women and the Public Sphere in the Age of the French Revolution*. Ithaca, NY: Cornell University Press.

Lane, Frederick S. 2000. *Obscene Profits: The Entrepreneurs of Pornography in the Cyber Age*. New York: Routledge.

Lanteri-Laura, Georges. 1979. *La Lecture des Perversions: Histoire de Leur Appropriation Médicale*. Paris, Fr.: Masson.

Laqueur, Thomas. 1990. *Making Sex: Body and Gender from the Greeks to Freud*. Cambridge, MA: Harvard University Press.

Larson, Jane. 1997. "'Even a Worm Will Turn at Last:' Rape Reform in Late Nineteenth-Century America." *Yale Journal of Law and the Humanities* 9: 1–71.

Lasch, Christopher. 1979. *Haven in a Heartless World: The Family Besieged*. New York: Basic Books.

Laumann, Edward O., John H. Gagnon, Robert T. Michael, and Stuart Michaels. 1994. *The Social Organization of Sexuality: Sexual Practices in the United States*. Chicago, IL: University of Chicago Press.

Leap, William, ed. 1999. *Public Sex, Gay Space*. New York: Columbia University Press.

Learmonth, Michael. 1999. "Siliporn Valley." *San Jose Metro*, November 17, 15(37): 20–29.

Lefler, Julie. 1999. "Shining the Spotlight on Johns: Moving Toward Equal Treatment of Male Customers and Female Prostitutes." *Hastings Women's Law Journal* 10(1): 11–37.

Le Franc, Elsie, ed. 1994. *Consequences of Structural Adjustment: A Review of the Jamaican Experience*. Kingston, Jamaica: Canoe Press.

Leidholdt, Dorchen. 2000. "Analysis of International Trafficking of Women and Children Victim Protection Act." October 15. www.uri.edu/artsci/wms/hughes/catw/ans600.htm.

Leidner, Robin. 1993. *Fast Food, Fast Talk: Service Work and the Routinization of Everyday Life*. Berkeley, CA: University of California Press.

Leigh, Carol, 1997. "Inventing Sex Work." In *Whores and Other Feminists*, Jill Nagle, ed. London, UK: Routledge. pp. 223–231.

Leigh, Carol. 1994. "Prostitution in the United States: The Statistics." *Gauntlet: Exploring the Limits of Free Expression* 1: 17–19.

Leitenberg, Harold, and Heidi Saltzman. 2000. "A Statewide Survey of Age at First Intercourse for Adolescent Females and Age of Their Male Partners: Relation to Other Risk Behaviors and Statutory Rape Implications." *Archives of Sexual Behavior* 29: 202–215.

Leo, John. 1981. "Cradle-to-Grave Intimacy: Some Researchers Openly Argue that 'Anything Goes' for Children." *Time*, September 7: 69.

LeVay, Simon. 1993. *The Sexual Brain*. Cambridge, MA: MIT Press.

Lever, Janet, and Deanne Dolnick. 2000. "Clients and Call Girls: Seeking Sex and Intimacy." In *Sex for Sale: Prostitution, Pornography, and the Sex Industry*, Ronald Weitzer, ed. New York: Routledge. pp. 85–103.

Levesque, Roger. 2000. *Adolescents, Sex, and the Law: Preparing Adolescents for Responsible Citizenship*. Washington, DC: American Psychological Association.

Levesque, Roger. 1999. *Sexual Abuse of Children: A Human Rights Perspective*. Bloomington, IN: Indiana University Press.

Lévi-Strauss, Claude. 1971. "The Family." In *Man, Culture and Society*, Harry Shapiro, ed. London, UK: Oxford University Press. pp. 333–358.

Levine, Judith. 2002. *Harmful to Minors: The Perils of Protecting Children from Sex*. Minneapolis, MN: University of Minnesota Press.

Levine, Kay. 2003. *Prosecution, Politics, and Pregnancy: Enforcing Statutory Rape in California*. Unpublished Ph.D., School of Jurisprudence and Social Policy, University of California, Berkeley, CA.

Lewin, Ellen. 1998. *Recognizing Ourselves: Ceremonies of Lesbian and Gay Commitment*. New York: Columbia University Press.

Lewis, Amanda E. 2003. *Race in the Schoolyard: Negotiating the Color Line in Classrooms and Communities*. Piscataway, NJ: Rutgers University Press.

Lewis, Diane. 1999. "Naming 'Johns': Suicide Raises Ethical Questions About Policy." *FineLine: The Newsletter on Journalism Ethics* 2(6): 3.

Lewis, Gregory, and Jonathan Edelson. 2000. "DOMA and ENDA: Congress Votes on Gay Rights." In *The Politics of Gay Rights*, Craig Rimmerman et al., eds. Chicago, IL: University of Chicago Press.

Lewis, Melvin, and Phillip Sarrel. 1969. "Some Psychological Aspects of Seduction, Incest and Rape in Childhood." *Journal of American Academy of Child Psychiatry* 8: 606–619.

Lewis, Neil. 2001. "Immigrants Offered Incentives to Help U.S. Fight Terrorism. *New York Times Online.* November 30. www.nytimes.com/2001/11/30JUST.html.

Lieshout, Maurice van. 1995. "Leather Nights in the Woods." *Journal of Homosexuality* 29 (1): 19–29.

Lindberg, Frederick, and Lois Distad. 1985. "Post-traumatic Stress Disorders in Women Who Experienced Childhood Incest." *Child Abuse & Neglect* 9: 329–334.

Loftus, Jeni. 2001. "America's Liberalization in Attitudes toward Homosexuality, 1973 to 1998." *American Sociological Review* 66 (October): 762–782.

Lombroso, Caesar, and Ferrero, William. 1895. *The Female Offender.* London, UK: Fisher Unwin.

Longo, Paulo Henrique. 1998. "The Pegaçáo Program: Information, Prevention and Empowerment of Young Male Sex Workers in Rio de Janeiro." In *Global Sex Workers*, Kempadoo and Doezema, eds. New York: Routledge. pp. 213–239.

Lopez, Steve. 2000. "Hold the Pickles, Please: This Drive-Through Has a New Menu Item." *Time,* October 2: p. 6.

Lorde, Audre. 1984 . *Sister Outsider.* Trumansberg, NY: The Crossing Press.

Luibheid, Eithne. 2002. *Entry Denied: Controlling Sexuality at the Border.* Minneapolis, MN: University of Minnesota Press.

Luker, Kristin. 1998. "Sex, Social Hygiene, and Syphilis: The Double-Edged Sword of Social Reform." *Theory and Society* 27: 601–634.

Luker, Kristin. 1984. *Abortion and the Politics of Motherhood.* Berkeley, CA: University of California Press.

Luker, Kristin. 1975. *Taking Chances: Abortion and the Decision Not to Contracept.* Berkeley, CA: University of California Press.

Lutz, Catherine. 2001. *Homefront: A Military City and the American Twentieth Century.* Boston, MA: Beacon Press.

Lynch, Michael. 1998. "Enforcing 'Statutory Rape'?" *Public Interest* 132: 3–17.

Maatman, Melanie, and Alexander H. Meijer. 1992. *Cruising als Ruimteclaim.* Amsterdam, the Netherlands: Planologisch en Demografisch Instituut.

Macaulay, Stewart. 1985. "Law, Private Governance, and Continuing Relationships: An Empirical View of Contract." *Wisconsin Law Review* May/June: 465–482.

MacDonald, William. 1978. *Victimless Crimes: A Description of Offenders and their Prosecution in the District of Columbia.* Washington, DC: Institute for Law and Social Research.

MacKinnon, Catherine. 1989. *Towards a Feminist Theory of the State.* Cambridge, MA: Harvard University Press.

MacKinnon, Catharine. 1987. *Feminism Unmodified: Discourses on Life and Law.* Cambridge, MA: Harvard University Press.

MacKinnon, Catharine. 1979. *Sexual Harassment of Working Women.* New Haven, CT: Yale University Press.

Macleod, Mary, and Esther Saraga. 1998. "Challenging the Orthodoxy: Towards a Feminist Theory and Practice." *Feminist Review* 28 (January): 16–55.

Mahler, Karen. 1998. "Global Concern for Children's Rights: The World Congress Against Sexual Exploitation." *International Family Planning Perspectives* 23(2): 79–84.

Mahood, Linda. 1995. *Policing Gender, Class and Family: Britain, 1850–1940.* London, UK: University College London Press.

Mahood, Linda. 1990. *The Magdalenes: Prostitution in the Nineteenth Century.* London, UK: Routledge.

Males, Mike. 1999. *Framing Youth: 10 Myths About the Next Generation.* Monroe, ME: Common Courage Press.

Manderson, Lenore, and Margaret Jolly. 1997. *Sites of Desire, Economies of Pleasure: Sexualities in Asia and the Pacific.* Chicago, IL: University of Chicago Press.

Månsson, Sven-Axel. 1988. *The Man in Sexual Commerce.* Lund, Sweden: Lund University School of Social Work.

Margolin, D. 1972. "Rape: The Facts." *Women: A Journal of Liberation* 3: 19–22.

Marinucci, Carla. 1995a."International Praise for S.F. 'School for Johns." *San Francisco Examiner,* November 14.

Marinucci, Carla. 1995b. "A School for Scandal." *San Francisco Examiner*, April 16.

Marotta, Toby. 1981. *The Politics of Homosexuality*. New York: Houghton Mifflin.

Marquis, Christopher. 2003. "A Crackdown on the Traffic in Humans." *New York Times Online.* February 26. http://nytimes.com/2003/02/26/international/26sex.html.

Martin, Biddy. 1994. "Sexualities Without Genders and Other Queer Utopias." *Diacritics* 24 (Summer): 104–121.

Marx, Karl. [1844] 1978. "The Economic and Philosophic Manuscripts of 1844." In *The Marx-Engels Reader,* R. Tucker, ed. New York: WW Norton. pp. 66–129.

Marx, Karl. 1959. *Economic and Philosophic Manuscripts of 1844*. London, UK: Lawrence and Wishart.

Masson, Jeffrey. 1984. *The Assault on Truth: Freud's Suppression of the Seduction Theory.* Harmondsworth, UK: Penguin.

Masson, Jeffrey. 1988. *A Dark Science: Women, Sexuality, and Psychiatry in the Nineteenth Century*. New York: Noonday Press.

Mayhew, Henry. [1851] 1968. "Those That Will Not Work, Comprising Prostitutes, Thieves, Swindlers and Beggars." In *London Labour and London Poor*. Vol. IV. New York: Dover.

McAdam, Doug. 1982. *Political Process and the Development of Black Insurgency 1930–1970.* Chicago, IL: University of Chicago Press.

McCann, Michael W. 1998. "How Does Law Matter for Social Movements?" In *How Does Law Matter*, Bryant G. Garth and Austin Sarat, eds. Evanston, IL: Northwestern University Press. pp. 76–108.

McCulloch, Hamish. 2001. "The Work of INTERPOL." *Five Years After Stockholm, The Fifth Report on the Implementation of the Agenda for Action Adopted at the First World Congress Against the Commercial Sexual Exploitation of Children Stockholm, Sweden: August 28, 1996.* Bangkok, Thailand: ECPAT International.

McIntosh, Mary. 1978. "Who Needs Prostitutes: The Ideology of Male Sexual Needs." *Women, Sexuality, and Social Control,* Carol Smart and Barry Smart, eds. London, UK: Routledge. pp. 53–65.

McKeganey, Neil, and Marina Barnard. 1996. *Sex Work on the Streets: Prostitutes and Their Clients.* Buckingham, UK: Open University Press.

McKinnon, Susan. 1995. "American Kinship/American Incest: Asymmetries in a Scientific Discourse." In *Naturalizing Power: Essays in Feminist Cultural Analysis*, Sylvia Yanagisako and Carol Delancy, eds. New York: Routledge. pp. 25–46.

McNamee, Gwen Hoerr. 1999. *A Noble Experiment?: The First 100 Years of the Cook County Juvenile Court, 1899–1999*. Chicago, IL: Chicago Bar Association.

McNeil, Ian. 1985. "Relational Contract: What We Do and Do Not Know." *Wisconsin Law Review* May/June: 483–525.

Melai, A.J., et al. 1980. *Eindrapport van de Adviescommissie Zedelijkheidswetgeving*. Gravenhage, the Netherlands: Staatsdrukkerij.

Mercer, Kobena. 1995. "Busy in the Ruins of Wretched Phantasia." In *Mirage: Enigmas of Race, Difference, and Desire*, R. Farr, ed. London, UK: ICA/Institute of International Visual Arts.

Messerschmidt, James. 1993. *Masculinities and Crime: Critique and Reconceptualization of Theory.* Lanham, MD: Rowman and Littlefield.

Meyer, David S., and Suzanne Staggenborg. 1996. "Movements, Countermovements, and the Structure of Political Opportunity." *American Journal of Sociology* 101(6): 1628–1660.

Miller, Alice. 1999. "Human Rights and Sexuality: First Steps Toward Articulating a Rights Framework for Claims to Sexual Rights and Freedom." *ASIL Proceedings*: 288–303.

Miller, Henry, and Corrine Miller. 1998. "Issues in Statutory Rape Law Enforcement: The Views of District Attorneys in Kansas." *Family Planning Perspectives* 30(4): 177–182.

Miller, Marjorie. 2000. "Immigrants Died 'a Most Terrible Death' in England." *Los Angeles Times* June 20. A1.

Mills, Mike. 1999. "City of Boulder Ponders Transgendered Rights." *Boulder Pride News,* Aug. 12. www.boulderpride.org/NewsArchive/1999/MikeMillsTransgenderRights.html.

Minority Views. 1999. "Democrats Dissenting Report on the Trafficking Victims Protection Act." www.house.gov/judiciarydemocrats/dissentinghr3244.htm.

Minter, Shannon. 2003. *Representing Transsexual Clients: An Overview of Selected Legal Issues*. San Francisco: National Center for Lesbian Rights. www.nclrights.org.

Minter, Shannon. 2000. "Do Transsexuals Dream of Gay Rights? Getting Real About Transgender Inclusion in the Gay Rights Movement." *New York Law School Journal of Human Rights* 17: 589–621.

Moerings, Martin, and B. Swier. 1997. *Recht rond zedendelicten*. Alphen aan de Rijn, the Netherlands: Samson.

Mohr, Richard. 1994. *A More Perfect Union: Why Straight America Must Stand Up for Gay Rights*. Boston, MA: Beacon Press.

Montgomery, Heather. 1998. "Children, Prostitution and Identity: A Case Study from a Tourist Resort in Thailand." In *Global Sex Workers*, Kempadoo and Doezema, eds. New York: Routledge. pp 139–150.

Monto, Martin. 2000. "Why Men Seek Out Prostitutes." In *Sex for Sale*, Ron Weitzer, ed. New York: Routledge. pp. 67–85.

Moraga, Cherríe, and Gloria Anzaldúa, eds. 1981. *This Bridge Called My Back: Writings by Radical Women of Color*. Watertown, MA: Persephone Press.

Morrison, Toni. 1990. *Playing in the Dark: Whiteness and the Literary Imagination*. Cambridge, MA: Harvard University Press.

Mosse, George. 1985. *Nationalisms and Sexualities: Middle-Class Moralities and Sexual Norms in Modern Europe*. Madison, WI: University of Wisconsin Press.

Muntarbhorn, Vitit. 2001. *Report of the Second World Congress Against Commercial Sexual Exploitation of Children, Yokohama, Japan: December 17–20, 2001*. The Ministry of Foreign Affairs of Japan.

Musick, Judith. 1993. *Young, Poor, and Pregnant: The Psychology of Teen Motherhood*. New Haven, CT: Yale University Press.

Myers, John, ed. 1994. *The Backlash: Child Protection Under Fire*. Newbury Park, CA: Sage.

Myron, Nancy, and Charlotte Bunch, eds. 1975. *Lesbianism and the Women's Movement*. Baltimore, MD: Diana Press.

NACLA. 1995. "Disposable Children: The Hazards of Growing Up Poor in Latin America." *Report on the Americas*. New York: Author.

Narvesen, Ore. 1989. *The Sexual Exploitation of Children in Developing Countries*. Oslo, Norway: Redd Barna.

Nagle, Jill, ed. 1997. *Whores and Other Feminists*. New York: Routledge.

"Names of Alleged U.S. Prostitute Client Released." 1999. Reuters, January 13. www.infonautics.com.

Nathanson, Constance A. 1991. *Dangerous Passage: The Social Control of Sexuality in Women's Adolescence*. Philadelphia, PA: Temple University Press.

National Center on Child Abuse and Neglect. 1988. *Study of National Incidence and Prevalence of Child Abuse and Neglect*. Washington, DC: U.S. Department of Health and Human Services.

National Gay and Lesbian Task Force Policy Institute. 1997. *Capital Gains and Losses: A State by State Review of Gay, Lesbian, Bisexual, Transgender, and HIV/AIDS-Related Legislation in 1997*. Washington, DC: NGLTRF Policy Institute.

National Gay Task Force. 1976. "Progress Report '75." *Opportunities for Action/Reports on Results* January (NGTF Action Report): 6.

National Organization for Women (NOW). 2000. "Legislative Update." June 12. www.now.org/issues/legislat/06-12-2000.html.

Nelson, Andrea, and Pamela Oliver. 1998. "Gender and the Construction of Consent in Child-Adult Sexual Contact: Beyond Gender Neutrality and Male Monopoly." *Gender and Society* 12(5): 554–577.

Nelson, Barbara. 1984. *Making an Issue of Child Abuse: Political Agenda Setting for Social Problems*. Chicago, IL: University of Chicago Press.

Nelson, Nici. 1987. "Selling Her Kiosk: Kikuyu Notions of Sexuality and Sex for Sale in Mathare Valley, Kenya." In *The Cultural Construction of Sexuality*, P. Caplan, ed. London, UK: Tavistock. pp. 217–239.

Ness, Carol, and Ryan Kim. 2001. "Enticing Informers." *San Francisco Chronicle*, December 3.

Nevins, Buddy. 1987. "Sodomy Law Test Planned." March 17 [newspaper illegible]

Newburn, Tim, and Elizabeth Stanko. 1994. *Just Boys Doing Business?: Men, Masculinities, and Crime*. London, UK: Routledge.

Nezlek, John. 2002. "Estimating the Incidence of Statutory Rape in Virginia." Richmond, VA: Center for Injury and Violence Prevention, Virginia Department of Health.

Nice, David C. 1988. "State Deregulation of Intimate Behavior." *Social Science Quarterly* 69(1): 203–211.

Nieuwenhuys, Olga. 1996. "The Paradox of Child Labor and Anthropology." *Annual Review of Anthropology* 25: 237–251.

De Nieuwe Sekstant 82(2), Summer 2002, 36.

Nieves, Evelyn. 1999. "For Patrons of Prostitutes, Remedial Instruction." *The New York Times*, March 18. A1, A20.

Nijboer, Jeanette. 1994. *Op de Lesbisch Toer in Amsterdam*. Amsterdam, the Netherlands: Vita.

Nordland, Eva. 1971. *Det Store Nederlaget*. Oslo: Universitetsforlaget.

NRC Handelsblad. 1999. Special issue on "Prostitutie." October 14.

NRC Handelsblad. 2001. Ook Virtuele Kinderporno Strafbaar. January 13.

Oberman, Michelle. 2000. "Regulating Consensual Sex with Minors: Defining a Role for Statutory Rape." *Buffalo Law Review* 48: 703–784.

O'Connell Davidson, Julia. 2001a. *The Sex Exploiter*. Theme paper for the NGO Group for the Convention on the Rights of the Child, in preparation for the Second World Congress Against the Commercial Sexual Exploitation of Children, Stockholm, Sweden.

O'Connell Davidson, Julia. 2001b. "The Sex Tourist, the Expatriate, His Ex-wife, and Her 'Other:' The Politics of Loss, Difference, and Desire." *Sexualities* 4(1): 5–24.

O'Connell Davidson, Julia. 1998. *Prostitution, Power, and Freedom*. Cambridge, UK: Polity Press.

O'Connell Davidson, Julia, and Jacqueline Sánchez Taylor. 1999. "Fantasy Islands: Exploring the Demand for Sex Tourism." In *Sun, Sex, and Gold: Tourism and Sex Work in the Caribbean*, Kamala Kempadoo, ed. Oxford, UK: Rowman and Littlefield. pp. 37–54.

O'Connell Davidson, Julia, and Jacqueline Sanchez Taylor. 1996. "Child Prostitution and Sex Tourism." *Research Papers* 1–7. Bangkok, Thailand: ECPAT.

Odem, Mary. 1995. *Delinquent Daughters: Protecting and Policing Adolescent Female Sexuality in the United States, 1885–1920*. Chapel Hill, NC: University of North Carolina Press.

Office of Juvenile Justice and Delinquency Prevention. 1999. *Minorities in the Juvenile Justice System*. Washington, DC: U.S. Department of Justice.

O'Grady, Ron. 1992. *The Child and the Tourist*. Bangkok, Thailand: ECPAT.

Olafson, Erna, D.L. Corwin, and R.C. Summit. 1993. "Modern History of Child Sexual Abuse Awareness: Cycles of Discovery and Suppression." *Child Abuse and Neglect* 17: 7–24.

O'Leary, Jean. 1978. "Legal Problems and Remedies." In *Our Right to Love: A Lesbian Resource Book*, Ginny Vida, ed. Englewood Cliffs, NJ: Prentice Hall. pp. 196–203.

Oliver, Melvin, and Thomas Shapiro. 1995. *Black Wealth/White Wealth: A New Perspective on Racial Inequality*. New York: Routledge.

Oliveri, Rigel. 2000. "Statutory Rape Law and Enforcement on the Wake of Welfare Reform." *Stanford Law Review* 53: 46–508.

O'Neill Richards, Amy. 1999. "DCI Exceptional Intelligence Analyst Program, Intelligence Monograph: International Trafficking in Women—A Contemporary Manifestation of Slavery and Organized Crime." Washington, DC: Center for the Intelligence.

Olsen, Frances. 1984. "Statutory Rape: A Feminist Critique of Rights Analysis." *Texas Law Review* 63: 387–432.

Olujic, Maria. 1995. "The Croatian War Experience." In *Fieldwork Under Fire*, Nordstrom and Robben, eds. Berkeley, CA: University of California Press. pp. 186–205.

Omi, Michael, and Howard Winant. 1986. *Racial Transformation in the United States From the 1960s to the 1980s*. New York: Routledge.

Oosterhuis, Harry. 2000. *Stepchildren of Nature: Krafft-Ebing, Psychiatry, and the Making of Sexual Identity*. Chicago, IL: The University of Chicago Press.

Oppermannn, Martin, ed. 1998. *Sex Tourism and Prostitution: Aspects of Leisure, Recreation and Work*. New York: Cognizant Communication.

Orr, Jacqueline. 2004. "Militarization of Inner Space." *Critical Sociology* (30)2, 451–481.

O'Toole, Laura, and Jessica Schiffman, eds. 1997. *Gender Violence: Interdisciplinary Perspectives*. New York: New York University Press.

Owens, Robert. 1998. *Queer Kids: The Challenges and Promise for Lesbian, Gay, and Bisexual Youth*. New York: Haworth Press.

Paans, Anna. 2002. "Seks Nog Taboe in Opvoeding." *Algemeen Dagblad* 25, February 15.

Pankhurst, Christabel. 1913. *Plain Facts About a Great Evil*. New York: The Medical Review of Reviews.

Pateman, Carole. 1988. *The Sexual Contract*. Stanford, CA: Stanford University Press.

Patterson, Orlando. 1998. "What is Freedom Without Privacy?" *The New York Times,* September 15.

Patterson, Orlando. 1991. *Freedom*. New York: Basic Books.

Patton, Cindy. 2002. *Globalizing AIDS*. Minneapolis, MN: University of Minnesota Press.

Pattullo, Polly. 1996. *Last Resorts: The Cost of Tourism in the Caribbean*. London, UK: Latin America Bureau.

Paz, Octavio. 1993. *La Llama Doble: Amor y Erotismo*. Barcelona, Spain: Editorial Seix Barral.

Pereira, Roberto, Carlos Basilia, Paulo Longo, and Sylvio Oliveira. 1992. "Intervention with Children and Teenagers Involved in Prostitution in the Streets of Rio de Janeiro." International Conference on AIDS. Amsterdam, the Netherlands, July 19–24.

Perrot, Michelle, ed. 1990. *A History of Private Life, Volume IV: From the Fires of Revolution to the Great War*. Cambridge, MA: Belknap Press.

Pfeffer, Rachel. 1997. *Surviving the Streets: Girls Living on Their Own*. New York: Garland Publishing.

Pheterson, Gail. 1993. "The Whore Stigma: Female Dishonor and Male Unworthiness." *Social Text* 37: 39–65.

Pheterson, Gail. 1989. *A Vindication of the Rights of Whores*. Seattle, WA: Seal Press.

Phipps, Charles. 1997. "Children, Adults, Sex, and the Criminal Law: In Search of Reason." *Seton Hall Legislative Journal* 22: 1–141.

Phillips, Lynn. 1999. "Recasting Consent: Agency and Victimization in Adult-Teen Relationships." In *New Versions of Victims*, Sharon Lamb, ed. New York: University Press. pp. 82–107.

Pichardo, Nelson A. 1997. "New Social Movements: A Critical Review." *Annual Review of Sociology* 23: 411–430.

Pickup, Francine. 1998. "Deconstructing Trafficking in Women: The Example of Russia." *Journal of International Studies* 27 (4): 995–1021.

Pierre-Pierre, Garry. 1994. "Police Focus on Arresting Prostitutes' Customers." *New York Times,* November 20. p. 51.

Pinedo, Danielle. 2003. "Veel Homo's Leiden een Keurig, Burgerlijk Leventje'; De Kruistocht van 'Beroepshomo' Henk Krol." *NRC-Handelsblad,* Zaterdags Bijvoegsel, p. 23.

Platt, Anthony. 1969. *The Child Savers: The Invention of Delinquency*. Chicago, IL: University of Chicago Press.

Plummer, Kenneth. 1989. "Lesbian and Gay Youth in England." *Journal of Homosexuality* 17: 45–63.

Pocina, Peter. 2001. "Forgive Them Their Debts." *Portland Press Herald,* March 17, 2C.

Pol, Lotte van de. 1996. *Het Amsterdams Hoerdom. Prostitutie in een Vroegmoderne Stedelijke Samenleving, 1650–1800*. Amsterdam, the Netherlands: Wereldbibliotheek.

Poovey, Mary. 1995. *Making a Social Body: British Cultural Formation 1830–1864*. Chicago, IL: University of Chicago Press.

Porter, Francis, Linda Blick, and Suzanne Sgroi. 1982. "Treatment of the Sexually Abused Child." In *Handbook of Clinical Intervention in Child Sexual Abuse*, Suzanne Sgroi, ed. Lexington, MA: Lexington Books. pp. 109–145.

Postman, Neil. 1982. *The Disappearance of Childhood*. New York: Random House.

Povinelli, Elizabeth, and George Chauncey, eds. 1999. "Thinking Sexuality Transnationally." *GLQ: A Journal of Gay and Lesbian Studies* 5(4), Special Issue.

Prasad, Monica. 1999. "The Morality of Market Exchange: Love, Money, and Contractual Justice." *Sociological Perspectives* 42(2): 181–215.

Prial, Dunstan. 1999. "IPO Outlook: 'Adult' Web Sites Profit, Though Few are Likely to Offer Shares." *The Wall Street Journal,* March 8. B10.

Prieur, Annick, and Arnhild Taksdal. 1993. "Clients of Prostitutes: Sick Deviants or Ordinary Men? A Discussion of the Male Role Concept and Cultural Changes in Masculinity." *NORA* 2: 105–114.

Prochaska, F. K. 1980. *Women and Philanthropy in Nineteenth-Century England*. Oxford, UK: Clarendon Press.

Pruitt, Deborah, and Suzanne LaFont. 1995. "For Love and Money: Romance Tourism in Jamaica." *Annals of Tourism Research* 22(2): 422–440.

Puar, Jasbir K., and Amit S. Rai. 2002. "Monster, Terrorist, Fag: The War on Terrorism and the Production of Docile Patriots." *Social Texts* 72 (Fall): 117–148.

Puri, Jyoti. 2002. "Nationalism Has a Lot to Do with It! Unraveling Questions of Nationalism and Transnationalism in Lesbian/Gay Studies." In *Handbook of Lesbian and Gay Studies*, Diane Richardson and Steven Seidman, eds. London, UK: Sage Publications.

Puzzanchera, Charles. 2000. "Delinquency Cases Waived to Criminal Court, 1988–1997." Washington, DC: U.S. Department of Justice.

Radin, Margaret Jane. 1996. *Contested Commodities: The Trouble with Trade in Sex, Children, Body Parts, and Other Things*. Cambridge, MA: Harvard University Press.

Raeburn, Nicole. 2000. "The Rise of Lesbian, Gay and Bisexual Rights in the Workplace." Ph.D. Dissertation, Department of Sociology, Ohio State University.

Rainville, Gerard, and Steven Smith. 2003. "Juvenile Felony Defendants in Criminal Courts." Washington, DC: Bureau of Justice Statistics.

Rajani, Rkesh, and Mustafa Kudrati. 1996. "The Varieties of Sexual Experience of the Street Children of Mwanza, Tanzania." In *Learning About Sexuality*, Sondra Zeidenstein and Kirsten Moore, eds. New York: The Population Council/IWHC, pp. 301–332.

Raymond, Janice. 1998. "Prostitution as Violence against Women." *Women's Studies International Forum* 21(1): 1–9.

Rayside, David. 1998. *On the Fringe: Gays and Lesbians in Politics*. Ithaca, NY: Cornell University Press.

Regan, Milton C., Jr. 1993. *Family Law and the Pursuit of Intimacy*. New York: New York University Press.

Renovoize, Jean. 1993. *Innocence Destroyed: A Study of Child Sexual Abuse*. New York: Routledge.

Richardson, Dianne. 1996. "Heterosexuality and Social Theory." In *Theorising Heterosexuality*, Diane Richardson, ed. Buckingham, UK: Oxford University Press. pp. 1–20.

Richie, Beth. 1996. *Compelled to Crime: The Gender Entrapment of Battered Black Women*. New York: Routledge Press.

Rimmerman, Craig, Kenneth Wald, and Clyde Wilcox, eds. 2000. *The Politics of Gay Rights*. Chicago, IL: University of Chicago Press.

Rind, Bruce, Philip Tromovich, and Robert Bauserman. 1998. "A Meta-Analytic Examination of Assumed Properties of Child Sexual Abuse Using College Samples." *Psychological Bulletin* 124: 22–53.

Roberts, Dorothy. 2001. *Shattered Bonds: The Color of Child Welfare*. New York: Basic Books.

Robson, Ruthann. 1992. *Lesbian (Out)Law: Survival Under the Rule of Law*. Ithaca, NY: Firebrand Books.

Rocha, Jan. 1991. "Introduction." In *Brazil: War on Children*, Gilberto Dimenstein, ed. London, UK: LatinAmerica Bureau. pp. 1–15.

Rose, Nikolas. 1989. *Governing the Soul: The Shaping of the Private Self*. London, UK: Free Association Books.

Rose, Nikolas, and Peter Miller. 1992. "Political Power Beyond the State: Problematics of Government." *British Journal of Sociology* 43(2): 173–205.

Rosen, Ruth. 1982. *The Lost Sisterhood: Prostitution in America, 1900–1918*. Baltimore, MD: Johns Hopkins University Press.

Rosin, Hanna. 2000. "Thai Boy Caught up in Fight Against Sex Trafficking. *Washington Post*, December 15. p. 15.

Rossen, Benjamin. 1989. *Zedenangst: Het Verhaal van Oude Pekela*. Lisse, the Netherlands: Swets en Zeitlinger.

Rountree, Will. Spring 2000. *Contracting Intimacy: Property, Parenting, and Meaning in Intimate Relationships*. Ph.D. Dissertation, Department of Sociology, University of California. Berkeley, CA.

Rubin, Gayle, 1999. "Thinking Sex: Notes for a Radical Theory of the Politics of Sexuality." In *Culture, Society and Sexuality: A Reader*, Richard Parker and Peter Aggleton, eds. London, UK: University College London. pp. 143–179.

Rubin, Gayle. 1991. "The Catacombs: A Temple of the Butthole." In *Leatherfolks: Radical Sex, People, Politics and Practice*, Mark Thompson, ed. Boston, MA: Alyson. pp. 119–141.

Rubin, Gayle. 1975. "The Traffic in Women: Notes on the 'Political Economy' of Sex." In *Toward an Anthropology of Women*, R. Reiter, ed. New York: Monthly Review Press. pp. 157–211.

Rush, Florence. 1980. *The Best Kept Secret: Sexual Abuse of Children*. New York: McGraw-Hill.

Rush, Florence. 1974. "The Sexual Abuse of Children: A Feminist Point of View." In *Rape: The First Sourcebook for Women by New York Radical Feminists*, Noreen Connell and Cassandra Wilson, eds. New York: New American Library. pp. 64–75.

Russell, Diana. 1986. *The Secret Trauma: Incest in the Lives of Girls and Women*. New York: Basic.

Russell, Diana. 1984. *Sexual Exploitation: Rape, Child Sexual Abuse, and Workplace Harassment*. Beverly Hills, CA: Sage Publications.

Sachs, Susan. 1999. "Fears of Rape and Violence: Women Newly Seeking Asylum." *New York Times Week in Review*, August 1.

Safa, Heidi. 1997. "Where the Big Fish Eat the Little Fish: Women's Work in the Free Trade Zones." *Report on the Americas, NACLA* 30(5): 31–36.

Said, Edward. 1978. *Orientalism: Western Conceptions of the Orient*. Harmondsworth, UK: Penguin.

Sánchez Taylor, Jacqueline. 2001. "Dollars Are a Girl's Best Friend." *Sociology* 35(3): 749–764.

Sánchez Taylor, Jacqueline. 2000. "Tourism and 'Embodied' Commodities: Sex Tourism in the Caribbean." In *Tourism and Sex: Culture, Commerce, and Coercion*, Stephen Clift and Simon Carter, eds. London, UK: Pinter.

Sanday, Peggy Reeves. 1990. *Fraternity Gang Rape: Sex, Brotherhood, and Privilege on Campus*. New York: New York University.

San Francisco Task Force on Prostitution. 1996. *Final Report*. Submitted to the Board of Supervisors of the City and County of San Francisco, California.

San Francisco Task Force on Prostitution. 1994. *Interim Report*. Submitted to the Board of Supervisors of the City and County of San Francisco, California.

Sax, Marjan, and Jules Deckwitz, eds. 1992. "On an Old Bicycle. Erotic and Sexual Relationships Between Women and Minors." *Paidika* 2: 4.

Schaffner, Laurie. 1999. *Teenage Runaways*. New York: Haworth Press.

Schaffner, Laurie. 1997. "Female Juvenile Delinquency: Sexual Solutions and Gender Bias in Juvenile Justice." *Hastings Women's Law Journal* 9(1): 1–27.

Scheper-Hughes, Nancy. 1992. *Death Without Weeping: The Violence of Everyday Life in Brazil*. Berkeley, CA: University of California Press.

Scheper-Hughes, Nancy, and Carolyn Sargent, eds. 1998. *Small Wars: The Cultural Politics of Childhood*. Berkeley, CA: University of California Press.

Schlafly, Phyllis. 2003. "Attacks on the Sanctity of Marriage Must Be Thwarted." October 13. www.townhall.com.

Schlosser, Eric. 1997. "The Business of Pornography." *U.S. News and World Report*, February 10, 43–52.

Schlossman, Steven, and Stephanie Wallace. 1978. "The Crime of Precocious Sexuality: Female Juvenile Delinquency in the Progressive Era." *Harvard Educational Review* 1: 65–94.

Schnabel, Paul. 1990. "Het Verlies van de Seksuele Onschuld." In *Het Verlies van de Onschuld*, Gert Hekma, Bram van Stolk, Bart van Heerikhuizen, and Bernard Kruitfhof, eds. Groningen, the Netherlands: Wolters-Noordhoff. pp. 11–50.

Schneider, Beth E., and Nancy E. Stoller, eds. 1995. *Women Resisting AIDS: Feminist Strategies of Empowerment*. Philadelphia, PA: Temple University Press.

Schroedel, Jean Reith, and Pamela Fiber. 2000. "Lesbian and Gay Policy Priorities: Commonality and Difference." In *The Politics of Gay Rights*, Craig Rimmerman, Kenneth Wald, and Clyde Wilcox, eds. Chicago, IL: University of Chicago Press. pp. 97–121.

Scott, Elizabeth. 2000. "Criminal Responsibility in Adolescence: Lessons from Developmental Psychology." In *Youth on Trial*, Grisso and Schwartz, eds. Chicago, IL: University of Chicago Press. pp. 291–324.

Scott, Ann. 1988. "Feminism and the Seductiveness of the 'Real Event.'" *Feminist Review* 28: 88–102.

Scott, Joan Wallach. 1996. *Only Paradoxes to Offer*. Cambridge, MA: Harvard University Press.

Scott, Joan Wallach. 1987. "L'Ouvriere, Mot Impie, Sordide . . . Women Workers in the Discourse of French Political Economy, 1840–1860." In *The Historical Meanings of Work*, P. Joyce, ed. Cambridge, UK: Cambridge University Press. pp. 119–42.

Seattle Commission on Sexual Minorities. 1999. Policy and Legislative Recommendations Concerning Seattle. www.ci.seattle.wa.us/scsm/.

Seidman, Steven. 2002. *Beyond the Closet: The Transformation of Gay and Lesbian Life*. New York: Routledge.

Seidman, Steven. 1994. "Gay Amsterdam, Een Mislukt Utopia?" *Krisis* 57: 69–71.

Seidman, Steven. 1991. *Romantic Longings*. New York: Routledge.

"Sex, News, and Statistics: Where Entertainment on the Web Scores." 2000. *The Economist,* October 7. www.economist.com.

Sgroi, Suzanne. 1982. "Family Treatment of Child Sexual Abuse." In *Social Work and Child Sexual Abuse: Journal of Social Work and Human Sexuality*, Vol. I, Issue 1 and 2, Jon Conte and David Shore, eds. New York: Haworth Press.

Shilling, Halle. 1999. Gender Identity Discussed. *Boulder Daily Camera*, August 17. 1C.

Shilts, Randy. 1987. *And the Band Played On: Politics, People, and the AIDS Epidemic.* New York: St. Martin's Press.

Shoop, Robert J. 1999. "See No Evil: Sexual Abuse of Children by Teachers." *The High School Magazine* 6(7) May/June: 8–12.

Showalter, Elaine. 1987. *The Female Malady.* London, UK: Virago Press.

Shrage, Laurie. 1994. *Moral Dilemmas of Feminism.* New York: Routledge.

Simmel, Georg. [1907] 1971. "Prostitution." In *On Individuality and Social Forms,* Donald N. Levine, ed. Chicago, IL: University of Chicago Press. pp. 121–126.

Skrobanek, Siriporn. 1990. *Child Prostitution in Thailand.* Report on the First National Assembly of Child Development, August 30–31. Thailand: UNICEF.

Smart, Carole. 1992. "Disruptive Bodies and Unruly Sex: The Regulation of Reproduction and Sexuality in the Nineteenth Century." In *Regulating Womanhood: Historical Essays on Marriage, Motherhood, and Sexuality,* Carol Smart, ed. London, UK: Routledge. pp. 7–32.

Smart, Carole, and Barry Smart, eds. 1978. *Women, Sexuality, and Social Control.* London, UK: Routledge.

Smidt, H. J. 1882. *Het nieuwe Wetboek van Strafrecht Vol. II.* Haarlem, the Netherlands: Tjeenk Willink.

Smith, Anna Marie. 2001. "The Politicization of Marriage in Contemporary American Public Policy: The Defense of Marriage Act and the Personal Responsibility Act." *Citizenship Studies* 5 (November): 303–320.

Smith, Christopher. 2000. Press Release. April 4. www.house.gov/apps/list/press/nj04 smith/040400.html

Smith, Lesley Shacklady. 1978. "Sexist Assumptions and Female Delinquency: An Empirical Investigation." In *Women, Sexuality, and Social Control,* Carol Smart and Barry Smart, eds. London, UK: Routledge and Kegan Paul. pp. 74–88.

Smith, Paul. 1997. *Millennial Dreams: Contemporary Culture and Capital in the North.* London, UK: Verso.

Snitow, Ann, Christine Stansell, and Sharon Thompson. 1983. *Powers of Desire: The Politics of Sexuality.* New York: Monthly Review Press.

Snyder, Howard, and Melissa Sickmund. 1999. "Juvenile Offenders and Victims: 1999 National Report." Washington, DC: Office of Juvenile Justice and Delinquency Prevention, U.S. Department of Justice.

Sorrentino, Constance. 1990. "The Changing Family in International Perspective." *Monthly Labor Review,* March, 41–58.

Spillers, Hortense J. 1992. "Interstices: A Small Drama of Words." In *Pleasure and Danger*, Carole Vance, ed. London, UK: Pandora Press. pp 73–100.

Spillman, Lynn. 1997. *Nation and Commemoration: Creating National Identities in the United States and Australia.* Cambridge, UK: Cambridge University Press.

Spira, Alfred, Nathalie Bajos, et le Groupe Analyse des Comportements Sexuels en France. 1993. *Les Comportements Sexuels en France.* Paris, Fr.: La documentation Francaise.

Spivak, Gayatri. 1990. *The Post-Colonial Critic.* New York: Routledge.

Squires, Judith, ed. 1993. "Perversity." *New Formations* 19. Special issue.

Stacey, Judith. 1996. *In the Name of the Family: Rethinking Family Values in the Postmodern Age.* Boston, MA: Beacon Press.

Staggenborg, Suzanne. 1995. "Can Feminist Organizations Be Effective?" In *Feminist Organizations: Harvest of the New Women's Movement,* Myra Marx Ferree and Patricia Yancey Martin, eds. Philadelphia, PA: Temple University Press. pp. 339–355.

"State Sex Laws Change." 1975. *Gay Blade,* June 1. p. 5.

Statutory Rape Vertical Prosecution Program (SVRP). 2002. "Project Description." State of California, Office of Criminal Justice Planning. www.srvp.net.

Stein, Arlene, ed. 1993. *Sisters, Sexperts, Queers: Beyond the Lesbian Nation.* New York: Penguin.

Steinberg, Laurence, and Elizabeth Cauffman. 1996. "Maturity of Judgment in Adolescence: Psychosocial Factors in Adolescent Decision Making." *Law and Human Behavior* 20: 249–271.

Stephens, Sharon, ed. 1995. *Children and the Politics of Culture.* Princeton, NJ: Princeton University Press.

Stockholm Declaration and Agenda for Action. August 1996. First World Congress Against Commercial Sexual Exploitation of Children. Stockholm, Sweden. pp. 27–31.

Stockinger, Jacob. 1979. "Homosexuality and the French Enlightenment." In *Homosexuality and French Literature: Cultural Contexts/Critical Texts*, George Stambolian and Elaine Marks, eds. Ithaca, NY: Cornell University Press. pp. 161–185.

Stoddard, Thomas. 1993. "Why Gay People Should Seek the Right to Marry." In *Lesbians, Gay Men, and the Law*, William Rubenstein, ed. New York: New Press.

Storrow, Richard F. 1997. "Naming the Grotesque Body in the Nascent Jurisprudence of Transsexualism." *Michigan Journal of Gender and the Law* 4: 275–334.

Sturkie, Kinly. 1986. "Treating Incest Victims and Their Families." In *Incest as Child Abuse: Research and Applications*. Brenda Vander Mey and Ronald Neff, eds. New York: Praeger. pp. 126–167.

Stychin, Carl. 1998. *A Nation of Rights: National Cultures, Sexual Identity Politics, and the Discourse of Rights.* Philadelphia, PA: Temple University Press.

Stychin, Carl, and Didi Herman, eds. 2001. *Law and Sexuality: The Global Arena.* Minneapolis, MN: University of Minnesota Press.

"Suburban Detroit Police Release Names of Prostitution Ring's Clients." 1999. *Associated Press Online*, January 15. www.freedomforum.org

Suffredini, Kara S. 2000. "Which Bodies Count When They Are Bashed?: An Argument for the Inclusion of Transgendered Individuals in the Hate Crimes Prevention Act of 1999." *Boston College Third World Law Journal* 20: 447.

Sullivan, Andrew. 1996. *Virtually Normal: An Argument about Homosexuality.* New York: Vintage.

Sullivan, Elroy, and William Simon. 1998. "The Client: A Social, Psychological, and Behavioral Look at the Unseen Patron of Prostitution." In *Prostitution: On Whores, Hustlers, and Johns*, James Elias, ed. Amherst, NY: Prometheus Books. pp. 134–155.

Summers, Anne. 1979. "A Home from Home: Women's Philanthropic Work in the Nineteenth Century." In *Fit Work for Women*, S. Burman, ed. London, UK: Croom Helm. pp. 33–63.

Summit, Ronald. 1983. "The Child Sexual Abuse Accommodation Syndrome." *Child Abuse and Neglect* 7: 177–193.

Sunder Rajan, Rajeswari. 2003. *The Scandal of the State: Women, Law, and Citizenship in Postcolonial India.* Durham, NC: Duke University Press.

Swaminathan, Samaya, Susan F. Crane, Ana Filgueiras and K. Row. 1991. "Reaching Marginalized Groups Through Local Non-governmental Organizations." Paper presented at International Conference on AIDS, 7(2): 37, June 16–21, Florence, Italy.

Swidler, Ann. 1980. "Love and Adulthood in American Culture." In *Themes of Work and Love In Adulthood*, Neil J. Smelser and E. H. Erikson, eds. Cambridge, MA: Harvard University Press.

Sykes, Gresham, and David Matza. [1957] 1985. "Techniques of Neutralization: A Theory of Delinquency." In *Theories of Deviance*, Stuart Traub and Craig Little, eds. Itasca, IL: F. E. Peacock.

Symbaluk, D. G., and K. M. Jones. 1998. "Prostitution Offender Programs: Canada Finds New Solutions to an Old Problem." *Corrections Compendium* 23(11): 1–2, 8.

Tappan, Paul. 1947. *Delinquent Girls in Court.* New York: Columbia University Press.

Tarrow, Sidney. 1998. *Power in Movement: Social Movements and Contentious Politics.* Cambridge, MA: Cambridge University Press.

Tarrow, Sidney. 1996. "States and Opportunities: The Political Structuring of Social Movements." In *Comparative Perspectives on Social Movements: Political Opportunities, Mobilizing Structures, and Cultural Framings*, John McCarthy, Doug McAdam, and Meyer N. Zald, eds. Cambridge, MA: Cambridge University Press. pp. 41–61.

Tarrow, Sidney. 1988. "National Politics and Collective Action: Recent Theory and Research in Western Europe and the United States." *Annual Review of Sociology* 14: 421–440.

Tarvis, Carol. 2000. "The Uproar Over Sexual Abuse Research and Its Findings." *Society* 37(4): 15–17.

Taylor, Verta, and Leila Rupp. 1993. "Women's Culture and Lesbian Feminist Activism: A Reconsideration of Cultural Feminism." *Signs* 19: 32–61.

Thibodeau, Wayne. 2003. "P.E.I. Cautions on Same Sex Unions." *The Guardian,* July 19.

Thompson, Bill. 1994. *Sadomasochism: Painful Perversion or Pleasurable Play?* London, UK: Cassell.

Thompson, Sharon. 1995. *Going All the Way: Teenage Girls' Tales of Sex, Romance, and Pregnancy.* New York: Hill and Wang.

Tibbets, Janice. 2003. "Historic Day for Gay Marriage: Ottawa Urges Provinces to Endorse Bill." *Calgary Herald,* July 18.

Tjensvoll, Hanne Marie. 1946. "Det seksuelle problem som samfunnsproblem." Norges Barnevern 4: 14–20.

Toldson, Ivory, ed. 1997. *Stolen Innocence: Preventing, Healing and Recovering from Child Molestation.* New York: CPHC Press and Products.

Tolman, Deborah. 1994. "Doing Desire: Adolescent Girls' Struggles for/with Sexuality." *Gender and Society* 8: 324–342.

Touraine, Alain. 1997. "Book Review: Challenging Codes and the Playing Self." *American Journal of Sociology* 103(3): 763–765.

Transgender Law and Policy Institute. 2003. *Transgender-Inclusive Non-Discrimination Laws.* www.transgenderlaw.org.

Treguear, Tatania, and Carmen Carro. 1994. *Niñas y Adolescentes Prostituidas.* San José de Costa Rica: UNICEF.

Tschirren, Rhea, Kirsty Hammet, and Penelope Saunders. 1996. *Sex for Favors, ACSA/Second Story.* Adelaide, South Australia: Youth Health Service/HIV/AIDS Worker Training Project.

"Two Face Jail Time for Smuggling Ring." 2001. *Associated Press, Fox News Online,* October 2. www.foxnews.com/national100201.prostitutes.sml.

U.S. Census Bureau. March 2000. *Current Population Survey.* Washington, DC: United States Department of Commerce.

U.S. Census Bureau. 1992. *Marriage, Divorce, and Remarriage in the 1990s.* Washington, DC: U.S. Government Printing Office Current Population Reports. pp. 23–180.

U.S. Census Bureau. 1989. *Studies in Marriage and the Family.* Washington, DC: U.S. Government Printing Office Current Population Reports. pp. 23–162.

U.S. State Department. 2000. "Trafficking in Women and Girls: Clinton Administration's Model Anti-Trafficking Legislation." June 5. http://secretary.state.gov/www/picw/trafficking/usmodel.htm.

Vaid, Urvashi. 1995. *Virtual Equality: The Mainstreaming of Gay and Lesbian Liberation.* New York: Doubleday.

Valdes, Francisco. 1995. "Queers, Sissies, Dykes, and Tomboys: Deconstructing the Conflation of Sex, Gender, and Sexual Orientation in Euro-American Law and Society." *California Law Review* 83: 3–128.

Van Bueren, Geraldine. 2001. *Child Sexual Exploitation and the Law.* A Report on the International Framework and Current National Legislative and Enforcement Responses, Theme paper for Second World Congress Against Commercial Sexual Exploitation of Children, Yokahama, Japan, December 17–20.

Vance, Carole. 1984. *Pleasure and Danger: Exploring Female Sexuality.* Boston, MA: Routledge and Kegan Paul.

van Lieshout, Maurice. 1995. "Leather Nights in the Woods: Homosexual Encounters in a Dutch Highway Rest Area." *Journal of Homosexuality* 29(1): 19–39.

van Zessen, Gertjan, and Theo Sandfort, eds. 1991. *Seksualiteit in Nederland: Seksueel Gedrag, Risico en Preventie van AIDS.* Amsterdam/Lisse, the Netherlands: Swets & Zeitlinger.

Vegheim, Berit. 1995. *Det Uforutsignare Systemet og det Sårbare Fellesskapet. Rapport om Kvinnelige Fangers Opplevelse av Fengselsstraff.* Oslo: Department of Criminology, University of Oslo.

Velde, Hans van. 2001. "From Trial Process to Reality: The Long Road to Civil Marriage." *De Gay Krant* 432 (March 31): 13–37.

Vermeulen, Frank. 1997. "Raadslid Pleit Voor Onderricht in Liefde." *Volkskrant,* May 15. 3.

Vicinus, Martha, ed. 1977. *A Widening Sphere: Changing Roles of Victorian Women.* London, UK: Methuen and Co.

Visser, Jan H., and Hetty C.D.M. Oomens. 2000. *Prostitute in Nederland in 1999.* Amsterdam, the Netherlands: Mr. A. de Graaf Stichting.

Vogels, Ton, and Ron van der Vliet. 1990. *Jeugd en Seks.* Den Haag, the Netherlands: SDU.

Waite, Linda, ed. 2000. *The Ties That Bind: Perspectives on Marriage and Cohabitation.* New York: Aldine de Gruyter.

Wagner, David. 1997. *The New Temperance.* Boulder, CO: Westview Press.

Wal, Geke van der. 1995. "Sex als Heidens Karwei." *DeVolkskrant,* October 4.

Walkerdine, Valerie. 1986. "Video Replay: Families, Films and Fantasy." In *Formations of Fantasy,* V. Burgin, J. Donald, and C. Kaplan, eds. London, UK: Methuen. pp. 167–199.

Walkowitz, Judith. 1992. *City of Dreadful Delight: Narratives of Sexual Danger in Late Victorian London.* Chicago, IL: University of Chicago Press.

Walkowitz, Judith. 1980. *Prostitution and Victorian Society.* London, UK: Cambridge University Press.

Walters, Suzanna Danuta. 2001. *All the Rage: The Story of Gay Visibility in America.* Chicago, IL: University of Chicago Press.

Ward, Elizabeth. 1985. *Father-Daughter Rape.* New York: Grove Press.

Warner, Michael. 2000. *The Trouble with Normal: Sex, Politics, and the Ethics of Queer Life.* Cambridge, MA: Harvard University Press.

Warner, Michael. 1993, ed. *Fear of a Queer Planet.* Minneapolis, MN: University of Minnesota Press.

Weeks, Jeffrey. [1981] 1997. "Inverts, Perverts, and Mary-Annes." In *The Subcultures Reader,* Ken Gelder and Sarah Thornton, eds. London, UK: Routledge. pp. 268–281.

Weeks, Jeffrey. 1995a. *Invented Moralities: Sexual Values in an Age of Uncertainty.* New York: Columbia University Press.

Weeks, Jeffrey. 1995b. "Desire and Identities." In *Conceiving Sexuality: Approaches to Sex Research in a Postmodern World.* R. Parker and J. Gagnon, eds. New York: Routledge. pp. 33–50.

Weeks, Jeffrey. 1981. *Sex, Politics and Society: The Regulation of Sexuality Since 1800.* London, UK: Longman.

Weeks, Jeffrey, Brian Heaphy, and Catherine Donovan. 2001. *Same Sex Intimacies: Families of Choice and Other Life Experiments.* New York: Routledge.

Weinberg, Kirson S. 1955. *Incest Behavior.* New York: Citadel Press.

Weiner, Niel, and Sharon Kurpius. 1995. *Shattered Innocence: A Practical Guide for Counseling Women Survivors of Childhood Sexual Abuse.* New York: Taylor Francis.

Weis, Lois, and Michelle Fine, eds. 2000. *Construction Sites: Excavating Race, Class, and Gender among Urban Young.* New York: Teachers College.

Weisberg, D. Kelly. 1984. "The 'Discovery' of Sexual Abuse." *UC Davis Law Review* 18: 1–57.

Weitzer, Ron. 2000a. "Why We Need More Research on Sex Work." In *Sex for Sale,* Ron Weitzer, ed. New York: Routledge. pp. 1–17.

Weitzer, Ron. 2000b. "The Politics of Prostitution in America." In *Sex for Sale,* Ron Weitzer, ed. New York: Routledge. pp. 159–181.

Weitzer, Ron. 2000c. *Sex for Sale: Prostitution, Pornography, and the Sex Industry.* New York: Routledge.

Wellings, Kaye, Julia Field, Ann Johnson, and Jand Wadsworth. 1994. *Sexual Behaviour in Britain: The National Survey of Sexual Attitudes and Lifestyles.* London, UK: Penguin.

West, Elliott, and Paula Petrik 1992. *Small Worlds: Children and Adolescents in America, 1885–1950.* Kansas City, MO: University Press of Kansas.

Westervelt, Don. 2001. "Defending Marriage and Country." *Constellations* 8 (March): 106–126.

West Group. 2003. *California Juvenile Laws and Court Rules.* St. Paul, MN: author.

West Group. 2003. *California Welfare and Institution Codes.* St. Paul, MN: author.

Weston, Kath. 1997. *Families We Choose: Lesbians, Gays, Kinship.* New York: Columbia University Press.

Weston, Kath. 1996. *Render Me, Gender Me: Lesbians Talk Sex, Class, Color, Nation, Studmuffins.* New York: Columbia University Press.

Wettley, Annemarie. 1959. *Von der "Psychopathia sexualis" zur Sexualwissenschaft.* Stuttgart, Germany: Enke.

Whittle, Stephen. 2000. *The Transgender Debate: The Crisis Surrounding Gender Identities.* London, UK: Garnett Publishing.

Wijers, Marjan. 1998. "Women, Labor and Migration." *In Global Sex Workers,* Kamala Kempadoo and Jo Doezema, eds. New York: Routledge. pp. 69–78.

Williams, Christine, and Arlene Stein, eds. 2002. *Sexuality and Gender.* Malden, MA: Blackwell.

Williams, Patricia J. 1992. *The Alchemy of Race and Rights: Diary of a Law Professor.* Cambridge, MA: Harvard University Press.
Williams, Patricia J. 1988. "On Being the Object of Property." *Signs* 14(1): 5–24.
Wilson, Elizabeth. 1995. "The Invisible Flâneur." In *Postmodern Cities and Spaces*, W. Watson and K. Gibson, eds. Cambridge, MA: Blackwell. pp. 59–77.
Wilson, Melba. 1993. *Crossing the Boundary: Black Women Survive Incest.* Seattle, WA: Seal Press.
Winick, Charles, and Paul M. Kinsie. 1971. *The Lively Commerce: Prostitution in the United States.* Chicago, IL: Quadrangle Books.
Winn, Marie. 1993. *Children Without Childhood.* New York: Pantheon.
Wintemute, Robert, and Mads Andenaes, eds. 2001. *Legal Recognition of Same Sex Partnerships: A Study of National, European, and International Law.* Oxford, UK: Hart Publishing.
Wolfenden Report: Report of the Committee on Homosexual Offenses and Prostitution. 1963. New York: Stein and Day.
Wolfson, Evan, and Robert S. Mower. 1994. "When the Police Are in Our Bedrooms, Shouldn't the Courts Go In After Them?: An Update on the Fight Against 'Sodomy' Laws." *Fordham Urban Law Journal* 21(4): 997–1055.
Woodhead, Martin. 1997. "Psychology and the Cultural Construction of Children's Needs." In *Constructing and Reconstructing Childhood*, Allison James and Alan Prout, eds. London, UK: Falmer Press. pp. 63–84.
Yang, Alan. 1997. "The Polls—Trends, Attitudes Toward Homosexuality." *Public Opinion Quarterly* 61: 477–507.
Yates, Gary, Richard MacKenzie, Julia Pennbridge, and Avon Swofford. 1991. "A Risk Profile Comparison of Homeless Youth in Prostitution and Homeless Youth Not Involved." *Journal of Adolescent Health* 12: 545–48.
Yokohama Global Commitment. 2001. Adopted at the closing session of the Second World Congress against Commercial Sexual Exploitation of Children. December 17–20. Yokohama, Japan.
Zelizer, Viviana. 1985. *Pricing the Priceless Child: The Changing Social Value of Children.* New York: Basic Books.

Legal Decisions and Public Documents

13 Vt. Stat. Ann, tit. 13 sec. 1458 (2000).
American Psychological Association (and American Public Health Association). Brief of *Amici Curiae* in Support of Respondents, *Bowers v. Hardwick*. (January 31, 1986).
Americans with Disabilities Act. 42 U.S.C. 12211(b)(1) (1990).
Ashlie v. Chester-Upland School District, No. CIV A. 78–4037, 1979 U.S. Dist. LEXIS 12516, at *8 E.D. Pa. (May 9, 1979).
Baehr v. Lewin. 74 Haw. 530, 562, 563, 567–70 (1993).
Boulder, Co. Code 12–1 sec. 4 (2000).
Boulder, Co. Ordinance. 7040 (Jan. 20, 2000).
Bowers v. Hardwick. 478 U.S. 186 (1986).
Boyd v. United States. 116 U.S. 616 (1886).
Boy Scouts of American and Monmouth Council et al. v. James Dale. (99–699) 530 U.S. 640 (2000).
Cal. Assembly Bill 196, Re.g., Sess. (2003).
Cal. Assembly Bill 458, Re.g., Sess. (2003).
Cal. Assembly Bill 2222, Re.g., Sess. (2000).
Cal. Ed. Code, sec. 220. (Deering 2000).
Cal. Penal Code, sec. 422.76. (Deering 2000).
Child Abuse Treatment and Prevention Act (CAPTA). Public Law 93–247 (1978).
City of Dallas v. England. 846 S.W.2d 957 (Tex. Ct. App. 1993).
Criminal Sexual Assault Act of Illinois of 2000. 720 Illinois Comprehensive Statutes Article 5 Sections 12–16 (2000).
Croft v. Westmoreland County Children and Youth Services. 103 F.3d at 1125 (1997).
Cruzan v. Special Sch. Dist. #1, 294 F. 3d 981 (8th Cir. 2002).
Defense of Marriage Act (DOMA). HR 3396 (1986).
Dobre v. National R. R. Passenger Corp. (AMTRACK). 850 F. Supp. 284 (E.D. Pa. 1983).
Doe v. Boeing Co. 846 P. 2d 531, 533, 536 (Wash. 1993).

Doe v. Yunits. 2001 WL 664942 (Mass. Super. Ct. 2001).

Eisenstadt v. Baird. 405 U.S. 438 (1972).

Employment Non-Discrimination Act. HR 3285, S 1705 (1994).

Equal Credit Opportunity Act (ECOA). 15 U.S.C. 1691 et seq. (1974).

Fair Employment and Housing Act. California. (1959).

Farmer v. Haas. 990 F.2d 319, 320 (7th Cir. 1993).

The Federal Gay and Lesbian Civil Rights Bill. HR 1430, S 574 (1975).

Goins v. West Group. No. 9818222 (Minn. Ct. App. Nov. 21, 2000).

Goodridge v. Department of Pubic Health. No. 2001–1647A (Suffolk County Super. Ct. Mass. March 2003).

Griswold v. Connecticut. 381 U.S. 479 (1965).

Grossman v. Bernards Township Board of Education. 11 E.P.D. P686, CCH Employment Practices Decisions (D.N.J. 1975).

Hate Crimes Prevention Act. Senate Bill 622 (1999).

106th Congress H. Con. Res. 107. (July 12, 1999).

Hernandez-Montiel v. INS. 225 F. 3d 1084 (9th Cir. 2000).

Hillary Goodridge and Others v. Department of Health and Another. SJC–08860 (2003).

Holloway v. Arthur Anderson & Co. 566 F. 2d 662, 659 (9th Cir. 1977).

Holt v. Northwestern Pennsylvania Training Partnership Consortium, Inc. 694 A. 2d 1134 (Pa. Commw. 1997).

Illinois Compiled Statutes 2003. ILCS 5/12 12 et. seq. 2003.

Iowa City Public Hearing on Ordinance Amending the Iowa City Code tit. 2, Human Rights Ordinance, ch. 2, sec. 2–2–2, and 2–1–1 (Sept. 26, 1995).

Jefferson County, Ky. Ordinance. 36 (Oct. 12, 1999).

Kirkpatrick v. Seligman. 636 F. 2d 1047 (5th Cir. 1981).

Lawrence v. Texas. No. 02–102 (2003).

Lexington, Ky. Ordinance. 201–99 (July 1999).

Louisiana Covenant Marriage Act. 1380 (July 15, 1997).

Louisiana Electorate of Gays and Lesbians, Inc. v. State. 812 So. 2d 626 (La. 2002).

Louisville, Ky. Ordinance. 9 (Feb. 1, 1999).

Mann Act. Ch 395, Stat. 825–827 (1910).

Michael M. v. Sonoma County. 1981. 450 U.S. 464. (C.A. Sup. Ct. 1981).

Minneapolis, Minn. Code of Ordinances, tit. 7, Ch, 139.20 (1975).

Minn. Stat. Ann., sec. 363.01, 557.035 (West Supp. 2000).

Minn. Stat., sec. 611A.79 (West Supp. 2000).

Mo. Rev. Stat., sec. 557.035.4 (2000).

Mo. Stat. Ann., sec. 363.01, 557.035 (West Supp. 2000).

New Orleans, La., Ordinance, 18, 794. (July 1, 1998).

New York City Bill, Int. No. 754 (2000).

New York v. Ferber. 458 U.S. 747, 759 (1982).

N.M. Stat. Ann., 28–1–2(Q).

Olympia, WA, Code sec. 5.80.020 (1997).

Parham v. J.R. 444 U.S. 584 (1979).

Price Waterhouse v. Hopkins. 490 U.S. 228, 235 (1989).

Prince v. Massachusetts. 321 U.S. 158 (1944).

Rehabilitation Act of 1973. 29 U.S.C. 706(8)(F)(i).

R.I. Gen. Laws, 11–24–2 (2001).

Roe v. Wade. 410 U.S. 113 (1973).

Rosa v. Park West Bank and Trust Co. 214 F. 3d 213 (1st Cir. 2000).

San Francisco, Cal., Ordinance 433–94. (1994).

Seattle, Wash., Code sec. 14.04.030 (1986).

Seattle, Wash. Ordinance, 119628 (Aug. 1999).

Stanley v. Georgia. 394 U.S. 557 (1969).

State v. Baxley. 633 So. 2d 142 (La. 1994).

State v. Baxley. 656 So. 2d 973 (La. 1995).

State v. Morales. 869 S.W.2d 941 (Tex. 1994).

Statutory Rape. California Penal Code Sec. 261.5 (2000).

Toledo, Ohio, Code ch. 5 554.01 (1998).

Trafficking Victim's Protection Act. HR 3244. (2000).

Troxel v. Granville. 530 U.S. 57 (2000).

Tucson, Ariz., Code Chapter 10 Section 17–11 (1999).

Ulane v. Eastern Airlines, Inc. 581 F. Supp. 821, 825 N.D. Ill. (1984).

Ulane v. Eastern Airlines, Inc. 742 F. 2d 1081, 1084–86, 1087 7th Cir. (1984).

Underwood v. Archer Management Services, Inc. 566 F. 2d 664 (9th Cir. 1977).

Underwood v. Archer Management Services, Inc. 857 F. Supp. 96, 98 (D.D.C. 1994).

United Nations. 1989. *United Nations Convention on the Rights of the Child.* Geneva, Switzerland: Author.

United Nations. 1949. *Convention for the Suppression of the Traffic in Persons and the Exploitation of the Prostitution of Others.* Geneva, Switzerland: Author.

United States vs. Morrison. 169 F. 3d. 820 (2000).

About the Contributors

LAURA AGUSTÍN has been studying the links between the sex industry and migration since 1994, after working in *educación popular* in Latin America and with Latin American migrants abroad. Her Open University doctoral thesis, to be a Zed Book, focuses on the discourses and practices of the social sector proposing to help women migrants. She has many publications in Spanish and English, has been an evaluator of projects for the European Commission's Daphne Program and for the International Labor Organization, and is the moderator of the romance-language list, *Industriadel Sexo*.

ELIZABETH BERNSTEIN is an Assistant Professor of Sociology and Women's Studies at Barnard College, Columbia University. She is currently completing a book titled *Economies of Desire: Sexual Commerce and Post-Industrial Culture*, which is a theoretical and empirical treatment of recent transformations in the global sexual economy, based upon ethnographic research in five countries.

MARY BERNSTEIN is an Assistant Professor at the University of Connecticut. Her research focuses on sexuality, social movements, law, and gender. Her recent anthology, *Queer Families, Queer Politics: Challenging Culture and the State* (Columbia University Press 2001), connects the microdynamics of gender, sexuality, and family with the macrodynamics of social movements, politics, and law. Currently, she is working on a book about how lesbian and gay activists choose political strategies and how those strategies impact legal change.

WENDY CHAPKIS is an Associate Professor of Women's Studies and Sociology at the University of Southern Maine. Dr. Chapkis is the author of two books, *Beauty Secrets: Women and the Politics of Appearance* (South End Press 1986) and *Live Sex Acts: Women Performing Erotic Labor* (Routledge 1997) and the editor of two anthologies, *Loaded Questions: Women in the Military* and *Of*

Common Cloth: Women in the Global Textile Industry (coedited with Dr. Cynthia Enloe). *Live Sex Acts* won the award for best scholarly work from the Organization of Language, Communication and Gender in 1997 and was a finalist for the 1998 C. Wright Mills award from the Society for the Study of Social Problems.

PAISLEY CURRAH is an Associate Professor in the Department of Political Science and the executive director of the Center for Lesbian and Gay Studies (CLAGS) at the City University of New York. He has published articles on the constructions of identity deployed in the rights claims of sexual minorities in the United States, including "The Transgender Rights Imaginary," and is a coeditor with Richard M. Juang and Shannon Minter of *Transgender Rights: History, Politics, and Law* (forthcoming from the University of Minnesota Press). He also does policy and legislative work for transgender groups and is a cofounder of the Transgender Law and Policy Institute.

JULIA O'CONNELL DAVIDSON is a Professor of Sociology at the University of Nottingham. Since 1993 she has been involved in research on prostitution and sex tourism. With Jaqueline Sanchez Taylor, she conducted research on child prostitution and tourism in Latin America, the Caribbean, India, and South Africa for the United Nations' End Child Prostitution in Asian Tourism (ECPAT) and authored "The Sex Exploiter," one of the background papers for the World Congress Against the Sexual Exploitation of Children. She currently is a coholder of an Economic and Social Research Council award for research on tourist-related prostitution in Jamaica and the Dominican Republic.

KJERSTI ERICSSON is a Professor of Criminology in the Department of Criminology and Sociology of Law at the University of Oslo. Dr. Ericsson has published several books on total institutions, juvenile delinquency, education, gender relations, and child welfare. She is also a writer of fiction and has published eight volumes of poetry and two novels.

GERT HEKMA teaches Gay and Lesbian Studies in Social Sciences at the University of Amsterdam. He is the coeditor of *Sexual Cultures in Europe* (Manchester 1999) with Franz Eder and Lesley Hall.

JANET R. JAKOBSEN is Director of the Center for Research on Women at Barnard College. She is the author of *Working Alliances and the Politics of Difference: Diversity and Feminist Ethics* (Indiana University Press 1998), *Love the Sin: Sexual Regulation and the Limits of Religious Tolerance,* with Ann Pellegrini. She is currently working on a book titled *The Value of Freedom: Sex, Religion, and America in a Global Economy.* Previously, Janet was a policy analyst and lobbyist in Washington, D.C.

KERWIN KAYE is in the Doctoral program in American Studies at New York University. He holds a Master's degree in Cultural Anthropology from San Francisco State University, where his thesis focused upon male street prostitution. He has also written about labor conditions in San Francisco's adult entertainment theaters.

ELIZABETH LAPOVSKY KENNEDY is a Professor of Women's Studies at the University of Arizona, Tucson, with affiliated appointments in History and Anthropology. She received her Ph.D. in social anthropology from Cambridge University, England, in 1972 based on her research with the Waunan of the Choco province, Colombia. Kennedy was a founding member of Women's Studies at the State University of New York at Buffalo, where she taught for 28 years. Her research pioneered the study of lesbian history, a subject on which she has published widely, including the prize-winning book, *Boots of Leather, Slippers of Gold: The History of a Lesbian Community*. She has also written about the development of Women's Studies as a field, and is coauthor of *Feminist Scholarship: Kindling in the Grove of Academe* (with Ellen DuBois et al.). She is currently working on *Many Strands, One Woman: Lesbianism, Marriage, and Sexuality in an Upper Middle-Class Life*.

SHANNON MINTER is the Legal Director at the National Center for Lesbian Rights in San Francisco, where he oversees impact litigation on behalf of lesbian, gay, bisexual, and transgender people in family law, immigration and asylum law, and other civil rights areas. He has written numerous articles on international human rights, family law, and transgender issues. He serves on the board of the Horizons Foundation and on the Advisory Board of the International Gay and Lesbian Human Rights Commission. He is an adjunct lecturer at Stanford Law School.

WILL ROUNTREE holds a J.D. from the University of Wisconsin Law School and a Ph.D. in Sociology from the University of California at Berkeley. He is a trial consultant at the National Jury Project in Oakland, California. His writings explore the role of contract in the transformation of modern kinship arrangements.

PENELOPE SAUNDERS received her Ph.D. in Latin American Studies from Flinders University of South Australia in 1997. In 1999 she was a Rockefeller Postdoctoral Research Fellow at the Center for the Study of Sexuality, Gender, Health, and Human Rights at Columbia University. Her postdoctoral research focused on homeless youth, sexuality, and the United Nations Convention on the Rights of the Child. She has extensive experience designing and directing programs for homeless youth and sex workers in Australia and in the United States. Currently, she is the Executive Director of Different Avenues, a non-profit organization working with homeless youth in Washington, D.C.

LAURIE SCHAFFNER, author of *Teenage Runaways: Broken Hearts and "Bad Attitudes,"* (Haworth Press 1999), is a sociologist at the University of Illinois at Chicago. She is working on her forthcoming book, *Girlhood on the Edge: Gender, Adolescence, and the Law* and is a cofounder of the Chicago Girls Coalition.

STEVEN SEIDMAN is a Professor of Sociology at the State University of New York at Albany. He is author of, among other books, *Beyond the Closet: The Transformation of Gay and Lesbian Life* (Routledge 2002), *Contested Knowledge: Social Theory in a Postmodern Era* (Blackwell 1998), *Difference Troubles: Queering Social Theory and Sexual Politics* (Cambridge 1997), and *Embattled Eros: Sexual Politics and Ethics in Contemporary America* (Routledge 1991). He edited *Queer Theory/Sociology* (Blackwell 1996), coedited with Linda Nicholson *Social Postmodernism: Beyond Identity Politics* (Cambridge 1995), and coedited with Jeffrey Alexander *The New Social Theory* (Routledge 2000). He edits the "Cultural Social Studies Series" with Cambridge and the "21st Century Sociology Series" with Blackwell.

JACQUELINE SÁNCHEZ TAYLOR is a Lecturer in Sociology at the University of Leeds. She coholds an Economic and Social Research Council award for research on tourist-related prostitution in Jamaica and the Dominican Republic, a study that builds upon her previous research on sex tourism in the Caribbean, Latin America, South Africa, and India and was commissioned by the United Nations' ECPAT. She has a particular research interest in the phenomenon of female sex tourism to the Caribbean as well as in the racialized, gendered, and sexualized discourses that tourist women and local men use to organize, explain, and justify their sexual interactions.

Index